Rome: Empire of the Eagles

Rome: Empire of the Eagles

Neil Faulkner

PEARSON
Longman

Harlow, England • London • New York • Boston • San Francisco • Toronto
Sydney • Tokyo • Singapore • Hong Kong • Seoul • Taipei • New Delhi
Cape Town • Madrid • Mexico City • Amsterdam • Munich • Paris • Milan

PEARSON EDUCATION LIMITED

Edinburgh Gate
Harlow CM20 2JE
Tel: +44 (0)1279 623623
Fax: +44 (0)1279 431059
Website: www.pearsoned.co.uk

First published in Great Britain in 2008

© Pearson Education Limited 2008

The right of Neil Faulkner to be identified as author of this work has been asserted
by him in accordance with the Copyright, Designs and Patents Act 1988.

ISBN: 978-0-582-78495-6

British Library Cataloguing-in-Publication Data
A catalogue record for this book is available from the British Library

Library of Congress Cataloging-in-Publication Data
A catalog record for this book is available from the Library of Congress

10 9 8 7 6 5 4 3 2 1
11 10 09 08 07

Typeset in 9.5/14pt Mellor by 35
Printed and bound in China
SWTC/01

The publisher's policy is to use paper manufactured from sustainable forests.

Contents

List of maps and plates

Maps

Plates

[In central plate section]

1   The Low Ham mosaic in Somerset depiciting a thousand-year-old
     myth that has the Roman race founded by the Trojan hero Aeneas,
     a story immortalised for Roman (and Romanised) audiences by the
     great Latin poet Virgil.

2   The 'Capitoline Wolf', an archaic bronze that reminded
     contemporary viewers that the Romans were spawn of Mars and
     sucklings of the She-Wolf.

3   A hut-urn, used to inter the cremated remains of Rome's
     8th century BC dead.

4   An Italic hoplite of the Early Republican period.

5   Temple of Hera at Paestum.

6   The quinquereme, essentially a muscle-powered ram; the battleship
     of the 3rd century BC.

7   Gaius Marius abandoned carts and made his soldiers carry their
     equipment on their backs: part of the growing professionalisation
     of the army under the Late Republic.

8   Coin of the Social War rebels.

9   Pompey the Great. The Late Republic was dominated by a
     succession of great warlords whose power eclipsed that of their
     senatorial colleagues and presaged that of the emperors.

10   Luxuria (the extravagant and conspicuous consumption of wealth)
     became more socially acceptable among the elite under the Late
     Republic.

11   The Roman Forum.

12   Cicero. Though a 'new man', he became the leading representative
     of senatorial reaction in the middle of the 1st century BC.

13   Julius Caesar, the greatest politician and general of the Late
     Republic, and the man who finally destroyed the power of the
     senatorial aristocracy and inaugurated the regime of the 'new men'.

14 The siege of Alesia, 52 BC; an apocalyptic climax to Caesar's eight-year conquest of Gaul.

15 Octavian-Augustus. A murderous civil-war faction leader is transformed into a heroic monarch in all but name by the spin doctors, in-house poets and court artists of the new Augustan regime.

16 Augustus's image-makers portrayed him both as a paternalistic 'father of his country' and as a statesman-like commander-in-chief who guaranteed national security and internal order.

17 The *Res Gestae* – Augustus's political testimony – inscribed in stone and placed on public view at various places across the empire.

18 The *Ara Pacis* (Altar of Peace) in Rome, rich in political symbolism, showing Rome's senatorial aristocracy.

19 The *Ara Pacis* again; showing the imperial family, women and children included.

20 Behind a mask of constitutional rectitude was the fist of military power. The Praetorian Guard was stationed in Rome, and, as events in AD 41 proved, it, and not the Senate, was the final arbiter of power.

21 The enemy within. Onto the floor of this room fell the debris – benches, tables, writing implements – of the first-floor *scriptorium* where the Dead Sea Scrolls were inscribed: a call to revolutionary holy war against the Roman Empire.

22 A Roman base in the Judean Desert outside the Jewish fortress of Masada, where the last of the revolutionaries of AD 66–73 defied the might of Rome.

23 The Colosseum is Rome's Auschwitz: built for the mass murder of slaves as a form of public entertainment.

24 Hadrian's Wall.

25 Temple of Olympian Zeus, Athens.

26 The Column of Marcus Aurelius in Rome has the form of a traditional victory monument – but this had been a war to eject Germanic invaders after the frontier defences on the upper Danube had collapsed.

Acknowledgements

I am very grateful to Tim Cornell, Richard Gosling, Steve Roskams and Philip de Souza for the time taken to read and critique this book in draft. Significant corrections are the result. Needless to say, none of these readers is in any way responsible for what follows. I am also grateful to the many, often very vocal, adult education students whom it was my great pleasure to teach and debate with at Richmond Adult and Community College and The City Literary Institute.

Publisher's acknowledgements

We are grateful to the following for permission to reproduce copyright material:

Bridgeman Art Library/Somerset County Museum, Taunton Castle, UK, for plate 1; Corbis/Araldo de Luca for plate 2; akg-images Ltd/Andrew Baguzzi for plate 3; the Bridgeman Art Library Ltd/Louvre, Paris, France for plate 4; Corbis/Marco Cristofori for plate 5; akg-images Ltd/Peter Connolly for plate 6; DK Images/Karl Shone for plate 7; the Trustees of the British Museum for plate 8; Alamy Images/Visual Arts Library (London) for plate 9; David Bellingham for plate 10; Punchstock/Brand X for plate 11; Corbis/Sandro Vannini for plate 12; akg-images Ltd for plate 13; akg-images Ltd/Peter Connolly for plate 14; Corbis/Roger Wood for plate 15; akg-images Ltd/Nimatallah for plate 16; DK Images/Mike Dunning for plates 17 and 23; Ancient Art & Architecture/C M Dixon for plates 18 and 19; DK Images/De Agostini Editore Picture Library for plate 20; Alamy Images/Robert Estall Photo Agency for plate 24; Alamy Images/Steve Allen Travel Photography for plate 25; Corbis/Araldo de Luca for plate 26; Marcus Prinis & Jona Lendering for plate 27; Alamy Images/Robert Harding for plate 28; TopFoto for plate 29 and akg-images Ltd/Pirozzi for plate 32.

In some instances we have been unable to trace the owners of copyright material, and we would appreciate any information that would enable us to do so.

Introduction

The world of Rome, with its wars of conquest, slave labour, bloody games and crucifixions, can seem a terrible one. Or, thinking of town planning, civil engineering, bath-houses, mosaic pavements and Latin literature, Rome can appear a peak of human cultural achievement. Which of these is dominant? Rome the bloody conqueror or Rome the great civilizer? Should we deplore the historical example of Rome, or admire it, perhaps even seek to emulate it?

Some are making open comparisons between Rome and today's American Empire. The office of Donald Rumsfeld, neo-conservative US Secretary of State under George Bush junior, sponsored a private study of great empires, including the Roman, asking how they had maintained their dominance and what the United States could learn from them. British diplomat Robert Copper, imagining 'a new kind of imperialism . . . acceptable to a world of human rights and cosmopolitan values' which might be promoted by the EU, has suggested that 'like Rome, this commonwealth would provide its citizens with some of its laws, some coins, and the occasional road'. When the Islamic militant Osama bin Laden called for 'a general mobilisation to prepare for repulsing the raids of the Romans', it was a metaphor for holy war against the American occupation of Iraq. Ancient historians Tom Holland and Peter Jones, writing in the *BBC History Magazine*, debated whether US power offered parallels with the Roman *imperium*. And Alex Callinicos, a leading left-wing intellectual, compared the US and British invasion of Iraq in 2003 with that of the 4th century Roman emperor Julian in the opening passages of his recent book *The New Mandarins of American Power*. The past, it seems, is about the present.

This book is a contribution to the debate. Though trained as a Roman archaeologist, I also taught Roman history for about ten years, mainly at two London adult education colleges. As a Marxist, I approached the subject in a distinctive way, but I also found myself at odds with 'orthodox' Marxist accounts of the ancient world. In particular, I found the concept of a 'slave mode of production' both empirically unsound and of little explanatory value. In the Roman world, most of the exploited were not slaves, and most of the surplus accumulated and consumed by the ruling class was produced by non-servile labour. Even when slaves were important – notably in Italy and Sicily during the 2nd and 1st centuries BC – this fact did not appear to have affected the character of Roman imperialism in any fundamental way. In relation to this, three points are worth stressing. First, the exploitation of slaves does not seem to have been so very different from the exploitation of other categories of rural labour (serfs, debt-bondsmen, tenants, seasonal wage-labourers). Second, the taxes, labour services and compulsory requisitioning imposed by the Roman state seem to have been as significant in generating surplus as the revenues raised by landowners from their estates; and the former was a type of exploitation that could be visited even on peasants who owned their own land. Third – and for me the most important point – war probably contributed more surplus in the Roman Empire than either taxes or rents. Rome was, in its very essence, a system of robbery with violence.

So what I offer is a story with a message: a narrative of Roman history driven by a single, comprehensive interpretation. I argue that Rome was a dynamic system of military imperialism – of robbery with violence – and that its rise and fall, its conquests and defeats, its revolutions and civil wars can best be understood as manifestations of this. Let me stress that the conceptual framework has not been 'imposed on the evidence': it has grown out of it. After all, as I say, mine is not an 'orthodox' Marxist interpretation; it is something that has been worked out afresh through long engagement with the narrative. Evidence and theories have interacted. Evidence demanded explanation and pointed in certain directions. Theories attempted to organize evidence meaningfully, but were sometimes changed by counter-evidence. And the working out was done partly through discussion with colleagues and students. The result is a narrative of Roman history reconfigured by a distinctive and substantially new interpretation.

Something must be said also about matters of detail. I aim to tell a story. I have turned what I know of the evidence into a narrative. In fact, the evidence is often weak and open to alternative interpretation; much of Roman history is fiercely argued, and one can say little of substance that is wholly uncontroversial. So, as I used to tell my students, what I offer is 'an interpretive narrative' – a story that makes sense, that respects the evidence, and that amounts to a possible history of what happened and why. But much is open to debate, and I do not engage in debate in the text. There is not the space for it. This, relative to its subject, is a short book. Also, it is aimed at the general reader (though I hope students will find it useful and scholars be interested by the interpretation). For these reasons, I have dispensed with the customary academic apparatus of argument, references and footnotes. Because the book is a broad synthesis, scholars will know the evidence and debates, while students will find the bibliographical essay an efficient introduction to the more specialized literature. But because the text is devoid of the rather tedious argument, qualification and referencing obligatory in more formal academic writing, it demands this all-embracing *caveat*: much of the detail in what follows is open to dispute, and the general interpretation in particular is highly controversial.

Controversy is inevitable. We live in an age of empire and war. As I write this, the American Empire is escalating its war in the Middle East, a war which has already killed two-thirds of a million people. But the Empire has powerful friends and many influential, well-funded, high-profile apologists. The American Empire can be a force for good, they tell us. Like the British Empire. Like the Roman.

The war in Iraq is being fought for oil, profit and US power. Yet the lie endures that it is about democracy and freedom. Rome was the same. The spin stressed peace, law and civilization. The reality was carnage and looting to enrich a few. That reality is this book's theme.

Neil Faulkner
St Albans
February 2007

Note on ancient monetary values

The coinage of the Roman Empire in the 1st and 2nd centuries AD was based on a golden *aureus*, silver *denarii* (25 to the *aureus*), and base-metal *sestertii* (100), *dupondii* (200), *asses* (400), *semisses* (800), and *quadrantes* (1,600). But many eastern cities continued to issue their own coins using a Greek system based on minas, drachmas and obols (with various multiples and fractions of these). In either case, the basic currency unit tended to be a silver coin – *denarius* or drachma/tetradrachma – but the weights of these could vary quite a lot (4.5 gm was about average for the *denarius*), and the actual silver content much more so (from 90 per cent to perhaps as little as 20 per cent). Larger amounts of money might, however, be expressed in terms of talents – though these were never coined – one talent being 26 kg of silver and therefore almost 6,000 *denarii* (or drachmae/tetradrachmae).

It is notoriously difficult to convert ancient monetary values into modern equivalents, especially since it is relative purchasing power, not nominal equivalents, that we are really interested in. A key question is: what constituted a living wage? Agricultural labourers received one *denarius* for a day's work, and it has been estimated that a typical peasant family of six would have needed about 180 *denarii* a year for basic subsistence. The annual pay of Roman soldiers was 225 *denarii* for a legionary, 150 for an auxiliary cavalryman, and 75 for an auxiliary infantryman. Deductions may have been made for food, fodder, clothes, equipment, and the regimental burial club, but on the other hand soldiers had free accommodation, generous bonuses, and did not pay tax.

Richard Reece proposes a modern British equivalent of about £25 ($49) for a *denarius* (or drachma/tetradrachma), which would give £4,500 ($8,900) as the minimum peasant family income, £5,625 ($11,128) for legionary pay, £3,750 ($7,419) for auxiliary cavalry, and £1,875 ($3,709) for auxiliary infantry. One talent would, on the same reasoning, represent £150,000 ($296,775) in today's values. These figures should not, of course, be compared with income levels in modern western societies, where the average standard of living is high; the ancient world was a pre-industrial society with much lower levels of material culture.

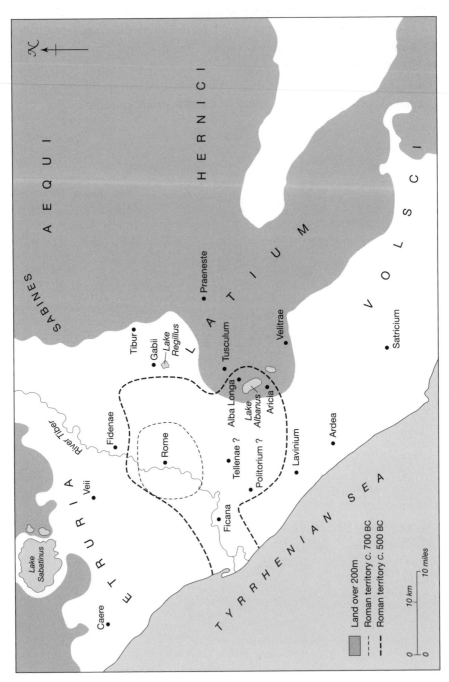

MAP 1 ✦ *Ancient Latium and its neighbours, 7th–5th centuries BC*

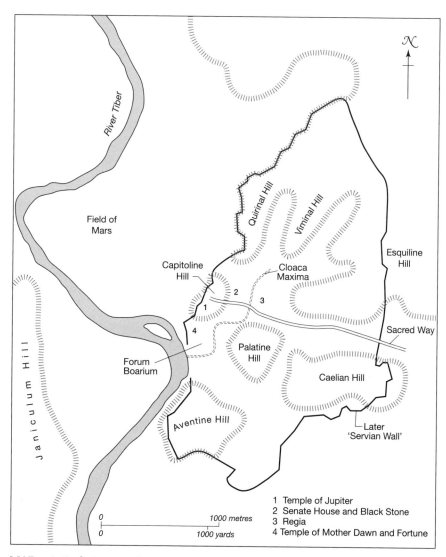

MAP 2 ♦ *Early Rome, 7th–5th centuries BC*

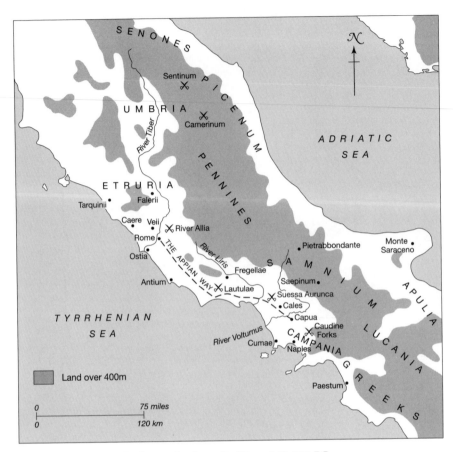

MAP 3 ♦ *Central Italy during the Samnite Wars, 343–290 BC*

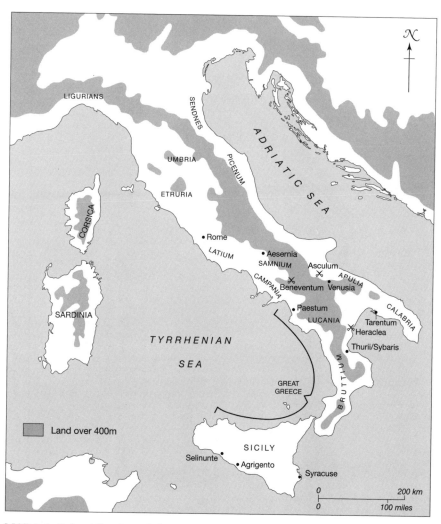

MAP 4 ♦ *Italy at the time of the wars against Tarentum and Pyrrhus, 282–275 BC*

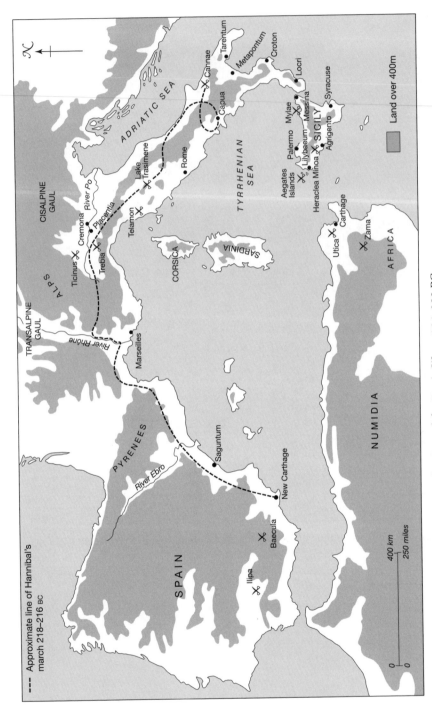

--- Approximate line of Hannibal's march 218–216 BC

Land over 400m

MAP 5 ◆ *The Western Mediterranean at the time of the Punic Wars, 264–202 BC*

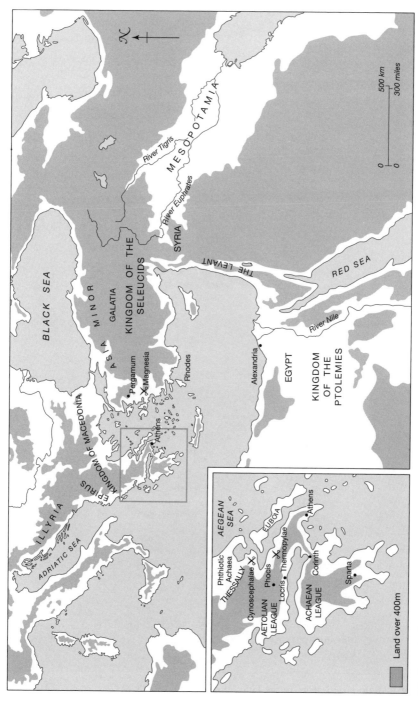

MAP 6 ◆ *The Eastern Mediterranean at the time of the Macedonian Wars, 215–146 BC*

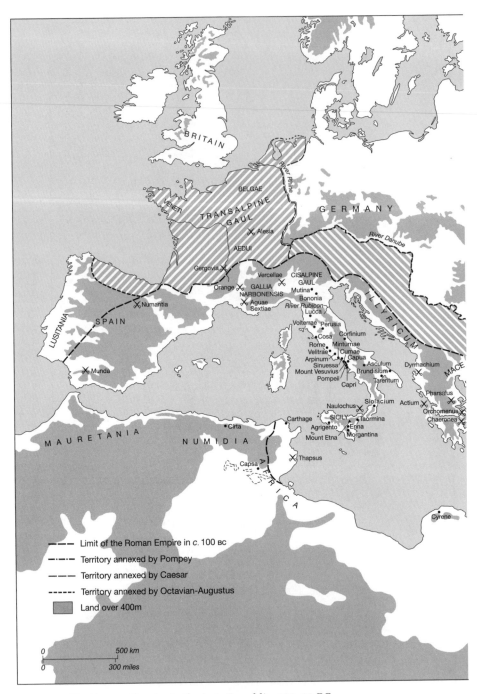

MAP 7 ♦ *The Roman Empire in the Late Republic, 133–30 BC*

NORTH SEA

Britannia

Germania Inferior

FREE GERMANY

River Rhine

ATLANTIC OCEAN

Lugdunensis

Belgica

Germania Superior

River Danube

Pannonia Superior

Raetia

Noricum

Pannonia Inferior

Aquitania

AP

AC

AM

Narbonensis

Italia

Illyricum

Moesia Superior

Lusitania

Tarraconensis

Macedonia

Baetica

Rome

MEDITERRANEAN SEA

Epirus

Mauretania

Sicilia

Atlas Mountains

Africa

Cyrenaica

AP Alpes Penninae
AC Alpes Cottiae
AM Alpes Maritimae

Sahara Desert

0   500 km
0   300 miles

MAP 8 ♦ *The provinces of the Roman Empire in the mid 1st century AD*

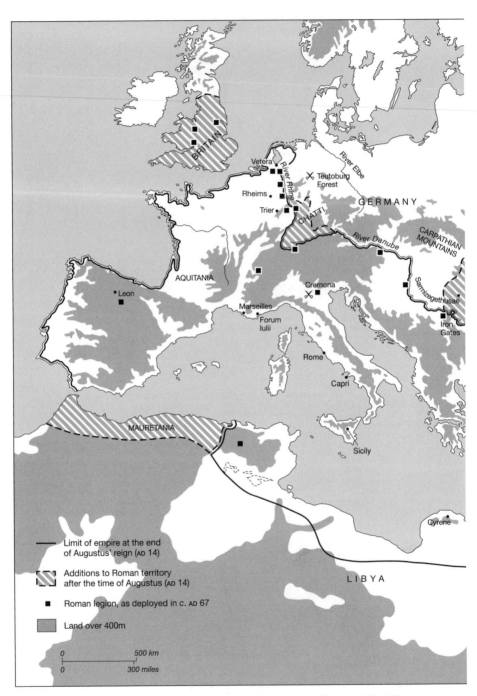

Vetera
River Rhine
Teutoburg Forest
Rheims
Trier
CHATTI
GERMANY
River Elbe
River Danube
CARPATHIAN MOUNTAINS
Sarmizegethusae
Iron Gates
AQUITANIA
Leon
Cremona
Marseilles
Forum Iulii
Rome
Capri
Sicily
MAURETANIA
Cyrene
LIBYA

—— Limit of empire at the end of Augustus' reign (AD 14)

Additions to Roman territory after the time of Augustus (AD 14)

■ Roman legion, as deployed in c. AD 67

Land over 400m

0   500 km
0   300 miles

MAP 9 ♦ *The Roman Empire from Augustus to Marcus Aurelius, 30 BC–AD 180*

Control of coastal strip only

DACIA

BLACK SEA

CAUCASUS MOUNTAINS

CASPIAN SEA

ARMENIA

CAPPADOCIA

River Tigris

Zagros Mountains

MESOPOTAMIA

PARTHIAN EMPIRE

IRAN

Antioch

SYRIA

Palmyra

Babylon

CYPRUS

PALESTINE

Damascus

River Euphrates

PERSIAN GULF

Beth-Horon   Jerash
Jerusalem   Herodium
                Masada

Alexandria

Petra   NABATAEAN
               ARABIA
Aqaba

River Nile

RED SEA

EGYPT

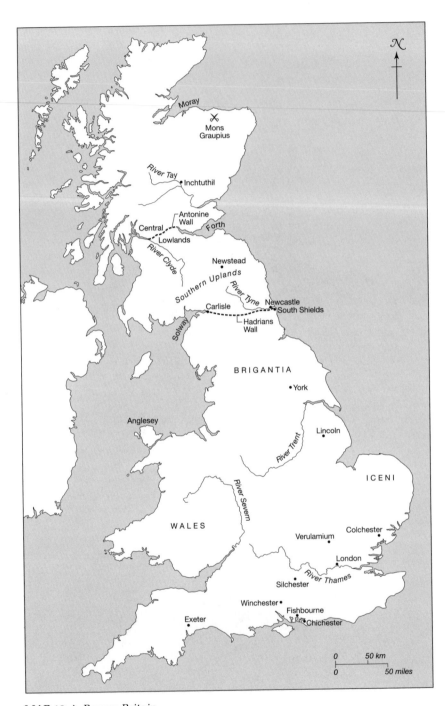

MAP 10 ♦ *Roman Britain*

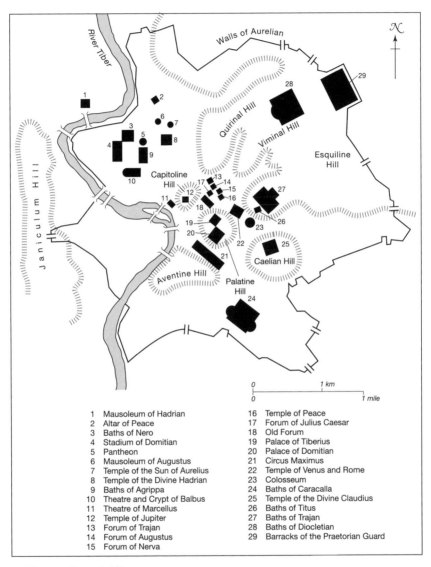

MAP 11 ♦ *Imperial Rome*

1	Mausoleum of Hadrian	16	Temple of Peace
2	Altar of Peace	17	Forum of Julius Caesar
3	Baths of Nero	18	Old Forum
4	Stadium of Domitian	19	Palace of Tiberius
5	Pantheon	20	Palace of Domitian
6	Mausoleum of Augustus	21	Circus Maximus
7	Temple of the Sun of Aurelius	22	Temple of Venus and Rome
8	Temple of the Divine Hadrian	23	Colosseum
9	Baths of Agrippa	24	Baths of Caracalla
10	Theatre and Crypt of Balbus	25	Temple of the Divine Claudius
11	Theatre of Marcellus	26	Baths of Titus
12	Temple of Jupiter	27	Baths of Trajan
13	Forum of Trajan	28	Baths of Diocletian
14	Forum of Augustus	29	Barracks of the Praetorian Guard
15	Forum of Nerva		

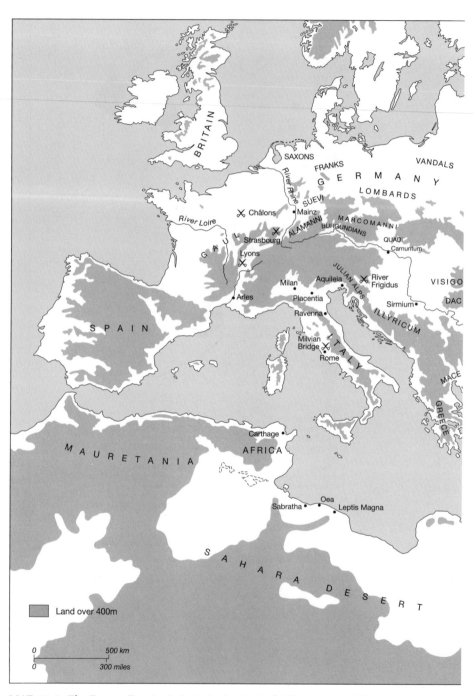

MAP 12 ♦ *The Roman Empire in Late Antiquity, 3rd–5th centuries AD*

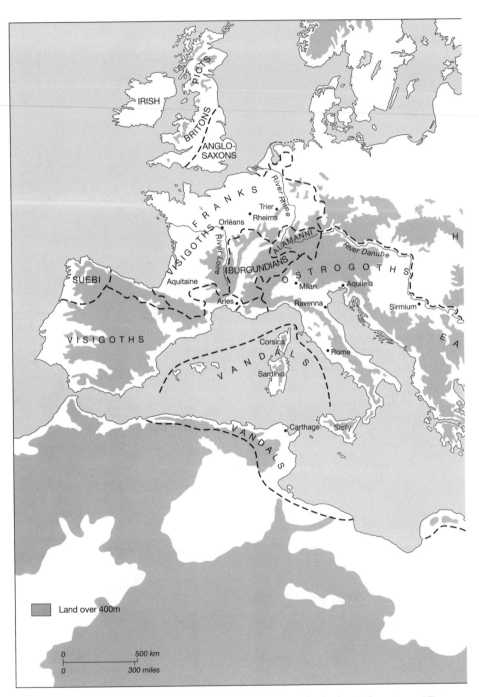

MAP 13 ♦ *A new world order: the Mediterranean region in the late 5th century AD*

HUNS

SLAVS

River Danube

WESTERN ROMAN EMPIRE

BLACK SEA

CASPIAN SEA

Constantinople

Antioch

River Tigris

River Euphrates

SASSANID EMPIRE

PERSIAN GULF

Jerusalem

Alexandria

River Nile

RED SEA

N

Prologue

Where do we come from? Who are our ancestors? Who built the place where we live? In short, who are we? The Romans were bound to ask such questions. By the time of the Emperor Augustus (31 BC to AD 14) – and probably long before – they had clear answers.

Stories about the origins of Rome and the Romans survive in the works of two of the Augustan Age's leading men of letters: in Virgil's epic poem *The Aeneid*, and in Book 1 of Livy's *History of Rome*. From them we learn that Rome – by then the capital city of a global superpower – was conceived as an imperial phoenix rising from the flames of burning Troy over a thousand years before.

It went like this. The hero Aeneas had escaped the destruction of Troy in 1184 BC, carrying his aged father Anchises on his shoulders, dragging his son Ascanius by the hand. Anchises clasped images of Troy's gods to his breast as he was borne along – saving the spirits of his race to ensure its regeneration. With other refugees, Aeneas fled by sea; but, harried by vengeful gods, he found no safe haven for seven years. Then storms tossed his ships on to the shore of Carthage, where the exiled Phoenician queen Dido was building a new city. Venus, divine mother of Aeneas, tried to protect her son through union with Dido, but Jupiter, lord of heaven, and patron of the future city of Rome, ordained otherwise: Aeneas was commanded to abandon his Afro-Punic lover and fulfil an historic mission in Italy. Dido, stricken with grief and anger, cursed Aeneas, pledged her people to eternal enmity with the Trojans, and then killed herself.

Making landfall in Italy near the Bay of Naples, Aeneas encountered the Sibyl of Cumae, a prophetess of the god Apollo, and mistress of the arcane arts. Guided by her, Aeneas descended into the Underworld to meet his recently deceased father Anchises, now, in death, privy to knowledge of his people's future. As a parade of great Romans – the spirit forms of those yet to come – passed before them, Anchises drew the lesson for his son: 'Others . . . shall hammer forth more delicately a breathing likeness out of bronze, coax living faces from the marble, plead causes with more skill, plot with their gauge the movements in the sky, and tell the rising of the constellations. But as for you, Roman, let your concern be to command the nations, and may this be your skill: to impose the rule of peace, to spare the submissive, and to crush the proud.'(1) Greeks might be better artists, orators and scientists, but it was Romans who were destined to rule the world.

The price, though, was to be high. 'Your Trojans will regret their coming,' the Sibyl screeched. 'I see war and all the horrors of war. I see Tiber streaming and foaming with blood.'(2) Sure enough, when Aeneas's followers landed at Latium, about a hundred miles up the coast, they were quickly plunged into a life-or-death struggle. Would Aeneas marry the King of Latium's daughter, secure an alliance with the Latin people, and thus win for his Trojans land, farms, and a place to build a city? Or would local warlord Turnus the Rutulian crush the interlopers? Venus persuaded Vulcan, the smith-god, to craft a fabulous panoply of helmet, sword, breastplate, greaves, spear and shield for her son. The face of the shield, made of bronze, silver and gold, was decorated with scenes of Rome's future triumphs. At the centre was an image of a great naval battle to come, that of Actium in 31 BC, an apocalyptic struggle between Eastern barbarism and Western civilization. Aeneas 'had no knowledge of the events, but nonetheless he found pleasure in their representations, as he lifted onto his shoulder the glory and the destiny of his heirs.'(3)

The dogs of war were unleashed. Bloody battle followed bloody battle. The fate of Italy – and the world – swayed in the balance. Would the Roman race live, or would it be ripped from its Trojan womb unborn? Finally, to decide, the two heroes met in single combat. At the climax of the fight, when the gods turned Turnus' skill and strength to jelly, Aeneas, champion of the new order, seized his opportunity and brought Turnus down with a spear cast that pierced his thigh. Then, 'in vengeful bitterness, his fury kindled, and terrible in his rage'(4), he smashed out the remaining life with a sword thrust through the breast.

Time passed. Aeneas died three years after the war. His son Ascanius succeeded him, but, leaving Lavinium, the settlement of his father, he founded a new city at Alba Longa in the hills nearby. Here his descendants ruled for 300 years. But the last of the Alban kings was a usurper and tyrant called Amulius, who drove out his brother Numitor, the rightful king, and made Numitor's only child, the maiden Rhea Silvia, a Vestal Virgin. Amulius aimed to terminate the line of Numitor, for Vestals were not allowed to marry. But Amulius was foiled, for Rhea Silvia was impregnated by Mars, god of war, and gave birth to the twins Romulus and Remus. When Amulius found out, he had Rhea Silvia thrown into prison, and her sons cast into the Tiber. He was foiled again. The boys were washed ashore and suckled by a she-wolf. Later they were found, taken in, and looked after by the royal herdsman Faustulus and his wife. When grown to manhood, learning the truth of their origins, Romulus and Remus slew Amulius, restored Numitor, and set out to found a city of their own at the place where, long before, they had been saved from the waters of the Tiber.

But the House of Aeneas was now polluted by killing; and blood begets blood. Romulus and Remus each claimed the kingship. Each waited for a sign from the gods, Romulus and his followers taking station on the Palatine Hill, Remus and his on the neighbouring Aventine. First, six vultures appeared in the sky for Remus. Then, immediately after-wards, twelve for Romulus. The gods had not spoken clearly: was priority decisive, or number? Claim and counter-claim degenerated into anger and abuse. Romulus assumed control and began to build a city. But as he and his followers worked to raise a wall along the boundary – a sacred line protected by ritual and taboo – Remus leapt across. Enraged by such defiance and sacrilege, Romulus slew his own brother. Thus, in 753 BC, in an act of fratricide, was Rome founded and Romulus made its king.

Romulus, needing settlers and soldiers, offered his city as a haven for exiles, brigands and fugitive slaves. To provide wives, he abducted the women of the neighbouring Sabines. And, after a period of warfare, he negotiated the union of Latin and Sabine, ruling Rome jointly with the Sabine king Titus Tatius in the later years of his reign. Romulus was the first of seven kings. The second was Numa Pompilius, revered for his wisdom and as founder of Rome's religious system, and the third Tullus Hostilius, a warmonger and imperialist, whose atrocities provoked Jupiter into setting his palace ablaze with a thunderbolt and burning him alive. Fourth to reign was Ancus Marcius, a moderate who preferred diplomacy abroad and public works at home – though he too could fight well enough when he had to. The fifth was Tarquinius Priscus, an Etruscan adventurer turned populist politician who charmed his way to power and then ruled as the proverbial 'benevolent dictator'. Then came Servius Tullius, a Latin protégé of the Tarquins, who succeeded after the assassination of his patron, and imposed radical reform on army and state. Finally, having murdered his predecessor, Tarquinius Superbus, a scheming and malevolent despot, ascended the throne of Romulus. The coup which overthrew him ended the Monarchy, founded the Republic, and inaugurated the Romans' enduring hatred of kings.

Thus was the story of Rome's origins told in the time of Augustus. We do not know how many people believed in its literal truth, though some were certainly sceptical. 'Events before Rome was born or thought of have come to us in old tales with more of the charm of poetry than of a sound historical record,' explained the historian Livy. On the other hand, he did not consider it his job to sort fact from fiction. The origin myths dignified the Roman past. They should be allowed to stand. Besides, 'so great is the glory won by the Roman people in their wars that, when they declare that Mars himself was their first parent and father of the man who founded their city, all the nations of the world might well allow the claim as readily as they accept Rome's imperial dominion.'(5)

The stories of Aeneas, Romulus, and the kings of Rome were not, then, a literal account of past happenings, but the revered texts of an imperial ideology grounded in a religious conception of the world. Rome was a superpower. Success depended on the will of the gods. Therefore, the Romans must be the gods' anointed. Why not, then, the gods' actual children? And who, in that pagan world where the boundary between sacred and profane was so blurred, who among the defeated and the subjugated could refute such claims? Power was the proof of myth.

Livy's scepticism is a good starting-point for us. The myth-history of ancient Rome was an 'invented tradition', stories created after Rome had become a great city to fill a gap at the beginning of time. They were fashioned from the materials to hand, evolving slowly over time towards their final form in the written epics of the Augustan Age. The result was a *mélange* of ancient fable, religious hokum, psychodrama, contemporary politics and traditional values. There were truths here, but they were not, by and large, historical ones. Rather, from the myths, we gain insight into the thought-world of ancient Rome: we see the Romans as they saw themselves, or as they wished to be seen, and we learn how they answered those pressing questions about origins and identity with which we began.

In fact, there was no 'Trojan' settlement in Late Bronze Age Italy. Nor was there a city on the site of Rome in the mid-8th century BC. Neither Aeneas nor Romulus ever existed. Indeed, the awkwardness of the double-myth – the obvious merging of two separate stories – exposes the whole as an elaborate concoction. It arose from the need to bridge two ideological worlds, that of the great gods and heroes of ancient Greece, and that of the local cults of a small and unsophisticated Italic people. Once a superpower, Rome needed to discuss its origins in the *lingua franca* of Homeric myth. Aeneas provides the connection between parochial folk-tale and cosmopolitan high-culture. Romulus, the local Italian boy, thereby gained a stature appropriate to the founder of an imperial city: though product of the seed of Mars and the milk of a wolf, he required descent from an Homeric hero with a divine mother to under-write his city's claims to global supremacy.

Not that Aeneas remained particularly Homeric in the hands of Virgil. Myths were devices for talking about the present, and Virgil's Aeneas bears little resemblance to Homer's Achilles: he was a hero for Augustan Rome, not Archaic Greece. Joyless and 'pious' (the Latin *pius* defies simple translation), Aeneas displays the sanctimonious rectitude of an imperial overlord, not the swaggering thuggery of a robber baron; and he acts not for himself and his self-glorification, but as a tool of divinely ordained destiny, an instrument of an imperial history about to unfold. The end therefore justifies the means. The Roman people, threatened with destruction at its moment of conception, born in the fires of an Italian civil war, charged with a mission to rule the world and impose order upon it, was of necessity a race of warriors. Rome's myth-history is her explanation for a thousand years of blood, slavery and empire. It presents the world-view of the Roman imperial ruling class at the height of its power.

Sometimes the link between mythic past and political present is explicit. Virgil has Aeneas girded for battle with a shield bearing an image of Octavian-Augustus at Actium. Usually the references are more elliptical. Virgil's contemporaries, though, could hardly have missed them. Aeneas fights and wins a terrible Italian civil war; as Octavian had a Roman civil war. He eschews seduction by an eastern *femme fatale*

(Dido/Cleopatra), unlike Octavian's bitter enemy (Antony). He thus arrives at the time and place appointed, ready to play his part in the grand performance of history-yet-to-be, as Octavian also might be thought to have done. After all, Octavian was great nephew and adopted son of Julius Caesar, who, not given to modesty, had claimed descent from Venus and Aeneas. Octavian had ended the civil wars, reconstructed the fractured Roman state, and, in a sense, founded the city anew. The spin, then, occasionally explicit, more usually implicit, was that Octavian was the new Aeneas-Romulus, a full-blooded reincarnation of his great ancestors, a second founder of the race and the city.

If Aeneas and Romulus were characters of myth, what of the other six kings of Rome? If no Trojans ever settled in Italy, and if Rome was not founded before *c.* 650 BC, what of the later events recounted in Book 1 of Livy's *History*, which continues the story up to 509 BC? Is it all fiction? After all, the writing of formal Roman history began only in the 3rd century BC, first in Greek, then in Latin. None of these early works survives complete: we have only fragments and extracts. The earliest surviving works are of 2nd century date, but there is little in them about the kings. We depend for the early history of Rome largely on the testimony of two late 1st century sources, of which Livy is one, and the Greek historian Dionysius of Halicarnassus the other. What can they possibly have known about real events 500 years before their own time, and 250 years before historical writing began? What primary sources, known to them but lost to us, might they have used?

Livy and Dionysius doubtless had access to the Roman state archives, as well as being sufficiently well-connected to gain entry to many private libraries. They would have found much useful material: written versions of old, orally transmitted epic poetry which, in the manner of Homer, perhaps preserved some authentic information about early Rome; an edited copy of the *Annales Maximi*, the whiteboards posted up for public view each year by the Roman priests, listing festival dates, election results, triumphs and portents; copies of important official documents like international treaties, decrees of the Senate, and treasury accounts; the works of 3rd century Greek historians and Roman annalists (who created formal year-by-year records of events); and – of more dubious value – aristocratic family histories which purported to list the high offices and great achievements of past members of the lineage.

These were tainted sources. History was manipulated by the powerful. Of this the ancients themselves were well aware. 'Of course,' explained the Roman politician Cicero, 'the history of Rome has been falsified by these speeches [aristocratic funerary orations], for there is much in them which never happened – invented triumphs, additional consulates, false claims to patrician status, with lesser men smuggled into another family with the same name . . .'(6) Despite such strictures, ancient historians were often uncritical of sources and sloppy about their writing. Livy transposed obvious errors, repeated mistranslations, reproduced without comment contradictory accounts, and even, drawing on different sources, sometimes recounted the same event twice without realizing there was only one. He was often little more than a hack.

But these things mattered less to ancient historians than to modern. Literal truth was, for men like Livy, 'a comparatively trivial matter'. If Greek historians were tragedians, Roman historians were moralists. 'I invite the reader's attention to the much more serious consideration of the kind of lives our ancestors lived, of who were the men, and what the means, both in politics and war, by which Rome's power was first acquired and subsequently expanded.' In this, there were lessons for the present, a period in which Livy detected serious moral decline: 'The study of history is the best medicine for a sick mind; for in history you have a record of the infinite variety of human experience plainly set out for all to see; and in that record you can find for yourself and your country both examples and warnings: fine things to take as models, base things, rotten through and through, to avoid.' The historian, then, was a man with a mission: to reform the morals of the age and save his fellow citizens from 'the vices of avarice and luxury'(7). Livy's history, no less than Virgil's poem, was an ideological tract.

As we approach the early history of Rome, therefore, we tread gingerly through a minefield of myth and moralizing. Archaeology is our guide. Many possibilities in the written texts can be tested against the hard evidence of surviving material culture. Excavations in the heart of ancient Rome; the analysis of grave-goods from archaic tombs; landscape surveys to locate and date settlement sites from scatters of potsherds; the tracing of trade routes from the find-spots of imported exotica: in these and other ways archaeologists are creating new evidence for early Rome. Rarely can archaeological material be tied to specific historical events; it deals more with the economic, social and cultural background, and with long-term changes in settlement, land-use and trade. But it creates a framework of possibilities. Stories that cannot be fitted to this framework must be rejected. The city of Romulus turns to myth when archaeology reveals nothing more than a village of wood, clay and thatch.

Let us take this as our starting-point, this Iron Age village found by archaeologists on the Palatine Hill, deeply buried beneath the aristocratic mansions of the Late Republic, and the imperial palaces of the Early Empire. What, from this and other evidence, do we know about the origins and early history of the small Latin city-state that would one day become the greatest empire in antiquity?

CHAPTER 1

· · · · · · · · · · · · · · · ·

The making of an imperial city-state, *c.* 750–367 BC

The people of Romulus: the Latin chiefdom, *c.* 750–625 BC

Not a city, but three or four hilltop villages were all that existed on the site of Rome around 750 BC. One of these – better known to us from excavation than the others – was on the Palatine Hill. In attempting to describe this place, in imagining it filled with people – living, working, trading, resting, playing, breeding, dying – much, inevitably, remains speculative. But from what we know – from excavation on the Palatine, from other excavations nearby, from myth, fragments of history, and the case-studies of anthropologists – we can perhaps visualize it as follows.

The Palatine must always have been a good place for Iron Age farmers and shepherds to settle. The ground rose steeply from the surrounding marsh to a wide plateau, an ideal refuge for men and beasts, where they were protected from both floods and raiders. Plough-land and pasture were in high demand at the time. Territory was often disputed in border clashes, and brigand-chiefs made a living rustling sheep and cattle. The village on the Palatine, girded by cliffs and a palisade, offered relative security, and a small Latin-speaking community had long been settled there. The people lived in small rectangular or oval huts, the floors cut into the bedrock, the frameworks formed of timber posts and rafters, the walls of wattle and daub, the roofs of thatch. We know the form of these not just from the postholes and slots excavated on the Palatine, but also from the ceramic containers modelled on the houses of the living in which the first villagers had laid to rest the cremated bones of their dead. For, near the bottom of the hill, just clear of the marsh, was an old cemetery, in use since the earliest days of the village in the 10th century BC, where at first the rite had been cremation, but afterwards, certainly by 750 BC, the villagers interred the intact bodies of the dead in trenches, along with ceramic jars containing food and drink. The spirits of the ancestors thus hallowed the ground, making good the claims of the living to possess it, guarding the approaches to the village above – though by now the settlement was beginning to spill down on to the low ground near the cemetery.

West of the Palatine lay the River Tiber, with trackways through the marsh leading to a crossing place and, on the far bank, the slopes of the Janiculan Hill. On the near bank were other hills besides the Palatine: the Aventine to the south-west; the Caelian to the south-east; the projecting spurs of the Esquiline, Viminal and Quirinal to the north-east; and an abrupt knoll, the Capitoline, immediately north-west (though these names may have been given later). Some of these other hills were also inhabited; they, too, made good refuges. And this spot next to the Tiber was one to which fugitives often came, for it lay in a marginal, frontier zone – a frontier between nature and agriculture, where much of the land was still a wilderness of swamp and forest; and a frontier between peoples, with Latins to the south, Etruscans to the north, and Sabines to the east. Humanity's flotsam and jetsam drifted here – the misfits and outcasts of more ordered societies elsewhere. Getting a living was tough, and you had to be ready to fight for what was yours. People clung together for safety, living on the high ground behind timber walls. These were raw new communities, with a rough-and-ready pioneering culture.

So mixed up were people here that not even on the site of Rome was everyone a Latin: there were Sabine settlers on the Quirinal. They were descendants of highlanders from the interior, who spoke a dialect of the Oscan-Umbrian language of the Apennine mountains. Relations between villages were often tense, but especially so when one was Latin and the other Sabine. The Latins were people of the plains, mostly farmers who combined the cultivation of wheat, barley, peas and beans with the raising of cattle, sheep and pigs. The animals provided meat, milk, hides and wool, as well as manure to keep the arable in good heart.

The Sabines, though they cultivated small fields in upland valleys, were mainly pastoralists – and, if the hostile testimony of Latin historians can be trusted, also sheep-stealers and cattle-rustlers. The exigencies of transhumant pastoralism – involving the movement of animals between upland summer pastures and lowland winter ones – complicated relations between the two peoples. Droveways criss-crossed the landscape, and access was often contested, for good grazing was precious. Old folk-tales memorialized the ethnic strife. *The Rape of the Sabine Women* told the story of a Latin chieftain who tricked his Sabine neighbours and abducted their women, and *The Legend of Tarpeia* that of a Latin traitor who met a grisly end during a war against the Sabines.

Close neighbours, though, usually tried to get along, else life's insecurities became insupportable. Sometimes, indeed, it was essential to combine against a common threat. This was probably easier in the frontier zone, where social bonds were looser, ethnic antagonisms less entrenched, and, if there were occasional fracas between Latin and Sabine – or even Latin and Latin – there was also much co-operation. Men from neighbouring villages entertained one another, exchanged gifts, became 'guest-friends'. They joined forces to deal with brigands and raiders. They made alliances, contracted marriages, sired mongrel children. In *The Legend of Titus Tatius*, the Sabine wives of Latin men intervened to stop a war between their fathers and husbands: another traditional story with perhaps a core of truth. Making a living and defending what was yours often meant peace with near-neighbours and a united front against more distant enemies. So the people of the hills by the Tiber got together. They meshed into a single community, and as they proliferated and grew strong, others came to join them from outlying farms, hamlets, and the wilderness beyond. Some, no doubt, were brigands and vagabonds, but, in troubled times, men uprooted in one place might, if they were tough, hard-working and handy in a fight, find a ready enough welcome in another.

The picture was the same across Old Latium. This was the land of the people who spoke Latin. As well as language, they shared history, religion and customs. But at this time, they can have numbered only a few thousands, for Latium was fairly small. It comprised in the main a coastal plain of irregular shape, 80 km in length, 50 km wide in the north where the Tiber valley formed a broad expanse, and narrower further south, where it eventually turned into an uninhabitable swamp. East of the plain, the Latins had also settled some of the high ground. Volcanoes and rivers had formed this landscape in geological time. The Alban Hills south of Rome were mounds of lava; 50 craters lay within a day's walk of the Palatine; and much of Latium was strewn with a layer of volcanic debris rich in phosphates and potash. The Tiber, its tributaries, and the smaller rivers that flowed directly to the sea further south had turned this debris into alluvial silt and spread it across the land, making it, with adequate drainage, into first-class soil for farming. The result was a mixed landscape of hill, plain and marsh, of arable, pasture and wilderness. Wherever the land could yield a living, it had, by the 8th century, filled up with Latin-speaking settlers.

To later generations, Latium seemed blessed by the gods. When dawn rose over the sea and Virgil's Aeneas saw from his ship 'a mighty forest through which the Tiber pleasantly flowed'(1), he knew that his travels were over, that he had reached the Promised Land. Horace, another of the Augustan poets, thought his Sabine farm at Tibur, in the hill-country 30 km inland from Rome, the finest place on earth: 'neither the sturdy Spartan hills nor the low lush fields of Larissa can knock at the heart as Tibur does, with Sibyl's booming grotto, Anio's fine cascade, Tiburnus' grove, the orchards whose rivulets weave a dance of irrigation, the winds blowing clear from the south, sweeping clouds out of a dark sky, and never breeding long rains.'(2) Poets are not peasants and they construct a rural idyll. But the point stands: Latium was good land, and for that reason from early times heavily settled.

The Latins first lived in numerous scattered villages, each of a few dozen families. Latterly, however, the smaller, more vulnerable settlements had been abandoned, and people had been brought together – perhaps not always willingly – into the larger, more defensible ones. During the 8th century, what had once been an open, usually peaceful landscape of farmers became more enclosed and defensive: the land, in fact, had come to bear the mark of a new class of chieftains and warriors who had emerged to rule in troubled times.

Men had lived in rough equality during the 9th century. Each family (*familia*) at that time comprised a small group of kin and dependants under the authority of a leading male (*paterfamilias*, head of household). This unit was largely self-sufficient, living off the produce of its own fields and flocks, which were tended by family members. There was no money for regular trade; essential transactions were done by barter or with ingots of bronze; and wealth was measured in head of cattle. In life, each family shared a complex of huts and enclosures within the village; and in death, a common plot in the village cemetery. The head of household's power was in theory absolute – including power over life and death within the family – and he was the acknowledged owner of the family's estate. In practice, family life must have involved negotiation, and patriarchy been moderated by custom, popular censure, and the need to find ways of living and working together.

From one family to another, there was little difference in rank and status, and each head of household played an equal part in village life, speaking in public assembly, making sacrifice to the gods, guarding the border with spear and shield. What bound him to other men, in his own village and beyond, were ties of extended kinship: his membership of a clan (*gens*). Once, in a golden age beyond remembering – or so it was believed – when it had always been summer, the earth had given of its bounty freely, and men had known neither toil nor war, the clans had held all things in common. Now, though, was the Age of Iron, when the price of life was sweat and aching limbs, and men claimed land as private property and would shed blood to defend it. Now, also, Hunger waited. It waited for the work-shy, the weak, and those who angered the gods. It was insecurity and fear that gave the clans their strength: they meant an insurance against hardship, a defence against enemies, and a pooling of prayers to placate the gods. Each father, family and farm, each atom of economy and society, was fixed in its place within village and clan by its dependence on the support of others.

During the 8th century, this simple society became more complex. As well as ties of family and clan, there were new obligations to men of power who claimed authority as priests, judges and war-chiefs. As communities coalesced and populations grew, as villages of a few dozen became large settlements of several hundred, concentrations of wealth acquired a certain critical mass. Reserves of grain and meat now sufficed to free some men from labour in the fields. Small villages cannot support full-time blacksmiths and potters; large ones can. Small communities cannot feed retinues of warriors that do no work; large ones might be made to. The chieftains who now raised themselves to power did so as collectors and distributors of the surplus, some of which they used as offerings to the gods, some to recruit and train soldiers, and some to reward loyalists who upheld chiefly authority. They were priests, war-lords and politicians combined. In the simple, small-scale, egalitarian societies of the 9th century, heads of household had met in assembly, per-formed holy rites, and arrayed themselves for war as co-equals in village and clan. In the more complex, larger-scale, stratified societies that had formed by the 7th century, authority in politics, religion and war had become the prerogative of a new ruling class of chiefs. Archaeology encounters them in the cemeteries of this time. If they were as richly caparisoned in life as in death, then they rode into battle in decorated chariots, wearing helmets and breastplates of bronze, equipped with shield, spear and sword. They must have feasted with household and retinue amid a clutter of drinking gear – folding metal tripods, griffin-headed cauldrons, and, shipped over from Corinth and Athens, a range of ceramic wine-containers, mixing-bowls and pitchers painted with scenes from myth.

Fighting and feasting welded the followers of chieftains into a warrior elite. Insecurity and a need for protection had forged this new class of men, but, once formed, the rivalries among them fed the clamour for war. Chiefs built up their war-bands to compete with other chiefs for territory, resources and followers; or they were overwhelmed, their lands annexed, their line extinguished. By the 7th century BC, Latin society was divided into chiefs, nobles and commoners, and war and preparations for war were endemic.

Among the new chiefdoms was that on the hills by the Tiber, where, by *c.* 700 BC, the separate villages had coalesced, other settlements nearby had been absorbed, and a succession of chiefs who styled them-selves 'kings' – Numa Pompilius, Tullus Hostilius and Ancus Marcius – had established their rule. (The Latin word *rex* is commonly translated 'king'. The Romans certainly used the word later to describe those we would recognize as kings. But the 'kingdom' ruled by Ancus Marcius was not much larger than an English parish.) The nobles – the leading men of the more powerful clans – formed a 'royal' council. Here was the embryo of the class of patricians and of their later assembly, the Senate. All the clans were grouped in one or another of three tribes (*tribus*) – called Luceres, Ramnes and Tities – and each of these was divided into ten cantons (*curia*). Though many people forgot this in time and came to imagine that the tribes and cantons had always existed, they were in fact devices of the king-chief, imposed for the efficient organization of political and military affairs. For the chiefdom was – as, in the circumstances, it had to be – first and foremost an armed body of men, a tribal militia for waging war against its neighbours.

When summoned, all free men attended the Assembly of the Cantons (*Comitia Curiata*), where, under the authority of clan-chiefs, canton by canton, they voted by acclamation for or against war. If they decided for war, they marched off in cantonal and tribal units, 100 men forming the 'century' (*centuria*) required of each canton, 1,000 men the tribal contingent, and 3,000 the army or 'legion' as a whole (*legio* meaning 'levy'). Only the king-chief, the nobles and the knights of their retinues wore any armour – perhaps a helmet and a small breastplate – or carried swords. The commoners were equipped simply with spears, some for throwing, some for close-quarters fighting, and with large round shields. Battle tactics were crude. Men fought defensively in dense but loosely structured masses, presenting to the enemy a wall of shields bristling with spear-points. Attacks were wild charges led by the armoured elite. Pitched battles were the exception, however, and most wars entailed little more than border raids and skirmishes.

New ideas were needed to make sense of life under the chieftains: ideas able to bind together disparate fragments of population, to make a unity of them, and to invest people with a shared sense of history and identity. Myths, ancestors and gods; holy rites and sacred places; customs in common and a collective destiny: these were the stuff of a tribal people's grit and solidarity.

Old cults and traditions remained, those of ploughmen and shepherds inherited from a simpler past. Religion mattered too much, was too deeply ingrained, for one set of gods simply to be swapped for another. Rather, new gods joined the old in an enlarged pantheon. People continued, as they had always done, to imagine the natural world around them animated by myriad spirits. The simplest act required its petty rite of propitiation. Fear of the gods – of divine disfavour – engendered an obsessive avoidance of taboo and endless repetition of ritual. The year was divided between days that were 'profane' (*dies fasti*), when work was permitted, and those that were 'sacred' (*dies nefasti*), when normal activity was suspended and a religious festival celebrated. Some land was available for men to plough, but other land was left wild because it belonged to the god of a sacred grove, with perhaps a wooden idol, a tree-stump for an altar, and branches hung with offerings. Every household had divine protection – a *lar*, the family's guardian spirit; the *penates*, who looked after the food-stores; and the *Manes*, the spirits of the ancestors, who received regular grave-side offerings. Groups of households met to honour the nymph of a local spring or the guardian of a crossroads. Then there were the great gods worshipped in public pageants on festival days by the whole people – the Earth Mother, source of fertility and fruitfulness; Vesta, goddess of the hearth, a luminous presence in every home; Faunus, protector of flocks, whose priests danced half-naked in goatskin skirts at the festival of the *Lupercalia*; and Saturn, whose winter festival held out the promise of returning spring and preserved the memory of a golden age before toil and war. All these were old gods – gods of families, fields and flocks such as farmers worshipped. To them, though, were now added, in the age of chieftains, new gods of war and power.

Most important was the triad of Jupiter, Mars and Quirinus, to each of whom a specialist priest (*flamen*) was allocated, chosen by the king from his patricians. Jupiter was the supreme sky-god, ruler over heaven and earth, protector of boundaries, laws and social rank. Mars was god of war. In March each year, the brotherhood of Salian priests led the rituals of Mars which opened the new campaigning season: the display of shields, the dedication of horses, the blessing of arms and trumpets. And in October, when the season ended, they led the sacrifices that gave thanks to Mars, and the ceremonies that purified the blood-polluted weapons. Then there was Quirinus, the spirit of deified Romulus, mythic founder of Rome, who ensured the peace, prosperity and well-being of his people.

These people were the descendants of shepherds, ploughmen and outlaws who had sought safety in the hills by the Tiber. They had been forged into a tribal state by a nobility of kings, clan-chiefs and warrior-knights. They now possessed a small territory extending some seven kilometres in each direction, around 150 sq km in all. They had come to believe in an imagined past and invented traditions, and these had helped them think of themselves as a single people. They had, in short, become the *Quirites*, the people of Romulus, the wolf-men of Mars. They had become the Romans.

City of the Tarquins: the Etruscan city-state, c. 625–509 BC

No city existed on the banks of the Tiber when the Romans first emerged as a distinct people. Until the late 7th century BC, they were a tribal community ruled by chiefs, and their main settlement contained no masonry or monumental buildings. Though hundreds lived there, Rome was still a place of earth banks, timber palisades, and small houses of wood, clay and thatch. And such it might have remained had not the Romans been sucked into the vortex of Etruscan military imperialism. Ancient cities rarely just evolved; usually they were founded and built by political decision. This, almost certainly, was the case with Rome.

The region north of Latium was ruled by a powerful Etruscan-speaking elite who derived their wealth from rural estates worked by serfs. They had begun to construct stone-built cities on defensible hilltops, and at these sites a sophisticated civilization developed during the 6th century. Civil engineers built stone bridges, carefully graded paved roads suitable for carts, and whole networks of underground drains for land reclamation and water supply. Architects designed large stone-built temples with colonnaded porches, and artists decorated these with brightly painted terracotta slabs. Potters produced a range of fine *bucchero* tableware – delicately shaped, thin-walled vessels with a glossy black finish. Greek and Phoenician merchants brought in shiploads of oil, perfume, ostrich eggs, bronze vessels, and ceramics decorated with superb figured scenes in black silhouette, exchanging these for copper, iron and slaves. And such was the demand for eastern exotica that local artists were soon copying the 'Oriental' styles. Many of the most treasured objects accompanied their owners in death, for outside the cities of the living were cities of the dead, with streets of tombs in which, behind sealed entrances, the spirits of the departed reclined on couches, feasts laid out before them, the walls painted with frescoes of games, music and drinking. In wealth, power and culture, the Etruscans were well ahead of the Latins, and by the end of the 7th century they had already achieved that critical mass of elite-controlled surplus that made civilization – life in cities – possible.

The Etruscans had also adopted a new way of war. A military revolution begun in Greece had spread rapidly to the Greek colonies and

Etruscan cities of Italy. The city-states of the time were, in essence, communities of citizens pledged to common defence of territory, property and families. Each free man was obliged to do military service, but his contribution was related to means, and, increasingly, the chief burden came to fall on the better-off citizens who could equip themselves with a full panoply – that is, as heavy infantrymen with helmet, body-armour, large round shield, thrusting spear, and sword: what the Greeks called 'hoplites'. These men, perhaps a third of the total in a typical city-state militia, formed the essential core of Greek armies. The upper-class cavalry were generally too few to matter. The lower-class light infantry, though numerous, played only secondary roles in battle. It was hoplites that were decisive. They formed up as a phalanx, a block of close-packed men, eight or more ranks deep, ranged shoulder-to-shoulder, the front rank presenting a wall of overlapping shields with spears projecting above. Though slow and inflexible, the phalanx was an ideal formation for deploying large numbers of poorly trained, amateur soldiers. In head-on confrontation, provided it maintained order, the phalanx was virtually unbreakable in defence and unstoppable in attack. Levies of tribesmen – lacking armour and in loose formation – were easily defeated by the concentrated killing-power of dense masses of city-state heavy infantry. Generally, to fight a phalanx, you needed your own phalanx. So those with the resources to do so – like the Etruscans – remodelled their armies for hoplite warfare during the 6th century.

Rearmed, the Etruscans became conquerors. Umbria, much of the Po valley to the north, and substantial parts of Latium and Campania to the south fell to Etruscan warlords. They founded many cities – among them, probably, Pompeii – each a planned 'new town' with a regular street-grid laid out by Etruscan surveyors. Neither conquests nor colonies were under unified control, however. There was no 'Etruscan Empire' formally constituted. The homeland itself was divided into independent city-states – traditionally twelve – and interventions abroad were mainly the work of military freebooters seeking glory, plunder and land. Groups of nobles organized expeditions – with or without the backing of their respective cities – by calling up men who owed them allegiance and service, and attracting others by offering a share in the spoils. Nor were the adventurers and would-be colonists recruited necessarily Etruscan. In much of Italy, especially on the Hellenized west coast, the upper classes shared elements of a common culture – a *koine* (strictly a common language, but often used metaphorically about culture in general). Ties of kinship and hospitality linked men together – Etruscans, Latins, Sabines, Greeks, others – across ethnic barriers. In a limited sense only, therefore, could Rome be said to have 'fallen to the Etruscans' in the 6th century BC. Tarquinius Priscus, the Etruscan warlord who made himself king, was a more or less independent operator. The dynasty he founded – unstable and relatively short-lived – was only in the loosest sense part of a wider Etruscan *imperium*. Nonetheless, the impact was profound: the Etruscan kings founded Rome anew as a city, a city-state, and a true monarchy.

Rome was ripe for taking. The Latin community was divided into political factions. The patrician aristocracy of clan-chiefs owned the best land and controlled the royal council. The burden of war service fell mainly on the commoners, especially on the *assidui*, a 'middling sort' made up of small property-owners able to equip themselves as proto-hoplites. As the tribal state became more dependent on them, the middling sort's resentment over such issues as debt, land shortage, aristocratic privilege, and over-long stints on campaign acquired greater urgency. With the balance of power at Rome tipping against the patrician retinues and in favour of a discontented hoplite class, the intervention of Tarquinius Priscus was the catalyst that collapsed the tribal state. He and his two sucessors, Servius Tullius (a Latin, but protégé of the Etruscans) and Tarquinius Superbus, were what a contemporary Greek would have called 'tyrants': populist strongmen who battered their way to power with mass support. And once in control, the Etruscans, like Greek tyrants, implemented a programme of domestic reform, monumental building, and imperial expansion.

Urbanization had in fact already begun at Rome when the Etruscans came to power. Around 650 BC, the marsh between the hills had been drained and an expanse of beaten earth laid out, creating a place of public assembly at the centre of the settlement: the Forum. Another low-lying area close to the river had also been drained, this to serve as a cattle market: the Forum Boarium. Shortly afterwards, the main forum had been paved in stone, and soon, before the end of the 7th century, the earliest stone buildings had been erected nearby. Whatever had already been done, however, it was probably Tarquinius Priscus who 'founded'

Rome in a formal sense. He thereby started the process which turned a stronghold into a city, villagers into citizens, a tribal chiefdom into a royal city-state.

To found a city was a most holy act. Plutarch records the ceremony at Rome in his biography of Romulus. (Plutarch's *Lives* were written around the end of the 1st century AD, and his account of the foundation ceremony at Rome is probably based on records of later rituals at other sites; something like it, however, may have happened at Rome in the time of Tarquinius Priscus.) First, Plutarch tells us, a circular trench was dug at the Comitium, the place of public assembly in the Forum, and into this were cast offerings of first-fruits and clods of earth taken from each citizen's farm. This spot, thus sanctified with symbols of fertility and fraternity, was the centre around which the city was to be laid out. 'Then the founder fitted to a plough a bronze ploughshare, and, yoking together a bull and a cow, drove himself a deep furrow round the bounds. The business of those that followed was to see that whatever earth was thrown up should be turned inwards to the city, and not to let any clod lie outside. With this line they described the wall, the *pomerium*, and where they designed to make a gate, there they took out the share, carried the plough over, and left a space. Because of this, they consider the whole wall as holy, except where the gates are, for had they judged them also sacred, they could not, without offence to religion, have given free ingress and egress for the necessaries of life, some of which are in themselves unclean.'(3) (Remus' offence in the famous myth, for which his brother Romulus killed him, was, of course, to leap across the *pomerium*, violating – and by implication denying – its sacredness.)

Archaeology has revealed what may be a 6th century defensive wall associated with a new city boundary. It was constructed from well-cut, carefully laid blocks of *cappellaccio*, a soft volcanic tufa quarried in the Roman countryside and widely used at the time as a building stone. The boundary enclosed the Palatine, the Esquiline, and the Forum in between, amounting to some 285 hectares, which – assuming our estimates of dates for this and an earlier boundary around the Palatine alone are correct – would have made the new city more than three times the size of the 7th century chieftain's stronghold.

A century of monumental building followed. The city's main sewer became a huge stone-lined culvert, the Great Drain (*Cloaca Maxima*), large enough, as a Roman writer observed several centuries later, to allow the passage of a wagon loaded with hay. In the Forum, new buildings included the Regia, the house of the king; the Senate House, where meetings of the royal council were held; and the Black Stone, a subterranean sanctuary containing a large stone block inscribed with ritual injunctions. Nearby, the Palatine Hill began to emerge as Rome's elite residential district, with large patrician houses (*domus*) of standardized design on the lower slopes. Entering one of these through a street-front passage, one came into a spacious cruciform courtyard (*atrium*), with a narrow opening to the sky that allowed rainwater to collect in a centrally placed basin (*impluvium*). Facing the courtyard were four symmetrically placed suites of rooms, together with a large reception-room (*tablinum*) directly opposite the entrance passage. (Several elements of this design were still being recommended by the Roman architect Vitruvius 500 years later. Examples can be seen at Pompeii.)

Most impressive among Etruscan buildings were the new temples. Of these, none could compare with the temple on the Capitoline Hill, the most ambitious project of all, and one that was still unfinished when the last king was overthrown in *c.* 509 BC. Dedicated by the consuls of the new Republic, it was, and would forever remain, Rome's greatest monument: the Capitoline Temple of Jupiter, Juno and Minerva, the three patron deities of Rome, the Roman people, and, ultimately, the Roman Empire. 'Builders and engineers were brought from all over Etruria,' Livy tells us, 'and the project involved the use not only of public funds but also of a large number of labourers from the poorer classes. The work was hard in itself, and came as an addition to their regular military duties, but it was an honourable burden with a solemn and religious significance, and they were not, on the whole, unwilling to bear it.'(4) The Capitoline Temple was about 55 m wide and 60 m long, making it one of the largest in the world. It was approached frontally up a steep flight of steps giving access to the high podium. A deep porch of 18 columns arranged in three rows of six covered the front of the podium, and a line of columns ran down either side of the building to meet lateral extensions of the rear wall. The shrine itself was a solid-walled structure divided into three long cells, each with a monumental door at the front and a cult image at the back. A gabled, tiled roof extended over both porch and shrine. Exterior architraves, cornices and eaves were decorated with lines of terracottas painted with floral and geometric patterns. Rows of gorgons and other mythic monsters glared down from the guttering. Life-sized gods perched on the roof, each wearing the same enigmatic 'archaic' smile. The temple and its cult symbolized the new order of the late 6th century: the monarchy, the city, the war-making state that Rome was becoming, and the growing dominance of the Roman *imperium* in Old Latium.

Etruscan Rome was a boom town for artisans and traders. Apart from great building projects, with their demand for quarrymen, surveyors, stone-cutters, architects, sculptors, tile-makers and general labourers, the city became a regional emporium. The Tiber was a funnel for people, goods and ideas, and Rome stood at the highest point navigable for ships of any size. It linked the Greek and Phoenician traders working the Mediterranean sea-lanes with the Italian aristocracy of the inland towns, whose growing wealth and 'Orientalizing' tastes made them eager to acquire luxury goods from the East. Moreover, this east-west funnel was crossed at Rome by an equally important north-south routeway. The city, 20 km from the sea, lay at the lowest convenient crossing-point on the river: the overland route down the west coast of Italy between Etruria and Campania ran through Rome. The late 6th century city was full of Greek and Etruscan pottery shops. New cult centres like the Temples of Mother Dawn and Fortune down near the docks served a growing merchant community. Great trading cities like Phoenician Carthage and Greek Marseille sought treaties with Rome's kings. The patrician elite laid their tables with Athenian black-figure ceramics and mixed wine in Etruscan bronze cauldrons. 'Hi, enjoy your drink!' exclaimed the Greek inscription on a 6th century wine-cup found in Rome. The moralists of a later age were wrong, it seems: there had never been a golden age of sober living; Rome's rich had always loved *luxuria* (a word which implied not only luxury, but the extravagant and conspicuous consumption of wealth as a mark of status). The city had ceased to be a farming settlement and become a centre of commerce, grandeur and 'taste'. Most of the inhabitants were not now peasants but the artisans, traders, labourers and slaves who served the city elite. Rome had become a parasitic 'consumer city', a place which produced less than it consumed and was dependent on inflows of surplus wealth from outside.

Much of the surplus was raised in the *ager Romanus* (Roman farmland), where the elite had their estates. But part was also raised through war – through, that is, the forcible seizure of surplus in the form of booty. Rome remained at root a war-making state – and a turbulent one at that, one whose social conflicts had enabled the Tarquins to rise to power in the first place, and which afterwards prompted them to attempt a major remodelling of Roman society. Their aim in this was to break the power of the patricians and the clans they dominated, and to reform an out-dated army composed of loosely organized tribal contingents. Instead, there was to be a constitutional monarchy based on popular consent, an empowering of the citizen-body as a whole, and a recasting of the army as a hoplite phalanx. These changes, involving as they did a decisive and permanent shift of power from clan-chiefs to citizen-yeomanry, were, in fact, of greater significance even than the building of the city: they were the very essence of the transition from tribal chiefdom to city-state engineered by the Etruscan kings.

Around 550 BC, in the aftermath of the violent convulsion that brought him to power, Servius Tullius, the second of the dynasty of usurper-kings, imposed a new property-based constitution on the state. All male citizens (except a minority who owned no property at all) were allocated to a military-service class (*classis*) according to the value of their estate as determined in a five-yearly census (*census*). The census, and the highly respected elected magistrates who conducted it (*censores*), were to be characteristic features of the Roman state throughout its history. Without the census, military service (*militia*) and war tax (*tributum*) could not have been administered fairly and efficiently. With the census, regularly updated, each man's contribution could be related to his means. Nothing demonstrates more clearly than the Roman census the basic nature of the city-state as a community of men organized for war.

According to their rating, citizens equipped themselves as cavalry, heavy infantry or light infantry, and according to age they served as 'juniors' in the field army or 'seniors' in the home guard. The new classifications were grafted on to a reformed tribal system. In place of the three 'Romulan' tribes of the 7th century chiefdom (Luceres, Ramnes and Tities), there were now 21 'Servian' tribes, four in the city corresponding to four urban areas, the rest in the countryside. Tribal membership was determined by place of residence and affirmed in a civil registration process. It was through the tribe that each man then exercised his rights and performed his duties. The tribe was required to supply four centuries of juniors and four of seniors. This yielded a field army of 8,400 men and a home guard of equal size. Each force was divided into two legions of 4,200 men, of whom 3,000 were 'of the hoplite-shield rating', and 1,200 were light infantry armed with javelins and slings. There were also six centuries of cavalry (later increased to 18), drawn from the wealthiest class, the knights (*equites*).

Rome's new hoplite army was the basis of new political institutions. Servius Tullius aimed to underpin royal authority and marginalize the patrician clan-chiefs who controlled the Assembly of the Cantons (*Comitia Curiata*) by creating a new popular assembly. It was to be controlled by the hoplite class, by citizens of the middling sort, the main supporters of the dynasty. It was, moreover, to be a military assembly, representing the people organized as an army, for it was here that henceforward decisions would be made about peace and war. This Assembly of the Centuries (*Comitia Centuriata*) met just outside the city on the Field of Mars (*Campus Martius*), the army's mustering ground, and it voted century by century. The higher classes – knights and hoplites – voted first, and their votes had greater weight. The whole mass of the propertyless poor, known as 'proletarians' (*proletarii*: those who had offspring but no property), men who were therefore 'counted only by head' (*capite censi*), were lumped together in a single 'century' to cast their votes. Property, military service and political power were thus intertwined: the Assembly of the Centuries was a stakeholders' assembly. The old Assembly of the Cantons was not dissolved, and the clan-chiefs ensured that it continued to function; but it was eclipsed and never recovered its former prestige.

The new army saw frequent action. Rome was surrounded by actual and potential enemies. Border disputes flared up with neighbouring Etruscan and Latin city-states, and hostile tribesmen, Sabines, Aequi and Volsci, mounted regular raids on the western and southern edges of Latium. The price of security was high. War, though, could be profitable, and this – the inner secret of Rome's whole history – was a discovery of the Etruscan kings. Given a superior army and troubled conditions, the temptation was to launch preventive wars: better to neutralize an enemy before he became a serious threat. Often, moreover, there was a victory dividend to be drawn: booty, slaves and land. In a world of peasant agriculture and primitive technology, where land and labour were the basis of wealth but the return from estates was more or less fixed, plundering enemies was the easiest source of new wealth – wealth to maintain armies, build cities, and reward supporters. So late 6th century Rome evolved in the hands of the Etruscan kings into something more than a military state seeking security through arms; she became an aggressive, predatory, imperial state, one that waged wars of plunder and conquest as deliberate policy. Militarism entered the soul of Rome.

Old legends recorded the destruction of ancient cities and the absorption of their people by the Roman state – Alba Longa, Tellenae, Politorium, Ficana: archaic settlements snuffed out in the shadowy era before historical records began. Once, in the mid 7th century, the *ager Romanus* had covered about 150 sq km and supported a population of no more than a few thousand. By the end of the 6th century, the *ager Romanus* was 20 km wide, covered some 800 sq km, and contained perhaps 35,000 people. The territory of Rome by then embraced a third of Old Latium. Moreover, as the most powerful of the Latin states, Rome controlled a league of independent cities, including Gabii, Tusculum, Aricia, Ardea and Lavinium, and these formed a defensive ring around her frontier. The Etruscan kings – conquering kings, mini-imperialists – had turned Rome into the Latin hegemon.

This was the new order that was so aptly symbolized by the Temple of Jupiter, Juno and Minerva rising on the Capitoline Hill. Paid for – as all the city's future temples would be – by war booty, it honoured Jupiter, god of property and power, Juno, goddess of marriage and the family, and Minerva, goddess of wisdom and (without apparent irony) war. The 8th century fertility cults of farmers were now overshadowed, in the late 6th century, by the black-hearted gods of empire.

Sixty years of strife: the patrician regime, c. 509–449 BC

By the late 6th century, the monarchy was in decay. The Tarquins had come to power with popular support, but their government became autocratic and repressive. The kings fought numerous wars of conquest and built many great monuments, but these policies came at a cost to the general population. When the kings also claimed descent from the gods and behaved like despots – in itself a response to declining popularity – their supporters abandoned them. Crucially, their main political base was eroded by the very success of their reforms: once the Assembly of the Centuries was securely established as a sovereign body, the hostility of the middling sort towards the patricians subsided, and the popular role of the Tarquins was largely played out. The focus shifted to secondary matters: the burden of war service, the cost of public works, abuses of power. In these conditions, the patrician aristocracy was able to reassert itself and, under the increasingly tyrannical regime of Tarquinius Superbus, to plot the overthrow of the monarchy.

The plotters' aim was not full-blooded counter-revolution. The patricians did not wish to – or were not strong enough to – abolish the Assembly of the Centuries and impose a narrow oligarchy. Broadly, they accepted the new political order, based, as it was, on the city-state's dependence on a mass army of citizen-hoplites. Indeed, in a sense, the army was the prize in contention between king and nobles. The growing wealth of the city was a result of successful war, but court government meant favouritism and whimsy in the distribution of spoils, a tendency exacerbated by the king's declining popularity and his consequent reliance on a small inner circle. The plotters wanted to destroy the system of royal patronage and put the state under collective aristocratic control. The aim was a government that would not restrict the distribution of offices and spoils to a court clique.

The king was with the army at Ardea when revolt broke out in Rome in *c.* 509 BC. He immediately marched back to the capital, but there he found the rebels in firm control and the gates shut against him. Meantime, some of the rebel leaders had reached Ardea and persuaded the army to join the revolt. Tarquinius and most of his family then fled to Caere in Etruria, setting up a court in exile which spent its time trying to drum up support for restoration. For some years, the final outcome remained uncertain. The Etruscan adventurer Lars Porsenna – acting ostensibly in the Tarquin interest but really in his own – invaded Roman territory and threatened the city. This effort, however, was among the last gasps of Etruscan imperial power. Stretched thin across their sprawling domains, the Etruscans were being driven back on several fronts. The Greeks of Cumae had inflicted a decisive defeat on them in distant Campania in *c.* 524 BC, and, responding to a request for help from the Latin cities, had recently sent a seaborne expedition north to challenge Etruscan supremacy in Latium. A Greek victory over an army led by one of Lars Porsenna's sons at Aricia in *c.* 506 BC enabled the Latin cities to assert their independence. Rome's anti-Tarquin revolution – part of a broader anti-Etruscan movement across west-central Italy – was not to be reversed.

Though the patricians enjoyed a measure of popular support – else the army would not have mutinied – they were neither nationalists nor democrats, and in fact had no particular political programme at all save to overthrow the king and advance themselves to power. The monarchy, latterly at least, had been centralized and authoritarian. The new government was the opposite, a loose alliance of rival families, each commanding an extensive network of personal dependants. The head of each patrician family had an inner retinue of kinsmen and servants – like 7th century clan-chiefs – but also an outer retinue of clients (*clientes*) who, though not related by blood or marriage, were tied to their patron (*patronus*) by reciprocal obligations of service and protection. Where the state's organs of justice were weak or partial, patrons provided support amid the vicissitudes of life: the resources and influence to secure legal redress; the means to execute judgments in the absence of official law enforcement; letters of introduction (from one great man to another) to facilitate travel and trade; loans, even gifts, to bridge the effects of harvest failure, war damage or accidental loss; the services of a doctor, a tutor, a cook, or a pretty slave-girl. The benefits to patrons were no less tangible. In a world where the measure of a man was the size of his retinue, clients were expected to attend any summons – to a feast, a court-hearing, an election contest, a street confrontation, even a pitched battle. And since a strong patron offered better protection and succour, all clients had an interest in the advancement of their own leader. Around 500 BC, 'the comrades (*sodales*) of Publius Valerius' set up a dedication to Mars at the Latin city of Satricum. Not as subjects of a king, citizens of a state, or members of a tribe did they define themselves, but as a group of men united by allegiance to an aristocratic patron. Even private wars were possible. The Fabii clan mobilized its retinue in *c.* 477 BC to wage its own war against the Etruscan city of Veii – and suffered shattering defeat at the battle of Cremera. Others turned on Rome herself: disgruntled nobles and their clients fought alongside Etruscans, Sabines and Volsci against the mother-city. The rivalry of patrician retinues contained destructive power. Baronial anarchy threatened the fledgling Republic.

The city constitution evolved as an attempt to contain the retinues and structure their rivalry. The composition of the aristocracy at first remained open. New families, some Roman, some foreign, joined the 136 reputedly recognized as patrician in the time of the kings. When the Sabine chieftain Appius Claudius migrated to Rome in *c.* 504 BC – with, it is said, 5,000 dependants and clients – he was granted patrician rank and admitted to the Senate. Subsequently, however, the ranks of the aristocracy closed against newcomers, and the patricians became an exclusive caste. The twin principles of collegiality and annual elections then served to channel and contain competition within this group. In place of the king, whose authority had been autocratic and for life, the Early Republic was administered by two supreme magistrates – at first called 'praetors' (*praetores*), later 'consuls' (*consules*) – elected annually from among the patricians. The latter formed an advisory council – the Senate (*senatus*) – but only gradually did *ad hoc* meetings of invited 'elders' (*patres*) evolve into a regular assembly of fixed composition.

The consuls inherited much of the king's political, military and legal authority – but only one third of his religious authority, which they shared with two other high priests, the chief priest (*pontifex maximus*) and the 'king of sacred affairs' (*rex sacrorum*). Consuls enjoyed wide executive powers – including that of life and death when acting as army commanders-in-chief in the field. But there were limits: each man was constrained by his colleague's power of veto, such that both consuls had to agree for action to be taken; each could be called to account at the end of his year in office (though not before, since serving magistrates were immune to prosecution); and each knew he would return to his seat on the backbenches, to sit again as an equal among peers, dependent on their support for any further honour.

The consulship had two great advantages. First, it directed the competition between aristocratic houses towards office-holding and military commands *within* – as opposed to *against* – the state. The highly prestigious supreme office was rotated, and many men could aspire to achieve it. Any patrician could hope one day to be Rome's first citizen, the leader of her armies, the master of her assemblies and pageants, the year of his tenure bearing his name forever (since the Romans employed a system of consular dates). Second, the consulship protected the state against overmighty subjects: by directing ambition's flow, by ensuring that authority was always shared, short-term and subject to critical review, the danger of civil war – a war of rival retinues – was minimized. It was from these special qualities of the consulship that the Senate derived its famed *auctoritas* – a word which means, in Latin, a combination of authority, influence and prestige. Strictly, the Senate had no formal power to make law or direct the executive: its constitutional role was purely advisory. In practice, before the late 2nd century BC, the collective sanction of the Senate over individual members was so great that few consuls ever defied a senatorial *consultum* (tellingly, the word means 'advice', but it came to have the force of 'edict'). The patricians of the Early and Middle Republic operated as a well-organized and united ruling class. It was as well for them that they did, for they faced many enemies, both at home and abroad.

The Tarquins had been empire-builders who had made Rome the most powerful state in Latium and the head of a league of Latin cities. The revolution at Rome and the break-up of the Etruscan *imperium* seemed to offer the Latins a chance of independence. So they severed relations with Rome and formed a new league without her, placing themselves under the protection of the goddess Diana at the ancient Grove of Ferentina at Aricia, and electing a 'Latin dictator' to command the free federate forces (the word *dictator* did not have its modern connotation: it signified an elected magistrate given sole and supreme authority for a limited period, either the duration of an emergency or a six-month maximum). Rome, her military pre-eminence threatened by withdrawal of Latin manpower, treated the secession as rebellion and declared war. The main Latin army was soon beaten at the battle of Lake Regillus (*c.* 499 BC), but the war then dragged on, the Romans unable to capture the Latin cities, their columns facing constant harassment from guerrillas. The peace agreement finally drawn up by the consul Spurius Cassius in *c.* 493 BC reflected the stalemate – the Latins were too strong to be crushed, but they lacked the offensive power necessary to overthrow Rome. Besides, Romans and Latins needed each other, threatened as they both were by the Itruscans and the hill-tribes. The former Latin League was restored. Within it, Rome, by far the strongest member, was bound to remain dominant – a political reality symbolized by the relocation of the cult of Diana from Aricia to a temple on the Aventine Hill. Despite this, in a real sense the Treaty of Cassius was an alliance of partners: by its terms, Romans and Latins were to remain at peace, enjoy the same legal rights, give support to one another in war, and have equal shares in land and booty. It was an agreement to work as a team, fighting, plundering and colonizing other people. It was destined to hold firm for 150 years.

In the first half of the 5th century BC, however, there was more fighting than plundering or colonizing. Every year, the Latin League found itself at war with the hill-tribes. Hard times in the Apennines were driving the tribesmen down on to the coastal plains to raid and settle. On the frontiers of Latium, Sabines attacked the north-east, Aequi occupied towns in the east, and Volsci settled a swathe of territory in the south. Among them were Roman and Latin renegades like Coriolanus. There was little glory or booty in this fighting; it was a gruelling struggle to defend frontiers and farms against elusive barbarian raiders. Roman land was laid waste. The cost of constant campaigning drained resources. The burden of military service weighed heavily on the people. Men with land near the frontier saw farms destroyed or annexed. The 6th century boom in temple building and pottery production came to an end. The Roman economy slumped, and life for many went sour. Some said it had been better under the kings.

Patricians, on the other hand, seem to have got richer. As they did so, they closed ranks against new blood and entrenched their constitutional power. Republican Rome was an agrarian society where most wealth came from farming and most men owned some land. The division of land, though, was unequal. Some patricians owned several farms, while many poor peasants had such tiny plots that they could not support families without supplementing income by domestic craftwork or seasonal wage-labour. The majority lay somewhere between these two extremes. They were either middle peasants, who had a family farm just sufficient for subsistence, or rich peasants, whose farms needed extra hands at harvest time and produced small surpluses. A man's whole social being was bound up with the size of that portion of the *ager Romanus* passed down to him by his forebears. To live independently of others, from the produce of one's own land and labour, was the mark of a free man. To be dependent for one's livelihood on others – to be a wage-labourer, debt-bondsman, slave or beggar – was to be something less than a man. It was a distinction enshrined in the constitution of the city-state: only property-owners did military service, and only substantial property-owners –

the middling sort who served as hoplites – fought in the all-important phalanx. These differential burdens of military service earned differential political rights – since block-votes were weighted by wealth in the popular assembly. Property-ownership, personal independence, hoplite service, a high-value vote: these things defined a citizen of substance in Early Republican Rome. But the livelihood – and therefore the status and respectability – of many men of modest means was under threat. With little in reserve, they lived in fear that a twist of fortune – crop blight, flooding, an enemy raid, cattle disease, a drought in spring, personal sickness, a war wound – might bring them down. They dreaded, above all, proletarianization: being reduced to the level of men who worked for others and whose citizenship counted for little.

Cumulatively, the failures of peasant farms were, in history's *longue durée*, the clicks of a mechanism that dispossessed the poor and enriched the already-rich. For, while each small farmer could, with luck, escape disaster much of the time, it was not the case that all small farmers could escape all disaster all the time. In the long run, nature, if not war, exacted a toll, and in their struggle to get through hard times, poor men would incur debts, and if hard times continued, they would be unable to repay them, and would then lose their land and sometimes their freedom. The loan sharks – in the absence of banks – were big landowners with surpluses to spare. By this means, the land and labour of the poor passed into the hands of the rich. It is, in fact, one of the iron laws of traditional agrarian societies based on private property that, over time – *without collective action to counteract the tendency* – big estates get bigger and small ones disappear. Loans were made, indeed, on the very expectation that they would *not* be repaid, and that land and freedom would be forfeit. Bad debt built patrician estates. The arrangement by which a citizen-debtor pledged his liberty as security for a loan – legally enforceable over centuries of Roman history – was known as *nexum*. Those who fell foul of it and became debt-bondsmen might find themselves working the land of their ancestors for a new owner-master. Or worse: they might be 'sold across the Tiber' to an Etruscan or Greek slave-dealer. Little wonder that the two great historic demands of the ancient poor were for cancellation of debts and redistribution of land.

In *c.* 494 BC, the patrician regime was knocked sideways by plebeian revolt. Prior to this, the Roman plebs had had no real existence: they were not organized as a corporate body in the same sense as clans, cantons and centuries, all of which had roles in the constitution. Nor were the plebeians a homogeneous class with uniform interests that lent themselves to coherent political expression: though most plebeians were relatively poor, some were as rich as patricians. The plebeians were simply everyone who was not a patrician, a condition that meant that even the richest of them was excluded from the Senate, the consulship, and the high priesthoods. The plebeian movement which developed in the early 5th century BC was, therefore, a class alliance: at the top were some of Rome's richest citizens, with aspirations to join the governing elite; at the bottom were impoverished debtors, the landless poor, and recent immigrants to the city's commercial district. What gave the movement its power, however, was the adherence of the hoplite class: small property-owners made insecure by patrician exploitation. War service, farm debt, and a rapacious ruling class turned the solid yeomen of Rome's legions into revolutionaries. 'The reaction of military events upon domestic politics runs like a red thread through Roman history,' argued one eminent ancient historian. 'In assuming the burden of regular military duty, the plebeians became more conscious of their own value to the state, and acquired habits of discipline and co-operation which enabled them to assert their rights more effectively. The leadership which they required in their political warfare was supplied by the more substantial landowners who stood outside the privileged circle and were not qualified for the consulship, but might hold subordinate commands as *tribuni militum* [military tribunes]'.(5)

The plebeians massed on the Aventine Hill south-west of the city, which, being close to the river, had become the main centre for Rome's artisans and traders. They met on consecrated ground, at a place where a new temple was being constructed for Ceres, Bacchus and Proserpina (the deities respectively of grain, wine and the bountiful earth), and it was the temple officials, known as 'aediles' (*aediles*), who were their first convenors. They declared themselves in a state of secession (*secessio*), which involved refusing military service until grievances had been met: in effect, on strike. (The plebeians would employ this form of protest at least five times in the 150 years that the Struggle of the Orders lasted.) But the patricians proved obdurate, for their powers of patronage were sufficient to prevent their clients deserting wholesale to the plebeian movement. Patrician retinues and plebeian crowds confronted one another on the streets. There was a rough balance between the two sides, producing political stalemate and a permanent division of the state into rival camps. For decades, the conduct of public affairs was frequently log-jammed – a condition readily recognized by contemporary Greeks, many of whose cities were consumed by similar conflicts between oligarchs and democrats, resulting in what they called *stasis*: paralysis of the state due to civil strife.

The stalemate turned plebeian protest into an organized movement with its own assemblies, officers and procedures – a permanent opposition to the patricians and the networks of clansmen and clients they controlled. The early mass rallies evolved into the Assembly of the Plebs (*Concilium Plebis*). The aediles were joined by ten annually elected 'tribunes of the plebs'. Voting *en masse* gave way to voting by tribe (to ensure that rural plebeians who could not attend meetings in the city would not be under-represented). Somehow, despite the conflict, Rome continued to function, but the unresolved issues in dispute ensured that the Struggle of the Orders flared up repeatedly in renewed agitation over food shortages, military service, and the debt question. Not until the middle of the century was some sort of settlement achieved.

Both patrician consuls and plebeian tribunes stepped down in *c.* 451 BC to make way for a 'Decemvirate', a provisional ruling committee of ten, charged with the task of establishing the constitution, codifying the law, and committing matters to writing so that every citizen should know his rights. Writing was not new – Latin texts go back to the 8th century BC – but its uses had been largely ritual and administrative. Now writing was to be used to record laws. Too much law had been based on memory, precedent, and the tendentious 'interpretations' of upper-class judges. Writing promised fairness. 'When the laws are written down,' wrote the Greek playwright Euripides around this time, 'weak and rich men get equal justice; the weaker, when abused, can respond to the prosperous in kind, and the small man with justice on his side defeats the strong.'

But when the Decemvirate published their laws – the Twelve Tables – there was dismay. Much, for sure, was uncontroversial, and it was convenient to have it summarized in plain and simple Latin; there were laws here that would endure as long as Rome. The centrality of the family was affirmed, and the powers of fathers in relation to wives, sons and daughters defined. Property rights were protected, infringements classified, and procedures for obtaining redress set out. Ostentatious display at funerals was discouraged. Secret meetings were banned. There was much about the laws that seemed public-spirited. But the laws of property in the Twelve Tables knew no limits, and the rights of the creditor in relation to the debtor were absolute. 'Unless they make a settlement,' boomed the law, 'debtors shall be held in bonds for 60 days. During that time, they shall be brought before the praetor's court in the meeting place on three successive market days, and the amount for which they are judged liable shall be announced. On the third market day, they shall suffer capital punishment or be delivered up for sale across the Tiber.' Just as shocking was the laconic injunction inscribed on Table XI: 'Intermarriage shall not take place between plebeians and patricians.' A closed caste society dominated by landlords and debt-collectors: this, it seemed, was the model city of the Decemvirate.

Plebeian Rome again rose in revolt. The Aventine was reoccupied for a great meeting of the Assembly of the Plebs, and the commons declared a renewed state of secession against the patricians. The Decemvirate, shedding its mask of propriety and impartiality, then announced it would remain in office to restore order and save the Republic. Its members brought their retinues on to the street to battle it out with the plebeian crowd. The state, whose frontiers were currently under attack, was in turmoil.

Now the real power of the plebeian movement revealed itself. Had the junta commanded sufficient physical force to suppress the protests, they would doubtless have done so and thereby earned the plaudits of the rest of the aristocracy. But it did not. Faced by what was, in effect, a revolt of the hoplite class, the decemvirs' street fighters could make little headway. It was the Roman army itself that was in secession, and against it the junta could not win. Once this was clear, the Decemvirate's support inside the wider ruling class collapsed. The decemvirs lost the confidence of the Senate and were promptly forced to resign their positions and retire to the backbenches. The victory sent a surge of radical expectation through the plebeian masses that the Senate dared not disappoint. New consuls, Lucius Valerius and Marcus Horatius, elected on a reform platform, introduced sweeping laws to recognize plebeian institutions and formalize the rights of commoners (c. 449 BC). First, tribunes of the plebs were recognized as Roman magistrates, their persons protected from harm by religious sanction, with a special right of veto over any measure they deemed to be against the interests of the commons. Second, the Assembly of the Plebs gained formal recognition, its decisions (*plebiscita*) henceforward having constitutional authority. Third, the common citizens earned a right of appeal to the popular assembly against any decision by a patrician magistrate. In combination, these measures signalled the end not just of the Decemvirate but of the patrician regime which had governed the Republic for 60 years. Rome remained an oligarchy: its executive (the consuls), its primary assembly (the Senate) and its leading priesthoods (*pontifex maximus* and *rex sacrorum*) remained patrician preserves. But, constitutionally, these could not rule alone; indeed, in the face of determined opposition, they could not rule at all, for the levers of power now in the hands of the tribunes were sufficient to halt government business. The patricians continued to govern, but subject to approval by plebeian officers and plebeian mass meetings. The Struggle of the Orders was not yet over; there were bitter battles yet to come; but a giant step had been taken towards a more inclusive and broad-based polity.

The compromise which ended the first stage in the Struggle of the Orders was pregnant with great events. Had the junta crushed the popular movement, Rome would have become a society of landlords and serfs. Instead, the popular victory launched it on quite another trajectory. By empowering, to a degree, the common citizen, the reformed constitution limited exploitation and preserved the small-farmer class from which Rome's armies were raised. More than that: not only did the middling sort survive, they became stakeholders with a positive interest in fighting for a Republic that safeguarded their land and granted them a share in the spoils of war. It is no exaggeration to say that, without the plebeian movement, the Struggle of the Orders, and the Valerio-Horatian laws of *c.* 449 BC, the legions of the Roman Republic could never have embarked on world conquest.

Hubris and Nemesis: the divided Republic, c. 449–367 BC

In the 60 years of patrician rule after the overthrow of the kings, Roman territory had hardly increased at all. Lars Porsenna had been defeated and Tarquin restoration prevented. Roman hegemony over the Latin cities had been restored. The Sabines, Aequi and Volsci had been repulsed and Latin territory safeguarded. But these had been defensive wars, and the cost of victory had been high. Nothing yet gave any clue that the divided and embattled city-state beside the Tiber would, within two centuries, control the whole of Italy, and two centuries after that, most of the Mediterranean. However, the plebeian triumph of *c.* 449 BC had given Rome's latent imperialism a new cutting edge. Loans, evictions and land-seizures – traditional methods for building up large holdings – were unpopular and now open to legal challenge. The booty, slaves and new land to be had through war therefore loomed larger in the ambition of Roman patricians. The Assembly of the Centuries, moreover, was more likely to vote for war, even foreign war, now that the common soldier could expect a decent share of the spoils. Mid-5th century Rome was a state whose inner tensions were being transformed into an outward-thrusting energy; a state where aspirations that might collide and produce *stasis* at home were about to be redirected into foreign conquest.

There was, at the time, a long-running dispute with the Etruscan city-state of Veii, which lay about 20 km due north of Rome. A short distance up the Tiber, Veientine territory extended on to the south bank of the river and included the strategically important town of Fidenae. This Veientine foothold on the Latin side of the Tiber posed a direct threat to Roman territory and to the city's control of the lucrative trade in salt and luxury goods in the valley. Veii itself occupied a rocky plateau completely surrounded by cliffs and waterways except for a narrow neck of land on one side: a natural fortress of great strength. It was enclosed by a defensive wall several kilometres in circumference running along the top of the cliffs. Temples towered over the city. Artists' workshops lined the streets. Roads radiated from the metropolis to the sea, to other Etruscan cities, and to Veii's own rich agricultural hinterland. Heavily populated and wealthy, one of the great cities of Etruria, Veii was defended by a hoplite phalanx thousands-strong. This was a very different sort of enemy from a Sabine war-band; Veii was fully the equal of Rome.

War first broke out between the two cities in *c.* 483 BC. It then lasted, on and off, for almost a century. In the First Veientine War (*c.* 483–474 BC), the Romans were defeated (the Fabii clan almost annihilated), and Veii retained control of Fidenae, the object of the struggle. In the

Second Veientine War (*c.* 437–435 BC), a reinvigorated Rome went on to the offensive, captured Fidenae by siege, and drove the enemy off the south bank. Both these wars were, in a sense, defensive responses to the threat posed by Veientine control of Fidenae. Not so the Third Veientine War (*c.* 406–396 BC), the first unequivocally aggressive war in Roman history, where the aim was total conquest.

Veii itself was put under siege, an operation that strained Roman resources to the limit. The logistics of maintaining siege lines; the numbers and resourcefulness of the defenders; the threat posed by Etruscan relief-columns; and attacks on Latin territory by Veii's barbarian allies: these in combination brought Rome close to defeat. In the crisis, the state declared martial law and appointed its leading citizen, Marcus Furius Camillus, dictator. Camillus reorganized the army, introduced pay so that men could afford to remain in the field outside the usual summer campaigning season, and began a more aggressive siege of Veii. The defences were penetrated along one of the main drainage tunnels beneath the city, some of which, it seems, had not been blocked. The Romans stormed in, and Veii was put to the sack. It is worth stressing what this implied: first, the soldiers ran amok, killing men, raping women; then, the survivors were rounded up and sold into slavery; finally, all movable property was systematically and comprehensively looted. The sack of Veii in 396 BC meant that the city and its people – according to some the wealthiest in Etruria – ceased to exist. The territory of the city was annexed, doubling the size of the *ager Romanus*, and this was later settled by Roman farmers, enrolled in four new tribes.

Veii had been destroyed in a new and terrible kind of war. Not a war for limited objectives to be ended by treaty when one of the protagonists sued for peace, but a total war whose aim was the annihilation of the enemy. And even as they fought this war, the Romans were active on other fronts, driving the Aequi and Volsci from parts of eastern and southern Latium. Rome had become something more than the leading city in a defensive alliance of Latins; she had become a predator state threatening the whole of west-central Italy. This was part of a wider change. The old international system – based on patchworks of small cities and tribes – was disintegrating. A new system dominated by great powers was emerging across the Mediterranean. For now, and for the next 200 years, it would remain uncertain which of the rising powers would win the contest for global supremacy. Rome's imperial future was not predestined; many times history might have taken a different course; even now, at the moment of the fall of Veii, her greatest victory so far, danger threatened. In the far north, another warlike people was on the move; and one strong branch of that people had just lunged southwards into the Italian peninsula. A great Celtic battle-host was heading for Rome.

In the 6th century BC, when Rome was a small city-state ruled by Etruscan kings, a distinctive warrior aristocracy – members of what archaeologists now call the 'Hallstatt culture' – controlled a group of territories in Central Europe north of the Alps. The Hallstatt lords spoke Celtic, lived in hill-forts, and were buried with funerary carts, bronze cauldrons and drinking horns. At first their numbers were few and the territories they controlled small and scattered, but during the 5th century Celtic influence spread. A new style – the 'La Tène culture' – was adopted by an increasingly numerous aristocracy. Drinking sets and fire-dogs, gold and silver torcs, elaborate horse fittings, and weaponry, especially iron swords in decorated scabbards, became essential status-symbols in much of Central Europe. The aristocracy was formed of chieftains and small retinues of warriors, who wore helmets and sometimes body-armour, fought on horseback or in chariots, and were expert in the use of long slashing swords. Though the military ethos affected the whole of Celtic society, such that military service with spear and shield was an obligation on all free men, military achievement was a particular mark of noble status. The standing of a chief was measured by the size of the retinue of followers he attracted through success in war and raiding. In the late 5th century, this Celtic warrior culture burst the bounds of its homeland and flooded across Europe in a succession of violent waves. In the age of migrations (c. 400–200 BC), the Celts reached the furthest fringes of the Continent and beyond: across France and into southern Britain and eastern Spain; eastwards to the lower Danube and the shores of the Black Sea; from there into Greece and across the Aegean to Turkey; and over the Alps into the Po Valley, where they clashed with Ligurians, Etruscans and Veneti. Thus the Celts entered the history of the Greeks, who called them *Keltoi*, and of the Romans, who called them *Galli*.

One of the first to set out, in 390 BC, was Brennus. Seeking whatever chance might offer – mercenary service, war booty, land on which to settle, at any rate something honourable – Brennus led his host south into the heart of Italy. Alerted to the danger, the Roman army mobilized and met the Gauls in the steep valley of the River Allia, a small tributary of the Tiber on Rome's north-east frontier. Here, for the first time, Roman soldiers faced a Celtic battle-array. A great mass of spearmen shouted war-cries and beat weapons against shields, many of them naked to the waist save for torcs, bracelets, painted tattoos and patterned cloaks. Trumpet blasts could be heard above the din, animal totems were waved aloft, and priests in the ranks called on the Celtic gods for assistance. In front were young warriors brandishing swords and shouting challenges to single combat. The battle was soon over. The Celtic charge was shattering. The whole line surged forwards at tremendous speed, its loose order and light equipment allowing the Gauls to sweep round the Romans' flanks and threaten their rear. The ponderous phalanx of the city-state – a tight-packed block of slow-moving heavy infantry – was defenceless against such tactics. The Romans broke and ran. Thousands were cut down in the rout. A remnant retreated to the ruins of Veii and entrenched themselves. Nothing then stood between Brennus and Rome.

The city was effectively undefended. The 6th century wall was dilapidated, and new suburbs had been built outside its protection. Besides, the circuit was too long to be held by the depleted forces left in the city. As the Gallic host approached, the citizens retreated to the Capitoline Hill, where they improvised a breastwork at the top of the cliffs. There they held out for months – while the Gauls occupied and plundered the city – until hunger compelled them to seek terms. The fate of Veii a few years earlier cast a black shadow over these days. Was Rome, so recently and so completely victorious, now in its turn to be ethnically cleansed? Brennus, though, was a Gaul: his motives were mercenary, but his ambition modest; he was content to be bought off for a ransom in gold. Long afterwards, the Romans told each other stories about the Gallic invasion – how the sacred geese of Juno had alerted the defenders to a night attack; how Camillus, the victor of Veii, twice defeated the retreating Gauls with a scratch force; and how Camillus also, when the Romans saw the devastation in their city and debated moving to Veii, persuaded them to stay and rebuild. But these edifying tales cannot alter the fact that the Gauls had had Rome at their mercy, and that, had they been a more ruthless enemy, they might have destroyed it as utterly as the Romans had destroyed Veii.

The Gallic invasion set Roman power back a generation. The city's imperial prestige was shattered, and old enemies sought to reverse past defeats. There were wars against the Etruscan cities of Falerii and Tarquinii, challenging Rome's seizure of Veientine territory. The Aequi and Volsci raided Latium again. There was conflict, too, with former allies: the Etruscan city of Caere, which had supported Rome against Veii; the Hernici hill-tribesmen, who had belonged to the Latin League; and some of the Latin cities themselves – Tusculum, Praeneste, Velitrae and Tibur. Gallic war-bands and Greek pirates were also active. Yet, though on the defensive on several fronts, Rome survived. Moreover, despite the demands of militia service, she mobilized her citizens to build a new wall around the city (known as the 'Servian Wall'). Ten metres high and four wide, built of masonry hauled from a Veientine quarry, the wall enclosed the whole of the then-existing city, a total length of more than 10 km. The work of quarrying, transporting and lay-ing the stone represented at least five million man-hours of labour. In the aftermath of the Gallic invasion, the Roman state revealed extraordinary resilience. The burden, however, was heavy and unevenly distributed, and the effect of this was to reignite the Struggle of the Orders.

The plebeians were the soldiers, navvies and casualties of the belea-guered city's ordeal. Heavy losses at the Allia had carried off the young workers on many peasant farms. Land had been laid waste and property plundered by the invaders. The ransom to buy them off had been high. Since then, unceasing war had meant frequent call-ups and high taxes, while the building of the wall had consumed the labour of thousands. These burdens, bad enough in themselves, had accelerated the grinding tendency for small proprietors to get into debt and lose their land and freedom. To this ancient feud between rich and poor was now added, especially since the fall of Veii, a new grievance over recently conquered 'public land' (*ager publicus*). Should this remain under state control – under the control, that is, of patrician magistrates inclined to offer it in large blocks to their friends? Or should it be divided into small plots and distributed to poorer citizens? Was conquered land, that is, to be farmed by patricians or plebeians?

The issues were bitterly contested. When the maverick patrician and war-hero Marcus Manlius Capitolinus championed the popular cause, paying off the private debts of many plebeians from his own resources and promising a general redress of grievances, he was met by a conservative counter-attack led by another war-hero, Marcus Furius Camillus, the man now acclaimed as 'the second founder of Rome' for his role in the city's recovery after the Gallic invasion. Capitolinus was prosecuted for sedition and executed in *c.* 384 BC. This provided a breathing-space but solved nothing. Plebeian agitation was renewed the following decade. Gaius Licinius Stolo and Lucius Sextius Lateranus were repeatedly re-elected tribunes of the plebs on a radical platform of debt, land and constitutional reform. For ten years, the patricians blocked their initiatives, and the tribunes in turn used their veto power to paralyse government. In *c.* 367 BC, the opposition finally crumbled and three major reforms were enacted: debt payments were reduced by deducting past payments from the capital owed and setting a three-year maximum period for the repayment of the remainder; *ager publicus* was henceforward to be sold off in private plots, with holdings limited to 500 *iugera* (300 acres); and the right of plebeians to stand for the consulship was legally recognized.

The Licinio-Sextian laws amounted to a comprehensive defeat for the patrician aristocracy – symbolized by the election of one of the two plebeian leaders, Lucius Sextius Lateranus, to the consulship the following year. The gains, moreover, were permanent, and additional laws strengthened the position of the plebeians further in succeeding decades. Interest on loans was first restricted; then debt-bondage was abolished outright. Plebeians were first guaranteed one of the annual consulships; then they gained access to most of the high priesthoods. Other laws increased the power of the popular assemblies, and one, the most important, gave edicts (*plebiscita*) of the Assembly of the Plebs equal status with laws (*leges*) proposed by the Senate and passed by the Assembly of the Centuries. This last measure, in 287 BC, was effectively the closing act of the Struggle of the Orders, which had begun over two centuries before.

Within two generations of the Licinio-Sextian laws, in fact, the plebeian movement had disappeared, its aristocratic leaders absorbed into an expanded governing class, its institutions, above all the plebeian tribunes and the Assembly of the Plebs, incorporated into the workings of the Roman state. The old patrician aristocracy was transformed into a new nobility (*nobilitas*) by the admission to its ranks of rich plebeian families. The reactionaries who had dominated the consulship in the first half of the 4th century BC lost control to a new party of moderates –

pro-reform patricians and plebeian newcomers. No longer was high office monopolized by an exclusive hereditary caste; an aristocracy based on wealth and public service, open to recruitment from below, was now in power.

Was the Struggle of the Orders ended, then, by the simple device of incorporating the popular leaders? Some plebeian radicals fearing this had certainly opposed their leaders' aspiration to the consulship during the Licinio-Sextian agitation. But had the grievances of poor plebeians remained acute, they would eventually have found new leaders – as they were to do in the Late Republic. Yet no great popular movements disturbed the internal order of the Middle Republic. From the late 4th to the mid 2nd century BC, the Roman state was remarkably stable. The Greek historian Polybius, writing towards the end of that period, was fascinated by the Roman constitution, seeing in it a large part of the explanation for Rome's victories over Greece. 'The elements by which the Roman constitution was controlled were three in number . . . and all the aspects of the administration were, taken separately, so fairly and so suitably ordered and regulated through the agency of these three elements that it was impossible even for the Romans themselves to declare with certainty whether the whole system was an aristocracy, a democracy or a monarchy. In fact, it was quite natural that this should be so, for if we were to fix our eyes only upon the power of the consuls, the constitution might give the impression of being completely monarchical and royal; if we confined our attention to the Senate, it would seem to be aristocratic; and if we looked at the power of the people, it would appear to be a clear example of democracy . . . the result is a union which is strong enough to withstand all emergencies, so that it is impossible to find a better form of constitution than this . . . Whenever one of the three elements swells in importance, becomes over-ambitious and tends to encroach upon the others, it becomes apparent . . . that none of the three is completely independent, but that the designs of any one can be blocked or impeded by the rest, with the result that none will unduly dominate the others or treat them with contempt. Thus the whole situation remains in equilibrium, since any aggressive impulse is checked, and each estate is apprehensive from the outset of censure from the others.'(6)

Polybius was an intelligent observer. To a degree he was right. Sovereignty rested with the People, not the Senate, so that popular consent was the precondition for all major acts of state – the 'democratic element'. The Assembly of the Centuries elected senior magistrates and voted on constitutional laws and declarations of war. The edicts of the Assembly of the Plebs had been given the force of law. And a new Assembly of the Tribes – originally set up as a conservative alternative to the Assembly of the Plebs – became virtually indistinguishable from the latter. (The ancient Assembly of the Cantons had by this time become little more than a decorative relic.) But the popular assemblies were controlled from above: the People could meet only on the summons of a higher magistrate, vote only on proposals submitted to them, and elect candidates for office only from an approved list. Laws could not be amended, merely accepted or rejected, and debate was limited to speakers chosen by the presiding magistrate. The block-voting system weighted things in favour of the better-off. Meetings were often packed by the clients of great men.

Meantime, as the state expanded, the number of elected magistrates gradually increased: two censors every five years and two consuls every year had become standard, but more praetors (judges and administrators), military tribunes (junior generals), plebeian tribunes (popular represent-atives), aediles (responsible for public works and municipal regulations) and quaestors (finance officers) were created as needed. The senior magistrates – censors, consuls and praetors – had *imperium*, a regal power of command during their term of office; they were accompanied on pub-lic occasions by lictors (*lictores*), each bearing a bundle of rods and an axe, symbolizing the senior magistrate's judicial authority. This was the 'monarchical element' in Polybius' scheme. The Senate, of course, repres-ented the 'aristocratic'. It was now an assembly of rich office-holders, men of property and distinguished family who had held a senior magis-tracy, some of patrician descent, many now plebeian. An obsession with rank and etiquette dominated proceedings. The leader of the house (*princeps senatus*) always spoke first, followed by others in order of their former office, and, when all were done, the 'sense of the house' (*sententia*) would be clear. The senators would then vote a 'decree of the Senate' (*senatus consultum*), technically only advice, but advice which, in view of the supreme *auctoritas* of the assembly, was all but binding on magistrates.

The mixed constitution that Polybius describes was indeed crucial to Rome's internal stability and her capacity to wage imperialist war. But he conflates form and content, attributing prime significance to legal niceties, and misses the most essential characteristic of the Roman constitution: its stability rested on the fact that, because it accurately reflected the balance of class forces in Roman society, it enjoyed a wide measure of popular support. Rome remained, at root, an oligarchy. It was governed by an aristocracy of top landowners and office-holders, a *nobilitas* formed of a few hundred top patrician and plebeian families. This ruling class was now relatively open to recruitment from below, and competition for state office, and the honour (*dignitas*) and reputation (*gloria*) associated with it, was intense. Only a minority of consuls in the 500 years between 300 BC and AD 200 had consular fathers: birth no longer guaranteed success; one had to fight for one's place among Rome's grandees. Achievement was proudly displayed, and men honoured by Rome reciprocated with rich benefactions. 'Appius Claudius Caecus,' announces the epitaph of one of the most famous figures of the late 4th century BC, 'son of Gaius, censor, consul twice, dictator, interrex three times, praetor twice, curule aedile twice, quaestor, tribune of the soldiers three times. He captured several towns from the Samnites, and routed an army of Sabines and Etruscans. He prevented peace being made with King Pyrrhus. In his censorship, he paved the Appian Way and built an aqueduct for Rome. He built the Temple of Bellona.'(7) Offices held, victories won, monuments built: these are paraded as tokens of the great man's prestige. Appius Claudius Caecus exudes the self-confidence of the Middle Republican ruling class.

The power of men like Caecus was not so much constrained by 'democracy' – as the Polybian model would have it – as shaped by a need to harness popular energies in the service of both rival aristocratic houses and the state as a whole. The People could not be taken for granted: they had to be wooed and placated. Stability was the result of class compromise in the Struggle of the Orders and the consequent emergence of a united citizen-body with a common interest in conquest. Most vital of all was the economic security of the Roman peasantry who formed the legions. Only in part was this due to new laws on interest, debt-bondage and land distribution. Equally important was Rome's explosive imperialism after the middle of the 4th century BC. The social contradictions that had produced the Struggle of the Orders in the Early Republic were resolved in the foreign conquests of the Middle Republic. For the nobles, there was wealth, power and glory in military achievement. For the commons, there was pay for military service, a share in the spoils, and new land for those who wanted it. For the state, there were inflows of booty, indemnities and tribute with which to buy off social discontent, monumentalize the city, and build yet bigger armies. To this – resulting in the transformation of a Latin city-state into a Mediterranean empire – we now turn.

CHAPTER 2

The rise of a superpower, 343–146 BC

The conquest of Central Italy: the Latin and Samnite Wars, 343–290 BC

The Celts of Central Europe were not the only people on the move in the 4th century BC. It was an age of migrations. The causes are not fully understood, but we can propose a general hypothesis. New states were being built as military competition forged larger political units. War leaders and their retinues took control of society, surpluses were invested in arms and armour, and men were trained and organized for war. The world became less safe, and only powerful polities were able to retain their independence and freedom of action, subsuming smaller cities and tribes under their hegemony. Probably, also, population was growing and pressure on resources – farmland, pasture, water, woods – was increasing. Perhaps, too, there was ecological crisis. A localized failure of the human ecosystem, especially in a marginal zone – such as a drought that drained the springs and parched the grasslands on which highland people depended – could, in a world densely peopled and heavily armed, set off a chain reaction of folk movements and wars. Some such event may have started the Oscan-speaking Samnite peoples of the southern Apennines in motion.

Once thought of as impoverished highland pastoralists with a taste for plunder, the Samnites are now known to have had a mixed farming economy supporting numerous rural settlements spread across the upland plateaus and valleys of their homeland. They cultivated cereals, vines and olives, as well as raising stock, and while some lived in isolated farmsteads, others lived in villages. Excavations at the Samnite village of Saepinum have revealed a cluster of buildings around a crossroads, where the main road was a droveway linking summer and winter pastures. Remote hilltops were crowned with circuits of rough polygonal walling to provide refuges in time of danger; and sometimes the more accessible of these, like that at Monte Saraceno, were also, like the more low-lying villages, permanently settled. In other places, there were rural sanctuaries, where, one imagines, the people of a district would periodically come together to settle community affairs, make sacrifice together, and thus refresh a common identity and solidarity; the excavated site at Pietrabbondante is an example, though the rather grand buildings revealed here are of later, 2nd century BC date.

The Samnites stuck together. One or more villages (*vici*) formed a canton (*pagus*), governed by an elected magistrate (*meddix*), and a group of such cantons constituted a tribe (*populus*), also with its ruling magistrate (*meddix tuticus*). There were four of these tribes, each with a distinct territory and, possibly, a special tribal sanctuary (Pietrabbondante may have been that for the Pentri Samnites). These four tribes formed the Samnite Confederation, which, in war, had a reputation for unity, resilience and martial prowess. These Samnites, moreover, were close cousins of other Oscan-speaking peoples in southern Italy, with whom they shared beliefs, customs and institutions. The Oscans had spread throughout the region during the 5th century, so that a single Oscan *koine* (cultural identity) now united the peoples of Samnium, Campania, Lucania, northern Apulia, and Bruttium.

Among other things they shared the myth of the *ver sacrum* or 'sacred springtime'. An origin myth which explained the existence of territorially based tribes, the sacred springtime was a response to a crisis – such as famine – that threatened the community's survival and compelled part of it to migrate. The year's harvest and all the beasts were sacrificed to Mars (widely venerated as a god of fertility in the Apennines). The children of the tribe were designated 'sacrificial', but instead of being killed, upon reaching maturity, they were sent into the wilderness, following the lead of a wild animal, until they found a place to settle and form a new tribe at the place where the animal came to rest.

The 5th century BC had been a time of sacred springtimes. The Oscan peoples of the hills had descended on the Greek and Etruscan cities of the coast, and one after another these cities had succumbed to 'barbarian' rule, until, by about 400 BC, only two on the entire west coast remained under Greek authority. The invaders, however, were not destroyers. Though they formed a new elite, they quickly adopted the refinements of urban life. Monumental architecture, great art, advanced technology, the luxury trades, the literature and learning of the East, all these continued to flourish under the Samnites at Capua or the Lucanians at Paestum. More than that: threatened by a new outpouring from the mountains in the mid 4rd century BC, the by-then very mixed populations of Greeks, Etruscans and Oscans in the coastal cities of the south looked around for external support. In 343 BC, the Romans received an embassy from the city of Capua in Campania offering an alliance in return for support against Samnite intruders. The Romans had previously been on friendly terms with the Samnites. But, as smaller states nearer home were absorbed, the dynamic of military competition in peninsular Italy was propelling these two power blocks, Rome and the Latin League on one side, the Samnite Confederation on the other, into collision. So Rome seized the chance for an alliance with one of the richest cities in the south – and launched herself into the First Samnite War (343–341 BC).

The result was anticlimax. Though a combined Roman-Capuan force drove the Samnites out of Campania, the Roman soldiers, unused to long service far from home, mutinied and demanded repatriation. Theirs was, in fact, part of a wider discontent, for the First Samnite War had brought the entire Latin League to the brink of revolt. The driving grievance was simple: while the Latins, as subordinate allies within the League, were obliged to fight Rome's wars – an increasing burden – it was the citizens of the dominant city who got most of the spoils. The Latins therefore issued an ultimatum demanding the restoration of equal shares (as required by the Treaty of Cassius, which had ended the First Latin War in c. 493 BC).

Faced with this new crisis, the Romans restored their previous treaty with the Samnites, and, leaving their Campanian allies in the lurch, hurried their mutinous army home. They refused the Latins' ultimatum, and, when the latter broke with Rome and formed an alliance with Campanians and Volsci, the Romans, in an extraordinary volte-face, launched a combined attack on them in concert with the Samnites. The main Latin and Campanian force was crushed at the battle of Suessa Aurunca, and the Campanians were then detached from their allegiance by favourable terms (340 BC). The Latins and the Volsci were gradually reduced over the succeeding two years. (Among the gains was the seaboard town of Antium, wrested from the Volsci, notable because the curved prows of pirate ships captured there were fixed to the speakers' platform in the Roman Forum and gave to it the name *Rostra*, meaning 'beaks' or 'prows'.)

Complete victory allowed the Romans to impose their own terms on the Latins, but those terms seem to have been designed to bridge the gap between victor and vanquished. 'Do you choose to adopt harsh measures against men who have surrendered or suffered defeat?' asks the Roman consul of his fellow senators in Livy's treatment of the story. 'You may destroy the whole of Latium, and create vast deserts out of the places from where you have drawn a splendid allied army to make use of in many a major war. Or do you want to follow the example of your ancestors and extend the state of Rome by admitting your defeated enemies as citizens?'(1) Livy's grasp of the principles at work was sound. Rome needed the Latins to fuel her expansion with men, war *matériel*, and sources of supply. Ancient empires were built not by serfs but by free men with an interest in what they did. True, the old Latin League was broken up, and each town entered into private contract with Rome; even the pretence of a federation of equals was abandoned. True also that, depending on their wartime stance, five towns were incorporated into the Roman state, while ten others remained of subordinate Latin status – creating a hierarchy of privilege that exacerbated local rivalries and made it easier for the hegemon to divide and rule. All the same, in other circumstances towns taken in war might be destroyed and their populations slaughtered or enslaved. The Latin towns survived as self-governing communities, and were soon to flourish under the Roman aegis. Probably, too, the settlement of 338 BC reduced the relative military burden on them, and, at the same time, offered them a serious share in both movable booty and land gained through war. 'The Roman system,' explains ancient historian Tim Cornell, 'has been compared to a criminal operation which compensates its victims by enrolling them in the gang and inviting them to share the proceeds of future robberies.' More prosaically, from the perspective of the subject towns themselves, 'By joining a large and efficient operation and sacrificing their political independence, Rome's Italian allies obtained security, protection and profit for a relatively modest premium.'(2) Consequently, when Rome next moved against the Samnites, there would be no mutiny. Nor, in fact, would Rome ever again find herself at war with the Latins. Over time, moreover, the very distinction between Roman and Latin would fade away.

The settlement of the Second Latin War launched Rome on 75 years of conquest that would give her effective control of the whole Italian peninsula. A measure of this expansion is the increase in Roman (as opposed to Latin or allied) territory, which grew from 5,525 square kilometres in 338 BC to 26,805 on the eve of the Punic Wars in 264 BC. Incremental increases in Roman strength through the centuries-long battle for supremacy in Latium and central Italy had suddenly reached critical mass. An Italian superpower had emerged from its Latin incubator. Only one other state in Italy could still compete on equal terms: the Samnite Confederation. Along a 100-km front, from the Liris Valley in the north to the Bay of Naples in the south, the two states bordered each other, and a decade of Roman encroachment was enough to provoke war, as the outward-thrusting energy of the Oscan sacred springtimes was increasingly boxed in.

Like the five newly enfranchised Latin towns, the Capuans had also been granted Roman citizenship – albeit a halfway-house citizenship, offering rights to marry (*conubium*) and trade (*commercium*) with other Romans, but not the right to vote (a status known as *civitas sine suffragio*, in contrast to the *civitas optimo iure* of full citizens). Others on the borders of Samnium had been enrolled as 'allies' (*socii*) of Rome. Though formally independent, the treaties which governed their relations with Rome were unequal, since, in return for the protection of the superior power, they were obliged to supply troops on demand. The Romans were also founding new colonies (*coloniae*).

This practice dated back to at least the 5th century BC, when the Latin League had planted colonies of settlers on its borders as a defence against the raids of Aequi and Volsci. Colonies were established on captive land. The colonists were probably volunteers, often a mix of Romans, Latins and others. Led by three commissioners, they would march to the site under a banner, and, once arrived, sanctify it by taking auspices, making sacrifice, and ploughing ritual furrows. The commissioners set the boundaries to the colony's territory (*territorium*), and surveyed the land and divided it into plots, allocating these by lot to the colonists. The results of their work (known as 'centuriation') often survive in modern field-systems and can be seen from the air: the land is arranged in a chequerboard of squares (*centuriae*), each divided into 100 two-*iugera* strips. These small strips (a *iugerum* – or 'yoke' – was two-thirds of an acre, the amount a single team could plough in a day) were the basic building-blocks of the colonists' plots. We know little about how the allocation was determined, but the common view that, at least in early colonies, the two-*iugera* strip constituted a plot must be wrong, since no citizen family could have made an adequate living from such a small patch of ground. Boundary stones marked the limit of each farm. Two bronze or stone inscriptions were later displayed in the local forum, one recording the law founding the colony (*lex coloniae*), the other the owner-ship of land in the territory.

Founding a town on a suitable site, laying out a regular street-grid, and designating plots for public buildings and private residences were also the responsibility of the commissioners. Ostia, at the mouth of the Tiber, an ancient city with exceptionally well-preserved remains of later date, was originally a Roman colony founded in the 4th century BC. Essentially a strongly fortified camp, it guarded the river approach to Rome, an estuarine harbour, and valuable coastal salt deposits. Though engulfed by the later expansion of the town, the original colonial settle-ment – known now as the 'Castrum' – is still represented by fragments of defensive wall and a fossilized street-plan. Only 2.2 hectares were enclosed, space for no more than two or three hundred settlers; other early colonies were bigger, sometimes numbering thousands. All the ear-liest colonies were probably of Latin status, Roman citizenship still being linked with residence close to Rome itself; later, colonies might be either Roman or Latin. Either way, and especially after 338 BC, the *coloniae* were effective instruments of Roman domination, guarding borders and strategic points, providing manpower for the army, and beginning the process of Romanization which would eventually produce a uniform Latin culture across Italy.

New colonies added to the ring tightening around Samnium. Cales was founded with 2,500 settlers in 334 BC. Planted in the Volturnus

Valley close to the Samnite border in a position to support the Campanians, it was at the time the most southerly of Rome's colonies. Fregellae was founded a few years later, in 328 BC, this time on former Samnite land in the Liris Valley, effectively blocking off that key north-south communications route between Latium and Campania. The following year, after the Samnites had sent a garrison to Naples in response to an appeal for help from the common citizens there, the Romans put the town under siege and engineered a pro-Roman oligarchic coup. The Samnites found themselves being driven from the western seaboard, rolled back into their gloomy mountains, away from the rich cities and harbours of the coast. War broke out in 327 BC.

The Romans immediately went on to the offensive and invaded Samnite territory. This was to be the pattern for the war. Only once did the Samnites reciprocate and invade Roman territory: the dynamism of Roman imperialism – its predatory aggression, its reserves of offensive strength – kept the Samnites on the defensive. But in their own mountains, they were formidable opponents. We learn something of their appearance and fighting methods from the panoplies found in graves, the paintings on the walls of stone sarcophagi, and an archaic bronze statuette in the Louvre known as 'the Samnite Warrior'. At first, it seems, like typical highlanders, they had fought as skirmishers, wearing little armour and equipped with javelins and lightweight shields. Latterly, however, after long contact with the Greek and Etruscan civilization of the coast, they had elaborated their military system by adopting new equipment and tactics. Spears and swords for close-quarters action had been added to javelins. More and better armour was worn: Attic-style helmets crowned with crests and feathers; cuirasses of the Samnite triple-disc or the Greek 'muscled' type; sometimes greaves for the lower leg; and always a wide bronze belt that was perhaps, among Samnites, some symbol of manhood. The round Argive shield sometimes replaced the lighter oval or rectangular shield traditionally favoured by Italic peoples. The Samnites thus equipped themselves for heavy infantry action as well as skirmishing, and were now able to hold ground at close quarters behind shield wall and hedge of spears. The Samnites also fielded – now if not before – large contingents of cavalry, both light javelin-throwers and armoured knights. Yet they retained the cunning of mountain fighters. At the Battle of the Caudine Forks in 321 BC, they manoeuvred the invaders into a trap between two heavily defended passes, forcing the surrender of the two Roman consuls and their entire combined army. Agreeing to Samnite peace proposals – that they should withdraw from occupied territory – they were allowed to go free, though only after each man had been reduced to wearing a single garment, and had submitted to the humiliating ritual of passing 'beneath the yoke' before the jeering victors.

The Romans treated the Caudine peace as mere respite. By 315 BC, with a new army of 35,000 men, they were ready to launch a fresh invasion. Though outwitted by the Samnites again – they were defeated and forced to retreat at the Battle of Lautulae – this time there was no break in hostilities. The Romans returned to the field the following season, and, carefully avoiding any more precipitate lunges into enemy territory, they used the years 314–311 BC to build a tight ring of colonies and allies around the Samnites, and a new road, the Appian Way, to facilitate rapid movement between Rome and Capua. Then, from these secure bases, every year from 310 BC onwards, the Romans attacked and devastated the Samnite heartlands. The fighting was heavy and the strain on both sides severe. Rome, moreover, was under attack elsewhere, from Etruscans, Aequi and Hernici taking advantage of her commitment in Samnium. So when the Samnites sued for peace, the Romans seized the chance of another pause. They kept their existing gains, but, for the time being, withdrew from the rest of Samnium.

The resilience of the Roman state had proved extraordinary. Not only had the Romans bounced back easily from the disasters of 321 and 315 BC, but, while corralling the Samnites in their mountains and bringing them to the brink of defeat in 314–304 BC, they had launched successful simultaneous offensives on their northern and eastern borders. The Second Samnite War had revealed that the drip-drip-drip of political change and military expansion by the Roman state had produced, by the late 4th century BC, a dynamic military imperialism of terrible power and intent. Its relentlessness was daunting: every year was a year of war, always on one front, sometimes two or three. The political system almost guaranteed this. Each of the two annually elected consuls was eager for his chance of military glory. But the whole Roman order was geared to encourage and sustain their efforts. It was a predator state feeding on the spoils of war – on hauls of bullion and slaves, on plundered stock and grain, on annexed land for new colonies. The only limit to its aggression and appetite was its reserve of men and *matériel*; the only possible impediment to its continued advance a coalition of comparable military power. In 298 BC, such a coalition, perhaps years in the making, emerged. In the Third Samnite War (298–290 BC), Rome faced an alliance of Etruscans, Umbrians, Samnites and Gauls; and the war would culminate in one of the most decisive battles in Italian history: a battle, in effect, to decide whether or not the whole of Italy would become Roman.

Such was its geographical extent, the enemy coalition had the Roman line across Italy stretched thin, and in 296 BC the main Samnite army broke through, moved north, and linked up with the Etruscans, Umbrians and Gauls. The following year, they repeated this feat, and this time turned on the pursuing Roman army and crushed it at the Battle of Camerinum. The Roman state was plunged into crisis. The constitution was suspended as special commands were created and incumbent officeholders continued beyond their normal terms. Older men and ex-slaves were mobilized to fill the ranks of new legions, and another two consular armies, 35,000 men in total, were sent into the field before the end of the summer of 295 BC. Even so, as the Romans approached the coalition army encamped at Sentinum on the border between Umbria and Picenum, they were heavily outnumbered. To improve the odds, a detached Roman force invaded Etruria, hoping that the threat of devastation would draw off the Etruscan and Umbrian forces; which it did. Despite this, when the Romans offered battle, the remaining Samnites and Gauls accepted the challenge (an almost essential precondition of combat in ancient warfare, since an army which chose to remain in its fortified camp, often defensively sited, could be attacked only at grave disadvantage).

The Samnites were deployed on the coalition's right flank, facing the consular army of Quintus Fabius, the Gauls on the left, facing the consul Publius Decius. Roman military doctrine was essentially offensive, though it counselled caution in preparing for this and choosing an opportune moment. On this day, the older consul Fabius represented caution, his younger colleague Decius the spirit of the offensive. Fabius was determined to hold back on the left, confident that the enthusiasm of the barbarian warriors opposite would erode more quickly in a long wait than that of the stolid citizen-peasants of Latium. But Decius was determined to attack on the right as soon as the battle opened.

The Roman army that fought at Sentinum was very different from the hoplite phalanx of the 5th century BC. A century of wars against lightly equipped enemies who fought in more open, fast-moving formations, wars often fought in difficult terrain favourable to the guerrilla and the skirmisher, had transformed Roman equipment, organization and tactics. The Second Samnite War may have completed the transition. The dense blocks of men with spears and overlapping shields who had formed the phalanx had become looser formations of men armed mainly with javelin (*pilum*) and a lighter oval or rectangular shield (*scutum*). Large units – the legion (*legio*) of approximately 4,200 men – were divided into small sub-units of 120 called 'maniples' (*manipuli* means 'handfuls'), and these were deployed in an open chequerboard formation and trained to manoeuvre independently. The new legions were designed for mobile, offensive warfare. Unlike the relatively slow, cumbersome and defensive phalanx, they were expected to deploy, advance, wheel and, if necessary, alter front rapidly; and when the time came to close, they would hurl javelins to disorganize the enemy ranks, and then charge in with sword and shield.

Even so, Sentinum was hard-fought. Decius' attack on the right was soon bogged down in a head-on clash with the Gallic line, and when he unleashed his cavalry on the far right in an effort to turn the enemy flank, they were met by the Gallic cavalry and, once embroiled, counter-charged and routed by the Gallic chariot force. The panic quickly began to infect the legionaries, and, as it did so and their line faltered, the Gallic infantry pushed forwards. Decius, unable to shore up the collapsing Roman right, was soon lost to a bizarre religious frenzy. Calling on Mother Earth and the Gods of the Underworld to accept the legions of the enemy along with himself as a sacrifice, he galloped his horse into the Gallic line and perished. Fabius offered more practical help. Detaching units from the rear line of his legions on the left, he was able to stem the rout and launch a counter-attack on the right – a complex sequence of manoeuvres made possible only by the greater flexibility of the new legions. The Gallic advance was halted, and, as the Romans reformed and renewed their attack, the Gallic warriors formed a defensive shield-wall. Meantime, probing on the left, Fabius found the spirit of the Samnites in front of him flagging – as anticipated. Launching his infantry frontally and his cavalry on the left flank, he broke the Samnite line after brief resistance, leaving the Gallic shield-wall isolated on the battlefield.

Mentally and physically exhausted by hours of fighting and now surrounded, the Gallic units disintegrated and fled. The carnage of battle and pursuit claimed, it is said, 25,000 Samnites and Gauls, with another 8,000 taken prisoner; but Roman losses, at 9,000, were also heavy, especially in the wake of yet heavier losses at Camerinum earlier that year. Nonetheless, Sentinum had secured Roman hegemony in Italy.

Events between 293 and 264 BC are obscure, since the relevant parts of Livy's *History of Rome*, our principal source, are lost. But if we do not know a precise chronology, the overall thrust and outcome are clear. Sentinum left the anti-Roman coalition broken backed, and relentless year-on-year Roman offensives thereafter precluded any possibility of its restoration. Samnium, Etruria, Umbria, and the land of the Gallic Senones were conquered and made subject to Rome, mainly as 'allies' bound by treaty, though some land was annexed to the Roman state or settled with Latin colonists. Victory at Sentinum made the Roman Republic the only Italian superpower, and within a generation it had absorbed most of the minor states. Some still clung to independence – such as the Greek cities of the far south, foremost among which was Tarentum. Others, unwilling allies of Rome, still aspired to break free – the democrats ruled by pro-Roman oligarchs in the cities of Campania, and many among the Oscan-speaking peoples of the central and southern Apennines. But, too weak to take on Rome alone, rebels against the *Pax Romana* were forced to look abroad for a more powerful ally. The Greeks, at least, soon found one – a latter-day Alexander, a military adventurer and would-be champion of Greek 'freedom': King Pyrrhus of Epirus.

The conquest of Southern Italy: the Pyrrhic War, 280–275 BC

Prior to the 3rd century BC, Roman contact with the Greeks of southern Italy and Sicily – 'Western Greece' – had been restricted mainly to the Oscanized cities of Campania. Further south, in the foot of Italy and across the straits, most cities were still under Greek rule. Admittedly, few of these were truly independent, but their suzerains were other Greeks – most likely the Tarentines in southern Italy, or the Syracusans in Sicily – and these settlements, known collectively to the ancients as *Magna Graecia* (Great Greece), formed part of a wider Hellenistic civilization.

(The term 'Hellenistic' is used to describe the Greek-speaking world after the death of Alexander the Great in 323 BC.) That civilization extended from a scatter of older cities in the far west, like Massilia (Marseilles), to a multitude of new foundations spread across the recently conquered East, some of which, like Alexandria in Egypt, were poised for greatness. Over much of this expanse, especially in the Orient, the Greek cities floated on a sea of indigenous people, mere blobs of Hellenic culture amid alien deities, unfamiliar customs, and 'barbarous' languages. But where the Greek settlements were older – in the Aegean and Western Asia Minor ('Eastern Greece': colonized *c.* 1050–800 BC), and in Western Greece (colonized *c.* 750–600 BC) – Hellenism had sunk deeper roots. In many parts of southern Italy and Sicily, the native people had been driven off the coastal plain or assimilated into Greek society. Here, Greek had become the language of country as well as town, and Hera, Athena, Artemis and Aphrodite, the Earth Mothers of Old Greece, were worshipped in remote sacred groves. Yet, however well-rooted in places, this Hellenistic civilization was in crisis – a fact of fundamental importance to the balance of forces in a succession of clashes between the Roman Republic and the Hellenistic states in the two and a half centuries after 280 BC. Because of this, we must digress briefly to explore the crisis before returning to pick up the story of the first of these clashes: Rome's war against Tarentum and King Pyrrhus.

Land shortage had driven the earlier waves of Greek colonization that had created Eastern and Western Greece. Only about 15 per cent of Old Greece can be cultivated, and the ancient population had repeatedly outgrown its meagre resources. Colonial expeditions had been funded and organized by the city-states, and groups of pioneers had set off in search of new settlement sites, seeking a place with plentiful good land, a ready supply of fresh water, and, ideally, a natural harbour and a defensible highpoint for an acropolis (or citadel). Once new cities had been established, they sometimes planted further colonies of their own. Paestum, for example – famous for its three still-standing temples – was founded in *c.* 600 BC by settlers from Sybaris in the Gulf of Taranto, while Sybaris itself (a rich trading city whose 'sybaritic' luxury became proverbial) had been founded by Achaean Greeks in *c.* 720 BC. The new settlements were modelled on their mother-cities; Greek colonization meant the spread of a specific form of social and political organization: the city-state (*polis*).

Membership of the city-state depended on citizenship. This was determined by birth and was linked to land ownership: the first citizens had probably all been allocated a plot of land in the territory of the city, and property-ownership remained closely associated with the idea of citizenship thereafter. The city-state was, in essence, a collective of patriarchal households (*oikoi*) that lived off the produce of their own land and labour. The basic function of the state was to organize the collective defence of territory, and the citizen's most important duty to the state was military service. Greek city-states were protected by citizen militias, crucially the hoplite phalanx, a dense block of heavy infantry spearmen formed by the better-off citizens who could afford the necessary equipment. The phalanx empowered the *demos* (the citizen-body). The institutions of the Greek city-state reflected its dependence on a militia of its own citizens. Popular assemblies, jury courts, and frequent elections gave ordinary citizens real power. The annual round of religious festivals expressed the solidarity and common identity of the citizen community. In contrast to monarchies and empires, where subjects were expected to be passive and obedient, participation in public affairs was actively encouraged. 'Here,' announced the Athenian politician Pericles, 'each individual is interested not only in his own affairs but in the affairs of the state as well. Even those who are mostly occupied in their own business are extremely well-informed on general politics. This is a peculiarity of ours. We do not say that a man who takes no interest in politics is a man who minds his own business; we say that he has no business here at all.'(3) For Greeks like Pericles, political engagement was a moral obligation and the measure of a fellow citizen's worth. Appropriately enough, the words were spoken at a public funeral for Athenian war dead – political activity and military service were twin faces of Greek citizenship.

By the early 3rd century BC, however, the substance of Greek citizenship had become diluted. The city-state form – at its zenith in the 5th century BC – had always contained the seeds of its own decay. Divided into a multiplicity of independent polities – one estimate is of 1,500 city-states in *c.* 500 BC – warfare was endemic to the Greek world. Ancient Athens, for example, was at war three years in every four during most of the 5th and 4th centuries BC. Military competition became a dynamic force propelling change. Armed leagues were formed, at first for mutual security, often later mutating into miniature empires ruled by the dominant member. Warfare became more specialized and protracted, beyond the capabilities of a part-time amateur militia, so funds were accumulated to hire professionals. Both developments compromised citizen democracy. Politicians dominated the governing councils of the leagues. Full-time generals commanded the new professional armies. Reduced dependence on citizen militia-service undermined the authority of the popular assemblies and shifted power in the Greek world away from the *demos* to autocrats and oligarchs.

The tensions had always been present. Wealth had never been equally distributed within the city-state, and the balance of power between the minority of landed aristocrats who favoured oligarchy (the rule of the few) and the majority of working farmers who supported democracy (the rule of the citizen-body as a whole) had often been a fine one. During the 4th century, however, the balance altered sharply, and many Greek cities succumbed to the rule of oligarchs, tyrants or kings. Indeed, even where democracies survived, they became the playthings of the great powers. Rome consistently supported oligarchs, so her enemies often backed the democrats; but 'freedom' bestowed from on high is hollow, 'democracy' by permission a contradiction. A decisive moment had been reached in Old Greece in 338 BC – the same year as Rome's suppression of the Latin League – when Philip II's army had smashed the city-state militias of Athens and Thebes at the Battle of Chaeronea, thereby establishing a lasting Macedonian hegemony. The old Greek cities were first dragooned into supporting the eastern campaigns of Philip's son Alexander, then subsumed in the years of anarchy after his death as the Successors battled for control of the Empire. It was a generation before a moderately stable system of Hellenistic states emerged in the eastern Mediterranean.

Decay of the city-state system had afflicted Western Greece no less than Eastern, and most cities here too had succumbed to superior power. The Samnites had overrun the Campanian coastal cities, and the mixed Greek-Oscan-Etruscan communities that resulted had then sought Roman protection against renewed onslaughts from the highlands. Further south, the city of Tarentum had become the principal bulwark of Hellenism. Most Western Greek cities were well past their peak by the time of the Samnite Wars. The great civic monuments – such as the temples which still stand at Paestum, Agrigento and Selinunte – had almost all been erected in the 6th or 5th century BC. Afterwards the military struggle consumed most of the surplus. Tarentum was exceptional in continuing to prosper. Its pastures were reputed to produce the best fleeces in Italy, and wool was made into fine cloth and dyed with purple from mussel-beds along the coast. Tarentum was located, of course, on the gulf which bears its name, and, with a fine harbour, its goods were traded the length of the Adriatic during the 4th century; fine Tarentine painted pottery is found liberally distributed as far as the Po Valley and even beyond the Alps. Successful farms, rich trade, and an inclusive democratic constitution made Tarentum stable and powerful. The city had an army of 15,000, the strongest navy in Italy, and the resources to employ a series of mercenary armies from Sparta and Epirus – a military capacity used both to extend Tarentine territory in the coastal plain, uniting many local cities under its hegemony, and to keep the Lucanians bottled up in their highlands.

Tarentum therefore feared the growing power of Rome. Tension mounted quickly after the Third Samnite War. The Romans had founded a strong Latin colony at Venusia in Apulia in 291 BC. Close to the Lucanian border, it was one of the ring of settlements designed to contain the Samnites and their allies; but, further south than any other Roman colony at the time, it was also in Tarentum's backyard. Ten years later, in 282 BC, when Thurii, another Greek city on the Gulf of Taranto, appealed to them for help against Lucanian attacks, the Romans sent a small relief army and fleet. The Tarentines responded immediately to this new encroachment. They attacked the Roman fleet and sank several vessels, while their army marched on Thurii, drove away the outnumbered Roman force, and overthrew the pro-Roman oligarchy in the town, replacing it with a democracy. Then, having rejected a Roman request for compensation and anticipating a wider war, the Tarentines recruited a powerful ally.

Viewed in retrospect, King Pyrrhus of Epirus can seem a paper tiger. He was not so regarded at the time. One of the last of the generation of warlords spawned by the wars of the Successors, he was accounted the finest general of his age. At a time when there were still men alive who had fought under Alexander, Pyrrhus's army of 25,000 experienced professionals was modelled on that which had destroyed the Persian Empire. Rome's legions, by contrast, for all their success against the minor city-states and hill tribes of Italy, were still essentially a citizen militia. The Tarentines had every reason for confidence in their ally. And Pyrrhus – the space for great military exploits having been squeezed in the East by the emergence there, finally, of relatively stable Hellenistic kingdoms – expected to find an open arena for his talents in Western Greece. The Greek chattering classes anticipated easy victories.

The military doctrine of both Romans and Hellenistic Greeks was similar: to seek out the enemy's main forces and achieve an immediate decision in pitched battle. When a Roman army approached Tarentum, laying waste the countryside as it came, Pyrrhus, even though not all his Greek allies had yet arrived, marched out to confront it. Pyrrhus's army comprised three key elements. First, deployed in the centre of the battle-line, a heavy phalanx of pikemen, each equipped with a pike (*sarissa*) at least 4.8 m long, such that several rows of blades projected forward of the front rank. Second, stationed on the wings, large contingents of first-rate armoured shock cavalry equipped with spears, swords and shields. Traditionally, the king placed himself at the head of the main cavalry force and aimed to lead a decisive charge to break the enemy line at the climax of the battle. Third, a force of 20 elephants, each with a mahout (a driver who sat on the animal's neck) and a howdah (a small tower on the animal's back accommodating two or three men armed with bows, javelins or long spears). The elephants themselves were also trained to fight, using feet, trunks and tusks in close-quarters fighting. The sight, sound and smell of them disabled enemy cavalry by panicking the horses; while defending infantry could be traumatized by the approach and impact of an elephant charge.

Even so, the Battle of Heraclea in 280 BC was no simple affair. The Romans were amateurs, but drilled and disciplined amateurs. 'Pyrrhus rode up to take a view of them,' reports Plutarch, 'and seeing their order, the appointment of their watches, and the method and general form of their encampment, he was amazed, and addressing one of his friends next to him declared, "This order, Magacles, of the barbarians is not at all barbarian in character; we shall presently see what they can do." '(4) Pyrrhus's first impression did not deceive: what the 'barbarians' could do in battle was indeed formidable. The king's all-important cavalry charge miscarried; his horsemen were pushed back and his centre exposed. He took a grave risk in then ordering his phalanx and elephants to charge. Resisted at first by the legionaries in front, Pyrrhus's army would have been destroyed had the victorious Roman cavalry been able to plunge into the flanks of the phalanx. But they were hopelessly disordered by the close proximity of elephants, allowing Pyrrhus's cavalry, whose horses were used to the beasts, to regroup and counterattack. The enemy horse was quickly driven off, exposing the Roman centre to attack. Terrorized by the elephants, exhausted by the struggle to hold back the hedge of pikes in front of them, and now finally charged by heavy cavalry in the flank, the legionaries broke and ran. The ancient sources disagree about the casualty figures, but the lower estimate is a loss of 7,000 Romans to 4,000 Greeks; at best, an expensive victory for Pyrrhus, whose professional veterans were harder to replace than Rome's citizen militiamen.

The battle, therefore, was far from decisive. In an effort to prevent her recently won Empire in southern Italy from unravelling, Rome attempted to restore her prestige in a fresh clash of arms. Despite the defection of Greeks, Lucanians and Samnites, and an intimidating advance north to within 80 km of Rome by Pyrrhus's army, the Romans rejected the king's peace overtures – amounting to a demand for their withdrawal from the south. The Senate was rallied to continuing resistance by the ageing hawk Appius Claudius Pulcher: 'Do not persuade yourselves that making him [Pyrrhus] your friend is the way to send him back; rather it is the way to bring over other invaders from thence, condemning you as easily reduced, if Pyrrhus goes off without punishment for his outrages on you, but, on the contrary, with the reward of having enabled the Tarentines and Samnites to laugh at the Romans.'(5)

Unable to win over allies in central Italy, Pyrrhus withdrew south again for the winter, and it was here that the Romans confronted him once more in 279 BC. Both armies were larger, perhaps twice the size of the previous year, Pyrrhus's having been augmented by his new allies, the Romans' by the deployment of both main consular armies in the south. The first day of the Battle of Ausculum was fought in rough and wooded terrain that limited the effectiveness of elephants and cavalry, and left little opportunity for turning movements. Largely an infantry battle, then, the ground also favoured legionaries over hoplites: both were types of heavy infantry, but while the legionaries fought in a more open formation using javelins and swords, the hoplites needed a tight formation to maintain the integrity of their hedge of pikes. Neither side gave ground, however, and at the end of the first day's fighting both withdrew to their camps for the night. The following morning Pyrrhus offered battle again, this time on more open ground. The Romans, aggressive and confident as ever, accepted. Now, though the javelins and short swords of the legionaries again proved a match for the unwieldy pikes of the phalanx, the Roman army was thrown back by an elephant charge late in the day and retreated to its camp. Ausculum had been another gruelling encounter, with 6,000 Roman casualties and 3,500 Greek. The king had lost many of his best officers; the veterans who had fallen could not be replaced; Ausculum won him no new allies; and the Romans gave no indication they were any closer to surrender. His army was wasting away in a war of attrition he could not win. So he turned from Italy and crossed the straits to try his fortune in the interminable struggles of the Sicilian Greeks against the Carthaginians.

Pyrrhus's Italian allies could not sustain themselves without his direct support, however, and in the three years of his absence in Sicily were pressed hard by the Romans. Finally, in desperation, they appealed to him to come back. Pyrrhus, having achieved no more in Sicily than in Italy, heeded their call. In his final Italian campaign, Pyrrhus displayed the same energetic spirit, detaching a force to divert one of the two Roman consular armies, then launching a daring march through the night with his main force to take the other by surprise. But night marches are hazardous and the Greeks lost their way. When the sun came up on the Battle of Beneventum (275 BC), they were badly deployed, and their vanguard was attacked and thrown back. Pyrrhus restored the chaotic battle with an elephant charge, which in turn drove the Romans back to their camp. But the elephants, their energy spent, found themselves too far out in front and without proper support. The Roman infantry, reforming in the safety of their camp, harried the elephants with missiles and then charged out at them, causing a stampede to the rear which sent the panic-stricken beasts crashing through their own lines and throwing them into chaos. Pyrrhus withdrew in haste from the battlefield – and soon, with the bulk of his remaining army, about a third of the original 25,000, returned to Epirus. (He was killed a few years later, rather ingloriously, by a falling roof-tile hurled by an old woman during a street battle in Argos.)

The south Italian war was not yet over, but Pyrrhus's allies were left fighting against the odds. Tarentum fell in 272 BC when Pyrrhus decided to withdraw the garrison he had left there, agreeing to hand the city over to the Romans in return for his men's safe passage out. None of the other Greek cities was strong enough to contemplate continued resistance. There was war for some years more, however, against the Samnite, Lucanian and Bruttian highlanders; the colonies planted at Paestum (273 BC), Beneventum (268 BC) and Aesernia (263 BC) symbolized their progressive subjugation and the annexation of their territory. Unable to win when allied with Pyrrhus, the peoples of southern Italy were bound to succumb when left to face Rome alone. What is more, the Pyrrhic War had demonstrated again the extraordinary resilience of the Roman state when thrown back on to the defensive by an opponent of comparable battlefield power. Pyrrhus's victories had given him localized and temporary strategic dominance. But when he advanced, he had found himself hamstrung by the solidity of the Roman commonwealth in central Italy. Epirus was a small, impoverished and distant state; the Greeks of southern Italy were militarily weak; the Samnites were a broken people: whereas Rome had vast reserves of military manpower and a network of fortified strong-points and supply-bases across the peninsula. Pyrrhus had been able to achieve momentary success; but victory in the war had eluded him because the core of Rome's Italian Empire had remained intact.

These realities of power would be tested again, 60 years later, on a far grander scale. For Rome, now unchallenged mistress of Italy, was poised for her first overseas adventure, one that would bring her into immediate conflict with the ancient mercantile empire of Carthage – a conflict that would eventually spawn an Italian war far more terrible than that against Pyrrhus.

The conquest of Sicily: the First Punic War, 264–241 BC

'From 405 until the Roman conquest, which began in 264 BC, the history of Sicily has to be written around the careers and fortunes of five rulers of Syracuse, punctuated by periods of civil war, dynastic strife and anarchy'(6): thus wrote the ancient historian Moses Finley. A succession of thunderous wars starting in 416 BC – against Athenians, Carthaginians and, increasingly, one another – destroyed the city-state system among the Sicilian Greeks. 'Henceforth Sicilians were to be subjects rather than citizens. All further political action took the form of destructive dynastic struggles, conspiracies and civil wars. From time to time the people were still summoned to meet, and there were even elections and decrees. But they were mere pawns in the power game, pulled about by adventurers when it suited their purposes. These adventurers and their armed mercenaries made the real decisions, not voters in the assembly.'(7)

Like dictators of a later age, the tyrants of Syracuse played the popular card when opportune, but any sign of real democracy was crushed. Tyrant (*turannos*) was the word used by Greeks for an autocratic ruler who held power by force rather than constitutional right; and the difference between a mercenary-captain and a tyrant was simply that one remained at large while the other had control of a city. Tyrants were the military strongmen who, in an age of blood and iron, ruled through control of fortresses, soldiers, warships and artillery. They filled the space left by the decay of city-state, citizen-militia and popular assembly.

The city of Syracuse was unable, however, to establish a stable *imperium*. The wars of Dionysius I (405–367 BC) exhausted Sicily, and Syracuse overreached itself attempting to extend its empire into mainland Italy. Civil war between rival successors in the mid 4th century further impoverished the city and left the island as a whole open to intervention by military adventurers. Thereafter, periods of order were fragile and brief; by the time the last of Finley's five rulers was assassinated in 289 BC, Hellenistic Sicily was little more than an anarchy of mercenary enclaves. It was one of these – the Mamertine enclave at Messina – that became the focus of a crisis which would draw Rome into the affairs of the island.

The Mamertines were a corps of Italian mercenaries built up over the years by the tyrants of Syracuse (the name means 'followers of Mars' in Oscan). Conflict broke out between them and the citizens of Syracuse in the 280s BC, and the Mamertines were offered and accepted haven at Messina – where they promptly massacred the old inhabitants and divided up their possessions among themselves. The Mamertine city-state – an anomalous barbarian-mercenary polity symbolic of Sicily's descent into anarchy – extended its control over much of the north-eastern part of the island, using this as a base for banditry and piracy. By the 260s BC the Syracusans had had enough: they resolved to extirpate the pest. They were now ruled by a new tyrant, Hiero II, one of King Pyrrhus's hench-men, who had been installed during the king's campaigns in the island in 278–275 BC. The Mamertines were quickly defeated and rolled back to the city of Messina itself; at which point they appealed for help – at first to the Carthaginians.

Though most of the Sicilian coastal plain had been settled by Greeks long before, in the far west of the island there were Phoenician cities equally old. The Phoenicians were traders from the Levant who spoke a Semitic language and worshipped Near Eastern gods. They had estab-lished a string of settlements in the western Mediterranean in archaic times, of which the most important was – or became – the city of Carthage, situated on the coast of North Africa at a site close to modern Tunis. The threat represented by Greek colonization had caused the Phoenicians to federate and put themselves under the protection of the most powerful of their number. Carthage thereby became an imperial city; but, composed of Mediterranean merchants and African landowners, the Carthaginian ruling class exercised only loose authority over its subject cities, charging modest harbour dues and tribute merely to support the mercenary armies and fleets on which security depended. At home, too, Carthaginian gov-ernment was moderate: though dominated by the aristocracy – which supplied the two ruling *suffetes*, a 30-strong council of elders, and a high court of 104 judges – the final power of decision rested with a popular assembly of all citizens. And, somewhat in contrast to the Roman Republic and Hellenistic Greece, military authority remained wholly subordinate to civil. Though there was a fleet of warships in a protected inner harbour at Carthage, there was no standing army or regular militia; instead, generals were appointed and mercenaries recruited when needed.

The city itself was huge. A mighty citadel – the Byrsa Hill – towered over it. The commercial harbour was one of the busiest in the Medi-terranean. The residential districts were filled with elegant, tall, narrow-fronted houses of uniform size and layout, each with its own underground cistern fed with winter rainwater piped off the roofs. On the rolling prairies beyond the city lay the estates of the Carthaginian elite, producing the grain, meat, hides, fleeces, vines and olives that supplied the city and filled its cargo ships. Carthage was powered largely by mer-chant profit; it was a city and an empire much like Renaissance Venice. Foreign wars were fought, if at all, to protect and advance trade; they were limited wars for commercial advantage; Carthaginian imperialism was a means to an end, not, like Roman imperialism, an end in itself. Sicily, unfortunately, had been especially expensive. Many had been the expeditionary forces dispatched there during the 4th century BC in an effort to contain the territorial ambition of the tyrants of Syracuse. Now, it seemed, the new tyrant Hiero II had restored Syracusan power and was attempting to regain control of eastern Sicily. If he succeeded, a renewed onslaught on the Carthaginian west was likely. The Mamertine enclave at Messina looked like being a useful ally. So the Carthaginians obligingly sent a garrison to help defend the city against the Syracusans.

Once there, however, they were reluctant to leave, even though their arrival had at once discouraged further Syracusan operations. The Mamertines then cast around for help in ejecting guests who had rather overstayed their welcome; and they chose the Romans. Their appeal arrived just as opportunities for military aggression in peninsular Italy were becoming exhausted. The dynamic of Roman imperialism was operating more frenetically than ever before. We can measure this in several ways. The size of the *ager Romanus* (land held by the Roman state or its citizens, as opposed to that of Latins and allies) had increased fivefold in the period 338–264 BC. The number of *cives Romani* (Roman citizens) had increased threefold in the same period, and at least 21 new (mainly Latin) colonies had been founded. The literary record attests 14 temple foundations between 302 and 264 BC (always a reliable indicator of successful warfare, since public monuments were financed by spoils). Roman pottery had become far more widely distributed – a measure of trade – and official state coinage was introduced for the first time – to make it easier to pay soldiers and share out booty. Rome itself was growing fast and probably already contained 100,000 people – far too many for the hinterland to support, making the city dependent on its Empire for basic subsistence.

This imperialism was inflationary. As Rome became more of a heavyweight in the struggle between states, the enemies she had to face were more formidable – first the Samnite Confederation; then King Pyrrhus and the cities of Western Greece; and soon the Carthaginian Empire. Geopolitical competition on a wider global stage put a premium on conquests rich enough to maintain Rome's advantage. And as the Empire's social base increased – as more former victims were 'enrolled in the gang and invited to share the proceeds of future robberies' – hauls of booty had to be bigger if there was to be enough to go round. Thus, as the Empire expanded, so did the appetite for more. Rome had become one of history's monster states, a polity whose very essence was robbery with violence, whose predatory aggression endlessly fed and enlarged itself. The immediate expressions of this were the ambition of its politician-generals and the city's permanent state of war.

Thus, when the Mamertines finally asked the Carthaginians to leave, the Romans were happy to underwrite the request – and the Carthaginians on the spot were too weak to argue. But this new intervention in the affairs of Sicily alarmed both Carthaginians and Syracusans, who formed an unprecedented military alliance and marched together to suppress the Mamertine bandit-city before it could evolve into a fully-fledged Roman client. The Romans immediately invaded with a consular army and broke the siege of Messina. Their opponents seem to have been stunned by the scale of the Roman reaction and the speed with which the crisis had spiralled out of control. The Syracusans retreated southwards, the Carthaginians westwards, both abandoning the struggle for Messina. The Carthaginians then attempted to open peace negotiations. They promptly received a second shock: the Romans refused either to talk or to present any specific demands; they simply geared themselves up for all-out war, landing a double consular army in Sicily the following year.

The First Punic War began, like most wars, in a squabble over a secondary objective. But usually there are great matters at issue. Not so here: both Syracusans and Carthaginians felt they could let Messina go. What drove the war was Roman aggression, and this, as the Carthaginians were to discover each time they sued for peace, appeared to have no finite limits. Carthage found herself trapped in a no-holds-barred conflict for the highest possible stakes with a relentless predator who refused to negotiate. The waste of men and resources was to be prodigious – in Polybius's view, for whom it was 'the greatest war in history' up to that time, unprecedented. Such a conflict found Carthage militarily, politically, and indeed culturally ill-prepared; and so traumatizing was it that it would cause her transformation from a cautious merchant city-state into a military dynamo.

In another sense, too, there was an imbalance between the principal protagonists. Carthage was a mercantile empire protected by a large and

experienced fleet. Rome was a land-based empire with a powerful army
and a huge pool of reserve manpower. The result – until the imbalance
could be rectified – was to be an asymmetrical war of whale and elephant. This quickly became apparent in the event. The massive Roman
invasion army of 263 BC rolled down the east coast to threaten Syracuse
and secure Hiero's surrender. He was required to pay an indemnity and
to supply the Roman army in its further campaigns. In return, however,
he got the protection of his new 'ally' against more traditional enemies
– not only the Carthaginians, but also other Greeks who might wish to
challenge Syracusan pre-eminence. He became, in fact, Rome's first
'client king': a puppet ruler buoyed up by Roman diplomatic, financial
and military support, whose nominal independence spared Rome the
expense and trouble of formal occupation. The Roman blitzkrieg had
other consequences, too: some of Carthage's Sicilian allies deserted,
and Carthage herself again made peace overtures. When the Romans still
refused to negotiate – despite now having effective control of eastern
Sicily – it was apparent that her tacit war aims had expanded into a threat
to the whole Carthaginian lodgement in Sicily. The Carthaginian government was left with no choice but to send an expeditionary force to Sicily.

This decision brought the land war rapidly to its climax in 262 BC.
With a large force besieged by the Romans in Agrigento, the main
Carthaginian army, more than 50,000-strong, marched along the coast
in an attempt to relieve the city. At the Battle of Heraclea Minoa it was
decisively defeated, losing 7,000 men, and forced to fall back westwards.
Agrigento was promptly captured and put to the sack: 25,000 were
enslaved and the city was emptied of everything of value. 'When the
news of the events at Agrigento was received in Rome, the Senate was
almost beside itself with rejoicing,' reports Polybius. 'In this exultant
mood their aspirations soared far above their original designs, and they
were no longer content with having rescued the Mamertines nor with
what they had gained in the fighting. They now cherished the hope that
they could drive the Carthaginians out of Sicily altogether . . .'(8)

Easier hoped than done. The ruthlessness and greed displayed at
Agrigento had shocked some of Carthage's erstwhile allies back to their
former allegiance. This further shored up an already strong defensive
position in the far west: though they had lost the land war, the
Carthaginians were securely ensconced at Lilybaeum and other coastal

fortresses, the garrisons now heavily reinforced, and supply from the sea assured by the power of the fleet. By 261 BC there was stalemate.

Rome could not win the war – or rather, could not win all that she wanted, which was the whole island – without maritime supremacy. The Carthaginian coastal fortresses were impregnable to land assault and could be taken only by blockade; and since they were supplied by sea, that meant naval blockade. Ancient naval warfare can seem to us a curious business. The battleships of the age were quinqueremes: galleys with three banks of oars, the two on top, where the hull was wider, each pulled by two men, the short one at the bottom, where the curve of the hull narrowed the space, by just one (thus *quinqueremis* from *quinque* meaning 'five' and *remus* meaning 'oar'). Though the vessels were quite small – perhaps 6 m wide and 40 m long – because they depended for speed and manoeuvrability on muscle-power, some 270 rowers were packed on to the benches. These men powered not only the ship, but also its main armament: a metal-headed ram projecting from the prow, designed to shear off oars and smash holes in enemy vessels. Another 30 men crewed the ship, and as many as 120 marines crowded the upper deck, some fighting as archers, others as armoured spearmen. The marines constituted the quinquereme's secondary armament: close-up they could shower the upper deck of an enemy vessel with missiles, and, if grappled, could cross over to capture it in hand-to-hand fighting.

Naval battles tended to be chaotic. Because of their vulnerability to ramming, fleets formed up in one or more closely spaced lines to deny the enemy opportunity to take vessels in the beam. On the other hand, a tight formation made ships vulnerable to collision, especially if an enemy attack caused some ships to veer off course and spread disorder down the line. At worst, a badly handled fleet could be reduced to a slow-moving jumble of vessels, highly vulnerable to ramming attacks and successful boarding operations. Tactical manoeuvres often amounted to attempts to bring an enemy fleet to such a condition while preserving the good order and effectiveness of one's own vessels. In such manoeuvres the Carthaginians, an established naval power, began the war with a clear advantage. The Romans, assembling a fleet in the winter of 261–260 BC, were the Johnnies-come-lately.

Doubtful of their ability to outmanoeuvre a Carthaginian fleet, the Romans adopted a new device, a combined grappling hook and gangway known as a 'raven' (*corvus*). The device was held vertical against a round pole mounted with a pulley and capable of swivelling. Coming close to an enemy vessel, the raven could be swung into position and then allowed to drop down, the iron spike at the far end of the gangway (from which the device took its name) burying itself in the enemy's woodwork with the force of its fall. Then the marines would swarm on to the hooked vessel. The raven was deployed for the first time at the Battle of Mylai in 260 BC. The Carthaginians, contemptuous of Roman seafaring, 'steered straight for the enemy and thought they could risk an attack without keeping any formation, as though they were seizing a prize which was already theirs for the taking,' explained Polybius. 'Then, as they came into collision, the Carthaginians found that their vessels were invariably held fast by the ravens, and the Roman troops swarmed aboard them by means of the gangways and fought them hand-to-hand on deck. Some of the Carthaginians were cut down and others were thrown into confusion by these tactics and gave themselves up, for the fighting seemed to have been transformed into a battle on dry land.'(9) The Carthaginian fleet turned and fled with the loss of 50 of its 130 ships. A serious struggle for control of the waters around Sicily had begun.

In the next few years, however, though they made further gains on land and sea, the Romans failed to break through the Carthaginian defences. They responded with a bold lunge at Africa in 256 BC, hoping to draw the Carthaginians from their Sicilian fortresses by an attack on their homeland; and hoping too, no doubt, for richer plunder. At first all went well. An attempt by the main Carthaginian fleet to intercept the armada off the coast of Sicily was beaten off with heavy loss. A Roman army under Atilius Regulus was landed in Africa, established a secure base, and won an easy victory over local Carthaginian forces. Then the Romans overreached themselves. With Regulus at their gates, Carthage again sued for peace, this time offering to surrender the whole of Sicily; but the Romans demanded more, and thereby goaded their enemy into last-ditch resistance. They hired a Spartan mercenary general called Xanthippus as a consultant, and raised a new army of 12,000 infantry, 4,000 cavalry and 100 elephants with which to confront Regulus' 15,000 infantry and 500 cavalry in pitched battle (255 BC). Anticipating the tactics of Hannibal in the Second Punic War, Xanthippus pinned the Roman infantry in the centre with his own infantry and elephants while smashing the Roman flanks with his greatly superior cavalry. He then unleashed an elephant charge which shattered the Roman infantry advance in the centre. The legions were then attacked frontally by the Carthaginian heavy infantry and in the flanks by cavalry and light infantry. The Roman mass disintegrated. Barely 2,000 succeeded in making their escape back to their camp.

The Roman invasion of Africa had been destroyed. But the agony was not yet over. The fleet, which had returned to Sicily for the winter, sailed back to Africa to pick up the survivors. It saw off the heavily outnumbered Carthaginian home fleet and completed the evacuation, but on the way home was struck by a violent storm off the coast of Sicily and lost all but 80 of its 350 ships.

The struggle resumed its course as an exhausting war of attrition centred on Sicily. The Romans built a new fleet of 300 quinqueremes and captured Palermo in 254 BC. The Carthaginians landed a new army – including no less than 140 elephants – but suffered defeat when they attempted to retake the city in 251 BC. The Romans put Lilybaeum under siege in 250 BC, but their attempted blockade was broken and their naval power obliterated in a double disaster the following year, as one fleet was outmanoeuvred and destroyed in battle, and a second driven on to the coast by a sudden gale and smashed to pieces. Both sides had repeatedly raised, equipped and fielded new armies of 50,000 men and new fleets of 300 quinqueremes. Both had suffered massive losses of men and *matériel*. Both were groaning under the strain: Carthage faced mutiny in her Sicilian garrisons and revolt by her African subjects, the Romans growing resistance to the annual levy from her Italian allies. Yet the war was no nearer a conclusion: it remained a stalemate of elephant and whale – the Romans lacked a large enough fleet to blockade the western ports, the Carthaginians a field army with which to attempt reconquest of the island.

Carthage sent out a new commander in 247 BC. Hamilcar Barca was a maverick aristocrat – unconventional, populist in political orientation, a firm advocate of imperial expansion. He crushed a mutiny in the Carthaginian army as soon as he arrived, and then, with his albeit modest forces, went on to the offensive, raiding the Italian coast, encouraging Roman allies to desert, and establishing a strong, forward, mountain-top position near Palermo from which to wage guerrilla war. But while Rome

continued to send large armies to Sicily, Carthage refused to send reinforcements to Hamilcar, and the Carthaginian's offensive power gradually declined; soon, the coastal raids were suspended, and the army was
pulled back westwards and became inert.

The Romans, meantime, were equipping themselves for another
all-out strike. In 242 BC a new fleet of 200 quinqueremes and 700 transports sailed to Lilybaeum and established a blockade. The following year,
to save the city, the Carthaginians dispatched a new fleet of their own,
comparable in size with the Romans', but, for once, less experienced
and skilful. Roles were reversed: Roman sea-salts who had spent a year
on blockade confronted raw Carthaginian crews just out of port. At the
Battle of the Aegates Islands the Romans sank 50 enemy ships and captured 70 more. With the Roman blockade secure for at least another year,
the Carthaginian garrisons at Lilybaeum and elsewhere were doomed.
The home government authorized Hamilcar to secure whatever peace
terms he could.

The terms imposed by Rome were heavy: all Sicily and the islands
around it were to be abandoned; Hiero and the Syracusans were to be
left alone; an indemnity of 3,200 talents was to be paid in ten annual
instalments; no Italian or Sicilian mercenaries were henceforward to be
recruited; no Carthaginian ships were to enter Italian or Sicilian waters;
and all Roman POWs were to be returned without ransom. Nor was
this all. When the Carthaginian government, financially crippled by war
expenditures and the indemnity, refused to pay arrears of wages to its
returning mercenaries, they mutinied, marched on the capital, and raised
the Libyan subject population in revolt. The result was a bitterly fought,
three-year war (240–237 BC). The Romans used the opportunity to grab
more territory – Sardinia and Corsica – and, when challenged, responded
first by threatening a war they knew the Carthaginians incapable of fighting, and then, when their victim backed down, demanding another 1,200-
talent indemnity not to attack anyway.

The Phoenician cities in the western Mediterranean had existed
for 500 years, surviving numerous great wars with the Greeks. Yet within
25 years of Carthage's first military clash with Rome, the settlements on
Sicily, Sardinia and Corsica had been liquidated, and the mother-city
was paying out vast sums each year to fill the coffers of her victorious
enemy. The First Punic War was the most shattering defeat in

Carthaginian history. Politically traumatized, the Carthaginian ruling class split into opposing factions of doves and hawks. The doves were led by Hanno and supported mainly by the landowning aristocracy: they favoured peaceful co-existence with Rome, defence of the African empire, and an avoidance of costly and potentially disastrous foreign wars. They assumed – almost certainly wrongly – that they would be safe at home; that Rome would never come for them there. For the merchant aristocracy, however, there was not even temporary respite in prospect. Much of their trade was already crippled, and it took little imagination to picture the consequences for what remained if Roman expansion went unchecked. The hawks who represented them favoured a ship-building programme, overseas expansion, militant hostility to Romans, Italians and Greeks on all fronts, and preparations for a war of *revanche* to recover what had been lost. Their leader was the veteran general Hamilcar Barca, the former commander in Sicily. The Barca faction quickly established its political ascendancy. And Hamilcar already had a son who could be expected to succeed him as leader of the faction: his name was Hannibal.

Enemy at the gates: the Second Punic War, 218–202 BC

Aggression and arrogance characterized Roman imperialism between the 3rd and 1st centuries BC, a combination that frequently caused it to over-reach itself, straining its military power to the point where it was broken in defeat. The Greeks, of course, had words for this: *hubris*, meaning gross, violent and abusive behaviour born of overweening pride; and *nemesis*, the righteous indignation and retribution which *hubris* provoked. It was Rome's bullying of its punch-drunk enemy during and after the First Punic War that inspired a new spirit and resolve in Carthage. And it was a new offensive in the north, against the Gauls of the Po Valley, that was to provide Carthage with powerful local allies when they launched a war of *revanche*.

Romans and Gauls had clashed violently in the Third Samnite War, and in its aftermath the territory of the Senones tribe, the so-called *ager Gallicus*, had been annexed. Fifty years later, with the passage of a new land law in 232 BC, Latin settlers began arriving in numbers, displacing local Gauls, who presumably escaped northwards as refugees to foster a sense of injustice and danger among their compatriots of the Po Valley. Who would be next?

In 225 BC, a great coalition of the Cisalpine tribes (those 'on our side of the Alps'), supported by contingents from Transalpine Gaul (those 'across the Alps'), mobilized an army of 70,000 warriors and invaded Roman Italy. The Romans, able to draw on the manpower and logistical resources of the whole Italian peninsula, raised 130,000 men against them. Though the Gauls promptly retreated across the Apennine passes into Etruria, the Romans eventually succeeded in manoeuvring them into a pitched battle. Undeterred by the odds, despite facing attack on two sides, the Gauls deployed with confidence. The sight of their great host was, according to Polybius, 'awe-inspiring'. The Romans, though encouraged by their tactical advantage, were 'at the same time dismayed by the splendid array of the Celtic host and the ear-splitting din which they created. There were countless horns and trumpets being blown simultaneously in their ranks, and as the whole army was also shouting its war-cries, there arose such a babel of sound that it seemed to come not only from the trumpets and the soldiers but from the whole of the surrounding countryside at once. Besides this, the aspect and the movements of the naked warriors in the front ranks made a terrifying spectacle. They were all men of splendid physique and in the prime of life, and those in the leading companies were richly adorned with gold necklaces and bracelets.'(10) But the Battle of Telamon was a massacre. Though the Gallic shield-wall held for a time against attacks front and rear, it was broken by a furious Roman cavalry charge into its flanks. Polybius records that some 40,000 Gauls were killed and at least 10,000 captured. After this victory, the Romans conquered Cisalpine Gaul in a series of campaigns between 225 and 220 BC, consolidating their triumph by founding two new colonies on the middle Po at Cremona and Placentia.

Altogether, between the end of the Third Samnite War in 290 BC and the outbreak of the Second Punic War in 218 BC, the territory of the Roman Empire roughly doubled, with the addition of Sicily, Sardinia, Corsica and Cisalpine Gaul. Some territories were integrated under traditional legal arrangements. Loyalists – like the rulers of Syracuse and Messina – were rewarded with nominal independence and ranked as 'allies' (*socii*). Rebels sometimes lost their land to Latin and Roman settlers brought in to form new 'colonies' (*coloniae*) – like Cremona and

Placentia on the Po. But most new territory was organized into 'provinces' (*provinciae*), each governed by a Roman magistrate (at this time a praetor, the number of whom elected each year gradually increased in line with the growth of Empire), and most local inhabitants were reclassified as members of 'foreign communities' (*civitates peregrinae*): they were, in other words, mere subjects of the Roman state, obliged to pay tribute but denied political rights. Integration was problematic: the rapid expansion of the empire, the lack of rights for most new inhabitants, and the greed of the empire-builders sometimes combined to produce explosive revolts. Roman officials were often corrupt. Private profiteers had the contracts to collect taxes. Settlers grabbed the land of local peasants. Native chiefs were befuddled by loan sharks and ran up hopeless debts. Those who protested were beaten up by soldiers. As the reality of conquest and 'foreign' status sank in, a sullen anger often bubbled beneath surface calm, an anger that could flash into revolt if organized. Cisalpine Gaul was such a place, when, at the end of 218 BC, a Carthaginian army burst over the Alpine passes and entered the Po plain.

This army had marched from Spain, where the Barca faction had been busy building a new empire since 237 BC. Led first by the great Hamilcar, then by his son-in-law and former first lieutenant, Hasdrubal, the Carthaginians had won control of much of the Iberian peninsula, sometimes by military conquest, sometimes by diplomacy and alliances with the Spanish chieftains. The peninsula was a patchwork of peoples and tribes with an Iron Age culture, each group centred on a hill-fort girded by defensive walls of dry-stone masonry and mud-brick. The ancients described the inhabitants as 'Celtiberians', a fusion of native Iberians and incoming Celts from the north, and there is much archaeological and place-name evidence to support the idea of a hybrid culture spreading across Spain from the Pyrenees. Tribes near the east and south coasts were also recipients of limited influence from the Greek and Phoenician trading cities established there: imported wine carriers and ceramic table-services turn up at some of the larger hill-forts. The Celtiberians had a strong military tradition fostered by endemic tribal warfare and an impressive array of iron weapons. Their heavy infantry fought mainly as swordsmen, using either the curved *falcata* or the straight-sided *gladius*, both cut-and-thrust weapons designed for slashing and stabbing. They wore little or no armour, but carried large oval body-shields, and may also have been equipped with javelins. Certainly there were Spanish light infantry so armed, their javelins including a barbed variety made entirely of iron, and a short *pilum*, which had a narrow head and a long thin metal shaft designed to penetrate shields and armour. The Spanish way of war – as first encountered in the Second Punic War – was to have a profound impact on the Roman army. The *pilum* and the *gladius* (the latter known to Roman soldiers as 'the Spanish sword') were both adopted by the legions.

Spain offered much to the Carthaginians: a barrier against further Roman expansion; mines that produced abundant copper and silver for paying mercenaries; a rich military recruiting-ground; and new markets for Carthaginian merchants. The conquests of the 230s and 220s, moreover, were no drain on the Carthaginian state: they were made to pay for themselves, and the new territories developed into a semi-independent Barca fiefdom, complete with its own capital city at New Carthage. Hamilcar probably envisaged Spain as the launch-pad for a war of *revanche* against Rome from the outset. Livy recounts an old story that implies as much: 'Hamilcar, after the campaign in Africa, was about to carry his troops over to Spain, when Hannibal, then about nine years old, begged, with all the childish arts he could muster, to be allowed to accompany him; whereupon Hamilcar, who was preparing to offer sacrifice for a successful outcome, led the boy to the altar and made him solemnly swear, with his hand upon the sacred victim, that as soon as he was old enough he would be the enemy of the Roman people.' Livy then explains that Hamilcar's ultimate purpose in the conquest of Spain was 'an enterprise of far greater moment'(11) that only his death in 229 BC prevented him seeing through.

But Roman writers have a reason to paint Carthage the aggressor. We cannot be sure of Hamilcar's intentions. We do know that, while Carthage was fighting the Celtiberian tribes and Rome the Cisalpine Gauls, the two states' relations were governed by an agreement that the River Ebro in north-east Spain should be the boundary of their respective spheres of influence. We know also that, contrary to this agreement, the Romans had an alliance with the city of Saguntum, which lay on the east coast far to the south of the Ebro line – deep within the Carthaginian sphere. Much has been written – apparently without irony – about the 'defensive' character of Roman imperialism, not least in relation to the dispute over

Saguntum at the outbreak of the Second Punic War. Yet the facts are plain enough: Rome had no existing interests south of the Ebro when the alliance with Saguntum was made, and therefore the only possible interpretation of the alliance is that she was introducing a Trojan Horse into a Carthaginian preserve. It was as if the Carthaginians had formed an alliance with the Cisalpine Gauls. Though the implications of the Saguntine alliance have remained unclear to some modern scholars, they were not so to the Carthaginians at the time: Rome had imperial ambitions in Spain. As William Harris, author of the most thorough deconstruction of the theory of 'defensive imperialism', puts it: 'A full explanation [of Rome's conduct towards Carthage between the wars] must include the usual advantages which were expected from successful warfare and the aggressiveness with which these from time to time informed Roman conduct. Spain in particular was probably regarded by Roman senators as a rich prize that could be won in a war against Carthage. Hopes of glory, power and wealth, together with the habit of armed reaction to foreign opponents, mingled with what were seen as the needs of defence.'(12)

In 220 BC the alliance between Rome and Saguntum was activated. The Romans intervened in a dispute in the city to shore up the authority of the pro-Roman elements. Soon afterwards a Roman embassy appeared at New Carthage demanding a guarantee of Saguntine independence. The new Carthaginian commander in Spain sent home for advice on dealing with the crisis. He promptly received the authority he needed: the Carthaginian army moved against Saguntum and captured it in 219 BC after an eight-month siege.

The Romans had sent no military assistance to Saguntum. To have done so would have been a logistically hazardous enterprise. But this was of no great concern to them. Saguntum did not matter for itself, but as a *casus belli*. When they received news of the fall of the city, they sent a delegation to Carthage to demand the surrender of the Carthaginian commander in Spain and the restoration of Saguntine independence. Livy describes a dramatic scene on the floor of the house once the Carthaginian council of elders had rejected the Roman demands. 'Fabius [leader of the Roman delegation], in answer, laid his hand on the fold of his toga, where he had gathered it to his breast, and, "Here," he said, "we bring you peace and war. Take which you will." Scarcely had he spoken, when the answer no less proudly rang out, "Whichever you please – we do not care." Fabius let the gathered folds fall, and cried, "We give you war." The Carthaginian senators replied, as one man, "We accept it; and in the same spirit we will fight it to the end." '(13)

The Barca faction had got the war they may long have hoped and planned for, but it was the Romans who started the Second Punic War – by making an alliance with Saguntum, by intervening directly in its affairs, and by issuing an ultimatum when it was suppressed: all in violation of the Ebro agreement. But this time they had truly overreached themselves, grossly underestimating the strength of the Carthaginian empire in Spain, the size and professionalism of the Carthaginian army assembled there, and, above all, the brilliance of the young Carthaginian general Hannibal Barca, whom the soldiers had acclaimed commander-in-chief after the assassination of his predecessor in 221 BC.

Aggressive intent and arrogant overconfidence – *hubris* – were implicit, too, in Rome's military strategy at the start of the war. She planned to send one consular army to Spain, the other to Africa. Both were moving to their destinations when news reached their respective commanders that Hannibal had imposed his own grand strategy on the war. Sending 15,000 men to guard Africa, he crossed the Ebro with his main force and headed north. Leaving 11,000 men to hold north-eastern Spain, he crossed the Pyrenees and headed into Gaul with an army of 50,000 infantry, 9,000 cavalry and 37 elephants. His final destination was the Po Valley, and his march there is one of the epics of military history. Gallic tribes contested his crossing of the Rhône and forced him into an unwanted battle. The Romans, diverted from their intended assault on Spain, landed at the mouth of the Rhône, defeated his cavalry, and drove inland looking for a fight; but the Carthaginian veered away northwards. Another Gallic tribe ambushed his army in a narrow Alpine pass; a desperately dangerous struggle ensued before the enemy was routed. Finally, snow and rockfalls turned the passage of the Alps into a nightmare trek in which thousands perished. When his army descended to the western edge of the Po Valley, it had shrivelled to less than half its original size. Those remaining were exhausted and isolated, adrift in hostile territory, threatened by winter cold, lack of supplies, and the imminent onset of powerful Roman armies coming by forced marches to the battle zone. A bold strategic move had left the Carthaginian cause hanging by a thread.

The whole world was watching. Especially the recently conquered tribes of Cisalpine Gaul were watching. Here was the key to unlocking the strategic door into Italy. A Carthaginian victory might set the region alight and provide the local allies needed to provide reinforcements, supplies, and bases for the winter. The consul Publius Cornelius Scipio, returning from his abortive landing in the Rhône delta, led out a strong force of cavalry and light infantry to reconnoitre and probe the Carthaginian position. Hannibal met them at the River Ticinus and immediately attacked with his much stronger cavalry, driving the Romans off with serious loss; the consul was wounded and had to be rescued by his own son. Scipio pulled his army back to Placentia on the middle Po, leaving Hannibal free to forage and recruit. But when the other Roman consul arrived with his army from the south – the intended conquerors of Africa – the Romans advanced again and pitched their camp close to Hannibal's. It was late December and winter had set in – the coming Battle of the Trebia was to be fought in sub-zero temperatures and falling snow – but both sides were eager to fight.

The consuls commanded 40,000 men, mostly heavy infantry, plus good numbers of light infantry, though rather inadequate cavalry. The men were a mixture of Romans, Latins and allies. The Romans (probably also the Latins, and possibly some at least of the allies: we do not know) were organized into legions of 4,200 men, each composed of 1,200 *velites* (light javelin-throwers), 1,200 *hastati* (younger men serving as armoured heavy infantry with javelin, sword and body-shield), 1,200 *principes* (older men equipped in the same way), and 600 *triarii* (older still and armed with a long thrusting-spear instead of a javelin). Traditionally, these formed four distinct battle lines, the *velites* providing a screen of skirmishers in front, the *hastati* in the second line and, if they were needed, the *principes* in the third forming the main shock forces, the *triarii* a final reserve around which the army could rally in the event of disaster. This was still, however, an amateur army: despite regular drilling and weapons practice, the rank and file remained a militia of peasant farmers, the officers and generals upper-class politicians. It was an army easily goaded into battle on unfavourable terms.

Early one morning Hannibal sent his light cavalry up to the Roman camp to taunt their enemies. Sempronius Longus, the consul command-ing that day, immediately led his men out – before breakfast in freezing winter weather – deployed them for battle, and led them forward to the attack. They faced a Carthaginian army of a size comparable to their own and with a large professional core. Hannibal himself had spent his youth and young manhood at war. He presided over a war council made up of veteran generals. The army he had brought from Spain was composed of long-service mercenaries. The Romans had deployed and advanced in the usual way. The Carthaginian deployment, by contrast, embodied a cunning tactical scheme. The superior Carthaginian horse was on the wings, made up of Numidian light javelin-throwers, and Carthaginian, Spanish and Gaulish heavy shock cavalry: about 10,000 in all. The infantry centre was held by newly recruited Gauls: tough fighters, but lacking discipline and the least reliable part of Hannibal's army. Between the Gauls in the centre and the cavalry on the flanks, the infantry elite was stationed: Libyan spearmen and Spanish swordsmen. There were perhaps 20,000 heavy infantry in all, ranged in separate battle lines, each one many ranks deep. In front of each of the infantry flanks was a block of elephants (all 37 of which had survived the crossing of the Alps). Out in front was a skirmishing screen of 8,000 light infantry, including slingers from the Balearic Islands and javelin-throwers from Spain. Finally, hidden in a stream-bed on the edge of the battlefield were 2,000 picked men under a trusted marshal.

The battle went almost according to plan. The main weight of the Roman infantry attack fell on the Gauls in the centre, who gradually gave ground, drawing their enemies forwards after them. The much weaker Roman cavalry were swept away on the wings, and as the Carthaginian horse reformed and charged the exposed flanks of the legions, there were simultaneous attacks by the elephants and the Libyan and Spanish heavy foot. To complete the disaster, the concealed force emerged and plunged into the Roman rear. The Carthaginian victory would have been total had not the Gauls collapsed completely in the centre and fled, allowing 10,000 legionaries to break clean through to the far side of the battlefield and escape. Even so, the Romans lost 15,000 men; and would no doubt have lost many more but for cold, sleet and snow hindering the Carthaginian pursuit. The consuls and the rump of their army survived – retreating to Cremona and Placentia – but Hannibal ended the year master of the north. The war – Rome's interminable war for empire – had come home with a vengeance.

The Roman strategic position was still strong, however. Africa and Spain were vulnerable to attack with the main Carthaginian army in the Po Valley, and there was every chance that Hannibal could be held there and denied entry into Italy, the real heartland of Roman power. Eleven legions were raised in 217 BC – an unprecedented number – and both consuls, with six of these legions, were sent north to block Hannibal's anticipated invasion. (Roman sources count only Roman citizen legions. Typically at this time, a Roman army included equal or larger numbers of Latin and allied troops organized in their own contingents. The unit numbers quoted here should therefore be doubled.) For his part, Hannibal was eager for a new victory in Italy. Trebia had secured the allegiance of Cisalpine Gaul. A battle won in Etruria or Umbria might begin to break up the Italian core of Rome's empire (so central was this aim that his standard practice was to release without ransom non-Roman POWs). The consul Gaius Flaminius – incompetent, witless, arrogant – was set on beating Hannibal before his colleague could arrive to share the glory. Hannibal lured him on, feigning a strategic retreat, until the Roman army was strung out for miles in a marching column between Lake Trasimene and high ground to the north. Suddenly, from the heights above them, sounding through an early morning mist, the legionaries heard the war-cries of tens of thousands of their enemies deployed for ambush in the defile. Within minutes the Roman column was engulfed, its way blocked front and rear, and under attack along its entire length. The Romans never had a chance to deploy, and within half an hour it was over, 15,000 dead (including the consul), 10,000 taken prisoner, a mere 6,000 escaping in the confusion.

The morale of the Roman ruling class collapsed. Quintus Fabius Maximus was elected dictator. Cautious and conservative, his solution to the crisis was to avoid pitched battle and wear down Hannibal's forces in a long war of attrition: he was dubbed *Cunctator* – 'the Delayer'. New legions were raised, but their role now was to shadow the enemy, to box him in, to harass his foragers, not to confront him in open battle. The armies marched the length of Italy laying it waste, the Romans employing scorched earth to deny Hannibal supplies, the Carthaginians plundering Rome's allies in an effort to feed their army and provoke the enemy to battle. The policy was unsustainable. If Rome could not protect her allies, if her generals were too scared to fight an invader, her Italian Empire

seemed bound to collapse. The Fabian policy was overturned the follow-
ing year, and the two new consuls, Gaius Terentius Varro and Lucius
Aemilius Paullus, were ordered to seek battle in the summer of 216 BC.
The armies met on a level open plain at Cannae in Apulia.

Varro was in command on the day of the battle. His plan was to
withhold his wings, which were weak in cavalry, while launching an
immediate attack in the centre with his legions. Hannibal's plan was a
precisely calculated mechanism for translating the energy of this attack
into the means of the Roman army's destruction. Cannae was a tactical
masterpiece. It requires no genius, of course, to realize that destroying an
enemy's flanks so that his centre can be surrounded and annihilated is a
guarantee of victory. What makes Cannae special is that Hannibal found a
way to do this in the concrete circumstances facing him. The Roman
legionary attack was massive but unsophisticated: it was like a steam-
roller that rumbled forwards with tremendous power but was impossible
to stop or turn. Each man in the mass knew little of the battle around him,
but he could scent victory over an enemy ahead who was faltering and
falling back, and, scenting it, his instinct was to drive forwards. The
Carthaginian mistake at Trebia was not repeated: the Gauls deployed in
the centre were supported this time by the Spanish, creating a line that
would give but not break through the long hours of battle. As the struggle
of infantry developed in the centre, the Carthaginian horse again mastered the Romans on the wings, and columns of Libyan spearmen pushed
forwards on the flanks of the legions. The trap was set. The mass of
Roman infantry was then assailed on every side – Gauls and Spanish in
front, Libyans on the flanks, cavalry against the rear. The ring of enemies
gradually compressed the legionaries into a tight mass without room to
manoeuvre, deploy or wield weapons. Hardly any broke out; they simply
died on the ground where they stood. In all, of the 80,000 or so Roman
troops who engaged that day, 65,000 perished.

Cannae finally shattered the solidity of Rome's Italian Empire. Livy
provides an impressive list of the communities that now came over to
Hannibal – all the Gauls, most of the Samnites, the Lucanians, the
Bruttians, and most of the Greek cities of the South. The greatest prize,
though, was Capua, perhaps the greatest city in Italy after Rome, whose
allegiance Hannibal won by supporting local democrats against the pro-
Roman oligarchy: they provided Hannibal with a first-rate base and an

army of 30,000 foot and 4,000 horse. Henceforward, Greeks, Samnites, Lucanians and Bruttians would provide a growing proportion of Hannibal's army. But for all that, the gains were limited and problematic. The whole of the north, most of the centre and some of the south stayed loyal to Rome. Hannibal now had allies and territory to protect: if he failed in this, he would lose what support he had gained; but in guarding his new fiefdom, he sacrificed the strategic mobility that had won him such startling battlefield success in the first two years of the war. Some of his new friendships, moreover, ensured the continuing enmity of others: Hannibal's war rekindled ancient fears of the barbarian 'other' – of the Gaul, the Oscan, the highland brigand, the cattle rustler – and reactivated old rivalries between neighbouring cities and tribes, while his support for democrats triggered upper-class fears of revolt from below and threats to property.

These tensions compounded the central strategic problem now confronting his campaign. Even Cannae – the greatest defeat the Romans had ever suffered – had not destroyed Rome's Italian confederation. The war, it seemed, could not be won by mere spectacle. Roman territory would have to be broken away bit by bit in a long struggle of sieges and attrition. But how could Hannibal win such a war? His offensive represented a powerful coalition of forces: the revanchist imperialism of the Barca faction and the hawkish wing of the Carthaginian ruling class; the anti-Roman nationalism of the subject peoples of Cisalpine Gaul and southern Italy; the hostility of democratic crowds towards pro-Roman oligarchs in the cities of *Magna Graecia*; and the attraction of pay and booty for the professional mercenaries who made up the rank and file of Hannibal's army. But against this was the extraordinary resilience of the Roman state. Polybius estimated its reserves of citizen and allied manpower at 700,000 foot and 70,000 horse; and in the years after Cannae, having doubled the rate of war tax, the Romans regularly mobilized 20 legions (170,000 men), more than ever before. It was sufficient not only to maintain an iron ring of containment and pressure around Hannibal and his south Italian allies – the Fabian strategy renewed – but to allow the Romans to go on to the offensive in Spain and win a crushing victory over the Carthaginian army there in 215 BC. Even then, Rome was not at full stretch. When the Greek revolt spread to Syracuse, Tarentum and other southern cities, Roman mobilization reached 25 legions (210,000 men), so that Capua and Syracuse were recaptured in 211 BC. As Polybius observed, the Romans had the strength to divide their forces, whereas Hannibal could be in only one place at a time.

The war reached stalemate in southern Italy. The wider anti-Roman movement gradually decayed, but Hannibal's skill and continuing successes enabled him to maintain a large mercenary army and keep Roman commanders at a distance. The war's centre of gravity shifted to Spain. Roman victory there might compel the Carthaginians to abandon Italy for the defence of their Empire. Carthaginian victory might free them up to send a second army to reinforce Hannibal in Italy. The struggle for Spain ebbed and flowed. The Roman victory of 215 BC was followed by a crushing double-defeat in 211 BC. The ex-consuls Publius Cornelius Scipio and his brother Gnaeus Cornelius Scipio were separately defeated and killed in the same month. It seemed a shattered blow both to the Roman cause in Spain and to the Scipiones family, who, with the Aemilii, had led the opposition in the Senate to the Fabii's defensive strategy. They had argued for an offensive war linked with empire-building. Denied the main command (against Hannibal) since 216 BC, they had been fobbed off with Spain; and, after a promising start, this had now ended in disaster.

Some among Rome's conservative senatorial majority hoped that the Spanish defeat would silence the hawks. They were quickly disabused. Publius Cornelius Scipio, son and heir of the ex-consul – who as a young man had rescued his wounded father on the battlefield, and who, though still only 26 years old, was already a veteran officer of eight years active service – stood for election to the Spanish command. The decision rested with the Assembly of the Centuries – made up of Roman soldiers – and Scipio was elected. Weary of the war – of the losses, of annual conscription and high taxes, and of land laid waste and trade decayed – the rank and file had rejected old age and caution for a young fighter. In doing so, they sent a shock wave through the political system. Such elevation was unprecedented for one so young; Scipio had never held a senior magistracy, never wielded the power of *imperium*; and the jealous old men on the backbenches of the Senate resented and feared this breach of tradition. But they could not prevent it: under the stress of war, the old order – of amateur generals and part-time armies – was crumbling. A new kind of politics – imperial rather than urban – was being forged in the storm and stress of the war against Hannibal. Scipio was to become the first of

Rome's great professional generals, and also the first of the populists, the conservative revolutionaries, who broke with their class, appealed to the people, and built a career as generals and empire-builders in defiance of the Senate. Scipio was the first of the men like Caesar who would eventually topple the Republic.

The young Roman general took war seriously – he studied it with the conscious aim of becoming its master. The army he commanded also took war seriously. The levy was imposed on communities, not individuals, and this allowed most places to be filled by volunteers. Many men returned to war each year or remained on campaign from one year to the next. For them, soldiering was becoming a career. This was especially so in Spain, an overseas posting in which men may have been obliged to serve for the duration. The Spanish army had been shattered in 211 BC, but around the surviving core of officers and men who had served his father and uncle, Scipio built it anew. He may have introduced new weapons – was it now that legionaries were first equipped with the *gladius* and the *pilum* of the Celtiberians? He certainly drilled his soldiers until they could carry out the complex battlefield manoeuvres that the division of the army into maniples (sub-divisions of 120) made theoretically possible. Proper intelligence and reconnaissance services were developed. Light infantry tactics became more elaborate. Not less, Scipio's charisma and confidence transformed the morale of the army, while his diplomatic finesse won over a coterie of Celtiberian chieftains. Suddenly, in 209 BC, with his new machine ready for testing, he struck. A combination of brilliant intelligence, rapid movement and total surprise allowed the Romans to storm into New Carthage, the enemy's Spanish capital, before any of the three widely dispersed Carthaginian armies could move to support it. By a *coup de main* Scipio had secured the most important fortress, naval base, munitions plant, and treasure-house in Spain.

The Carthaginian generals had to fight if their empire was not to unravel. Scipio met Hasdrubal, brother of Hannibal, at the battle of Baecula in 208 BC. The enemy occupied a strong defensive position on a plateau at the top of cliffs. Scipio pinned Hasdrubal's centre with a large and well-supported force of *velites*, while the bulk of his men were formed into two mobile columns to advance on to the enemy's flanks and attack them from either side. The Carthaginian line quickly collapsed. Two years later, confronting another Hasdrubal at Ilipa, this time on an open battleground, Scipio repeated the tactics: a weak and withdrawn centre to pin the enemy; elaborate manoeuvres on the flanks; devastating attacks that broke the enemy line at both ends and rolled it up. Ilipa destroyed the last Carthaginian army in Spain, and any remaining strongholds were swiftly overrun. Scipio returned to Rome the victor of New Carthage, Baecula and Ilipa, and conqueror of the Carthaginian Empire in Spain. His ambition now was for the supreme command, but he envisaged this not as a command in Italy, but as a new command to lead an invasion of Africa, with Carthage itself as target, a threat almost guaranteed to secure Hannibal's recall to fight in defence of the home-land. The Fabian strategy of an Italian defensive was to be transformed into a Scipionic strategy of African empire-building.

A political storm raged around Scipio in the winter of 206–205 BC. He was elected consul by the popular vote, but it was for the Senate to assign provinces and commands. The final compromise was for Italy to be given to his colleague – denying the young superstar the chance to form an invasion force from its legions – but for him to have Sicily as his province, with the authority to attack Africa 'if he judged it to be in the public interest' – and so long as no state expenditure was involved. If he wanted an army for an invasion, therefore, he was going to have to build it himself. This he did, starting with the several thousand survivors of Cannae – whom Scipio now inspired with a chance of redeeming glory – and some 7,000 volunteers, many of them his Spanish veterans. He spent 205 BC encamped at Syracuse, recruiting, arming, drilling. With his com-mand prorogued (extended beyond its normal term), he sailed early the following year in a fleet of 40 warships and 400 transports, carrying a small but highly trained and motivated army of 26,000 men. His African campaign was as brilliant as his Spanish. He established a new coastal base at Castra Cornelia, won the allegiance of the Numidian prince Masinissa, and, with his assistance, ambushed and destroyed the local Carthaginian cavalry. The following year he destroyed a combined Carthaginian-Numidian army by having his men set fire to the enemy camps in the night and then massacre the panic-stricken fugitives issuing from the gates. And when the Carthaginians and their Numidian allies began to build a second army in the hinterland, Scipio marched inland and destroyed it at the Battle of the Great Plains. The desperate Carthaginian government then recalled Hannibal.

Attempts at reinforcement in Italy had failed. An alliance with King Philip V of Macedon had yielded no practical support. The revolts of Capua, Tarentum and Syracuse had long since been suppressed. Hasdrubal, after his defeat in Spain in 208 BC, had marched to northern Italy, hoping to effect a junction with his brother in the south, but his army had been destroyed at the battle of the Metaurus in 207 BC (the first that Hannibal knew of the disaster was receipt of his brother's severed head). By 203 BC Hannibal, in control of only an enclave around the city of Croton in the toe of Italy, had been reduced to little more than a chief of brigands and mercenaries. The Italian campaign was at its lowest ebb, whereas the homeland was in mortal danger. Even now, though, the Romans feared the great general: such was his reputation that they made no attempt to interfere with the evacuation of his small army, content merely to see him go. (Or perhaps the Fabii secretly hoped he would destroy Scipio.)

Taking command in Africa, Hannibal did not move until he was ready, needing time to build a new army around his core of Italian veterans. But in the spring of 202 BC he set out for the Bagradas Valley, determined to bring Scipio to battle, and the two armies, each close to 50,000 men, met at Zama. Hannibal's was by far the weaker: he was heavily outnumbered in cavalry, and most of his infantry were either demoralized by earlier defeats or newly recruited and without battle experience. Even his huge corps of 80 elephants was poorly trained. Only the 'Old Guard' of Italian veterans was first-rate. Scipio, by contrast, commanded an army of sea-soned volunteers, laurelled with victory and supremely confident; the only nagging doubt, perhaps, was that they were now to be tested for the first time by the master of war himself.

Hannibal's plan took full account of his own weaknesses. He knew he would lose the cavalry action on the wings, and his aim was to crush the Roman infantry in the centre quickly, before their cavalry had a chance to join in. But the Roman infantry were first-class troops, so his only hope was to wear them down before he committed the Old Guard. His first line was formed of elephants, but their charge miscarried: met by trumpet blasts and javelins, many stampeded back on their own men; others passed through gaps opened by Scipio's highly drilled legionaries and were then dispatched in the rear. The Roman *hastati* then closed with Hannibal's first line of infantry and broke it. As the fugitives streamed to the rear, they disordered and panicked the men in Hannibal's second line, and as the *hastati* pressed forwards this line also collapsed. The Old Guard forming the third line had been held well back to keep it clear of any débâcle in front. So there was a lull and a period of mutual readjustment. The *hastati* were reformed and kept in the line, while the *principes* and *triarii* were moved up either side of them. Then there was a further pause as the two lines faced each other across a few dozen yards of African plain: some tens of thousands of veteran soldiers who perhaps sensed that this was a supreme moment of historical decision. Then the lines charged, and for a time hacked and lunged and crashed shield against shield in the chaos of heavy-infantry collision. But it was an unequal contest. The Roman infantry had not been weakened: the *principes* and *triarii* were fresh, the *hastati* had their blood up, and together they greatly outnumbered Hannibal's Italian veterans. Then the Roman cavalry, returning from the fight on the wings, joined the infantry action, charging into the Carthaginian rear. The Old Guard disintegrated – and with it, the Carthaginian cause.

Hannibal Barca had launched a total war to destroy the Roman state. But the mercenary and barbarian army of a mercantile empire was no match for Rome's Italian confederation. A combination of local self-government, widespread citizenship rights, shares in land and booty, and consistent Roman support for city oligarchs gave to the confederation a mass social base solid enough to withstand the shock of 100,000 casualties at Trebia, Trasimene and Cannae – a shock that in Livy's view 'no other nation in the world could have suffered and not been overwhelmed'. Because of this, Hannibal could not drain away that huge pool of manpower reserves that enabled Rome to put up to 200,000 men into the field each year regardless of losses. Hannibal had launched a total war, but only Rome had the resources to fight one.

The Carthaginian Empire was destroyed by the peace terms now imposed: the loss of Spain and all overseas territories; a financially crippling indemnity of 10,000 talents payable over 50 years; a navy reduced to ten ships; and a ban on waging war without Roman consent. Zama thus reduced Carthage from a first- to a third-rate power. Rome, by contrast, was left the only superpower in the Mediterranean. As events would soon show, the Hellenistic states of the East, her nearest rivals, were hollow by comparison, and none would offer the sustained and bloody resistance that ancient Carthage had done in the First and Second Punic

Wars. The pivot on which Roman imperial history turned was the war against Hannibal. Before it, Rome could still perhaps have been stopped; afterwards, the power and dynamism of her imperialism could not be checked, and she was propelled inexorably to supremacy in the Mediterranean and Europe.

The conquest of the Mediterranean: the Macedonian Wars, 200–146 BC

A different kind of state from Rome might have sunk back exhausted after the exertion of the Second Punic War; in fact, military mobilization continued at a similar level, even reaching in 191–190 BC the same peak as in the gravest crisis of that struggle. It was not that any single enemy posed a comparable threat; indeed, *none* of the enemies engaged in this period posed *any* substantial threat. Rather, Rome chose to fight wars because it was profitable to do so, and, wielding greater power than any other state, was able to fight two or three wars simultaneously.

The interrupted conquest of Cisalpine Gaul was resumed in 203 BC, and by 191 BC the main resistance – that of the powerful Boii tribe – had been overcome. During the 180s BC, to control this territory, the Romans built a new road, the Via Aemilia, and founded several new colonies. Then, in a series of campaigns in the 170s, they pushed west from the Po plain into Liguria, and east to the Istrian peninsula.

Also, having driven the Carthaginians out in 206 BC, the Romans set about organizing and exploiting their new territories in Spain. They provoked a widespread revolt, however, one that began in the new Roman provinces in the south-east, but quickly drew in the unconquered tribes of the interior. The 'Spanish ulcer' was destined to suppurate for two centuries: the terrain was difficult, distances were huge, the tribes decentralized, and the Spanish first-rate guerrilla fighters. The Second Spanish War (taking the First as that of 217–206 BC against Carthage and her Celtiberian tribal allies) lasted from 197 to 179 BC, ending well short of total conquest. Victorious on the battlefield, Tiberius Sempronius Gracchus offered moderate terms to secure peace, leaving the Celtiberian tribes semi-independent though obliged to pay tribute to Rome. The Lusitanians of the far west, by contrast, who had also participated in the war, remained wholly unconquered.

The Gracchan settlement held for 25 years, until Roman oppression provoked a new generation to revolt. The Third Spanish War (154–133 BC) was more bitter than the Second. The first phase, against the Celtiberians, was ended quickly by conciliation (153–151 BC), but acts of genocide in Lusitania (modern Portugal) detonated a grim guerrilla war in the mountains there. A full-scale invasion under Servius Sulpicius Galba persuaded the Lusitanians to sue for peace. He demanded wholesale transplantation of highland populations to lowland sites, but when the Lusitanians gathered on the appointed day at three separate assembly-points, they were disarmed, surrounded and massacred – men, women and children. The atrocity reignited the resistance. Among those who took up arms again was a shepherd called Viriathus, who proved to be a brilliant guerrilla fighter, and had by 147 BC become the leader of the Lusitanian struggle. Between 146 and 141 BC he won an almost unbroken series of victories over five successive Roman commanders. The example – of native forces beating the imperial power – inspired the Celtiberians of the interior to a renewed attempt to throw off foreign rule. The 130s BC began with demoralized Roman soldiers defeated by Lusitanian guerrillas in the south-west and by Celtiberian defenders of the fortress of Numantia in the north. The Spanish ulcer would soon infect the core of the Roman body-politic. Certainly, there was little glory or gold to be had in the peninsula's interminable wars. Roman generals preferred the East.

The contrast between the barbarian cultures of the West and the ancient urban civilization of the East was extreme. The Hellenistic kingdoms built by Alexander's Successors had existed for a century. Many of the Greek cities they encompassed were 500 years old. Some of the cities of Asia Minor, Syria, the Levant, Egypt and Mesopotamia now ruled by Greeks were thousands of years old. Rich irrigation agriculture; hundreds of cities; a wealth of exotic trade goods; great centres of learning, art and refined living: the East offered dazzling spoils to the conqueror. Nor was eastern wealth particularly well defended. A relatively stable system of Hellenistic states existed around 200 BC. The major kingdoms were Macedonia in the Balkans (ruled by the Antigonid dynasty), Pergamum in western Asia Minor (under the Attalids), Syria and Mesopotamia (the Seleucids), and Egypt (the Ptolemies). The minor states included Athens, Sparta, Rhodes, the Achaean League (in the northern Peloponnese), the

Aetolian League (in north-west Greece), and Epirus-Illyria (in the far north-west). But even the greatest of these states was more pomp and glitter than substance. Their kings might control large and densely populated territories; they might draw huge tax revenues; but the social roots of Seleucid Syria and Ptolemaic Egypt were shallower than those of the Roman Republic. The Greeks were organized in small, privileged, urban enclaves. The mass of native people in the countryside felt little affinity with their Hellenistic monarchs. Greek armies comprised a professional military elite rather than a citizen-militia. Tactics had changed little since the time of Alexander. Moreover, though Macedonia was sociologically more cohesive than the other Hellenistic monarchies, it was a relatively small mountain kingdom – with none of Rome's reserves of manpower and treasure.

The earliest Roman ventures across the Adriatic had occurred before the Second Punic War. The First and Second Illyrian Wars (229–228 and 221–219 BC) had been fought ostensibly to suppress piracy, but the interference with a minor state in Macedonia's backyard had alarmed King Philip V sufficiently for him to form an alliance with Hannibal in 215 BC. The First Macedonian War (215–205 BC) proved a damp squib, however: Philip never sent support to Hannibal in Italy, and the Romans left their Aetolian allies to fight alone in Greece. But this reflected not pusillanimity on Philip's part so much as his preoccupation with the Aegean – where his war with Pergamum and Rhodes provided a pretext for Roman intervention against him in 200 BC. The alliance with Hannibal, and his wars against fellow Greeks, including Roman allies, made it easy enough to portray Philip's Macedonia as a dangerous 'rogue state'.

In fact, Philip was no threat to Roman interests. The very fact that he did *not* send troops to Italy in the wake of Cannae is proof enough of that; Philip's fighting front was to the south and the south-east, not towards the Adriatic. The Roman decision to back Pergamum and Rhodes and intervene in an eastern war was an act of aggression. Significantly, when the consul to whom responsibility for Macedonia had been given proposed a declaration of war, the Assembly of the Centuries turned it down. When he next summoned the assembly, he deployed a new concept: that of pre-emptive aggression against a would-be (and in fact imaginary) enemy. The decision was not 'whether you will choose war or peace; for Philip will not leave the choice open to you, seeing that he is actively preparing for unlimited hostilities on land and sea. What you are asked to decide is whether you will transport legions to Macedonia or allow the enemy into Italy; and the difference this makes is a matter of your own experience in the recent Punic Wars . . . It took Hannibal four months to reach Italy from Saguntum; but Philip, if we let him, will arrive four days after he sets sail from Corinth.'(14) The Assembly now voted for war. A real hatred of the draft had been overcome by an invented fear of invasion. For invented it was, the speciousness of the consul's argument apparent from the most superficial review of the events of the Second Macedonian War (200–196 BC). The largest Roman army sent to Greece was only 30,000 strong – a mere 2.5 per cent of Rome's total military manpower, or 7 per cent of her maximum mobilized strength in the Second Punic War. Yet this small army was sufficient to bring Macedonia to defeat – a defeat Philip anticipated judging by his interim peace offers and initial avoidance of battle. Hannibal, by contrast, had destroyed a Roman army of 80,000 – and still lost the war. These simple calculations demonstrate how suicidal a Macedonian invasion of Italy would in reality have been: doubly so, since not only would the invaders have been crushed, but Philip's kingdom would meantime have been overrun by his enemies in Greece.

The first two years of the war were inconclusive, but in the spring of 197 BC Titus Quinctius Flamininus invaded Thessaly, and Philip, finally resolved to risk battle rather than prolong a war of attrition he knew he could not win, marched towards him with 25,000 men. The ground was unsuitable for battle where the armies first met, and both withdrew along parallel routes separated by low hills, each soon unaware of the other's progress. A messy encounter battle then developed unexpectedly at Cynoscephalae when Macedonian and Roman detachments clashed in the mist on the heights overlooking a pass between the main armies. As more units were drawn into the fight for the high ground, a general engagement began. The Macedonian right reached the top of the pass before the Romans. When Philip saw this, he ordered the right phalanx to close up into a deep formation, increasing its shock power, and then to charge. Flamininus, seeing the desperate struggle that had begun on the Roman left, ordered in turn an attack by his right, which struck the left phalanx before it was properly deployed and routed it. The battle divided into separate halves, with the Macedonian right pushing down one slope, the Roman right down the other, such that a wide gap opened. At this point, a Roman military tribune seized the initiative. Taking the 20 maniples of *triarii* forming the rear line of the legions on the right, he reformed them and charged into the rear of the phalanx attacking the Roman left. The effect was devastating. The right phalanx was also routed. The battle had been hard-fought but decisive. About 8,000 Macedonians had been killed and 5,000 captured for a loss of 700 Romans. Philip V's only army had been destroyed and he was compelled to make peace.

Polybius was fascinated by the clash between phalanx and legion. The whole fate of the Hellenistic world – his world – had seemed to hinge on it. The outcome appeared paradoxical, for the compact formation and projecting pikes of the phalanx meant that in close-quarters combat each Roman legionary, fighting in a much more open formation, faced no less than ten spear-points. 'What is the factor which enables the Romans to win the battle and causes those who use the phalanx to fail? The answer is that in war the times and places for action are unlimited, whereas the phalanx requires one time and one type of ground only in order to produce its peculiar effect.' Broken ground disordered the phalanx, creating fatal gaps in the hedge of pikes. To be effective, it had to operate in a large block, making it slow, cumbersome and unresponsive to a changing battlefield situation. The Roman formation, by contrast, was flexible and mobile. While part could pin a phalanx frontally, other parts could manoeuvre to attack flank and rear. 'Every Roman soldier, once he is armed and goes into action, can adapt himself equally well to any place or time and meet an attack from any quarter. He is likewise equally well-prepared and needs to make no change whether he has to fight with the main body or with a detachment, in maniples or singly.'(15) Cynoscephalae illustrated these dictums. It showed that the legions were coming of age, that a complex evolution of the Roman military tradition under Etruscan, Greek, Samnite, Gaulish, Punic and Spanish influence was now producing the finest fighting formations in the ancient world.

Philip was left in control of his kingdom, but he was required to disband his fleet, withdraw his garrisons from the Greek cities, and pay a large indemnity of 1,000 talents, half immediately, the rest over ten years. (The size of the indemnity – only a tenth of that imposed on Carthage eight years before – is further evidence of Macedonia's relative weakness.)

Then, at the Isthmian Games in 196 BC, the trumpeter having called for silence in the stadium, the herald came forward to issue a special proclamation before the huge crowd of Greeks assembled there: 'The Senate of Rome and Titus Quinctius Flamininus the proconsul, having defeated King Philip and the Macedonians in battle, leave the following states and cities free, without garrisons, subject to no tribute and in full enjoyment of their ancestral laws: the peoples of Corinth, Phocis, Locri, Euboea, Phthiotic Achaea, Magnesia, Thessaly and Perrhaebia.'(16) Polybius reports such euphoria that Flamininus was almost killed by the pandemonium around him. Many scholars since have been equally starry-eyed, claiming the Isthmian proclamation of 196 BC as prime evidence for 'defensive imperialism'. If Rome was the aggressor, why this extraordinary decision to withdraw her armies and leave both Macedonia and the Greek cities free?

But Philip, we have seen, was no real threat. So we are left with no explanation of the intervention in Greece lest it be that the Romans had selflessly cast themselves in the role of honest broker and impartial policeman. In truth, of course, no great power goes to war except in what its leaders perceive to be its own interest. The Romans attacked Macedonia not because it was a threat, but simply because in subjugating it they could expect a rich reward in military glory, hauls of booty and slaves, and, perhaps most importantly, indemnity payments. The text of the treaty between Rome and the Aetolian League in the First Macedonian War (a document dated 212–211 BC) has survived. It is a highly revealing document. Part of it reads: 'If the Romans take by force any cities belonging to these people [enemies in war], the cities and their territories shall . . . belong to the Aetolian people; anything the Romans get hold of apart from the cities and their territories [i.e. portable valuables] shall belong to them. If the Romans and the Aetolians operating together take any of these cities, the cities and their territories shall . . . belong to the Aetolians; anything they get apart from the cities shall belong to them jointly.'(17) Booty, in short, was so important that the division of spoils had to be agreed between allies before hostilities began.

Then there were indemnities. These had become established as one of the principal mechanisms by which surplus was pumped out of defeated states. By imposing them, Rome was, in effect, diverting revenue from local rulers by interposing her own claim to a share of the tribute paid by the peasants of other states. Without any of the cost involved in direct rule, the mere threat of a renewal of war was enough to guarantee payment of a large proportion of the available surplus – with the additional benefit, of course, that defeated ruling classes were kept weak and compliant. The indemnities make nonsense of any claim that Rome was not motivated by gain.

Rome's second major war in the East followed a similar pattern. Hegemony over Macedonia and Greece brought her into contact with the Seleucid kingdom. The Aetolian League, which had expected greater territorial gains in the Second Macedonian War, invited King Antiochus III to support them in challenging the Roman settlement of Greece. When Antiochus sent over a small army in 192 BC, the Romans counter-attacked, defeating Antiochus and the Aetolians at the Battle of Thermopylae the following year. The Romans then crossed into Asia, and in 191 BC fought and won a pitched battle at Magnesia against the main Seleucid army. Antiochus was stripped of his territories in Asia Minor, forced to surrender his fleet and his elephants, and required to pay a 15,000 talent indemnity, 500 immediately, 2,500 when the Roman government ratified the agreement, and thereafter 1,000 annually for 12 years. The Aetolian League also lost territory and faced an indemnity of 500 talents.

In 189 BC, as these terms were being settled, Gnaeus Manlius Vulso launched a savage attack on the native peoples of Asia Minor, especially the Galatians, descendants of Gauls who had settled in central Anatolia about a century before, contingents of whom had served in the Seleucid army at Magnesia. The aim was plunder and Manlius' army ran a form of protection racket. Examples were made of communities that resisted, and payments were then extorted to secure Roman 'friendship' (immunity from attack). Fifty talents was usually enough to save a city. Places that resisted were taken by force, comprehensively plundered, and their people sold as slaves. The capture of the Gaulish stronghold at Mount Olympus, for example, yielded 40,000 captives. 'On a reasonable view,' comments William Harris, 'plundering was the main purpose of the war.'(18) Indeed, such were the spoils of 189 BC that even the Roman Senate was moved to question Manlius' probity, and he was to be credited by later writers with first introducing *luxuria* (extravagant, conspicuous and morally corrupting consumption) to Rome; nonetheless, he was granted his triumph.

Then, in 188 BC, just as they had done in 196 BC, the Romans withdrew, not only from Asia, where the territory confiscated from the Seleucids was divided between Pergamum and Rhodes, but even from Greece. Why should they stay? Huge annual revenues were now flowing into the Roman treasury. In just 14 years (202–188 BC) the Roman state had imposed indemnities worth at least 26,500 talents on defeated states (a figure which takes no account of small indemnities perhaps not recorded in the sources, and the countless hauls of booty, the distribution of which was tightly organized and included a fixed proportion for the state). There was personal enrichment, too. Manlius Vulso was not the only Roman politician who found empire-building profitable. Another was Scipio Africanus, victor of Zama. He had gone to Asia as military advisor to the Roman commander, his brother Lucius, and on his return to Rome a financial scandal broke around his head. After the Battle of Magnesia, it seems, Antiochus had been required to pay 18 million *denarii* for the upkeep of the Roman army as long as it remained in Asia: no adequate account of what happened to this money was ever forthcoming. So much eastern wealth was dropping into outstretched private hands, in fact, that Lucius Aemilius Paullus, the victor of the Third Macedonian War (171–168 BC), was considered poor among aristocrats in having a fortune of only 360,000 *denarii* at the time of his death.

Not that his campaigns had been unprofitable. The Romans found cause for a renewed assault on Macedonia when Philip's son and successor, King Perseus, attempted to rebuild his kingdom's power. Whereas his father's imperialism had left him friendless and isolated 30 years before, Perseus won support in the Greek cities, where democrats in particular were now hostile to the Roman hegemony. It did him little good. Though he was able to put 40,000 men into the field, even slightly outnumbering the Romans, the phalanx was defeated again at the battle of Pydna in 168 BC, where it was once more the victim of its own cumbersomeness. The pikemen charged in a solid mass, 20,000 strong – the Roman commander afterwards declared it the most terrifying thing he had ever seen – and the impact thrust the Roman line backwards. But the legionaries withdrew and reformed on rising ground, while the phalanx, surging forwards in the excitement of success, began to lose cohesion and split apart. The legionaries counterattacked, maniple by maniple, driving wedges into the gaps, where the *gladius* made short work of the pikemen close up.

Perseus surrendered and his kingdom was dissolved. Its territory was divided into four separate republics, and to preclude attempts at reunification these were denied the right to enter into mutual diplomatic relations. The inhabitants were obliged to pay tribute to Rome. Pergamum and Rhodes lost territory: they had not participated in the war, but neither had they supported Rome, and their motives were suspect. There was a general purge of the Greek aristocracy. In particular, 1,000 leading citizens of the Achaean League were deported to Rome. (Among them was the former politician Polybius, who became, in detention, a close friend and advisor to Scipio Aemilianus; and thus had both the leisure and privileged access to source material – not to mention the motive – to write his famous history.)

The most terrible fate was reserved for Epirus (modern Albania). Though she had given no practical support, Epirus had supported Perseus in the Third Macedonian War. Paullus was therefore ordered by the Senate to liquidate the Epirote people. The Roman army went there in 167 BC, broke up into small detachments, and then fell simultaneously upon all the towns and villages. They made a haul of 150,000 men, women and children, all of whom were sold into slavery. Some may have been kept back for a victory parade in Rome, an important construction project, or simply for the enjoyment of soldiers. Most were probably sold immediately to the Roman army slave-dealers, who would have shipped them to a slave market, like that on the island of Delos in the Aegean. We have no reliable figures for the total numbers enslaved in the Roman Empire. One estimate is that by the late 1st century BC there were two or three million slaves in Italy and Sicily, and that 100,000 new slaves were required each year to keep the market supplied. Rome's wars were in part giant slave-raids, in which entire populations were uprooted and dispersed across the Mediterranean to places where they were required to labour for the Roman ruling class. As for Epirus, where 25,000 peasant families had once lived, it was turned into sheep-pasture for the benefit of absentee landowners.

Macedonia and Greece were to fight one final time. An adventurer called Andriscus, claiming to be the son of Perseus, made a bid to reunite Macedonia and restore the monarchy. Quintus Caecilius Metellus crushed the revolt with two legions in 148 BC, and Macedonia was then converted into a Roman province. At the same time, in Greece itself, the conflict between pro-Roman oligarchs – who were taunted in the streets as 'traitors' even by children – and the democratic citizenry boiled over in major street clashes. A Roman attempt to break up the Achaean League then provoked an open revolt centred on Corinth and led by a revolutionary democrat called Critolaus. Metellus rushed south from Macedonia to crush the revolt, but resistance was such that only a rein-forced army of four legions under his successor Lucius Mummius was sufficient to restore Roman authority. An example was now made of the Greek 'commune' at Corinth: Mummius was ordered to destroy the city by handing it over to the soldiers. All the inhabitants, presumably many thousands, were either massacred or sold as slaves. The town was thoroughly looted, its great works of art shipped to Rome or simply destroyed. 'I was there,' declared Polybius. 'I saw paintings trampled underfoot, and soldiers sitting down on them to play dice.' When it was empty, the city was put to the torch. If you visit today, you find nothing of Classical Corinth save the ancient Temple of Apollo, which even the Romans were moved to spare; otherwise the ruins are those of a new Roman city of imperial times. The Achaean League was dissolved, oligarchy restored, the Greek cities forced to pay indemnities, and the Roman governor of Macedonia was authorized to intervene whenever necessary to maintain order.

Corinth was not the only great city destroyed in 146 BC. Carthage had recovered somewhat from the disaster of the Second Punic War. The indemnity was paid off and the city's trade prospered again. But hawkish politicians in the Roman Senate were bent on its destruction – Marcus Porcius Cato, known to us as Cato the Elder, became famous for ending every speech with the words *delenda est Carthago* ('Carthage must be destroyed'). A pretext was found in Carthage's half-hearted attempts to defend herself against the attacks of her neighbour, the pro-Roman King of Numidia, Masinissa. In 149 BC the Assembly of the Centuries voted for war. Carthage made a desperate appeal for peace, handing over hostages and all war *matériel* (including 2,000 catapults). But as each demand was fulfilled, the Romans added new conditions, until finally they required the Carthaginians to abandon their city on the coast and retire to an inland site: a sentence of extinction on a mercantile people.

The Carthaginians then prepared for armed resistance, working feverishly to strengthen the fortifications, restock the arsenals, train for military service, and fill the warehouses. What the Romans had expected to be a one-summer campaign turned into a gruelling four-year siege (149–146 BC). Publius Cornelius Scipio Aemilianus eventually assumed command. Son by blood of Aemilius Paullus, the victor of Pydna, and grandson by adoption of Scipio Africanus, conqueror of Hannibal, he represented the union of two great aristocratic houses, Scipiones and Aemilii, who shared a similar vision of Rome's imperial mission.

Aemilianus drove the siege hard against a garrison weakened by hunger, finally breaking through the outer wall, and then, in a week of the most savage street-fighting, battling his way to the capture of the citadel. Dying Carthage fought back to the very end. The ancient writers describe apocalyptic scenes: the Roman soldiers deluged with missiles from roofs and upper windows; buildings torched and levelled with people still inside to make an approach ramp for the Roman assault; the Carthaginian commander's wife, dressed in her finery, standing at the last redoubt on the highest part of the town, hurling her children into the flames of destruction before following herself. Of the 700,000 people supposed to have crowded into the city at the start of the siege, only 50,000 were left for the slave-dealers. The booty, though, was as rich as could be had anywhere in the world, and for several days the soldiers were free to plunder, saving only the gold, silver and votive offerings in the temples. This was reserved for official distribution – some to the soldiers, more to the generals, most to the state. The remaining buildings were then demolished. The great city of Carthage and its people – like Corinth, like the Epirotes, like so many others – ceased to exist.

By the middle of the 2nd century BC, Roman military imperialism had reached peak intensity. Superior power enabled the Roman ruling class to plunder the peoples of the Mediterranean almost at will. But all was not well at home. Roman Italy was exporting soldiers and importing spoils of war – primarily bullion and slaves, but also base metals, rich cloth, fine tableware, works of art, perfumes, ointments, spices, and much, much else. The flood of wealth was destabilizing the old social order. Some became fantastically rich and flaunted *luxuria*. Many, having benefited to a degree, now chafed at traditional barriers to further advancement. Others did not do well at all. Military service and agricultural depression ruined many poorer citizens. Big landlords were buying up failed farms. Slave labour replaced free men on Italian farms. The dispossessed packed the slums of Rome. A great, prolonged, multi-faceted social crisis was brewing in the heart of the empire. The Roman Republic – whose violence and greed had conquered the Mediterranean – was about to be shaken to destruction by the forces it had unleashed.

CHAPTER 3

• • • • • • • • • • • • • • •

The Roman revolution, 133–30 BC

A failed revolution: the Gracchi, 133–122 BC

Tiberius Sempronius Gracchus was a scion of one of the most illustrious families in Rome. He was grandson of Scipio Africanus, conqueror of Hannibal in 202 BC; son of Tiberius Sempronius Gracchus, who had ended the Second Spanish War in 179 BC and secured a quarter century of peace; and son-in-law of Appius Claudius Pulcher, the Senate's most senior member, 'the father of the house'. His brother Gaius, a close political ally, had also married well: his father-in-law was reckoned the richest Roman of his age. Tiberius the father, moreover, had earned a reputation as a stickler for traditional values when serving as *censor*, while the son had pursued a conventional yet distinguished career in the army – he had been first over the wall at the capture of Carthage, and later, in Spain, playing on his father's good name, had negotiated an agreement with the Celtiberians that saved a Roman army from destruction. Nothing, in fact, about Tiberius Gracchus, his family or his connections gave any indication that he was other than a typically conservative member of the Roman ruling class. Yet, elected tribune of the plebs in 133 BC, he so enraged his senatorial opponents with the radicalism of his politics that within barely a year they had murdered him in the streets.

His principal offence had been to propose a land reform bill, and, anticipating opposition in the Senate, to have taken it direct to the Assembly of the Tribes, where a large turnout by poor citizen-farmers had ensured its passage. The Senate had then persuaded another tribune to veto the bill (this being the constitutional right of any tribune); but Gracchus had reconvened the Assembly, secured his fellow-tribune's deposition, and then set up a land commission to implement the new law, its members being himself, his younger brother Gaius, and his father-in-law Claudius.

Crisis point was reached when Gracchus, determined to maintain the political momentum, decided to stand for election as tribune for a second year. Argument flared over whether this was constitutional, and it was the struggle around Gracchus's disputed candidacy that became violent. A leading senatorial conservative, the ex-consul and chief priest Publius Cornelius Scipio Nasica, mobilized his supporters and led a vicious armed attack on the land-reform party. Tiberius Gracchus and 300 of his followers were clubbed to death. A special senatorial commission executed many more in the weeks that followed.

In the space of a year, Roman politics had been transformed by street violence, political assassination, and a bloody assize. Nothing like it had happened since the Struggle of the Orders over 200 years before. A deep fracture had suddenly opened in the Roman body-politic. This fracture would widen in the years to come and eventually destroy the Republic in a series of civil wars. Attempts to dismiss the conflicts of 133 to 30 BC as little more than factional infighting among rival aristocratic houses are unconvincing. The social forces mobilized on each side were different, and two opposing ideologies and sets of policies were in dispute. The events of this period cannot be understood except as the expression of a rising ferment of discontent and struggle in Italian society as a whole.

The crisis was rooted in war and growth of empire. 'War and conquest transformed the economy of Italy,' explained Brunt, 'and helped at first to resolve, later to exacerbate social conflict. Internal struggles and foreign wars were often entangled, and reacted on each other. Expansion in itself distorted the working of political institutions, the machinery would-be social reformers had to use. It even changed the very meaning of the term "Roman".'(1)

The demands on Italian military manpower had remained high since the war against Hannibal. There had been wars of conquest in Africa, Spain, Gaul and the East, often followed by wars of subjugation when the recently conquered rose against their new masters. Rome faced national revolts in Cisalpine Gaul, Sardinia and Corsica, Macedonia and Greece, and, above all, Spain.

The guerrilla war in Lusitania (Portugal) lasted more than ten years. In 141 BC, Viriathus, having defeated five successive annual invasions, trapped the sixth Roman army to be sent against him and extracted a peace agreement in return for its release. The Romans broke the agreement the following year, but remained incapable of defeating Viriathus. Instead, they bribed some of his men to murder him in his sleep, whereupon Lusitanian morale collapsed and the Romans were finally able to annex the territory in 139 BC. Elsewhere in Spain resistance continued, centred on the Celtiberian fortress of Numantia, which defied the Romans for nine years. The site is well known to students of the Roman army because both the fortress and nearby Roman siege-camps have been explored by archaeologists, while the Greek historian Appian offers a full account of the military operations in his *Iberica* (*Spanish History*).

Numantia occupied a strong natural defensive position on a hilltop overlooking ravines and rivers: too strong to be taken in direct assault. Its defenders may have numbered about 8,000, the Roman siege forces – judging by the size of the succession of camps built between 142 and 133 BC – perhaps twice that. Despite the effort invested, the Romans made little progress; indeed, on one occasion, in 137 BC, the Numantines went on to the offensive, laid siege to the main Roman camp, and secured the surrender of the Roman army (this being the occasion when Tiberius Gracchus negotiated the army's safe passage). Popular clamour secured an extraordinary command for a member of the Scipio family: Rome's foremost soldier, Scipio Aemilianus, victor in the Third Punic War, was now sent to Spain. He restored army morale, reduced the outlying Celtiberian forts, and then, to seal Numantia off from the world and starve it out, surrounded the fortress with a 10 km-long stone wall and ditch, strengthened with 100 wooden interval towers and seven forts placed along the perimeter. Numantia surrendered after a few months in 133 BC. Its buildings were razed, its people enslaved.

Though there was eventual victory over both Lusitanians and Celtiberians, the Third Spanish War (154–133 BC) had incurred terrible costs – in casualties, in wasted resources, in diminished imperial prestige, and, not least, in its effects on Italian peasant agriculture and the cohesion of Roman society. Ever since Rome first acquired interests there during the Second Punic War, Spain had needed a permanent garrison of first two, then four legions, totalling (when allied forces are included) between 17,000 and 34,000 men. For much of the time these men were bogged down in long sieges or fruitless counter-insurgency sweeps. The soldiers faced boredom, discomfort, a sense of futility, years away from home – and the real fear that they might perish, tortured and mutilated, in a remote ravine. Tiberius Gracchus, serving as a junior officer at Numantia, was shocked by the poor morale of Roman troops.

At home, recruitment demands were necessarily high, and the draft was unpopular. The average size of the combined Romano-Italian army levied each year during the 35 years after the Second Punic War is estim-ated at 130,000 men. Overall, in the last two centuries of the Republic, an average of perhaps 13 per cent of adult male Roman citizens was serving in the legions at any one time. Thus, a majority of adult male Roman cit-izens must have spent at least seven years of their lives on campaign. In the 2nd century, moreover – in contrast to earlier practice, when armies campaigned in the summer and were demobilized in winter – troops were sent abroad and kept in the field without leave for years at a time.

This level of mobilization was disastrous for Italian peasant agriculture. Family farms were deprived of essential manpower for long periods – or permanently if men were killed or disabled – and many went to ruin. War accelerated the long-term tendency of small farmers to lose out to big landowners. I discussed this above – in relation to the Struggle of the Orders – as a function of the small farmer's lack of surplus to tide him over hard years, making debt, the mortgaging of farms, and the alienation of peasant land chronic features of rural life. Collective action – through the institutions of the city-state – was necessary to counteract this tend-ency. In the case of 2nd century BC Rome, however, a key mechanism had fallen into disuse. Brunt estimates that as many as 50,000 small farms may have been created in the generation after 200 BC, either in new colonies (*coloniae*) or through 'viritane' allotments (where farms were given to new settlers on an individual basis in existing communities). But after the 170s, agrarian resettlement virtually ceased; certainly there were no further colonies until the time of the Gracchi. So the draft was impact-ing on a situation where economic forces ruled unchecked. To have a man at the front could be just as devastating as drought, flooding or crop blight. Some peasants sold up and drifted into the city. Others struggled on but got into debt and were then evicted. Contemporary sources claim force was sometimes used to drive people off their land. So peasant land passed into the hands of the rich, sometimes speculators exploiting an emerging market in Italian real-estate, more commonly established local landowners keen to enlarge their holdings. The result was a profound change in the Italian countryside. In place of small land-units worked by peasant families for their own subsistence, there were now large estates (*latifundia*) producing cash crops or stock for a burgeoning market.

The flood of new wealth into Italy from the empire fed this growth of estates. It had the direct effect of inflating land prices and creating an active real-estate market; and the abiding prejudice of Roman society for land as the only proper expression of elite status reinforced it. Generals, officials, tax-farmers, merchants, slave-dealers, anyone making money in the empire, wanted to invest in land at home. Italian estates conferred respectability. They were also profitable. A further consequence of imperial wealth was that it generated demand for agricultural produce by fuelling the growth of the army, the towns, the construction industry, and the luxury trades. Small, mixed subsistence-farms were replaced by extensive orchards, vineyards, olive groves, sheep pastures and cattle ranches. Agriculture became a business. Economies of scale on special-ized *latifundia* conferred decisive advantages. Big operators could wield political influence to gain market access and secure public contracts. There were even manuals on estate management. Those by Cato, Columella and Varro have survived.

Cato's manual was aimed at the proprietors of medium-sized farms run for profit. The ideal was a holding of between 24 and 60 hectares – at least three times the size of a substantial peasant farm – which may have been fairly typical of the new commercial farms. It would have been difficult to build up single parcels of land substantially larger, and most top landowners probably had multiple holdings rather than one great estate. There were, anyway, limits to specialization and economies of scale: too violent a disruption of the traditional regime that kept the land in good heart risked undermining productivity. There was security, too, against the hazards of fortune in scattered holdings. When Pliny the Younger (*c.* AD 61–113), a rich senator with multiple holdings, wrote a letter to a friend seeking advice about a possible land purchase, he set out the pros and cons. The estate for sale adjoined his own – 'the land runs in and out of mine' – but the principal economy of scale he envisaged involved not greater specialization, but administrative downsizing: it would be necessary to maintain only one manager, household and work-force, he explained. The implication was that, if the purchase went ahead, the agricultural regime would remain much the same: 'The land is fertile, the soil rich and well-watered, and the whole made up of fields, vineyards and woods which produce enough to yield a steady income if not a very large one.'(2)

The chronology of Italian villa archaeology confirms the change. The town and territory of Cosa on the Etruscan coast 145 km north-west of Rome have been explored in detail. Though founded as a colony in 273 BC, and reinforced with a further draft of colonists in 197 BC, evidence for rural settlement up to this point is sparse, and, as far as can be judged, urban buildings were modest in scale. Only during the 2nd century BC did this begin to change, with more elaborate houses in Cosa itself, and the first appearance of substantial residences in the countryside. A building excavated at Giardino Vecchio was 25 metres square, with some rooms grouped around a courtyard, including living-rooms with cement floors and plastered walls. The house at Giardino Vecchio was not, however, a true villa. It may have been the house of a rich peasant, and it is perhaps significant that it did not outlast the Republic. True villas appeared only in the early 1st century BC. A famous example is that at Settefinestre, probably built around 75 BC, its location on a low hill overlooking a valley and its façade of a wall decorated with miniature turrets designed to assert the status of the owner. The main residence measured 44 metres square and comprised an *atrium* (front court), a peristyle (colonnaded court), each with grand rooms leading off, and a loggia that ran the length of the house and commanded splendid views. Most rooms were decorated with sumptuous mosaics and frescoes. Settefinestre may have belonged to a well-known senatorial family, the Sestii, and if the estate, possibly in excess of 120 hectares, had specialized in viticulture, as seems likely, the yield could have been as high as 1.2 million litres a year; wine-*amphorae* stamped *SES* have been found at the port of Cosa just over two miles away. The Settefinestre estate is known to have been one of about a dozen on this scale in the territory of the town.

The transformation of Roman agriculture may have been limited – more often multiple holdings than single great estates – but its social consequences were traumatic for the body-politic. 'When Tiberius [Gracchus] went through Tuscany to Numantia,' wrote Plutarch, 'and found the country almost depopulated, there being hardly any free husbandmen or shepherds, but for the most part only imported barbarian slaves, he then first conceived the course of policy which in the sequel proved so fatal to his family.'(3) Here was the essence of a supreme contradiction. As Keith Hopkins pointed out, in effect, Roman peasant soldiers were fighting for their own displacement: their victories supplied the slaves, their ruined farms the land, and the two combined made possible the *latifundia*. The change, in other words – it might be called 'the villa revolution' – rested on the simultaneous dispossession of the Italian peasantry and the flooding of the market with cheap slaves, both consequences of continual warfare and imperial expansion. The economy and society of Italy were being transformed by war. The rich, explained Appian, the Greek historian of the Late Republic, 'used persuasion or force to buy or seize property which adjoined their own, or any other smallholdings belonging to poor men, and came to operate great ranches instead of single farms. They employed slave-hands and shepherds on these estates to avoid having free men dragged off the land to serve in the army.'(4) The process was not complete – many small farms did survive – but the shift in land-ownership was sufficient to alter the character of Italy and plunge Rome into political crisis. A distinctive form of permanent war economy had created new social conditions, and, because the traditional institutions of an Italian city-state could not accommodate these conditions, mass struggles and civil wars erupted.

Gracchus's immediate concern was army recruitment and internal security. The problem was acute: previous tribunes, responding to popular clamour against conscription, are recorded impeding the levy in 151, 149 and 138 BC. The burden was falling too often on too few people – on a shrinking population group. The dispossession of the peasantry was draining Italy of its military manpower. Not only did slaves not fight, nor at the time did the free poor, notably the fast-growing population of Rome's slums. Military service in the city-state was linked to the economic independence and social status afforded by property-ownership. Only at moments of extreme crisis – after Cannae, for example – had the *capite censi* (those counted only by head in the census) been enrolled in the legions. The reasons were simple enough. Originally, soldiers had supplied their own equipment, and the full panoply of a heavy infantry-man had been expensive. In recent times, when the state supplied all or most equipment, the concern had been political: small farmers had a stake in the system, whereas the landless poor were a potential threat to property and were therefore best kept militarily and politically inert. The size of the citizen-farmer class – the *assidui* as they were sometimes called at the time – was therefore critical to military recruitment. More-over, as the numbers of 'stakeholders' declined, and the proportion of slaves increased – reaching perhaps a third of the population in Italy as a whole, and perhaps half in Sicily and parts of the south – the countryside became dangerously insecure. There are scattered references to small localized slave revolts at various times during the 2nd century; then, in 136–132 BC, the resistance exploded. A hundred and fifty slaves staged an uprising in Rome itself; 450 were crucified after another outbreak at Minturnae; no less than 4,000 are reported participating in a third at Sinuessa. These abortive risings on the mainland were probably inspired by events on Sicily. Here, two independent but simultaneous risings, one at Enna in the centre of the island, the other at Agrigento on the south coast, spread rapidly and fused into full-scale slave revolution.

The First Sicilian Slave War (136–132 BC) began on the estate of Damophilus, a leading citizen of Enna, 'who surpassed the Persians in the sumptuousness and costliness of his feasts'. The brutality of Damophilus drove his slaves to the desperate decision to kill their mas-ter. The conspirators sought advice from a Syrian miracle-worker and prophet called Eunus. Encouraging the revolt, he led 400 slaves into Enna, where they were joined by much of the urban population and quickly seized control of the city. Damophilus was brought from his villa, tried before a large crowd in the theatre, and summarily executed. His yet more vicious wife was handed over to her former female slaves, who first tortured her and then tossed her from the battlements. (The daughter, by contrast, who had always attempted to shield slaves from her parents' brutality, was given safe passage to the coast.) Other slave-owners were either executed or put to work manufacturing arms for the slave army that now began to form. Eunus was proclaimed king. He made the Syrian slave woman with whom he lived queen. And Enna itself – a towering natural fortress never taken in direct assault – made an excellent base. The army of the embryonic slave state soon numbered 10,000. Meantime, a slave herdsmen from Cilicia in Asia Minor called Cleon had raised a second revolt at Agrigento. When Eunus invited him to assume command of the combined slave army, he accepted and united his 5,000 men with those massing at Enna.

The revolution spread across much of the island. Eunus won control of Morgantina, which, like Enna, is near the centre of the island, and, more spectacularly, Taormina and possibly Messina on the east coast. His army is said to have numbered 60 or 70,000 at the height of the revolt, defeating several local Roman armies sent against it. The slave state was highly organized. It seems to have been modelled on the Hellenistic monarchies with which most of the slaves were familiar in their former homes: Eunus called himself 'Antiochus', the most popular name among the Seleucid monarchs; he wore a diadem and other regal insignia; and he minted coins depicting the corn goddess Demeter (who was especially revered at Enna) and inscribed with an abbreviation of his assumed name. Cleon, his commander-in-chief, was styled *strategos*, the Greek word for general; and there was a royal council, a royal bodyguard, and a royal household complete with butcher, baker, bath-attendant and buffoon. Sound orders were issued for the conduct of the war and the administration of liberated territory: not to burn down farmhouses, for example, or destroy agricultural tools and crops, or kill farm labourers. We should resist, therefore, the temptation to dismiss the Hellenistic trappings of the slave regime as mere farce. Revolutionary slaves had little choice but to construct a state, since the act of rebellion plunged them into war with their oppressors. The Sicilian slaves, faced with this task, simply used the only alternative to the Roman model that they knew. Form – that of a Hellenistic monarchy – and content – a struggle against slavery – may have been in contradiction, but the two could have co-existed well enough for the short period that the revolution lasted.

A third feature of the slave movement – for which we have only the most shadowy hints – was perhaps some sort of messianic-nationalist religious ideology. Our sources describe Eunus as a prophet of the Syrian goddess Atargatis. She was a primeval fertility deity, a great Earth Mother, and it seems likely that Demeter, the Greek corn-goddess worshipped at Enna and depicted on Eunus's coins, was equated with her. In the East, the cult of Atargatis, like other eastern 'mystery' cults, involved ecstatic forms of worship. Apuleius, in *The Golden Ass*, gives a vivid description of a troupe of her eunuch priests parading through a village in Thessaly, 'all dressed in different colours and looking absolutely hideous, their faces daubed with rouge and their eye-sockets painted to bring out the brightness of their eyes. They wore mitre-shaped birettas, saffron-coloured chasubles, silk surplices, girdles, and yellow shoes. Some of them sported white tunics with an irregular criss-cross of narrow purple stripes.'(5) The priests went about with bared shoulders, wielding great swords, wailing to the sound of pipes and horns, throwing their bodies about like dervishes, lacerating themselves with sharp knives, and lashing their own backs with whips strung with knuckle-bones. It is easy to imagine how the frenzy of the fertility cult that Apuleius describes could fuse with the mystical vision of a land cleansed of oppressors and restored to those who worked it – the devotees of Atargatis-Demeter, the followers of the prophet-king Eunus.

Eventually the Romans sent a consular army powerful enough to crush the revolt, first driving the slaves from the open field, afterwards taking the fortresses of Taormina and Enna by treachery. Thousands were tortured and executed in the aftermath. When Tiberius Gracchus was first elected tribune of the plebs, however, the matter still hung in the balance: the Sicilian slave revolution raged as a beacon of liberation that might yet set all Italy alight, its victories over Roman troops further evidence of the inadequacies of the Republic's army. An inscription from Polla in Lucania records the participation of runaway slaves in the Sicilian war – clear evidence of the links between slaves on opposite sides of the straits implied by the outbreaks at Rome, Minturnae and Sinuessa. It was the class struggle of slaves, therefore, and the direct threat it posed to Italian and Sicilian property, that split the senatorial aristocracy in 133–132 BC, with a minority around Gracchus convinced that land reform was essential to maintain the army and guarantee order in the countryside, an opposing minority deeply hostile to any redistributive measures that threatened the integrity of estates, and a mass in the middle confused by the crisis but conservative by instinct. Thus, when Gracchus proposed his bill, he had no confidence it would pass the Senate. He did not reach this judgement out of the blue. A number of recent popular measures – the appointment of Scipio Aemilianus to the Spanish command, the tribunes' resistance to the draft, laws introducing a secret ballot – had provoked strong opposition. Even land reform had been proposed not long before – by Laelius 'the Prudent', who, significantly, had earned his epithet by bowing to senatorial pressure to back down. Rather than have his bill burdened with a formal senatorial rejection, Tiberius Gracchus took it straight to the People without consulting his peers.

The proposed land reform was neat and moderate. It concerned all *ager publicus* – land taken from disloyal allies and converted into 'publicly owned farmland' – seized since the Second Punic War. Much of it had passed into the hands of the rich, who had come to regard it as their own, building villas and family tombs on it, and using it in dowries, mortgages and sales, such that any claim by the state to repossess it would be regarded by them as expropriation. But many of them were technically in breach of the law, and the Gracchan bill aimed to release parcels of *ager publicus* by enforcing the original statutory limit on the size of holdings: 500 *iugera* (120 hectares) per person, plus 250 more for each child. A land commission was to investigate all claims on *ager publicus*, to confiscate excessive holdings, and to redistribute the excess to new occupants (possibly in units of 30 *iugera*). The big land-holders were to be compensated with a rent-free hereditary lease on the land they retained. The new small-holders were to pay a small quit-rent and agree not to alienate their land for a fixed period of years.

Scholars have debated why opposition to this bill was so embittered and finally violent. Noteworthy is the fact that the land commission continued to function after the defeat of the Gracchan party in 132 BC. The Senate majority had probably been won to moderate reform by a combination of Gracchan arguments and the pressure of events – the slave revolt, popular agitation, the problem of army recruitment, the illegality of large holdings of *ager publicus*, the potential benefits of reform. But it had also been terrified by the eruption of mass struggle on the streets of the capital: whereas land reform by a senatorial commission was gradual and measured, the street demonstrations and packed popular assemblies were potentially uncontrollable. Where would it all end? After all, Gracchus had sidelined the Senate at the outset by taking his bill direct to the People. He had revived the traditional role of the tribune of the plebs as defender of the common citizen – or rather, had accelerated a worrying trend that was apparent since at least 151 BC. And in raising himself up as a popular leader – by making himself a commissioner under his own law, and by seeking a second term as tribune – he threatened the convention by which offices were rotated among senators as a way of controlling competition and maintaining cohesion within the ruling class. Was this the beginning of a new popular politics that might reduce the Senate to irrelevance?

Particular concern arose when King Attalus III of Pergamum bequeathed his entire kingdom to the Romans in 133 BC. Gracchus seized on this extraordinary windfall – Pergamum was very rich – by proposing that the royal treasures should be distributed to the beneficiaries of the land reform to assist them in stocking their farms. The Senate was outraged by this further threat to its traditional prerogatives, which included virtually untrammelled control over diplomacy and finance. It was not, it seems, reform as such that the Senate feared, but the popular movement necessary to bring it about. There was no contradiction, therefore, between the senators' support for the pogrom and assize court which shattered the Gracchan party, and their tolerance of the land commission's work thereafter.

This, though, was not enough to end the crisis. Without the pressure of the popular movement, the Senate's support was lukewarm, and the obstructiveness of big landowners slowed the pace of reform. The potential for political filibustering and legal challenges was immense. A number of inscribed boundary stones have been found which record Gracchan land allocations – so we know the commission was working. But there is no reliable way of quantifying the transference of land, and we have at least one clear example of deliberate obstruction – in 129–128 BC, when the land commission's responsibilities were shifted to one of the consuls, who promptly departed to the provinces, causing all work to be temporarily suspended. By 123 BC, the Gracchans appear to have resolved upon a new political offensive to drive forward reform. Gaius Gracchus, Tiberius's younger brother and one of the land commissioners, stood successfully for election as tribune of the plebs on a radical platform. Since, moreover, he would be elected again the following year, when another Gracchan would also be elected to one of the two consulships, this amounted to a more serious – and, to its opponents, more threatening – bid for governmental power than that of ten years before. The experience of Tiberius's tribunate and the struggles of the intervening years had taught sharp lessons. What emerged in 123 BC was nothing short of a full manifesto – in effect, an entire programme for government: something unprecedented in Roman politics, and revolutionary in its implications. Moreover, careful political calculation was implicit in the range of policies offered: there was a deliberate attempt by the Gracchans to construct a broad, popular, anti-senatorial coalition – a coalition powerful enough, it may have seemed, to defeat reaction, marginalize the Senate, and transform Roman politics and Italian society.

Gaius Gracchus is often assumed to have been a greater orator and popular leader than his brother, and to have been the more creative and audacious reformer. He is described as such by ancient writers, and modern scholars have been inclined to agree. The truth is that we know too little about either of the brothers to be sure. Political programmes – and the leaders and parties that carry them – take time to crystallize. The tribunate of Gaius Gracchus took place in the context of that of his brother ten years earlier: it was the experience of reactionary violence, and the time since spent debating the politics of crisis and change, that determined the far more radical course the reformers now followed. Four sets of policies, each reflecting the interests of a key social group, constituted the new Gracchan programme.

First, the original land law was revised, and the work of the commission was then pushed forward with renewed vigour. There may have been a new stipulation that *ager publicus* could – perhaps should – be distributed in relatively large plots of up to 200 *iugera* (48 hectares). Small farms created under earlier allocations may have failed. Brunt has commented, 'There was an inherent contradiction in the Gracchan objective of increasing the number of Rome's peasant soldiers, when it was soldiering that did much to destroy the peasantry.'(6) Why should new smallholdings have been any more successful than old, given high conscription, the growth of commercial agriculture, and the perennial marginality of the subsistence farmer? It may have made sense to increase the size of holdings. The Gracchans also revived the long-lapsed policy of founding colonies. Though their scheme for one at Capua fell through, colonies were founded at Tarentum and Scolacium in the far south of Italy, and, more controversially, at Carthage, the first example of a Roman colony overseas. The aim of colonies was different from before: instead of providing military security, Gracchan settlements were intended to provide farms for needy Roman citizens. Finally, to facilitate the marketing of agricultural produce, a new programme of road-building began.

Roads were not the only public works initiated by the Gracchans; they also built new granaries in the city of Rome. These were necessary for the state corn-supply, another Gracchan initiative – one pregnant with implications for the future – whereby the government purchased and stored corn in bulk, releasing it on to the market when necessary to support the bread price, which was fixed at an affordable rate. Both policies – public works and the corn supply – were designed to benefit the landless poor, mainly the huge population of Rome itself, perhaps already close to half a million. The urban crowd was probably decisive in most votes in the popular assemblies, because votes were cast in person. Though voting was by tribe (in the Assembly of the Tribes) or by century (in the Assembly of the Centuries) – the popular assemblies were therefore electoral colleges – the decision of these constituent groups was made by counting the votes cast by individual members. City-dwellers dominated for the obvious reason that countrymen had to make an exceptional effort to vote. Tiberius Gracchus had been attacked and killed at harvest time – that is, when most supporters of land reform were away from the city. Gaius Gracchus was consciously attempting to build a firm base of support in Rome itself.

Land for the *assidui* (the small farmers). Jobs and cheap bread for the *proletarii* (the landless poor). To these was added a third raft of reforms designed to attract the support of the equestrians. The Roman aristocracy was divided into three groups: senators, equestrians and decurions. At the top were the senators, a group of 300 or so of the richest men in the Empire, who had seats in the Senate and qualified for election to the most senior state offices. The equestrians formed a second division. They also were rich, some of them exceptionally so, but the basic property qualification was only 100,000 *denarii*, less than half that of a senator, and it is likely that the equestrian order had come to number many thousands. The numbers, wealth and influence of equestrians had grown enormously with the rise of empire. They were army officers, business contractors, slave-dealers and money-lenders. Most were also landowners: without land as security, few could have established themselves in business in the first place; and because of the Roman prejudice against commercial property, profits from business were frequently ploughed into new land purchases. Of particular importance were the *publicani* (public contractors). Probably the easiest way for an equestrian to become really rich was to secure a public contract to provide a specific commodity or service – perhaps to supply military equipment to the army, to run state-owned mines, or, most lucrative of all, to 'farm' taxes in the provinces. This was 'private-public partnership': the state avoided expenditure and responsibility; the contractors were rewarded with a hefty rake-off. A company of tax-farmers, for example, would undertake to collect the taxes due from one or more cities in a province, and their reward would be a proportion of the takings – plus whatever extra they could extort along the way.

Relations between senators and equestrians were sometimes tense. They might come into conflict in the provinces, perhaps in a clash of economic interests, if a senatorial governor was promoting a company in which he had an interest, or where a governor concerned with maintaining good order sought to check extortion. This sense that equestrians were under the thumb of senators – that economic success was dependent on currying favour – fed a wider political frustration. Although some equestrians gained admittance to the Senate as 'new men' (*novi homines*) – the Equestrian Order has been described as the 'seed-bed' of the Senate – the numbers involved were too few to satisfy aspirations. Equestrian empire-builders found themselves pushing at a barrier of senatorial privilege. Most failed to break through and were denied access to the highest offices (and rewards) in the state. A social group with new economic weight found itself politically confined. The Gracchans set out to exploit the tension between the two orders, and to build up equestrian power as a counterweight to that of the Senate. Gracchus's aim, according to one ancient commentator, was to make the state 'two-headed'.

The treasury of Pergamum – now the province of Asia – had already been tapped for funds to stock new farms created by Gracchan land allotments. It seems, however, that the cities of Asia were not at first subject to taxation, revenue being drawn only from the former royal estates, from customs dues, and from a tax on cattle. Gaius Gracchus ended the immunity of the cities and gave responsibility for collecting the taxes to companies of *publicani*, whose operations were governed by contracts let at Rome and renewable every five years. Gracchus's policy for Asia – the richest of Rome's provinces – was to exploit it both to enrich the equestrians and to fund land reform, public works and welfare measures. It is a policy that illustrates perfectly the politics of 'democratic imperialism'.

Left-wing historians have sometimes been rather dewy-eyed about the reformers of the Late Republic, so it is necessary to stress that the conflict between reformers and conservatives – *populares* and *optimates* as they came to be called by contemporaries – was a dispute over the division of spoils. The issue at stake in Asia was whether senators, equestrians or common citizens would benefit most from the exploitation of native peasants. For a measure of the hatred with which foreign tax-collectors were viewed, we need go no further than *The New Testament*, which makes frequent disparaging reference to *publicani*. Jesus could be vilified by his enemies as 'a glutton, a drunkard, and a friend of tax-collectors and sinners'. Jesus's advice to tax-collectors who sought salvation was to 'collect no more than the amount prescribed'; presumably they commonly extorted more. The popular view – in ancient Palestine at least – was that *publicani* were corrupt and on a moral level with prostitutes. The Gracchi were as much imperialists as the most reactionary senator; indeed, their whole programme was designed to strengthen the Roman Empire, and its realization depended upon efficient exploitation of the provinces and the deployment of accumulated surpluses in Italy.

A second key measure was an attempt to shift the balance of political power in Rome from the Senate to the Equestrian Order. Gracchus's aim was to strip the Senate of its role as a high court, abolishing its authority to set up special tribunals with capital powers (of the kind used against the Gracchans in 132 BC), and removing its right to investigate charges of corruption brought against its own members during their service as provincial governors – a notorious abuse that had led to a series of cover-ups. Though some details are obscure because the ancient sources do not agree, Gracchus's main concern seems to have been to create a new high court with juries formed exclusively of equestrians. This had major implications. Senators in imperial service had been almost invulnerable to prosecution for abuse of power. Now, by contrast, senators who clashed with the *publicani* were in grave danger: Roman justice was highly politicized, and it would have been easy enough to concoct a case to destroy an obstructive provincial governor.

The final strand of Gracchan reform proved the most problematic. In 125 BC, Marcus Fulvius Flaccus, an associate of the Gracchi, a replacement member of the land commission, and in that particular year one of the two elected consuls, had proposed a franchise bill which would have granted Roman citizenship to all free members of Latin and allied communities in Italy. The reformers favoured an extension of citizenship as a way of consolidating Rome's Italian manpower base. Up to two-thirds of a Roman army might be formed of Latins and allies. Yet it was Romans, those with voting rights in the imperial city, who got the main share of booty, land, public contracts, and government posts. The regular army tax (*tributum*) had been abolished in 167 BC, so that Romans – unlike other Italians – now paid no direct taxes. The Gracchan land commission had almost certainly sometimes redistributed *ager publicus* from non-Romans to Romans. The equestrian *publicani* favoured by Gracchan policy were all Roman. Elevation to the Senate was impossible for a Latin – however rich. The Roman courts protected their own – not simply because they were corrupt (though they were), but because the whole justice system was rooted in the citizen community. Roman magistrates were accountable to 'the Senate and People of Rome', not to Latins and allies: their decisions therefore reflected Roman interests.

These imbalances between contribution and reward had mattered little in the 3rd century BC. Romans, Latins and allies had fought side-by-side in defence of their homeland against Gauls, Samnites, Greeks and Carthaginians; there had been great sacrifice, but only modest gains. The wars of the 2nd century BC, by contrast, were foreign wars of conquest in which Latins and allies could have no interest unless they shared fully in the now ample rewards. This fracture line between Romans and non-Romans not only compromised military recruitment and morale, but also, by dividing the ranks of the free, undermined the security of property in a countryside now filled with slaves.

Such was the opposition to Flaccus's franchise bill, however, that it was never even put to the vote. Learning from this failure, in 122 BC Gaius Gracchus proposed a more moderate franchise bill, offering Roman citizenship to Latins, and Latin citizenship to allies, the latter as a halfway-house towards full enfranchisement. Even this was so controversial, however, that it shattered Gracchus's own popular base. Most senators were hostile because the flooding of the Roman political system with new, pro-Gracchan citizens threatened to swamp their own networks of clients and supporters. As the ups and downs of Gracchan populism demonstrated, power in the popular assemblies was finely balanced. Because voting in person restricted political activity largely to those who lived in or close to the city, many tribes and centuries – the units that delivered the block votes in the Assemblies of the Tribes and the Centuries respectively – were probably controlled by small caucuses; some, no doubt, were little more than pocket boroughs for great families. Even where attendances were larger, many in the city mob were enrolled as clients (*clientes*) in one or another aristocratic retinue and could be relied upon to vote in their patron's interests. Tiberius Gracchus's supporters had been overpowered when the small farmers were out of the city at harvest time: the Roman mob was far from being solidly Gracchan.

But for the first time the conservatives were able to reach beyond their own networks and build a wider opposition to the reformers. The senatorial leaders engineered a sophisticated two-pronged attack. First, they opposed the franchise bill on the grounds it would dilute citizen privileges – not least the very welfare reforms the Gracchans themselves had introduced. Second, they set up another tribune, Marcus Livius Drusus, to outflank the Gracchans on the left by proposing to abolish the rent imposed on new land-holders and to increase the number of new colonies to twelve. The aim was to drain support from the Gracchans – the genuine party of reform – on both the left and the right, so that they could be isolated and destroyed.

The attack was highly successful. Whereas Gracchus had secured a second term as tribune in 122 BC, he failed at his third attempt, a political defeat which opened the way to a generalized onslaught against his supporters. Fearing a repeat of the violence of 132 BC, the Gracchans armed themselves for self-defence and took refuge on the Aventine Hill, a predominantly plebeian part of Rome and traditional centre of radical protest. The Senate then declared martial law (issuing a *senatus consultum ultimum*), on the basis of which the consul Lucius Opimius proclaimed a general levy of the citizens of Rome and raised a force sufficient for an assault on the Aventine. Gaius Gracchus, Fulvius Flaccus and many others were cut down in the streets, and then mass arrests and executions, amounting to some 3,000 victims, completed the destruction of the revived Gracchan party. Much Gracchan legislation was also swept away by the tide of reaction: the colony at Carthage was annulled; the grain law was amended; a free market in public land was restored; the land commission was wound up.

In the turmoil of 123–122 BC, a reform movement led by aristocratic radicals and supported by crowds of common citizens had begun to grow over into full-blown democratic revolution. But it had run into an impenetrable barrier of reaction and privilege. A majority of aristocrats – both senators and equestrians – were either nervous or hostile, perceiving the popular movement as a potential threat to the traditional order and the rights of property. Many ordinary citizens became hostile once persuaded that their privileges would be diluted by an extension of the franchise; many were confused by the fake reformism of Drusus; and many were so rooted in the retinues of aristocratic patrons that they had never been open to Gracchan arguments in the first place. In sum, the numbers of Roman citizens consistently committed to all-out reform were too small – the cross-currents of self-interest too strong – to achieve the critical mass necessary to bring about a democratic revolution from below. Even the limited reforms achieved were reversed in the years after Gaius Gracchus's death; and the growth of the *latifundia* proceeded thereafter unchecked. The Gracchan route to a resolution of the crisis of the Late Republic was blocked. Another would have to be found.

A popular general: the supremacy of Marius, 107–88 BC

The Roman Revolution – the slow-motion breakdown of the Republican system of government and its replacement by the dictatorship of the Caesars – was a revolution without a revolutionary class. It is for this reason that it was so protracted and chaotic. For this reason, too, it is easily misunderstood, its deeper meaning hidden by the clash of aristocratic factions and their private armies. Rome was in the grip of a deep-rooted crisis in the years 133–30 BC, but the peculiar configuration of Roman society prevented any simple resolution through the action of a powerful class-based party like the Independents of 1649, the Jacobins of 1793, or the Bolsheviks of 1917. None of the main groups constituting the Roman citizen-body – senators, equestrians, decurions, *assidui*, *proletarii* – was able to play an effective revolutionary role.

The senatorial aristocracy was split by the crisis. A small minority favoured radical reform. A larger minority opposed reform of any kind and was determined to defend senatorial property, privilege and power against dilution. The 'centre' was open to argument, but, as part of a property-owning elite, most senators were instinctively cautious and conservative, becoming openly reactionary in the face of revolt from below. The Senate was therefore congenitally incapable of leading the reform of Roman society: feeble at best, hostile at worst, it was a barrier to change that had to be physically broken.

The equestrians were hardly more capable of providing new political leadership; they were certainly not the basis for some sort of 'bourgeois revolution'. The equestrians were themselves top aristocrats, men of property who feared revolt from below no less than senators; they had no wish to unleash a revolutionary struggle against the Republic that might place them at the mercy of radicals demanding cancellation of debts and redistribution of land. Equestrian hostility to the Senate was, in any case, muted. It is not as if the equestrians constituted an independent business class with interests sharply opposed to aristocratic landowners; they were not a bourgeoisie in the modern sense. Most equestrians were them-selves landowners. Many had no business interests at all. Those who did, or who pursued careers in public service – especially the most successful of these, like the leading *publicani* – depended heavily on senatorial patronage. The Roman Republic offered neither a free market to enter-prise nor a career open to the talents: it was a controlled society in which opportunities for enrichment and advancement were embedded in polit-ical structures. Public contracts and government appointments were in the gift of senators. The equestrians who prospered were those who enjoyed the favour of powerful patrons. The highest aspiration of an equestrian was to enter the Senate as a 'new man'. There was, in short, no firm economic, social or political ground on which the Equestrian Order might have taken a stand against the Senate.

Senators and equestrians were the grandees of Roman politics. Below them was a class of lesser aristocrats or gentry who formed the local governing elites in Italian towns. The composition of town councils was regulated by the census, which ranked people by property ownership, so that Roman towns were safely in the hands of landed oligarchs. (Later, under the Empire, they were known as *curiales* or *decuriones* – members of the Curial Order, the class of town councillors.) While there was some basis for tension between grandees and gentry – as between senators and equestrians – this was more than offset by myriad factors promoting collaboration. For one thing, the Roman state had always backed oligarchs against democrats, and could be relied upon to intervene in support of any established municipal authority threatened by popular disorder: for many Italian gentry, political loyalty to the Republic was synonymous with social order. Hannibal's attempt to raise the Italian towns against Rome had, after all, foundered on the rock of oligarchic resistance to city-state democracy.

Secondly, many towns enjoyed the patronage of senatorial and equestrian grandees – as did many decurions individually – and this was an important source of largesse and influence. Quintus Cicero, writing to his more famous brother about canvassing for the consulship, explained how the aspiring Roman politician should cultivate the support of leading men in the towns, whom he would find most eager to form political friendships. It is easy to see why. Though the example is of later date – *c.* AD 113 – the inscription recording Pliny the Younger's benefactions to his home town of Comum is instructive of long-established practice: 'He left [. . .] sesterces in his will for the construction of baths, with an additional 300,000 sesterces for decoration, and in addition to that 200,000 sesterces for upkeep; and for the support of his freedmen, a hundred persons, he likewise bequeathed to the municipality 1,866,666 sesterces, the income from which he desired to have applied thereafter to an annual banquet for the public. In his lifetime he also gave 500,000 sesterces for the support of the boys and girls of the lower class, and also a library and 100,000 sesterces for the upkeep of the library.'(7) The material interest binding country-town gentry to the senatorial elite could hardly be more obvious.

Not only were decurions cocooned within a system of patronage; they were also divided among themselves. The gentry competed fiercely with one another for advancement within their towns – as Pompeii's numerous painted election-notices testify – seeking election as *duovirs* (mayors), aediles (in charge of public works and municipal regulation) or quaestors (city treasurers). The most successful could even aspire to rise from the Curial to the Equestrian Order – with perhaps the Senate itself on the distant horizon of ambition. There were intense rivalries, too, between neighbouring towns, sometimes going back centuries; so intense that they occasionally erupted into violence, as when, in AD 59, the ancient antagonism between Pompeii and Nuceria degenerated into an amphitheatre riot in which 11 people were killed. Roman policy had, of course, exacerbated such feuds, creating a hierarchy of privilege which set Roman, Latin and ally at loggerheads, diverting political energy into a struggle for the franchise and equal rights. As well as being divided, the Curial Order was scattered in separate townships across Italy, with no overarching organization – in contrast to senators and equestrians – such as might have facilitated concerted action. The decurions were no more a revolutionary force than senators or equestrians.

That left the common people. The small citizen-farmers certainly had no love for the senatorial elite – or the rich generally – but their position was weak, and growing weaker. The peasantry was a scattered class of individualists, difficult to organize in the first place, harder still to keep together as a coherent force. The peasant farmer's ambition was restricted to his own farm; he wanted to defeat his oppressors and then be left alone to work the land with his family; he had no vision of a wider social transformation involving the collective action of peasants in general. That is why the peasants backed the Gracchi in their struggle against land poverty, but had no independent existence as a party, no leadership of their own, no political staying-power once the aristocratic reformers who had called them forth had been cut down. The Roman peasants of the Late Republic were further weakened by two specific circumstances: first, heavy conscription and the growth of commercial farming had combined to undermine traditional subsistence agriculture and erode peasant numbers; second, the still-substantial privilege of Roman citizenship prevented Roman peasants making common cause with Latins, allies and slaves in the Italian countryside. The *assidui* therefore lacked the economic weight, social coherence, and political organization necessary to constitute a serious revolutionary force.

Then, finally, there was the city mob. Most citizens lived in Rome or another Roman town, and it was here that the political, social and cultural life that defined 'civilization' was lived. But ancient cities were centres of consumption, not production. They were parasitic on the countryside, leeching away agricultural surpluses to be invested in monumental architecture, luxury living, and the 'bread and circuses' which, increasingly, sustained the urban poor. The senators and equestrians in Rome and the decurions in other towns were mainly landowners – not an independent mercantile elite as in medieval cities – and the urban masses were linked to them by ties of economic dependence and political affiliation. The archaeology of Pompeii is especially instructive. There was no zoning into rich and poor neighbourhoods. Many of the working population lived in the grand houses, either as part of the household, or through renting workshops and first-floor apartments along the street front. There were, of course, no factories – all production was at workshop level – but nor, it seems, was there an independent petty bourgeoisie of workshop masters organized in guilds. Instead, workshops belonged to the owners of grand houses, and guilds were subordinate to aristocratic patrons. Urban economic activity was embedded in an oligarchic power structure.

The mob – the *plebs media*, 'the middling sort' – was not, then, an independent political player. There was to be no equivalent in the Roman Revolution of the English Levellers or the Parisian *sansculottes*. The Late Republican crowd never detached itself from its aristocratic leaders. Because cities were parasitic and citizens privileged, the *plebs media* could intervene in urban politics in support of a reformist senator, but it could not break its ties of dependence, forge links with the rural masses, and challenge the power of the senatorial aristocracy as a whole. Indeed, the corruption and fickleness of the Roman mob – famously caricatured by Shakespeare in *Julius Caesar* – were real enough. The mob was bribed by largesse (effectively a share in the spoils of empire) and was loyal to the aristocratic patrons who dispensed it. One example will suffice: the grain dole – soon to be distributed free to all those on the citizen roll – was brought to Rome in fleets of ships from Sicily, North Africa, and (later) Egypt. It was a tithe levied on provincial peasants for the benefit of the Roman mob. Dependent for their privileges on imperialism and the aristocratic elite, the citizens of Rome were incapable of becoming an independent political force; indeed, they were only marginally more likely to back a reformer than a conservative, and often they split into warring gangs at the behest of rival aristocratic factions.

Each constituent element of the Roman citizen-body was disabled by a combination of self-interest and weakness from playing a revolutionary role. Yet the crisis grew worse, not better, and the clamour for reform, albeit from a formless *mélange* of competing and contradictory interests, grew louder. Chaos, the ancients believed, spawned Night and Day, Earth and Heaven, Gods and Mortals – all things. Chaos now would conjure armies, wars, military coups, a Caesar, an Augustan Age – a new world order. When a clash of class forces produces chronic instability but no clear outcome – when there is no revolutionary class able to seize power for itself and remodel society in its own image – leadership may devolve on military 'strongmen' who lift themselves above the factions, building support by promising both reform and a restoration of order, and maintaining power by balancing – or wobbling – between evenly balanced opposing forces. The first such military strongman – the first of the great warlords of the Late Republic – was Gaius Marius.

The occasion of Marius's rise to power was a severe military crisis comparable with that of the 130s BC. It gradually unfolded between 113 and 104 BC, involving a long guerrilla war in Africa, a devastating Celtic-Germanic invasion in the north, and a second great slave revolt in Sicily: multiple threats, none of which was easily mastered. The story, so far as Marius is concerned, begins in Numidia (roughly modern Algeria) in North Africa. A huge territory immediately west of the Roman province of Africa, Numidia comprised a rich coastal plain and river valleys where arable agriculture was practised, and a vast hinterland of mountain and desert. Since the end of the Second Punic War it had been ruled by two exceptionally long-lived client-kings – Masinissa (202–148 BC), the founder of the dynasty who as a young adventurer had fought alongside Scipio Africanus against Hannibal, and his son Micipsa (148–118 BC). Then the succession was disputed between two full brothers, Hiempsal and Adherbal, and their older, more accomplished, but bastard half-brother Jugurtha. When Jugurtha murdered Hiempsal and appeared poised to take over the kingdom, Adherbal invited the Romans to mediate. Reluctant to see Numidia united under a vigorous ruler of doubtful allegiance, the Romans divided the kingdom, giving the richer east to Adherbal, the more desolate west to Jugurtha.

The integrity and independence of Numidia were compromised, and Jugurtha raised the more resolute nobles to challenge the division of the kingdom. Cirta, the principal town of western Numidia, was captured, Adherbal assassinated, and the Italian merchant community massacred (113–112 BC). To restore control to their clients, the Romans then commenced a series of annual invasions by consular armies; but the Numidians proved formidable opponents. The desert was their ally. Limited water, food and forage crippled the mobility of Roman forces.

When they did march, the invaders were swallowed up in the vastness of the landscape, unable to bring their opponents to battle. For the Numidians were mainly light cavalry, able to move fast and strike at will, employing the tactics of ambush and skirmish, against which Rome's legions were cumbersome and ineffective. Jugurtha was master of these methods – one of ancient history's great guerrilla leaders. (Though rumour had it that some of Rome's commanders were bribed with African gold, and the capture of a Roman army in 110 BC provoked the passage of a law for investigating the corruption of senator-generals.)

The war entered its second phase with the appointment to command of the consul Quintus Caecilius Metellus in 109 BC. Metellus was no aristocratic fop: he restored morale, took the offensive, beat off a determined surprise attack on his main column, and captured a number of enemy strong-points. But the Romans still controlled little more than the ground they occupied. Jugurtha and his army continued their war of avoidance and attrition, making good their losses by recruiting new allies, Gaetulian tribesmen from Numidia's southern border, and King Bocchus of Mauretania (Morocco) in the west. The war dragged on through 108 BC. Late that year, Metellus's second-in-command, Gaius Marius, took home leave and returned to Rome to stand for election to the consulship.

Marius was a 'new man' (*novus homo*) from the small hill-town of Arpinum in central Italy. The town had gained Roman citizenship only in 188 BC, and Marius was the first of his family to achieve senatorial status. After serving in Spain in the 130s BC, he had held a series of magistracies in Rome from the late 120s onwards, culminating in the praetorship in 115 BC. In the same year, he contracted a marriage alliance with the ancient patrician family of the Julii. For Marius, the plebian new man from Arpinum, association with the patrician Julii represented spectacular social advancement. But it suited the Julii too, for the family had won little distinction of late, and Marius, whatever his background, was a rising star. (Rarely can such calculation have been better rewarded. Marius was destined to achieve unprecedented political honours. But even his achievement was to be eclipsed by that of his nephew – Julius Caesar. And then, between 30 BC and AD 68, the family was to produce a line of emperors.)

After faltering briefly, Marius's career had resumed when Metellus, needing good officers, invited him to become his second-in-command in Africa in 109 BC. But when Marius returned to Rome in the winter of 108–107 BC, he campaigned for the consulship on a populist ticket, criticizing the conduct of the war and blaming military failure on the domination of Roman politics by an aristocracy of birth that was corrupt and incompetent. Marius was duly elected and awarded Africa as his province. So he returned to Numidia to displace his old commander and bring the war to a successful end.

Marius's strategy was to increase the mobility of Roman forces by shedding baggage and marching light. In 107 BC he led a column through the desert to surprise, capture and destroy Jugurtha's southern stronghold of Capsa. In 106 BC he repeated the feat, this time marching 600 miles to reach the western edge of Numidia, where he captured the king's principal treasury in a near-impregnable fortress. When the Numidians and Mauretanians counter-attacked, the retreating column beat them off (albeit with heavy losses). Demoralized by the range and punitive power the Romans had acquired, and by his and Jugurtha's inability to defeat them in the open field, King Bocchus resolved to abandon the struggle and betray his ally. Jugurtha was kidnapped, handed over to the Romans, and executed in Rome in 105 BC. By then, however, a more serious military crisis had arisen on the Roman Empire's northern limits.

A rambling folk-movement by two large hordes, the Cimbri and the Teutones, perhaps a mixture of Celts and Germans, had been causing widespread disruption in central and western Europe for a decade. Several Roman armies had been defeated, either by the Cimbri and Teutones themselves, or by Celtic tribes in southern Gaul that the prevailing chaos had also set in motion. Finally, in 105 BC, the Cimbri and Teutones launched a full-scale invasion of the Roman province of Gallia Narbonensis. This large segment of what the Romans called 'Transalpine Gaul' (Gaul beyond the Alps), roughly corresponding to modern Provence, had been annexed as recently as 121 BC; Roman control remained fragile. The response to the invasion was correspondingly robust: a second consular army was dispatched to Gaul to reinforce the one already there. But the two commanders bickered, action was not co-ordinated, and the combined Roman force was destroyed at the Battle of Arausio (Orange) in perhaps the worst military disaster since Cannae, resulting, the ancient sources say, in some 80,000 casualties. The way to Italy lay open, and if the victors did not immediately take it, Rome was nonetheless gripped by panic-fear at the prospect of an imminent onslaught by northern barbarians. Marius, the returning conqueror of Jugurtha, was immediately elected to a second consulship and given the command in Gaul; he would continue to be re-elected each year of the emergency from 104 to 100 BC, holding an unprecedented five consecutive consulships.

Repulsed from the parts of Spain and Gaul to which they had migrated after Arausio, the Cimbri and Teutones finally descended on Italy in 102 BC. They came in separate columns, and Marius planned to defeat them in detail; but first he manoeuvred and avoided battle, seasoning his own troops while sapping the energy of the barbarian hordes. Then he struck, bringing the Teutones to battle on unfavourable ground at Aquae Sextiae and defeating them utterly, so that hardly a man escaped slaughter or slavery. For a time the Cimbri remained at large, settling on the rich plains of the Po Valley for the winter. But the following year Marius repeated his success, first wearing his enemy down with long campaigning in the north Italian summer heat, then bringing them to battle at Vercellae and winning a second crushing victory.

Nor was this the only victory of Marian armies in 101 BC. One of Marius's leading lieutenants, Manius Aquillius, had been dispatched with a force of veterans from the northern wars to suppress a new slave revolt in Sicily. As in the 130s BC, the rising had coincided with military crisis elsewhere. Concerned that the military manpower of allied states was being drained away by the activities of slave-raiders, the Senate had ordered the release of any allied subjects who had been enslaved. The consequent rush of slaves to Syracuse to demand their freedom in 104 BC overwhelmed the Governor of Sicily, who released 800 and then ordered the rest to return to their masters. Despite the memory of grisly retribution following the First Sicilian Slave War a generation before, the promise of freedom suddenly withdrawn, coupled with the crowding together of a great mass of the recently enslaved, was enough to detonate a second revolt. The slaves marched from Syracuse to the Shrine of the Palici. This was located at a small lake in the crater of an extinct volcano not far from Mount Etna. The water there still bubbles and exudes gaseous vapours; in antiquity it was livelier still, spouting two geyser-like jets, and the Palici, the ancient deities believed to reside in the lake, were considered the special protectors of the island's native people. They had supported an anti-Greek resistance movement in the 5th century BC. Now they would give their support to slaves in revolt against Rome.

There were two major outbreaks and two leaders emerged, one called Athenion, who was from Cilicia in Asia Minor, the other Salvius, of uncertain origin. At first in conflict, the two leaders were reconciled and, as Eunus and Cleon had done, combined their forces. Also as before, the slaves established a proto-state, though this time it took on Roman form, Salvius wearing a purple toga and appointing lictors bearing fasces in the manner of a consul. Though many rural slaves joined the revolt, both men and women fighting in the rebel army, the urban slaves remained loyal to their masters, and the Romans retained their grip on all the towns. The highest figure cited in the ancient sources for the size of the slave army is 40,000, far less than in the previous revolt. Nonetheless, the rebels, facing incompetent commanders and demoralized soldiery, held the countryside for three years. It was only with the arrival of Manius Aquillius and his veteran legionaries in 101 BC that the Second Sicilian Slave War was ended. Betrayal was a hallmark of the Empire's vengeance: urban slaves promised their freedom in return for loyalty during the war were kept in slavery; a thousand rebels promised their lives if they surrendered were sent to die in the arena.

In the space of five years, the soldiers of Gaius Marius had conquered Numidia, destroyed the Cimbri and Teutones, and crushed the Sicilian slaves. The Republic had been saved. The People's faith in their champion had been vindicated. Marius found himself the greatest Roman of his age, elevated so far above his erstwhile peers that the edifice of the state tottered top-heavy under his weight. The conservative majority in the Senate could only view their new master with gloomy suspicion.

No doubt this self-made man, basking in the popular acclaim that his achievements had earned, regarded the snobbery of hereditary nobles with a mixture of contempt and irritation. Barriers to the advancement of parvenus like himself, barriers whose effect was to shield incompetence from the competition of better men, must have seemed unjust and detrimental to the public interest. Yet it would be wrong to see Marius as a revolutionary – or even a radical reformer – opposed to senatorial government. On the contrary, access to the Senate, and the offices and rewards in its gift, were the summit of his political ambition, as they would be that of other great populists, not least his nephew Julius Caesar. Marius's faction included many of the senatorial elite, some from the oldest families, of which the Julii were merely the most prominent. The Roman aristocracy had always been divided into factions – alliances of great senatorial families and their networks of clients, competing for honour, power and wealth at the top of society. In the past, such clashes over policy as there had been rarely concerned matters of substance. The new wealth of empire in the 2nd century BC had encouraged some, like Scipio Africanus and his family, to adopt an ostentatious and luxurious lifestyle modelled on the Hellenistic East. And traditionalists like Cato the Elder had denounced them, the Scipiones in particular, speaking out against the supposed corruption of Roman public life, demanding a return to the imagined sobriety of the past. But a squabble about Greek art was hardly going to turn the world upside down.

Some have argued that the struggle between *populares* (populists: those who took the side of the People) and *optimates* (the 'best men': those who supported oligarchy and order) was no different: that policy differences remained secondary to the scramble for office, and if the competition became more vicious – indeed, lethal – that was only because the stakes for which men played were higher. New wealth fed intra-aristocratic competition, the argument goes, but did not alter its essentially factional, self-serving character.

Yet it was not wealth as such that had escalated the intensity of conflict within the Roman elite. The whole arena of conflict had been enlarged, allowing political protagonists to forge more powerful weapons and deploy a repertoire of new tactics. Things had moved beyond dinner-party gossip and bath-house cabals. Politics had ceased to be the exclusive pastime of aristocratic plotters. Everyone was now involved, since the whole shape and future of Rome and its empire were at issue. Though confusion and chaos often characterized their interventions, decayed patricians, 'new men', equestrians, decurions, common citizens, non-Romans, even slaves, all now entered the political process. Here was a potential base (except for the slaves) for men like Marius, a base independent of senatorial favour, one that could lift them clear of the carve-ups and compromises of factional politics. Thus had Marius triumphed at the polls – as the People's general against Old Corruption. But matters could not rest there. For Marius had become the over-mighty subject whose pre-eminence threatened the collegiate principles and closed shop of senatorial government. Traditionally, high offices had been shared out by agreement among the great families. Traditionally, policy had been consensual, and the 'advice' of the Senate had been as good as law. Not any more. The Gracchi had been vanquished, but, it seemed, their demon had been reborn as a military tyrant.

If so, his sprite was a radical tribune of the plebs called Lucius Appuleius Saturninus, who had emerged as a scourge of incompetent generals and a champion of the common soldier. The Senate resisted his measures and there had again been open clashes on the streets of the capital. The stakes were raised further when Marius and Saturninus formed an alliance in 101–100 BC to ensure a proper settlement for dis-charged soldiers and a new appointment for the general. Saturninus introduced a bill to provide land-allotments for military veterans in Gallia Narbonensis, and another authorizing new colonies in Sicily, Achaea (Greece) and Macedonia. Senatorial opposition was led by Quintus Caecilius Metellus, Marius's former commander in Numidia, and it was motivated in large part by fear that the proposed communities of veteran-settlers would constitute a permanent bloc of Marian loyalists, further entrenching the general's power. Saturninus's measures therefore faced defeat. At that point something extraordinary and unprecedented happened: Marius brought his veterans into the city to drive the sen-atorial mob off the streets, pack the popular assembly, and vote through Saturninus's bills.

Soldiers had entered the political arena. The populists had found a new weapon. It was one that Marius himself had forged. He had done so without conscious political intent; his famous army reforms were of strictly military purpose; yet their effect was to transform Rome's soldiery into a force of semi-professional mercenaries with real power. Marius had reformed the Roman army to make it a more effective military instru-ment in his campaigns against Numidians and Germans. Effectively a career officer who rose to the top through personal achievement, he was perhaps less hidebound than generals from the hereditary nobility. Certainly he was prepared to break rules to deal with the inherited weak-nesses of the army: lack of manpower; poor discipline and training; low morale; limited strategic mobility; and equally limited tactical flexibility. Some changes may have been introduced by other Roman commanders (our sources are hazy). Some may have been intended only as temporary measures (but then became permanent). What is certain is that the Roman army was substantially remodelled at the end of the 2nd century BC, and Marius was the dominant military figure of the period. The army of the Late Republic – the army destined to win the victories of Sulla, Pompey, Caesar and Octavian-Augustus – was, in effect, the army Marius created.

The single most important change was to abolish the property quali-fication and allow the *proletarii* – citizens without property counted by head in the census (*capite censi*) – to join the legions. This had occasion-ally been done in previous emergencies – after Cannae, for example – but this time, whether intentional or not, the change turned out to be per-manent. The problem represented by the decay of the Italian peasantry was suddenly turned on its head. The legions were no longer formed of reluctant conscripts from a shrinking social class. Enlistment became voluntary and open to all able-bodied citizens, including the large and growing class of *proletarii*, for many of whom army pay and a military career were attractive alternatives to unemployment and poverty. At a stroke, Marius solved the problems of recruitment, training, discipline and morale that had plagued Roman military operations for so long. He created a large army of long-service soldiers willing to campaign in distant theatres for years at a time, and, as professionals, to train, march and fight harder. He thereby transformed the army's strategic and tactical potential.

'Marius's Mules' they came to be called: because their general, deter-mined to increase mobility, slashed the size of the army's baggage train and loaded essential equipment on to the backs of the soldiers. It was now that the marching Roman soldier became – when he needed to be: when the army had to move fast – a pack-animal. Henceforward, in addition to wearing heavy tunic and military cloak, legionaries bore more than 20 kg of arms and armour, and humped up to 30 kg of equipment, including cooking utensils, palisade stake, entrenching tool, several days' rations, water flask, and personal belongings. Thus had Roman columns marched across 600 miles of North African wastes in the struggle against Jugurtha.

No less important was the abolition of the old distinction between *hastati*, *principes* and *triarii*, along with the division of the legion into maniples of 120 men. Instead, all legionaries were now equipped the same, with *pilum* and *gladius*, and the cohort, a battalion-sized unit of approximately 500 men, a tenth of a legion's strength, became the basic tactical unit. Legionaries were still heavy infantry, wearing helmet and chain-mail, and carrying large oval or rectangular shields, but, instead of being anchored in a relatively static and essentially defensive line, they were now mobile shock troops organized in independent units. It was the new Marian legions' combination of professional discipline, tactical flexibility and shock effect that had destroyed the northern hordes at Aquae Sextiae and Vercellae. The Roman army was fast approaching its zenith – and a period of military dominance that would last for 300 years.

But there was a political price. The soldiers fought for pay, and also, since many of the new recruits had no family plot to return to, an allotment of land to support them after discharge. They came to view their general as their patron (a conventional enough Roman view of the matter), and he regarded them (no less conventionally) as his clients. The soldiers looked to their patron to pay regularly and ensure adequate supplies while in service; to lead them to victory and bring them glory and shares of booty; and to provide farms and largesse at the end of their service. The general, for his part, found in his soldiers a powerful instrument for the advancement of his political career. One can hardly improve on the summary of the ancient historian Max Cary in 1935: 'In the riots of 100 BC, the most ominous feature was the intervention of Marius's soldiers. This incident revealed that the new army, which had proved itself the saviour of the Republic, might in turn become its destroyer. Composed mainly of proletarians without a stake in the country, and serving continuously with the colours for long terms of years, it gave its loyalty to the officer who enlisted and led it rather than to the Senate and People. The collision between Marius and the Senate over provision of land grants for his veterans also raised in an acute form the question of pay and pensions for the new army.'(8)

Rome's new soldiers were no vanguard of democratic revolution. A privileged special interest group, they fought for themselves alone. They would back the man who paid them regardless of politics. There was a foretaste of this in 99 BC. With political violence escalating, Marius broke with his new allies and redeployed his veterans in the cause of order. As Plutarch describes it: 'At length, when the Senate and Equestrian Order concerted measures together, and openly manifested their resentment, he [Marius] did bring his soldiers into the Forum, and driving the insurgents onto the Capitol, and then cutting off the conduits, forced them to

surrender by want of water. They, in this distress, addressing themselves
to him, surrendered, as it is termed, on the "public faith". He did his
utmost to save their lives, but so wholly in vain that, when they came
down into the Forum they were all basely murdered.'(9) It was the
Gracchi again, but now the agents of reaction were military veterans.
Though it was far short of full-blooded counter-revolution – Marius and
the supporters of moderate reform were to remain the dominant force
in Roman politics for a decade – it was evidence that soldiers, like the
urban mob, were loyal to patrons not principles. The next great crisis in
the history of the Late Republic would see soldiers fight as willingly for a
conservative dictator as a popular reformer. Here was the germ of the
civil wars.

A reactionary general: the supremacy of Sulla, 88–79 BC

Marcus Livius Drusus, tribune of the plebs in 91 BC, was not a populist
in the mould of the Gracchi; his father, indeed, had led the campaign
against Gaius Gracchus, and the son was an avowed supporter of senatorial government. Yet he took it upon himself to propose a law giving
full Roman citizenship to the Italian allies. When his bill ran into predict-
ably stiff opposition, and Drusus himself was felled by an unknown
assassin, the revolt of the allies which this eleventh-hour reform had been
designed to avert was finally detonated. It started at Asculum in central
Italy, where an especially arrogant magistrate provoked a massacre of
Roman residents. The rising then spread like a bushfire among the
Oscan-speaking peoples of the central Apennines. They quickly formed
a rebel confederation centred on Corfinium, complete with senate, mint,
political administration, army command, and a distinct identity as
'Italians'. One of the coins issued by the Corfinium mint shows a female
personification of Italia on the obverse, and eight warriors – perhaps
representing the eight peoples who formed the core of the rebellion –
swearing an oath of allegiance on the reverse.

Italy was at war. Broadly, the rebels controlled much of the east and
the south, mostly poorer hill-country, while the Romans held the west,
where most of their own territory and that of the generally loyal Latins
and Greeks was located. But this is to oversimplify: in many areas the

split between rebels and loyalists produced a complex patchwork of opposing allegiances, such that the 'Social War' (*socii* was the Latin for allies) was a war of many fronts.

At first the rebels were successful: the Romans had been taken by surprise, and their opponents moved fast to consolidate and expand the territory they controlled. While the hill-country was poor, it was easy to defend, and the Romans rediscovered the lesson of the Samnite Wars: that the Italian interior was ideal terrain for tribal guerrillas. A string of Roman defeats in the first year encouraged many whose allegiance was wavering to rebel, doubling the size of the Italian confederation and enabling it to put 100,000 soldiers into the field. Desperate to stop this potentially fatal haemorrhaging of support, the Romans took a moment-ous decision in 90 BC: they granted full Roman citizenship to all loyal-ists and any rebels who voluntarily laid down their arms. Those who had not already done so now lacked any reason to join the rebellion, while the resolve of many who had was gravely weakened by the offer of the franchise if they gave up. The Etruscans and Umbrians, who had been mobilizing their forces, quickly abandoned their planned rising, and the Romans, until now on the back foot against a spreading rebellion, were able to go on to the offensive. Separate campaigns were waged in central Italy, in Apulia and in Campania. The guerrilla bands were harried across the hills, and one by one the rebel cities fell. By 88 BC resistance was fizzling out everywhere.

Rome's military victory had cost the optimates a huge political conces-sion: the rebellion had revealed the hopelessness of continued resistance to the extension of the franchise, and victory had depended on granting it. Few after 88 BC can have doubted that all free Italians – including former rebels – would eventually be enfranchised: the long-term stability of the state and the strength of its army clearly hinged on this. Reformers had been arguing as much for half a century, during which time the anger of Rome's allies had steadily mounted. The war against the Cimbri and Teutones had put a particular strain on the loyalty of allies, with as many as two in three of Marius's soldiers non-Roman, and the general himself a firm supporter of the Italian franchise. But in the ten years since, the conflict between populists and optimates at Rome, swinging first one way, then the other, had repeatedly stymied reform. Years of frustration, of hopes raised and dashed, lay behind Drusus's failed bill in 91 BC.

So much was at stake: a say in political decisions at Rome; the protection of Roman courts; an equal share in war booty and land allocations; access to those in power and a fair hearing for pleas and petitions; the chance of a career in the imperial service; lucrative contracts for Italian entrepreneurs. Citizenship determined political rights, legal protection and economic opportunity, and the contradiction between the military contribution of non-Romans and their second-class status had become unsustainable as the empire continued to expand. Crudely, a bigger empire needed more soldiers, and armed men cannot easily be denied political rights.

But problems remained. The allies had been granted the vote. The impact this would have on Roman politics was uncertain. The state might yet be destabilized. The whole balance of power among the great aristocratic houses that dominated the Senate might be up-ended – with consequences no-one could predict – by a sudden, uncontrolled influx of new citizens; of voters, that is, not enrolled in factional retinues.

For more than ten years, ever since Marius, returning victorious from the north, had led his veterans into Rome to vote through Saturninus's land law, senatorial conservatives had been buffeted by radical attacks. Sometimes they had struck back successfully. The consuls had cracked down in 95 BC on Italians who had registered unlawfully as Roman citizens; and, as we have seen, it was conservative opposition to Drusus and his franchise bill that had provoked the Social War. Now, in the aftermath, the radical threat re-emerged greatly strengthened by the potential influx of new voters. The tribune Publius Sulpicius Rufus proposed a package of popular laws centred on franchise reform. First, the equestrian money-lending interest was accommodated with the proposal that all senators with outstanding debts above 2,000 *denarii* should be unseated. Second, the new citizens were to be empowered through a scheme to distribute them among the existing 35 voting tribes. This was a direct challenge to the Senate, for the original franchise concession of 90 BC had been neutered by the proviso that the Italians were to be enrolled in 10 new tribes – which, since the popular assemblies had a block-voting system, would have left them a permanent minority. Third, a new military command in Asia Minor against King Mithridates of Pontus was to be transferred from the conservative general Lucius Cornelius Sulla to the old popular favourite Gaius Marius. The political struggle around these

proposals quickly became, as so often in the recent past, a physical battle
for control of the streets as rival factions competed to pack the popular
assemblies with their own supporters. The Marians were successful, and
Rufus's three bills were passed. But matters were not allowed to rest
there. This time too much was at stake.

Sulla, the general divested of the eastern command, was an ambitious,
dissolute and unprincipled young aristocrat from a decayed family who
had first won renown as a senior officer under Marius in the wars against
Jugurtha and the Germans. He had since commanded with great distinction in Campania during the Social War, and had, in fact, only recently
left his army to return to the capital and stand for election there as consul. Sulla was not very political: his instincts were conservative, but his
ambition made him an opportunist. What turned him into a counter-
revolutionary leader was his hatred for Marius, his envy of the older
man's greater reputation, and the way in which his own chance for glory
– in an eastern war – had been snatched away. Sulla's reaction stunned
Rome. He returned to his army, appealed to the soldiers for support, and,
when they gave it, led six legions of Social War veterans against their
own capital city. The speed of this political and military coup destroyed
any possibility of effective resistance. Marius and many of his followers
fled before the soldiers arrived. Rufus and some others not so quick were
summarily executed. The fugitives were declared outlaws. Sulla's eastern
command was restored. To guarantee his position while away, Sulla
attempted to remodel the Roman constitution, stripping the Assembly of
the Tribes of its legislative power, and allowing the Assembly of the
Centuries only to debate matters already passed by the Senate. Sulla's
career was to be safeguarded by the hobbling of the popular party.

Then to the East in pursuit of glory and riches. The enemy, King
Mithridates VI of Pontus (120–63 BC), was the ruler of a prosperous
kingdom centred on territory along the southern shore of the Black Sea.
Its part-Hellenized population was governed by a dynasty of Persian
kings. The present incumbent was the sixth of the line and by far the
most ambitious and able. He had greatly extended his kingdom, first
occupying the northern shore of the Black Sea, then pushing eastwards
into Armenia. Soon he threatened the buffer states of Bithynia (to the
west) and Cappadocia (to the south), states which separated his kingdom
from the Roman province of Asia. Repeated incursions were beaten back,

until, in 89 BC, with Rome distracted by the Social War, Mithridates launched a huge invasion, sweeping through Bithynia and Asia, bringing his army and fleet to the Aegean. Many people, long oppressed by the officials, tax-collectors and businessmen who had battened on to Asia, the richest of all Roman provinces, welcomed him as liberator. Many, at his command, turned upon and massacred the Italian residents in their midst. There was to be no going back: the Roman Empire in Asia Minor was to be liquidated. Dizzy with success, still posing as the crusading champion of Hellenism, Mithridates then sent his forces into Greece. The pro-Roman oligarchy at Athens was overthrown. The Italian commercial community at Delos (the main centre of the slave trade) was massacred. The Pontic fleet established its base at Piraeus (the port of Athens). All southern and most of central Greece came over to Mithridates. Only now, in 87 BC, did Sulla finally arrive, landing in Greece with an army of five legions.

The Pontic Empire was no bubble. The bitterness accumulated over decades of Roman rule had fuelled Mithridates's campaigns. Corruption and extortion were endemic. Debate has raged over whether the highly publicized cases we hear about are representative. The most famous is that of Verres, Governor of Sicily in 73–71 BC, who was prosecuted in the Roman courts by Cicero. Verres was accused of every conceivable malpractice to enrich himself – tax evasion, appropriating public funds, accepting bribes, business fraud, selling honours, imposing extraordinary levies, and straightforward extortion with threats. He seems to have been the very embodiment of greed, and, moreover, to have been confident that bribery, powerful allies, the services of a top defence lawyer, and the traditional indifference of the Roman courts to provincial corruption would secure his release. He was mistaken: crushed by the weight of Cicero's attack, he fled into exile (with, however, much of his plundered wealth).

But how typical was Verres? We know of the case because Cicero published his speeches and these have survived. Probably he was worse than most. But a more moderate level of corruption and extortion seems to have been normal. When Cicero himself went out to Asia Minor as Governor of Cilicia in 51–50 BC, he found it 'in a state of lasting ruin and desolation' owing to the depredations of tax-farmers, money-lenders, and army billeting and requisition officers (who routinely took bribes from the richer towns to go elsewhere). The evidence emerges in surviving letters from Cicero to his friend Atticus. What is equally plain here is that the sanctimonious governor – 'I have bound myself to it [the province] by the principles of government expressed in my six books [*The Republic*]'(10) – was hopelessly compromised by his intimate relations with other members of the Roman ruling class – men like Marcus Brutus – 'the noblest Roman of them all' – who was deeply involved with a racketeering consortium that had lent money to the Greek city of Salamis on Cyprus at the illegal rate of 48 per cent compound interest. Cicero could have imposed a settlement; instead, importuned by Brutus's agent, he allowed the debt to roll over. Cicero lamented 'how hard it is to be good'. The truth of empire lay with the profiteers not the philosophers – a truth laid bare by the extraordinary success of the Mithridatic blitzkrieg across the East in 89–87 BC. Sulla – champion of the Roman rich – had arrived to fight a war for tax-collectors and loan-sharks.

Greece did not fall easily. Athens held out until reduced by famine in early 86 BC, pinning Sulla down in central Greece while two large Pontic armies pushed through Thrace and Macedonia. Tough battles followed at Chaeronea and Orchomenus, the Roman legions fighting defensively against the enemy's scythe-chariots and massed cavalry, securing victory on both occasions only through well-timed counter-attacks by reserves late in the day. The campaign of 86 BC opened a road into Asia, however, and the following year Roman armies pushed deep into Pontic territory, knocking aside whatever hastily assembled forces opposed them, and sacking the Greek cities that had sided with Mithridates. The king, having narrowly evaded capture, sued for peace. At the Treaty of Dardanus (near Troy), Mithridates accepted Sulla's terms, agreeing to give up all his recent conquests in Asia, surrender his Aegean fleet, and pay a moderate indemnity. These were, in the circumstances, easy terms, but Sulla needed a quick finish: the political situation in Rome had deteriorated alarmingly, and there was urgent need for him to return home. The king's former allies, the Greek cities of Asia, were less fortunate: first comprehensively plundered by the soldiers, they were then forced to pay an indemnity of 120 million *denarii*. Thus was Sulla's eastern war made to yield a handsome profit.

The counter-revolution of 88 BC had, in fact, been reversed as soon as Sulla departed for the East. The popular party had been scattered but not smashed, and once Sulla's veterans were removed from the scales, the balance of forces had tipped back in favour of Marius and his supporters. A short civil war in 87 BC had settled matters: the radical consul Lucius Cornelius Cinna, defeated by his more conservative colleague in street fighting in Rome, raised an army of newly enfranchised Italians and old Marian veterans in the countryside and marched on Rome. The garrison, weakened by hunger and disease, melted away, and the popular forces entered the city. The government was overthrown and its supporters decimated in a bloody purge. The severed heads of the executed were displayed in the Forum. Cinna, the new firebrand of radical politics, and Marius, the ageing war hero, declared themselves consuls for the following year. Marius soon fell ill and died, leaving Cinna virtual dictator in the period 87–84 BC. He chose Gnaeus Papirius Carbo to share his successive consulships, and when Cinna was assassinated by mutinous soldiers in 84 BC, Carbo succeeded as effective head of government.

Sulla's legislation was swept away, and power was restored to the popular assemblies. The new citizens were enrolled in the existing 35 voting tribes, making them the equals of old citizens. Generous debt-relief was instituted. The coinage was reformed. But as the regime consolidated its base at home, it lived in fear of Sulla's army in the East and of a resurgence of reaction when it returned. Cinna's government was authoritarian and unconstitutional not by choice but because threatened with imminent destruction by powerful and vengeful enemies. Though declared an outlaw, Sulla controlled the East, had accumulated a fortune in booty and indemnities, and led tens of thousands of veteran soldiers. An army sent out by the government with secret orders to relieve him of command had simply deserted. And now he was coming home.

Sulla landed at Brundisium early in 83 BC. Leading nobles quickly rallied to his cause, bringing his army to 50,000 men. Anticipating this, Carbo had organized a general levy across Italy, raising some 100,000 men, and these were further augmented by contingents of newly enfranchised Italians determined to defend their political rights. But Sulla was an experienced general with a bulging war-chest and a veteran army. The popular forces sent against him were destroyed either in battle or by a stream of desertions, and by the end of the year Sulla controlled southern Italy.

The year following, however, the fighting was harder: the new government legions had had time to train, and Rome's temples had been plundered to provide the money to equip, pay and sustain them. But Sulla – ably supported by subordinate commanders such as Marcus Licinius Crassus and Gnaeus Pompeius Magnus – outgeneralled his enemies in a whirlwind campaign which saw the popular forces defeated and dispersed in Latium, Etruria and the Po Valley. The last sizeable force – 70,000 men, some of them fugitives from earlier defeats, many of them newly raised Samnites – was crushed at the Battle of the Colline Gate outside Rome. The battle was bitterly contested, the Samnites dying to the last man, for the few who did surrender were promptly butchered on Sulla's orders. Residual resistance continued in parts of Italy – Etruscan Volterrae was not starved out until 80 BC – and major campaigns continued in Sicily, Africa and, above all, Spain, where the renegade Marian leader Quintus Sertorius was to remain in the field until 73 BC. But Sulla was master of Rome – and effective ruler of the Roman world – from the moment of his victory at the Colline Gate late in 82 BC. It was a victory tainted with the blood of massacre, and it heralded a counter-revolutionary terror of unprecedented ferocity: this time the party of the Gracchi, of Marius, and of Cinna and Carbo, the party of popular reform, was to be destroyed beyond hope of recovery.

Many of Sulla's enemies had perished in the civil war, whether killed in battle, in the sack of cities, or in massacres of prisoners. Now in Rome and across Italy, Sulla's death squads hunted down political opponents and murdered them. Soon, bringing system to the terror, the general had official lists posted up of the 'proscribed': anyone whose name appeared on a list – known enemies, those denounced by informers, some whose names were included through the malice of personal enemies or an accident of false intelligence – was declared an outlaw and could be killed with impunity. The lists, moreover, were regularly updated with supplementary notices, so that those whose names did not at first appear could not feel safe. Several thousands perished, including 40 senators and 1,600 equestrians, and their property was appropriated by the state and distributed as rewards to Sulla's supporters. Italian cities that had fought against him also had land confiscated for the resettlement of 120,000 legionary veterans. Pompeii is a famous example: besieged and captured by Sulla in the Social War ten years earlier, the city was remodelled as a Roman colony in 80 BC.

Sulla had himself appointed *dictator rei publicae constituendae* – 'dictator for the reform of the state' – in 82–81 BC. To ensure his reforms took effect, he then retained power as consul through 80 BC, before retiring from public life the following year. His power in this period – what Cary called 'the temporary monarchy of Cornelius Sulla' – was absolute, rested on military force, and was used to destroy completely the popular party and shore up the authority of the Senate. The veto powers of the tribunes and the law-making powers of the popular assemblies were drastically curtailed. The state-subsidized grain supply was abolished. Marian senators were purged and either fled or were killed. Three hundred new senators were drafted in to create an enlarged and conservative-dominated assembly.

A formal career structure – the *cursus honorum* ('course of honours') – was created for senators. First one sought election to one of 20 quaestorships at the minimum age of 30, success in this guaranteeing a seat in the Senate, a measure which helped maintain the number of senators at around 600. This was followed by the praetorship, with eight posts available, and a minimum age of 39; Sulla's increase in the number of posts from six to eight enlarged the pool of men qualified to govern provinces in an expanding Empire. Finally, for the fortunate few, there was election to one of the two consulships, for which the minimum age was 42. Sulla's purge, enlargement and reordering of the senatorial order were the prerequisites for the dominant role its members were expected to play in the new political order. As well as commanding armies, governing provinces, and directing government departments, senators alone – not equestrians – were to sit as judges in a series of new specialist tribunals that Sulla set up to deal with different types of crime.

Five times now – in 132, 122, 100, 88 and 82 BC – the popular party had been crushed in a reactionary coup. But the last had been by far the worst, and it must have seemed to the traumatized survivors a decisive blow. But the violence, avarice and naked illegality of Sulla's regime – a response to the depth of the crisis in Roman society – provoked a reaction. When the dictator retired and the terror ended, when 'normal' politics resumed, men found themselves outraged by what had happened and few, even among the most conservative, wished to be known as supporters of Sulla. Many had benefited and were glad to have done so, but, opportunists and trimmers, they found little advantage in any lingering association with the bloody tyrant of counter-revolution. When the politically ambitious looked about them, moreover, they found those great streams of popular discontent that had once carried Marius to glory still flowing strongly. Decayed noble families, equestrian entrepreneurs, upwardly mobile Italian gentry, debt-ridden small farmers, the mob of the city slums: Roman society was still a cauldron of discontents. Above all there were the soldiers – senator-generals, equestrian-officers, and the common citizens who formed the rank and file: tens of thousands of highly trained, tightly disciplined, heavily armed men. The army, Rome's instrument of imperial conquest, had always been the very essence of the state. Never more so than now. The crisis of the Late Republic had militarized politics. Armies had become arbiters between reaction and reform. Blood and iron determined history's course. This was the new reality. It would soon be apparent that at such a time the restored rule of the Senate had no secure foundation.

The rising sun: the supremacy of Pompey, 77–60 BC

'More worship the rising than the setting sun': so the young general Gnaeus Pompeius Magnus – Pompey the Great – is supposed to have said when comparing his own career with that of his former patron in the late 80s BC. It was the rival ambitions of the men who had formed Sulla's victorious civil-war faction that undid the counter-revolution of 82–81 BC. Sulla's response was world-weary – 'I see, then, it is my destiny to contend with children in my old age' – and the young Pompey was granted his desire: a triumphal procession through the streets of Rome.

'In his youth,' explained Plutarch, 'his countenance pleaded for him, seeming to anticipate his eloquence, and win upon the affections of the people before he spoke. His beauty even in his bloom of youth had something in it at once of gentleness and dignity; and when his prime of manhood came, the majesty and kingliness of his character at once became visible in it.'(11) By Plutarch's time, the later 1st century AD, Pompey had become a legendary golden boy, but even contemporaries had compared him – in appearance and achievement – to Alexander himself. After victory over Marian diehards in Africa in 81 BC, his soldiers had hailed him, just 26 years old and not yet a senator, *Imperator* (Conqueror) and *Magnus* (the Great). Pompey welcomed the acclaim, indeed revelled in it. Coming at such an early age it deepened the outlines of his emergent character: though dynamic and brilliant, Pompey was essentially shallow and self-serving, a man driven to great achievement not by high purpose but by vanity. One of Sulla's brood, once launched in life he quickly broke with a patron whose carefully crafted constitution was designed precisely to smother such politically precocious men as himself. Already famous as one of Rome's most successful generals, Pompey, under Sulla's system, would have had to wait four years for a seat in the Senate, 13 for the governorship of a province, and 16 for the consulship. Pompey, to advance himself, broke with the Senate and appealed to the People.

But men make history in the circumstances given to them. The ambition of its members may have broken up Sulla's faction, but Pompey's challenge to the authority of the Senate was possible only because the People offered an alternative way to power. The proscriptions had crushed the popular regime of Cinna and Carbo, but they had not settled the myriad discontents to which that regime had given distorted expression. Reforming magistrates, militant demonstrations, the packing of popular assemblies: these methods of change had been defeated by force of arms. But the chaotic swirl of interests that powered the Roman Revolution soon found another channel: in the ambition of a young politician-general – an opportunist willing to sell his aristocratic soul for popular favour.

It was a new military crisis – or rather a series of crises rooted in the empire's exponential expansion – that gave 'the rising sun' its chance to ascend. Huge and growing inflows of plundered wealth from the Empire had inflated the cost of competition for high office. Generals and their soldiers were enriched by war booty and slave hauls. The state coffers were filled by indemnities and tribute payments. Businessmen grew rich on tax-farming and money-lending, senators and their staffs on the bribes and perks of colonial service. Land was seized and parcelled up to make ranches for the rich and farms for veterans. The art market was flooded with Greek masterpieces. The beautiful coastline of the Bay of Naples – the ancient Roman riviera – was soon ringed with luxury villas. Pompeii became a boom town. Its art and architecture reveal much about the Italian elite in the age of Pompey and Caesar. What had once been a town of small houses and workshops became a city of grand residences and *luxuria*.

The owners of the House of the Vestals – recently excavated by a Bradford University team – absorbed two houses to the north of their own property and carried out wholesale remodelling of the resultant complex, creating an elaborate series of reception rooms around two peristyles (colonnaded courtyards). Such houses were decorated with an abundance of mosaics, frescos and statues. This was the age of Pompeii's 'Second Style' wall-painting. Fresco artists covered entire walls with highly elaborate *trompe-l'oeil* schemes, where depictions of architectural structures in three dimensions, often with gardens beyond, gave an impression of surpassing grandeur and wealth – in contrast to the austere simplicity of the earlier 'First Style'. *Luxuria* was the conspicuous and extravagant consumption of wealth as a signifier of rank, status and influence – of the ability to pull strings and do favours. *Luxuria* was about building a political base: recruiting the retinue of clients whose role as voters, canvassers, and, if it came to it, heavies for a street fight, was essential to political success. Hosting dinners in fashionably redecorated peristyles was, for the elite of Pompeii, a strategy for pursuing public acclaim and the honour of elective office. So too was the private patronage by which the public face of the town was transformed. 'Gaius Quintus Valgus, son of Gaius, and Marcus Porcius, son of Marcus, in their capacity as quinqennial *duoviri* [dual mayors in a census year], to demonstate the honour of the colony, erected this place of spectacles at their own expense and donated it to the colonists for their perpetual use'(12): thus do two of the leading citizens of Pompeii announce their generosity in paying for the construction of the amphitheatre on a stone plaque in *c.* 80–70 BC. 'Twenty pairs of gladiators of Gnaeus Alleius Nigidius Maius, quinquennial, and their substitutes will fight without any public expense at Pompeii'(13): here another Pompeian politician advertises the free games he is paying for on a painted wall-poster. Dozens of similar inscriptions reveal a whole town built and serviced by private patronage. In this, the local gentry of Pompeii mimicked the imperial statesmen of Rome – who played, of course, for far higher, and equally inflationary, stakes.

Conquerors returning to Rome would celebrate with triumphal processions, free games and banquets, and the building of public monuments and private palaces. Pompey's spectacles, benefactions and *luxuria* would eventually surpass that of all his predecessors, but his in turn would be surpassed by those of Caesar, Octavian-Augustus, and the Julio-Claudian emperors. Pompey's triumph after his return from the East in 62 BC, Plutarch tells us, lasted two days, the pageant representing the subjugation of 15 nations, the capture of 1,000 fortresses, 900 towns and 800 pirate ships, and the foundation of 39 new cities. The booty was commensurate, much of it displayed in the procession, while placards raised overhead recorded 'an account of all the tributes throughout the empire, and how that before these conquests the revenue amounted but to 50 million *denarii*, whereas from his acquisitions they had a revenue of 85 million, and that in present payment he was bringing into the common treasury coins, gold and silver plate, and ornaments to the value of 20,000 talents, over and above what had been distributed among the soldiers, among whom the smallest share was 1,500 drachmas.'(14)

It was from such hauls that Roman politicians built power-bases. One among many of Pompey's benefactions was Rome's first large stone-built theatre. A later marble map of Rome and the evidence of archaeology show it to have been a massive barrel-vaulted structure able to seat around 27,000; associated with it was a large garden with surrounding portico. Less permanent but no less politically potent were handouts, banquets and shows. 'Pompey spent some time in Rome before the opening or dedication of his theatre,' explains Plutarch, 'where he treated the people with all sorts of games, shows and exercises, in gymnastics alike and in music. There was likewise the hunting or baiting of wild beasts, and combats with them, in which 500 lions were slain; but above all, the battle of elephants was a spectacle full of horror and amazement. These entertainments brought him great honour and popularity; but on the other side he created no less envy to himself.'(15)

The inflationary cost of competitive 'political accumulation' – the building and maintaining of rival power-bases in domestic politics – meant aggressive wars of plunder, and super-exploitation of conquered territory. Military action was used, in effect, to redistribute large quantities of surplus wealth from native ruling classes on the rim of the imperial system to the Roman ruling class at its centre. Different sorts of evidence allow occasional glimpses of the impact on the subjugated. We have seen that Sulla's eastern war of 87–84 BC yielded – among much else no doubt – 120 million *denarii* from the indemnity payments imposed on the Greek cities of Asia. This, however, proved far more lucrative than it first seems, for the ransacked cities – they had already been comprehensively plundered by Sulla's troops – were forced to borrow to pay, and within a decade their compound-interest debt to Roman money-lenders had reached a staggering 720 million *denarii*. Pompey's eastern war in 66–63 BC appears to have cost its victims much more. If Plutarch can be trusted (mistakes in recording numbers are easily made, not least in the copying of manuscripts), then we seem to have the equivalent of £3 billion ($5.9 billion) in booty for the treasury, perhaps £2 billion ($3.9 billion) in booty for the soldiers, and almost a £1 billion ($1.9 billion) extra each year in tribute (*see* Note on ancient monetary values).

But that, it seems, was not the whole story. While Pompey used much of his own share to further his political career in Rome, he also invested some to ensure a steady income for the future. Cicero discovered something of this during his governorship of Cilicia in 51–50 BC. Pompey had lent money to the King of Cappadocia at a very high rate of interest, and he was subsequently being paid 198,000 *denarii* a month – though even this was not enough to cover interest, let alone pay off capital. The cost was passed on to local taxpayers: the peasants of Cappadocia. Our knowledge of this is an accident: it is mentioned in a surviving letter of Cicero to his friend Atticus. We have no way of knowing the extent of such practice. However, the debasement of the Egyptian silver coinage, the bullion content of which roughly halved between the 60s and the 40s BC, may well be circumstantial evidence for the overall level of Roman exploitation in the East. King Ptolemy XII Auletes is known to have borrowed and bribed on a massive scale to secure Roman military support for his restoration to the Egyptian throne after a coup in 58 BC. It is very tempting to agree with Michael Crawford, numismatist and ancient historian, and link the debasement with the corruption.

It is a common misconception that Rome brought peace and order to the world. The misconception is rooted in Roman myth. According to Virgil, it was only 'the proud' who were ground down by war, while 'the submissive' were spared to enjoy the benefits of peace, order and good government. It was the barbarian 'other' that threatened violence, not the imperial superpower. In truth, the predatory aggression of Late Republican Rome plunged the world into violence and chaos. It provoked an explosion of resistance across the Mediterranean in the 70s BC, resistance facilitated by Rome's victories over the Hellenistic states of the East. Once-powerful empires had been fragmented by defeat into a myriad of imperial provinces, client kingdoms, and carefully contained 'rogue states'. Rome did not yet constitute an effective suzerain. Its interventions took the form of smash and grab. The pieces left behind, the broken states of a disintegrating geopolitical system, could not always hold in check the furies of discontent and disorder aroused. This provided Pompey's opportunity. Vain, ambitious and self-serving, he now stepped forth as saviour of Rome and seeming architect of a new *Pax Romana* for the Mediterranean world.

The conflict raged across Spain, Asia Minor, the Mediterranean Sea, and Italy itself. In 80 BC, after Sulla's victory in the civil war, the Marian leader Quintus Sertorius had fled to Spain (where he had served as a provincial governor) to continue the struggle against the new regime. With a small retinue of Roman officers, he raised the Spanish tribes and sustained a guerrilla insurgency across the peninsula for eight years. Roman commanders found themselves in the coils of a people's war, facing hostility in every village, and the risk of ambush by numerous but elusive guerrillas whenever their cumbersome columns crossed country. At about the same time, fleets of pirate ships achieved naval dominance in the Mediterranean. Many men displaced by the political and military upheavals of the 80s BC found service on fast light warships that could be used to overhaul merchant vessels, raid coastal towns, and kidnap high-ranking Romans for ransom. King Mithridates regarded the pirates as potential auxiliaries alongside his own fleet – many were perhaps his own subjects, or at least supporters – and he offered them safe havens. The king had also formed an alliance with Sertorius, some of whose Roman officers were engaged to modernize the Pontic army. These hostile alliances and war preparations reflected Mithridates's growing fears for the survival of his kingdom, regarded by the Romans as the principal 'rogue state' in the East.

The crisis broke in 74 BC. Mithridates's allies in Spain and at sea were under heavy military pressure. Sertorius faced Roman armies augmented to 50,000 men pushing into the Celtiberian heartland of central Spain. The pirates lost most of their bases along the southern shore of Asia Minor to a systematic Roman campaign begun in 77 BC, and finally risked being driven from the Eastern Mediterranean entirely. The Kingdom of Bithynia, a buffer state between the Roman province of Asia and Mithridates's Pontus, was bequeathed to the Republic by the childless King Nicomedes III, a bequest the Senate readily accepted. As well as providing rich revenues, the acquisition threatened to bring the Roman army on to the Pontic border, and to close off the Black Sea entrance to Pontic trade and warships. In rapid response, Mithridates's remodelled army launched a pre-emptive strike and overran Bithynia.

At this moment, committed to major wars in Spain, the Mediterranean and Asia Minor, the Republic was suddenly confronted with a mortal threat to its survival in Italy itself. In 73 BC, in the South Italian town of Capua, some 70 gladiators armed themselves with kitchen utensils, killed their guards, and escaped from their training school. They headed for nearby Mount Vesuvius – looming menacingly over the *luxuria* of the Bay of Naples – and from here they raided aristocratic estates, freed the slaves, and shared out booty equally. As news of their exploits spread, others came to join them. When they defeated a detachment of soldiers sent from Rome, the trickle of recruits became a flood.

The number of slaves in Italy was now very high, perhaps a third of the population in total, and more like half in parts of the South. As well as working in mines and quarries, on public construction projects, in the arena and the brothels, and as servants in rich households, huge and increasing numbers were used to work the land. Replacing the free Italian peasants who had once voted for the Gracchi or marched with Marius, the slaves worked mainly on large and medium-sized estates formed from the absorption of failed farmsteads. Brigaded together, brutally coerced and overworked, yet often with vivid memories of families, farms and a life of freedom now lost, they formed a potentially revolutionary class. Though drawn from all parts of the empire, many were from the East, and the Greek spoken there became the language of slaves generally. Many, moreover, were educated, had worked as minor officials, or were former soldiers. Herein lay the rudiments of political and military organization. All that was required to detonate slave revolution was the spark of brilliant leadership. This was now provided by the trainee gladiator who had led the original breakout at Capua: a former soldier from Thrace (Bulgaria) called Spartacus. Within a year, the whole of Roman Italy was convulsed by revolt. Tens of thousands marched with Spartacus, from the Bay of Naples to the Po Valley, and several Roman armies sent against them were crushed. Rome seemed face-to-face with *Nemesis*. It had trans-ported millions of the victims of its wars to labour as slaves on Italian estates, and now the slaves had turned on their masters with bitter anger. The war had truly come home.

It threatened, moreover, to spread further and fuse with the struggle elsewhere. Marching south again in 72 BC, his followers having aban-doned the idea of crossing the Alpine passes and dispersing to their respective homelands, Spartacus made contact with the pirates, planning to use their ships to transport his army to Sicily and reignite the slave revolution that had burned there a generation before. Links were being forged that might have united Sertorius in Spain, the slaves of Italy and Sicily, the pirates of the eastern Mediterranean, and the Greeks of Asia Minor in a common anti-Roman front. The years 74–71 BC were among the most dangerous in the history of the empire. Certainly the crisis proved fatal for the senatorial government restored by Sulla ten years before.

It was the failure of Sulla's colleague, Quintus Caecilius Metellus Pius, to crush Sertorius that allowed Pompey to press for and secure a special command in Spain in 77 BC. Metellus and his army remained in the field, however, and the rivalry between the two commanders contributed to further defeats. Even after reinforcement, the war ground on for years, as Metellus and Pompey attempted to reduce one hilltop fortress after another. It was ended not by strategic brilliance but by treachery. The coherence of Sertorius's high command was weakened when the Senate passed a law pardoning most of the rebels. One of them then murdered Sertorius, usurped his position, and was then promptly defeated by Pompey. Quite suddenly, all resistance collapsed and the long war was brought to an end in 72 BC. On the other side of the empire also, the Roman counter-offensive was successful. Though the Romans were defeated in a sea battle with the pirates off Crete, Lucius Licinius Lucullus, appointed to a special command against Mithridates, destroyed the main Pontic army and fleet, recovered the territory that had been lost, and then invaded Pontus itself. At the Battle of Cabira he won another decisive victory, and Mithridates fled his kingdom to take refuge with the King of Armenia, his kinsman and ally, whose mountain territory seemed at the time beyond the reach of Roman power. By the end of 73 BC the threat from Mithridates had been greatly diminished, and Lucullus spent the following year settling the affairs of Asia Minor.

That same year, 72 BC, traumatized by the slave revolution at home, the Romans appointed Marcus Licinius Crassus, one of the richest men in the empire, to a special command against Spartacus. Conscription, hard drilling and brutal discipline – including the decimation of units routed in battle against the slaves (by which each tenth man was executed) – created a new army of ten legions (50,000 men). For six months the war continued in the South, where an embryonic slave state had emerged, in control of several towns and having official storehouses, arms factories, and tight collective discipline. But Spartacus found himself unable to supply his vast host once Crassus had closed off the toe of Italy with a huge entrenchment running from sea to sea. Breaking out northwards and resuming a war of movement in 71 BC, he was eventually boxed in and fell back into the mountains of Petelia in Apulia, threatened now by three converging Roman armies – that of Crassus, that of Pompey returning from Spain, and that of Lucullus recalled from the East: the whole military might of the Roman Empire deployed to crush the slave revolution in Italy.

Spartacus tried to break out again by seeking battle with Crassus before other Roman armies could join him. The historians record that the rebels fought with great determination, and that Spartacus, having killed his horse beforehand as a symbolic rejection of flight, died trying to hack his way through the mêlée to reach Crassus himself. His body was never found. The remnants of his army were pursued back into the mountains, Pompey's men now joining the manhunt. Some 6,000 captives were later crucified along the Appian Way, the road from Rome to Capua, where the revolt had begun three years before.

Pompey immediately sought further advancement for himself. This was far from guaranteed: his supremacy in the state was not yet firmly established. Spain had afforded him little glory: he had suffered several defeats, the war had been long and costly, much of the credit for such success as there was belonged to his colleague Metellus, and it was treachery that had finally brought Sertorius down. Lucullus, victor over Mithridates, and Crassus, conqueror of Spartacus, seemed at least equally meritorious. But Pompey had created a powerful base of support in Spain, where a network of client chiefs now worked in his favour, and he stood at the head of a veteran army that looked to him for pay, a share of plunder, and land for retirement. This army Pompey now led to within striking distance of Rome, at which point he issued a demand that he be allowed to stand for the consulship. Under Sulla's constitution this was illegal on two counts: Pompey was too young, and he had not yet qualified by holding more junior magistracies. More importantly, the Senate feared a new Marius, a general who championed the People, an advocate of reform who threatened property and privilege, a would-be popular dictator hostile to the power of conservative oligarchs.

The Senate, however, lacked an army. Lucullus had one, but most of it had been left back in the East. There was only Crassus, whose ten highly trained and battle-hardened legions might be a match for the Spanish veterans. Only Crassus might checkmate Pompey. But would he be willing?

That it should come to this was itself evidence that the Sullan constitution was all but dead. The oligarchy's powerlessness was apparent in its dependence on one warlord to defeat another. Now and henceforward it was reduced to little more than this: wooing, cajoling and bribing one senior general after another, each a prospective military dictator, the highest point of senatorial politics being to divine which of them was the lesser evil. At present it was Crassus in preference to Pompey. Later it would be Pompey over Caesar. Then Octavian over Antony. Sometimes the cynical opportunist whose favour was sought would judge it expedient to stamp his drive for power with the imprimatur of the Senate. And sometimes not, as now, when Crassus chose an alliance with Pompey instead of the Senate.

Crassus is a more shadowy figure than Pompey, his motives often difficult to fathom, but it seems likely that his natural caution inclined him to baulk at the risks of civil war – especially against Pompey and his veterans – and to prefer the safe option of a share in power. After all, both men were feared by their colleagues; not only was there the risk of defeat, but risk too in a victory which restored the power of the Senate and allowed it the chance one day to strike down Crassus in his turn. Whereas Pompey, also in fear of war, was willing to cut a deal: he and Crassus would stand for the consulship together, guaranteeing a combination of political power – of clients, of wealth, of votes – that would be unbeatable. And though the tension between the two rivals remained acute, their armies still in being during and after the election, the consuls did finally agree to demobilize, to reform the state, and to parcel out future high offices and honours between themselves and their respective retinues. Many features of the Sullan constitution were overturned. Senators lost their exclusive control of the jury-courts. The Senate was purged of many of Sulla's appointees. And the powers of the tribunes of plebs were restored. The events of the winter of 71–70 BC amounted in fact to an anti-oligarchic *coup*. Its principal agents may have been two rival politician-generals – suspicious and squabbling, each out for himself – but to secure their power they were compelled to weaken the Senate and strengthen the People.

Pompey aspired to a command in the East, and he remained in Rome until 67 BC, apparently awaiting the right opportunity. This came when the pirates attacked the ships that carried grain to the city. A bill was passed granting Pompey *imperium infinitum* – authority without boundaries – over the whole Mediterranean and all the coastal districts. With the right to levy on both the treasury and the tax-farmers, he raised a force of 500 ships and 120,000 men. Dividing the Mediterranean into 13 zones and organizing his forces into separate flotillas under 24 commanders, Pompey commenced a series of marine counter-insurgency sweeps that cleared the sea of pirates and shut down their coastal bases within three months.

A second bill in 66 BC then granted Pompey the command against Mithridates and his Armenian ally King Tigranes. Lucullus had returned to the East after the defeat of Spartacus, but his campaign in the Armenian mountains had badly misfired. The prize was Mithridates himself, an exotic eastern potentate who had become Rome's most intractable enemy. Lucullus craved the glory of his capture. Invading Armenia in 69 BC with a small army, he won a brilliant victory at Tigranocerta over vastly superior eastern forces. But tactical success does not always translate into strategic dominance. The following year, in pursuit of Mithridates, Tigranes and the remnants of their forces, he pushed deeper into the mountain wilderness of Armenia. His wily enemies lured him on, refusing battle, letting time, terrain and climate eat away at the morale of his legionaries. Finally, as the first autumn blizzards struck, they mutinied and demanded a retreat. Lucullus was forced to pull back, harassed as he did so by Pontic and Armenian guerrillas. His discomfiture was complete when Rome denied his small force reinforcement. Lucullus had become the target of a hostile political coalition at home – the loan-sharks resented his rescheduling of the debts of the

Greek cities of Asia, and Pompey had designs on his eastern command. Lucullus, who had crushed Mithridates and conquered Pontus, was recalled to Rome so that Pompey's sun might rise higher.

Pompey resumed the war with a much bigger army – perhaps three times the size of Lucullus's. With it, between 66 and 63 BC, he won a stunning series of military and diplomatic victories. Mithridates was again defeated and the last Pontic army destroyed. (The king escaped again, this time to the Crimea, but his attempts to renew the war from this base were frustrated by a revolt against conscription and taxation led by his own son; and Mithridates, blockaded inside a fortress by his own people, committed suicide in 63 BC, successfully evading his Roman enemies even at the end.) Pompey turned aside from the pursuit of Mithridates and quickly reduced Tigranes to submission. He then launched murderous attacks on the Albanians and Iberians of the Caucasus (66–65 BC), before being forced to pull back by an increasingly restive army. Other rich prizes soon beckoned. In 64 BC he intervened to restore order in Seleucid Syria, which feuding in the royal family had reduced to political chaos. Then, in 63 BC, he pushed on southwards down the Levantine coast towards Palestine and Arabia. Succession to the throne of the Jews was contested by two brothers, and both claimants submitted their suits to Pompey's arbitration. Naturally, the Roman war-lord decided in favour of the weaker, provoking the stronger to revolt, whereupon Pompey unleashed his army on Jerusalem, the holy city of the Jews. After a lengthy siege, the legionaries stormed into the Temple, the world centre of Judaism, cutting down soldiers, civilians and priests indiscriminately, and their leader then violated religious taboo by entering the Holy of Holies and profaning it with his unclean presence. Roman civilization had reached the Holy Land.

Sulla, Lucullus and Pompey had destroyed the Hellenistic system of states and created a power vacuum in the East. A new Roman supremacy was needed to keep the Parthian Empire at bay, to defend property and order, and to permit efficient exploitation of conquests. Pompey's 'eastern settlement' of 63 BC centred on the rich and heavily garrisoned Province of Syria, which was annexed at the outset and thereafter remained under direct Roman rule. Ranged around it was a penumbra of smaller provinces and client states, the latter retaining nominal independence but ruled by pro-Roman puppets. But the new East was not simply

Roman-dominated; it was also a personal fiefdom of Pompey himself. The region would remain his principal power-base in the years to come – controlled by his appointed vassals, milked of revenue to support his political campaigns at home, and a source of military manpower, *matériel* and supplies to sustain the Pompeian cause in civil war. Pompey by 63 BC had become probably the richest and most powerful Roman in history. His return to Rome was anticipated with a mixture of fascination and fear.

Pompey's special commands had been proposed by the tribunes and granted by the popular assemblies. His alliance with Crassus had delivered winning majorities. The Senate had been eclipsed in the years 71–67 BC. Afterwards, however, with Pompey himself in the East, the Senate had attempted to reassert itself. Ironically, the reaction had been led not by one of the traditional aristocracy, but by a 'new man' who was the first of his family to enter the Senate: Marcus Tullius Cicero. We know him mainly from the large corpus of his own writings that has survived – collections of letters and speeches, and treatises on philosophy, politics, oratory and religion. As well as being the greatest man of letters of his age, he was also a highly successful lawyer and a leading conservative politician from 67 BC until his death in 43 BC. From the outset a defender of the Senate, Cicero developed the concept of the *Concordia Ordinum* – the Union of the Orders – an attempt to unite senators and equestrians in a political bloc that would stand against what Cicero saw as the forces of disorder and breakdown: the warlords, the tribunes, the popular assemblies, and all those who supported reform. More clearly than any other Late Republican politician, Cicero theorized and articulated an ideology of senatorial reaction, that is, of the *optimates* (best men) who stood opposed to the *populares* (populists). In practice, however, the *Concordia Ordinum* quickly degenerated into political hysteria and a right-wing pogrom.

Cicero was elected consul in 64 BC in opposition to the popular candidate Lucius Sergius Catilina, against whose policy of cancelling debts (*novae tabulae*) the victor had run a veritable 'red scare' campaign. Afterwards, we are told, Catiline decided to organize a coup to overthrow the government, but his plans were betrayed, he fled the capital with some of his supporters, and he was then defeated and killed trying to raise an insurrection in the Etruscan countryside. Cicero, in this account, was the man of the hour. Acting promptly on intelligence received from informers, he arrested many of the leading conspirators, made the capital secure with improvised patrols and checkpoints, and dispatched the forces necessary to disperse Catiline's rebel army. This is the version of events presented by the historian Sallust in *The Conspiracy of Catiline*; and his version is essentially that of Cicero himself. Catiline, according to Sallust, had 'a vicious and depraved nature', delighted in 'civil war, bloodshed, robbery and political strife', and was possessed by 'an over-mastering desire for despotic power to gratify which he was prepared to use by any and every means.'(16)

Most classical scholars admire Cicero and assume the essential veracity of his account. In fact, he was a snob, a hypocrite, a liar and, as Michael Parenti has recently put it, 'a self-enriching slaveholder, slumlord and senator [who] deplored even the palest moves towards democracy'.(17) By dissecting the traditional account of the Catiline Conspiracy and exposing its numerous oddities and inconsistencies, Parenti brilliantly exposes it as a fabrication in which a hapless populist politician was hounded to death in a 'war on terror' directed at opponents of the Senate. In the fevered atmosphere engendered, senators ran for cover, supporting whatever repressive measures were demanded lest apparent weakness betray them as 'conspirators' in league with Catiline. First a state of emergency was declared; then the men arrested were summarily executed in the state prison; and finally the fugitives from Cicero's death-squads in Rome were hunted down by government forces in the countryside. *Cui bono?* Who benefits? This *bon mot* we owe to Cicero, who, though he did not invent it, made it famous by using it in his first big court case. The answer in this case is clear: the consul, the Senate, and the supporters of the *Concordia Ordinum*, now once again firmly in control of Rome.

Late the following year, 62 BC, Pompey returned from the East. Cicero hoped to enlist him as the figurehead leader of the *Concordia Ordinum*. The signs were good: in contrast to his behaviour in 71 BC, Pompey demobilized his soldiers, came immediately in person to Rome, and there respectfully addressed the Senate.

The honeymoon was brief. Pompey came to Rome seeking ratification of his eastern settlement and land allotments for his veterans. But the first would underwrite his power-base in the East, the second create a new one in Italy itself, and the Senate, encouraged by Crassus and Lucullus, jealous of Pompey's pre-eminence, and by Cato, fearful of the over-mighty citizen, put off decisions from session to session. Pompey let matters drift. Not so, however, one of the few powerful men to support his demands, a man whose career had also been stalled by the hostility of enemies in the Senate. An intelligent, dignified and steely presence in the swirling politics of the 60s BC, it may partly have been fear of him that had caused Cicero to hope that Pompey would lead the *Concordia*. If so, Cicero was right in judging Pompey the lesser evil. For the man in question was destined to become the greatest *popularis* of them all: Gaius Julius Caesar.

Crossing the Rubicon: the First Triumvirate, the Civil War, and the dictatorship of Caesar, 59–44 BC

Until 59 BC, when he was 41, Caesar's career had been unspectacular. A nephew of Marius and son-in-law of Cinna, he was closely associated with the populist faction in Roman politics, and, to escape the chill wind of Sullan reaction at home, he had spent much time in the East in early adulthood. After returning to Rome, he supported Pompey's coup of 71–70 BC, a political alliance further consolidated when in 67 BC he married into Pompey's family after the death of his first wife. He also became closely associated with another political giant of the 60s BC, borrowing heavily from Crassus to fund campaigns for election to a succession of offices – quaestor, aedile, *pontifex maximus* (high priest), praetor – culminating in his appointment as Governor of Further Spain in 61 BC. This posting involved both opportunities for enrichment, such that Caesar was able to pay off his debts, and a field command, which revealed hitherto hidden talent for generalship. But the higher he rose, the more suspicious and obstructive his senatorial colleagues became. For Caesar was no ordinary politician.

It was not simply that he was an exceptionally intelligent, charismatic and ambitious demagogue. Nor that his family connections with Marius, Cinna and Pompey placed him firmly within the populist camp. Nor even that his association with Pompey and Crassus, the predominant 'over-mighty' citizens of the 60s BC, showed him to be no respecter of senatorial proprieties. There was something else. Most Late Republican politicians were tractable. They were at root opportunists, open to compromise and realignment as the wind of favour turned, men whose worldly-wise cynicism meant that a deal could usually be cut. Not so Caesar. In him there was something solid, consistent and far-seeing that seemed to elevate him above the haggling of everyday politics. Caesar was a conviction politician. His ruthless ambition was wedded to a political certainty: that Rome had to reform, that change was inescapable, and that the man who became the People's champion, the man whose opposition to oligarchy and reaction was unflinching, might some day dominate the state.

What made Caesar frightening to opponents was his consistency. In the witch-hunting atmosphere engendered by Cicero's campaign against Catiline in 63 BC, for example, it was Caesar who stood up in the Senate to defend the rule of law against state terror. 'Those executions [the first by Sulla in 82 BC] were the first step that led to a ghastly calamity,' he declared. 'For before long, if anyone coveted a man's mansion or villa – or in the end merely his household plate or wearing-apparel – he found means to have him put on the list of proscribed persons. So those who rejoiced at the death of Damasippus [a notorious Marian] were soon haled off to execution themselves, and the killing did not stop till Sulla had glutted all his followers with riches. I am not afraid that any such action will be taken by Cicero, or in this present age. But in a great nation like ours there are many men, with many different characters. It may be that on some future occasion, when another consul has, like him, an armed force at his disposal, some false report will be accepted as true; and when, with this precedent before him, a consul draws the sword in obedience to a senatorial decree, who will there be to restrain him or stay his hand.'(18)

On this occasion, Cato had counter-attacked and rallied the Senate behind Cicero. The suspects had been murdered in prison without trial. Power had shifted – or so it seemed – in favour of the *Concordia Ordinum*. So when Caesar returned from his governorship in Spain three years later – richer and more famous – most senators saw no advantage in his further advancement. Nor in that of Pompey, whose eastern settlement had still not been ratified, and whose veterans were still denied farms. The three most powerful men in the state – for Crassus risked eclipse if he excluded himself from an alliance between Caesar and Pompey – were

PLATE 1 ♦ *Myth-history. The Low Ham mosaic in Somerset depicts a thousand-year-old myth that has the Roman race founded by the Trojan hero Aeneas, a story immortalised for Roman (and Romanised) audiences by the great Latin poet Virgil.*

PLATE 2 ♦ *Myth-history. Though the twins, Romulus and Remus, were added in the Renaissance, the 'Capitoline Wolf' is an archaic bronze that reminded contemporary viewers that the Romans were spawn of Mars and sucklings of the She-Wolf.*

PLATE 3 ◆ *Ceramic, and occasionally bronze, hut-urns were used to inter the cremated remains of Rome's 8ᵗʰ century BC dead. Presumably they show something of the appearance of the wattle-and-daub houses of the living – inhabitants not of a city, but of an Iron Age village.*

PLATE 4 ◆ *An Italic hoplite of the Early Republican period. Ancient polities were essentially armed bodies of men; military service was the defining duty of the citizen male.*

PLATE 5 ♦ *Temple of Hera at Paestum. The Greeks had colonised half the Mediterranean, but the city-states of the 5ᵗʰ century BC had morphed into the pawns of kings, dictators and warlords by the 3ʳᵈ, making them vulnerable to easy Roman conquest.*

Source: Corbis/Marco Cristofori

PLATE 6 ♦ *The quinquereme, essentially a muscle-powered ram, was the battleship of the 3ʳᵈ century BC. To defeat the mercantile empire of Carthage, and win an overseas empire, Rome had to become a naval power.*

Source: akg-images Ltd/Peter Connolly

PLATE 7 ♦ *Strategic mobility was the key to victory over lightly equipped, fast-moving guerrillas like the Numidians. Roman general Gaius Marius abandoned carts and made his soldiers carry their equipment on their backs: part of the growing professionalisation of the army under the Late Republic.*

Source: DK Images/Karl Shone

PLATE 8 ♦ *Coin of the Social War rebels. The revolt of Rome's Italian subjects meant a revolt by half her army that could have brought the empire down. The rebels were defeated – but were granted Roman citizenship.*

Source: The Trustees of the British Museum

PLATE 9 ♦ *Pompey the Great. The Late Republic was dominated by a succession of great warlords whose power eclipsed that of their senatorial colleagues and presaged that of the emperors.*

Source: Alamy Images/Visual Arts Library (London)

PLATE 10 ♦ *Luxuria (the extravagant and conspicuous consumption of wealth) became more socially acceptable among the elite under the Late Republic.*

Source: David Bellingham

PLATE 11 ♦ *The Roman Forum. Late Republicam warlords invested much of their plunder in monumentalising the city – building a downtown symbolic of slaughter and slavery.*

Source: Punchstock/Brand X

PLATE 12 ♦ *Cicero. Though a 'new man', he became the leading representative of senatorial reaction in the middle of the 1*[st] *century BC, attempting to build a conservative bloc against the popular forces behind politicians like Caesar, Antony and Octavian.*

Source: Corbis/Sandro Vannini

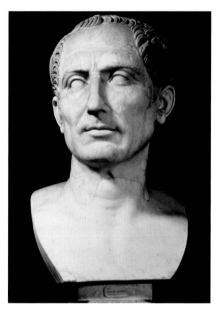

PLATE 13 ♦ *Julius Caesar, the greatest politician and general of the Late Republic, and the man who finally destroyed the power of the senatorial aristocracy and inaugurated the regime of the 'new men'.*

PLATE 14 ♦ *The siege of Alesia, 52 BC, was an apocalyptic climax to Caesar's eight-year conquest of Gaul. The war made Caesar the most powerful player in Roman politics – at a cost of a million dead and a million enslaved.*

PLATE 15 ♦ *Octavian-Augustus. A murderous civil-war faction leader is transformed into a heroic monarch in all but name by the spin doctors, in-house poets and court artists of the new Augustan regime.*

Source: Corbis/Roger Wood

PLATE 16 ♦ *Augustus's image-makers portrayed him both as a paternalistic 'father of his country' (wearing a toga) and as a statesman-like commander-in-chief who guaranteed national security and internal order (wearing a cuirass).*

Source: akg-images Ltd/Nimatallah

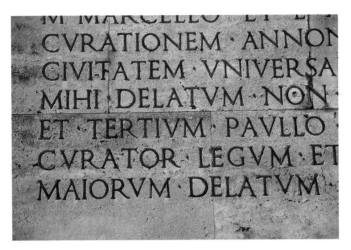

PLATE 17 ♦ *The* Res Gestae *– Augustus's political testimony – was inscribed in stone and placed on public view at various places across the empire. Today he would tour the TV studios.*

Source: DK Images/Mike Dunning

PLATE 18 ♦ *The* Ara Pacis *(Altar of Peace) in Rome is rich in political symbolism. Augustus, Rome's new military dictator, claimed to have 'restored the Republic'. Here, then, to make the point, are Rome's senatorial aristocracy.*

Source: Ancient Art & Architecture/C M Dixon

PLATE 19 ♦ *The* Ara Pacis *again, but now we see the imperial family, women and children included – the new power of the dynasty and apparently a complement to the old authority of the Senate.*

Source: Ancient Art & Architecture/C M Dixon

PLATE 20 ♦ *Behind a mask of constitutional rectitude was the fist of military power. The Praetorian Guard was stationed in Rome, and, as events in AD 41 proved, it, and not the Senate, was the final arbiter of power.*

Source: DK Images/De Agostini Editore Picture Library

PLATE 21 ♦ *The enemy within. Onto the floor of this room fell the debris –*
benches, tables, writing implements – of the first-floor scriptorium *where the*
Dead Sea Scrolls were inscribed: a call to revolutionary holy war against the
Roman Empire.

PLATE 22 ♦ *A Roman base in the Judean Desert outside the Jewish fortress of*
Masada, where the last of the revolutionaries of AD 66–73 defied the might of
Rome. Classical civilisation was sometimes bitterly contested by its victims.

PLATE 23 ♦ *Nero the lyre-player had laid out a pleasure park here, but the 'blood and iron' Flavian dynasty preferred an amphitheatre for the games. The Colosseum is Rome's Auschwitz: built for the mass murder of slaves as a form of public entertainment.*

Source: DK Images/Mike Dunning

PLATE 24 ♦ *Hadrian's Wall. For more than half a millennium, Rome had expanded. But the wilderness was unconquerable, and by the early 2nd century AD the frontiers had become permanent.*

Source: Alamy Images/Robert Estall Photo Agency

PLATE 25 ♦ *Temple of Olympian Zeus, Athens. Built by Hadrian, the temple symbolises the emperor's policy of constructing a commonwealth of the civilised behind the frontier walls he was also raising.*

Source: Alamy Images/Steve Allen Travel Photography

PLATE 26 ♦ *The ride turns. The Column of Marcus Aurelius in Rome has the form of a traditional victory monument – but this had been a war to eject Germanic invaders after the frontier defences on the upper Danube had collapsed.*

Source: Corbis/Araldo de Luca

PLATE 27 ♦ *A return to normality? On the Arch of Septimus Severus at Leptis Magna in Libya, the new emperor, victor in civil war, appears with his two sons, Caracalla and Geta, in a conventional scene. In fact, the developing 'military monarchy' represented a radical break with the past.*

PLATE 28 ♦ *A victory monument with a difference. The Sassanid emperor (mounted) receives the submission of the captive Roman emperor Valerian (kneeling) on a rock carving at Naqsh-i-Rustarn. Defeats were many in the mid-3rd century AD.*

PLATE 29 ♦ *The end of the* pax Romana. *Portchester Castle, a Roman fort on the 'Saxon Shore' – one of many new frontier defences built by the embattled empire of the 3rd and 4th centuries AD.*

Source: author's collection

PLATE 30 ♦ *Roman towns were also walled by the Late Empire – even as urban life within declined – turning them into the strong points of a developing system of defence-in-depth.*

Source: author's collection

PLATE 31 ♦ *A bureaucratic empire. The* Notitia Dignitatum *of c. AD too, with its titles, lists and badges of office, bears testimony to a bloated centralised state expanding at the expense of civil society.*

PLATE 32 ♦ *Theodosius the Great, the last emperor of a united empire, whose political authoritarianism and Christian militancy was not enough to reconstruct a viable polity.*

thus driven together by optimate resistance to their respective ambitions. What we call 'the First Triumvirate' was a secret pact formed in the winter of 60–59 BC, in which the wealth, client-retinues and popular appeal of Caesar, Pompey and Crassus were combined to give these three men unassailable dominance within the Roman polity.

Caesar was elected consul for 59 BC. His legislative package included confirmation of Pompey's eastern settlement, land for his veterans (as well as a large number of impoverished citizens), and a reduction in the contract price for the taxes of Asia (a measure that benefited equestrian tax-farmers and probably Crassus). The pact was cemented by Pompey's marriage to Caesar's daughter. And for Caesar? For him, at the end of his term as consul, there was the Governorship of Illyricum, Cisalpine Gaul, and Transalpine Gaul – a prize pregnant with immense historical significance.

Caesar's eight-year war in Gaul gives the lie to those, like Michael Parenti, who see the *populares* as champions of democracy. In truth, *optimates* and *populares* were equally committed to imperialist war and ethnic-cleansing; theirs was a squabble of victors over the distribution of spoil. On the evidence of Caesar's own testimony – his famous *Gallic War* chronicle – it seems likely that a million were killed, a million enslaved, and several hundred settlements torched. The people of Gaul were consumed in a military onslaught without precedent in their history.

Their land had been divided into numerous tribal polities, each dominated by chieftains, druids and warrior retinues, and ruled from imposing hilltop fortresses (*oppida*) girded with timber-laced drystone walls. Though highly militarized and placing great value on martial achievement, Gallic society did not engage in total war. The Gauls fought limited wars for booty, tribute and tribal supremacy. The archetypal form of Gallic warfare was the raid, the measure of its success the head of cattle rustled or weight of metal lifted. Rome, by contrast, was a centralized imperial state whose professional army was committed to pitched battle, all-out war, and the total subjugation of its enemies. When Caesar received his imperial governorship in Gaul, he was handed an opportunity to wage war against one of Rome's traditional and most feared enemies. Yet Free Gaul, in truth, posed no real threat to Rome. Nor did Caesar's claim that he intervened there to defend Rome's Gallic allies stand the test of time, for the holocaust he unleashed on this pretext eventually drove even the staunchest of former friends into bitter resistance. Caesar's war was not a measured application of force, but all-out robbery with violence. Gaul was heavily settled and farmed, and Rome's legions came for plunder – grain, cattle and horses, bronze, silver and gold, and the people themselves, taken as slaves.

At first the Gauls fought tribe by tribe, and so went down to defeat. Caesar's blitzkrieg expelled invaders from central Gaul in 58 BC, crushed the Belgae in the north-east in 57, and the Veneti in the north-west in 56. He launched raids into Germany and Britain in 55 and 54, and then shattered a Belgic rebellion in the north-east in 53. All the time, to feed his war, he drained his allies, like the powerful Aedui tribe of central Gaul, of food, fodder and manpower. Finally, traumatized but unsubdued, the Gauls united in a single struggle to expel the invader. Vercingetorix was elected supreme war-leader of a confederation that during 52 BC came to include almost every tribe in Gaul. The strategy he adopted might have won the war. Though his cavalry was first-rate, being formed of nobles and their retainers, his infantry was a tribal levy of farmers, no match for the disciplined, armoured, high-tech mercenaries of Caesar's legions. So Vercingetorix adopted a strategy of scorched earth and guerrilla attacks: he avoided pitched battles in the open, seeking the safety of great hilltop fortresses, while farms and grain-stores in the enemy's path were burnt, and enemy foraging parties ambushed. Roman aggression had conjured its alter-ego: an insurgent people among whom the exigencies of self-defence had engendered an embryonic Celtic nation-state under unified politico-military leadership.

The struggle was hard-fought. At Gergovia, with an assault on the *oppidum* bloodily repulsed, supplies exhausted, and the insurgency spreading across his rear, Caesar was forced to retreat. Later, at Alesia, he felt obliged to eschew direct assault: instead he had his men construct 45 km of siege-lines – with ramparts, palisades, towers, ditches, booby-traps and entanglements – designed both to bottle up Vercingetorix's 80,000 men inside the *oppidum*, and to repel the attacks of the anticipated Gallic relief-army from outside. When it came, maybe 250,000 strong, the relief-army was almost certainly the largest force ever assembled in the history of the Gauls. The succeeding four days saw some of the most ferocious fighting recorded in antiquity. For their last effort the Gauls mounted simultaneous attacks at numerous points on Caesar's lines, pinning his men to their positions and preventing them reinforcing those facing the main assault by 60,000 picked warriors. Again and again, in dense masses, covered by walls and roofs of shields, the Gauls came on. But each time the violent surge recoiled without breaking through. Then, as the light failed, Caesar led in person the counter-attack of his last reserve, and the Gallic host, physically and mentally exhausted, shattered like a pane of glass. The rout at Alesia sealed the fate of Gaul – and the triumph of Caesar, his army, and the populist cause at Rome.

These years of foreign war had been long years in the turbulent politics of the time. Much had changed while Caesar was in Gaul. His interests had been represented in Rome by the radical tribune of the plebs, Publius Clodius, who had built a following among the urban mob by such measures as a new corn law. Subsidized grain had been introduced by Gaius Gracchus and then abolished by Cornelius Sulla. Now Clodius reintroduced the principle but made it a free and regular handout: a grain dole for the citizens of Rome. Other measures included the legalisation of guilds (*collegia*), which facilitated the political mobilization of the urban masses, and the exclusion of conservative opponents, notably Cicero, who was exiled for the murder of Catiline's associates.

At first, Clodius had seemed to act as an ally of all the triumvirs. But he had created his own popular base, and when he clashed with the instinctively conservative Pompey in 58 BC, the latter had transferred his support to another tribune, Titus Annius Milo, enabling him to build up his own base of followers in the city during 57 BC. Clodius's supporters were attacked in a series of street battles, Cicero was recalled from exile, and Pompey was given a special five-year 'command' to organize Rome's corn-supply – an obvious attempt by the authorities to undercut the radical tribune's appeal. The shift to the right in the capital threatened the Triumvirate. Cicero was back and in some sort of alliance with Pompey. Milo's thugs were doing the Senate's dirty work in the backstreets. The populist cause – and therefore Caesar – was under attack.

Caesar, Crassus and Pompey met at Luca in Cisalpine Gaul in 56 BC to discuss the political situation, resolve their differences, and renew the secret alliance which, though shaky, still served them well enough. Caesar wished to retain his Gallic command: the war was only half won. Crassus obtained Syria and an opportunity to lead a campaign against the Parthian Empire in the East. Pompey received Spain, though he would choose to govern through deputies, remaining in Rome to over-see the corn-supply, maintain public order, and monitor the opposition. The arrangements were planned to last five years. In the event, it was only three.

Three events unhinged the First Triumvirate. First, in 54 BC, Pompey's wife died, severing the family tie that had linked him with Caesar, and hastening the growing political estrangement between the two that the clashes between Clodius's and Milo's supporters in Rome had come to symbolize. The second event occurred the following year, when, at the Battle of Carrhae, the first clash of arms between the Parthian and Roman Empires, Crassus was killed and his army destroyed. The Parthian army, with its roots in the Iranian steppes, was quite unlike anything the Romans had confronted before, comprising cataphracts (armoured shock cavalry) and horse-archers. However, the cataphracts could not break the solid ranks of Roman heavy infantry, nor could the legionaries get to grips with their more mobile opponents. The horse-archers were therefore decisive. After a Roman detachment was lured away from the main body and annihilated, Crassus attempted to retreat, but his column was assailed by clouds of horse-archers impossible to shake off. Resupplied with arrows by pack-camels, the Parthian bowmen destroyed the Roman army, killing 20,000, capturing 10,000, and taking possession of the revered Roman eagle-standards. By eliminating Crassus, moreover, the Parthians accidentally destroyed the balance of the Roman government.

The third event completed the Triumvirate's disintegration, putting the relationship of Caesar and Pompey beyond repair. Early in 52 BC, Clodius was ambushed and murdered by Milo's supporters on the Appian Way outside Rome. In response, an insurrectionary crowd burnt down the Senate House. For a time, a wave of violent disorder consumed Rome, and the government lost control of the capital. Though order was eventually restored by Pompey, whom the Senate had appointed sole consul for this purpose, the political tension remained acute. News of Caesar's victory over Vercingetorix, and his imminent return to Rome at the end of his term as governor, raised it further. What were Caesar's intentions now? With blood on the streets, what role would he play in the fraught domestic politics of Rome? For Caesar, by the end of the 50s BC, had become the most powerful man in the empire. Brilliant generalship in the Gallic War had brought him wealth, clients, glory, and, above all, a first-class army of some 50,000 loyal, battle-hardened legionaries. Would these men, Caesar's Gallic War veterans, prove to be the gravediggers of the Roman Republic? Would they raise up their master to be champion of the mob and king of Rome?

Little wonder that many in the capital were less than overjoyed at the news of Caesar's victory. A small hardline group of senators around Cato were in no doubt that events were fast moving towards some kind of decision: Caesar's war was now a mopping-up operation, and the great man would soon be back in Rome, more powerful and dangerous than ever before. Yet Pompey and the Senate majority vacillated, fearing Caesar's ambition, but fearing no less the chaos and risks of civil war if he was thwarted. Caesar, too, wanted peace: when ordered to surrender two of his legions for service against the Parthians, he let them go; though in fact they were promptly added to Pompey's forces in Italy. His aim was a second consulship and a new command (in the East?), and he sought an extension of his existing command to bridge the gap between the two and preserve his magisterial immunity from prosecution. But his enemies would not concede either, and they carried the Senate with them. A moderate proposal that both Caesar and Pompey should end their magistracies and demobilize their armies at the same moment was overwhelmingly endorsed. But this helped little, for still there remained the fact that it was Caesar, not Pompey, who was threatened with vindictive prosecution. The joint disarmament proposal ran aground on this rock: the hardliners persuaded Pompey to keep his legions in anticipation of Caesar's defiance, and Caesar, given the hostility to him, could not contemplate a return to Rome as a private citizen. The Roman courts were politicized and corrupt. Powerful enemies could engineer the destruction of virtually any man forced to face them. Caesar's only safety was a new magistracy conferring renewed immunity. This his enemies refused to grant.

On 7th January 49 BC, the Senate ordered Caesar to lay down his command and passed an emergency decree empowering the consuls and proconsuls – that is, the consuls and Pompey – to take whatever measures were necessary to defend the Republic. The Caesarian tribunes – including Mark Antony – fled the capital. Three days later, after an anxious hour of private reflection, Caesar made the decision to lead his army across the Rubicon, a small stream on the north-east frontier of Italy: 'If I refrain from this crossing, my friends, it will be the beginning of misfortune for me; but if I cross, it will be the beginning of misfortune for all mankind.' Yet his enemies had willed it so, and his officers and men, whose fortunes were so inextricably bound up with his own, would not have it otherwise. When he appealed to his soldiers, they clamoured their support. 'And speaking like a man possessed,' says the historian Appian, 'he crossed quickly, quoting the proverb, "Let the die be cast."'(19)

Pompey appeared the stronger contender. He had the backing of the Senate and was in formal control of most of the empire. The Roman imperial elite was overwhelmingly Pompeian in sympathy. Caesar was an outlaw and usurper whose regional power-base and army looked puny against the resources available to his enemies. The great retinue of self-appointed consultants who attached themselves to Pompey's head-quarters for the duration of the campaign – the Roman senators – was certainly convinced that victory would be easy. But Caesar enjoyed three advantages – advantages that would ultimately prove decisive. First, he was a brilliant strategist and tactician, one whose speed, aggression, mastery of improvisation and surprise, and willingness to take great risks in pursuit of great prizes would shortly transform the military situation. Second, his army of 50,000 Gallic War veterans was the finest fighting force in the world at the time. Third, this force was highly concentrated and therefore able to strike with maximum speed and power.

Caesar swept south to take Rome without a fight, herding Pompey and his as-yet inadequate forces before him. Keeping his soldiers well in hand, Caesar won general support in Italy; Pompey retreated across the Adriatic to build a bigger army among his eastern clients. Before follow-ing to confront him, Caesar secured his rear with a second whirlwind campaign in Spain (though his subordinates were meantime worsted in Africa, which became a Pompeian base). The following year (48 BC) Caesar crossed to Greece and advanced on Pompey's army, which fell back on the city of Dyrrhachium, its principal coastal base. Hoping to besiege and blockade Pompey's army, Caesar constructed mile upon mile of enclosing defence-works and hilltop redoubts. But he could not close the port of Dyrrhachium, and Pompey's army was sustained by seaborne supplies. Then, when the Pompeians, who outnumbered their oppon-ents, went on to the offensive, they broke through Caesar's defences and threatened to roll up his line. Caesar was compelled to retreat – eastwards, into the Greek hinterland, deeper into Pompey's vast eastern fiefdom.

Here, surrounded by enemies and threatened with starvation, Caesar's army might so easily have perished, victim of its own commander's relentless aggression and self-confidence. This, we are told, was Pompey's judgement: that hunger would devour the beast in a waiting game. But around him were the amateur strategists of the Senate, who sensed weakness and an easy kill. Pompey was induced to offer battle – the very battle that was Caesar's only chance. The armies met at Pharsalus in Thessaly, 35,000 or more Pompeians against 22,000 Caesarians. Almost all Caesar's men were legionaries, whereas the Pompeians were strong also in archers, slingers and, above all, cavalry, in which they outnumbered their opponents seven to one. For Caesar the odds were not good, and his battle plan was a masterpiece of improvisation designed to compensate for his disadvantage. The battle was fought beside a river, with one flank secure, so Pompey's plan was to hold Caesar's centre with his infantry while concentrating all his overwhelmingly superior cavalry and light infantry for a decisive attack on the enemy right. Anticipating this, Caesar's plan involved the extraordinary expedient of having heavy infantry charge cavalry. Ancient armies traditionally deployed their infantry in three lines. Caesar created a fourth, which was deployed at a right angle to the rest facing the right flank. His small Gallic cavalry force was also deployed here, its role to bait the trap by goading the Pompeian left into full-scale assault. The eastern cavalry surged forwards and the Gallic cavalry fled. But as the Pompeians thundered towards the Roman rear, they were struck in the flank by the 3,000 legionaries of Caesar's fourth line, under orders to use their javelins as thrusting-spears. Chaos and panic were followed by the rout of the entire Pompeian left. By this time the infantry battle was well advanced. Though heavily outnumbered, Caesar's legionaries were veterans, while Pompey's lines contained many raw recruits. In the second phase of the battle, Caesar committed his third line, until now held back as a reserve against the possibility of success by Pompey's cavalry. His fourth line meantime swept forwards on the right to assault the exposed left flank of the Pompeian infantry. Pompey's entire line disintegrated and rout became general. For the loss of 1,200 men, Caesar had killed 6,000 Pompeians. The fugitives, moreover, found no respite. Their camp was overrun by the Caesarians' tireless pursuit, and then a temporary refuge on a nearby hilltop was surrounded and ringed with defence-works: some 24,000 Pompeians promptly surrendered. Pompey himself abandoned his army and fled to Egypt. Here, however, he met his end, murdered by the government of King Ptolemy XII in the hope of winning the victor's favour.

Pharsalus was a tactical masterpiece and one of history's most decisive battles. The Pompeian cause was henceforward broken-backed. Even so, the war dragged on. Caesar pursued Pompey to Egypt with a small force, but the cavalier and partisan manner in which he intervened in an internal dynastic dispute between Ptolemy XII and his sister and co-regent Cleopatra provoked a violent response, and Caesar spent the winter of 48–47 BC under siege in the city of Alexandria. Relief came in the spring, but by that time Pompeian resistance had flared up across the empire. Caesarian *celeritas* (speed) was never more evident. First he went to Asia Minor to crush the revolt of a Pompeian client-prince in a five-day war (*veni, vidi, vici*: I came, I saw, I conquered). Then to Rome to confront and defuse a mutiny of returning veterans – including men of Caesar's crack Tenth Legion – disappointed by their rewards after Pharsalus. The following year (46 BC) he invaded Africa, where Quintus Metellus Scipio had raised an army of ten Roman and four Numidian legions. Caesar crossed in winter gales and immediately sought battle. He engineered a confrontation on a narrow headland near Thapsus, without room for manoeuvre or outflanking, so that his enemies' shaky infantry were compelled to face a frontal charge by Caesar's veterans. So confident were Caesar's men that they charged before the order was given, catching the Pompeians still trying to deploy; in the rout that followed the veterans gave no quarter and the battle degenerated into massacre. Ten thousand were killed, including almost all the Pompeian hierarchy. Marcus Cato, left in charge of a garrison, committed suicide when he got the news.

The final and most ghastly battle was fought in Spain, the oldest of Pompey's fiefdoms. Here his sons had raised an army of 13 legions, and when Caesar, with an army barely half the size, found them holding a strong defensive position on a hill near Munda in the spring of 45 BC, his decision to attack was a calculated risk: the Pompeians could not be drawn to fight on equal terms, yet the war would not end unless their army was destroyed. The Caesarians launched a difficult uphill attack and were soon bogged down in protracted and murderous close-quarters fighting. The line wavered under Pompeian counter-attacks. Caesar himself entered the front ranks to stiffen resolve. Before his men finally broke through they had lost 6,000 – the heaviest casualties of Caesar's career – and as their enemies ran, the Caesarian soldiery, driven mad by blood and fear, killed everyone they could reach, amounting to some 30,000 Pompeians.

Caesar and his men had won the civil war because they were masters of the battlefield. Their opponents were weakened by divided counsels, a dispersal of strength, and dependence on raw levies in Greece, Africa and Spain. But there was something more: Caesar was both conciliator and *popularis*. Magnanimous towards defeated enemies and solicitous of civilians endangered by war, he easily won the sympathy of the uncommitted. And wearing the mantle of the Gracchi and of Marius, he garnered strong support from that inchoate coalition for reform – the equestrians, the Italian municipal aristocracy, the city poor, the farmers, the newly enfranchised, those aspiring to citizenship, soldiers past and present – that had rendered Late Republican Rome ungovernable. It is surely significant that after the campaign of 49 BC Rome and Italy, though stripped of troops, were safe for Caesar: there was no Pompeian rising here.

Those, moreover, who had supported Caesar in the war were not to be disappointed. After decades of obstruction by the oligarchs of privilege, a raft of reforms was initiated between 49 and 44 BC: state regulation of credit and a reduction of debts; remission of rents; proper town planning and traffic regulation in Rome; a major programme of public building, including a new forum adjacent to the old; tighter regulation of the corn-dole; a succession of spectacles and feasts in the capital; a pay rise from 120 to 225 *denarii* for legionaries, and a huge bonus of 5,000 *denarii* each for Caesar's veterans in 46 BC; 30 new colonies for the settlement of 80,000 citizens and their families; regulation of municipal government in Italy; major land reclamation works in the Italian countryside; the enfranchisement of the Cisalpine Gauls; selective grants of Roman citizenship to many other upper-class provincials, and the award of 'municipal' status to their towns; reductions in provincial taxation. Pharsalus had opened a new era. The *ancien régime* was overthrown, and a stalled revolution burst into creative life, remodelling the Roman Empire for the centuries to come.

But there was no clean end. Caesar in Rome in the winter of 45–44 BC found himself surrounded by embittered, unreconstructed enemies. His constitutional position was, perforce, highly irregular. He had taken emergency powers as *dictator rei publicae constituendae causa* (dictator for the reconstitution of the state) for the duration of the civil war, but he could hardly abdicate that position now and hand back to his enemies the power to destroy him they had lost on the battlefield. His beleaguered government was staffed with loyalists – the Senate was packed with Caesarians, virtually all higher magistracies, including provincial governorships, were held by appointees, equestrians were welcomed to the highest councils of the state, and a burgeoning administration of minor officials was constructed. The Senate was sidelined. A parallel state structure formed alongside it. Civil war had created a military dictator who had usurped a position of dominance over his former peers in the Senate. To maintain himself, to reward his followers, to reform state and society, he was compelled to make his dictatorship permanent and create a government bureaucracy to ensure its effectiveness. A cult of personality developed around him – he was dubbed 'Father of the Fatherland', his head appeared on coins, and expressions of political loyalty to the ruler were already morphing into acts of worship for a god. He appeared to stalwarts of the old order a king in all but name, his pointed rejection of the hated title *rex* the flimsiest fig-leaf. On 14th February 44 BC, Caesar made himself *dictator perpetuus* (dictator for life), donned the purple robes of a king, and seated himself on a new ivory and gilt throne. He was known to be preparing for a great campaign of conquest in the East: a new Alexander was in the making, one in whose shadow all other men might shrivel. Such was not the Roman way. A month later, on 15th March, as he entered a meeting of the Senate in the Theatre of Pompey, Gaius Julius Caesar was boxed in by a crowd of senators and felled by multiple dagger wounds. He died in a pool of blood at the base of the statue of his greatest enemy.

A new Caesar: the Second Triumvirate, 43–31 BC

The Republic was dead but not yet buried. Tim Cornell has summarized matters well: 'With the beginning of the Civil Wars, the Republic, defined as the rule of magistrates, senate and people of Rome, was already dead.

Since 60 BC control of affairs had passed from the oligarchy to the dynasts, who were supported by their private armies and *clientelae*, and were constitutionally provided for by special commands which freed them from the restrictions of the system of annual collegiate magistracies. The oligarchy that Sulla restored had shown itself to be irresponsible, corrupt, self-seeking and indifferent, and no longer commanded the respect or loyalty of any significant group in society. The propertied classes of Italy had no confidence in a regime which excluded their leading men from senior positions and was unable to guarantee order and stability; the poor happily surrendered their spurious freedoms and ineffectual political rights in favour of individual leaders who depended on them for support and who consequently took care to supply their material needs. The position of Pompey in the mid-50s . . . already foreshadowed that of the emperors.'(20) To this I would add that the dynasts had been able to usurp power because the oligarchy's social base had been eroded by the expansion of the empire, the rise of new classes, and the consequent dislocation of the old order of state and society – changes which had engendered a revolutionary crisis. But because the dynasts at the same time fought for themselves – for personal power within the *existing* system – the leadership they offered remained inchoate. For this reason there was no clear break: the end was messy and protracted, and the Republic remained a wraithlike presence now and for a century or more to come.

Pompey, for instance, was diverted from the role of reforming dictator by his rivalry with Caesar. But Cornell is surely right to see the First Triumvirate as a transitional government heralding the end of the Republic and the creation of the Principate. Until this time, Roman politics had been intermittently shaped by the intervention of warlords, but, between bouts of open war, the politicians, the Senate and the *Concordia Ordinum* had retained a fragile grip. Never again after 60 BC. The highest point of senatorial politics henceforward was to choose between masters. The Senate, anyway, was transformed in the civil-war generation: many of the old families, some claiming descent from noble ancestors centuries before, were consumed by battle, execution and purge; the triumvirs filled the empty seats – and more (the Senate grew from several hundred to a thousand) – with loyalist 'new men'. An 'aristocracy of the robe', sitting by hereditary right, was gradually replaced by an 'aristocracy of office', men who had risen to the top through military and administrative service under the triumvirs.

Some men, though, could not stomach the subservience on which careers now depended. They resented the regal airs of those who had once been their peers; the arrogance of the sometimes low-born favourites and flunkies of the triumviral retinues; the shrivelling away of ancient nobility, of Roman traditions, of an ordered world where men knew their place, where privilege, property and power were safe. It was 60 to 80 such men, led by Marcus Brutus and Gaius Cassius, who had formed the conspiracy to assassinate Caesar. In its aftermath, there was at first turmoil, and some must have hoped to reverse the outcome of the Civil War. But they deluded themselves. As men adjusted and the new situation crystallized into alliances and blocs, it was soon apparent that the birth of a new order was irreversible.

First, however, the confusion, the fog of events unfolding. The Roman polity that Caesar's dictatorship had momentarily strapped together had burst apart; no one was sure what would replace it. Mark Antony and other Caesarian leaders, as eager as other members of the ruling class to avoid a repetition of the riots that had followed Clodius's death in 52 BC, at first formed a common front with the Senate against disorder. Leading assassins were even appointed to top posts. But conservatives feared Antony as the new Caesar. Cicero delivered a series of excoriating speeches modelled on those of Demosthenes against Philip II of Macedon three centuries before (thus, the *Philippics*). Ironically, it was the dead man who seemed to have bequeathed the optimates their strongest weapon. Lacking a legitimate son, Caesar had named his 19-year-old great-nephew Gaius Octavianus his adoptive son and heir to his estate. The young man thus became Gaius Julius Caesar Octavianus, conventionally known (now but not then) as Octavian.

Octavian was a complete unknown. Though his maternal grandmother was Julius Caesar's sister, his father belonged to an obscure Italian municipal family from Velitrae. Octavian himself was still in the East when news reached him of his elevation. Surely this youth and 'new man' suddenly cast into the storm-centre of Roman politics would allow himself to be guided by the great men of the Senate? So at first it seemed. Courted and flattered by Cicero and others when he arrived in Rome, Octavian raised an army in alliance with the Senate and advanced against Antony early in 43 BC. Antony, who had been conducting a half-hearted siege against the assassin Decimus Brutus at Mutina in northern Italy, retreated in the face of overwhelming force into the old Caesarian power-base of Gaul. By the summer he had raised a new army and resumed the offensive. He drove Decimus Brutus from Mutina and opened the way south to Rome. All-out war between the two Caesarian leaders seemed possible.

But Octavian's position straddled a contradiction and was unsustainable. He had raised an army in Caesar's name but was asking it to fight for the Senate against a Caesarian army. The soldiers were restless and their loyalty could not be guaranteed. Even if they fought and won, their victory could only weaken the Caesarian cause overall. And if they lost? There is evidence that Octavian was a physical coward. Certainly he was no general. He cannot have been sanguine about the prospect of battle against Antony's legions. He was untried. His reputation rested on his adoptive name alone. Defeat might extinguish his career at the outset. Above all was the simple fact that, because Octavian was his adoptive father's son and a Caesarian leader, he could not risk fighting a civil war within Caesar's party as the candidate of the Senate. Determined as he was to destroy his rival for the party leadership, he had been naïve to think he could achieve this in alliance with Cicero. In July 43 BC, therefore, Octavian took control of Rome in a military coup and revoked the amnesty for Caesar's assassins. He then made overtures to Antony.

Three Caesarian leaders, Octavian, Antony and Marcus Lepidus, commander of the Gallic legions, met at Bononia in northern Italy to form 'the Second Triumvirate' (though real power rested with the first two, Lepidus's most important role being to offset the rivalry of the principals). They then set about destroying their enemies. Three hundred senators (including Cicero) and 2,000 equestrians were proscribed and executed, and their family estates confiscated. A new cult of *divus Iulius* (divine Julius) was inaugurated. The empire was divided into three geographical zones, each ruled by a triumvir, but with Italy for the time being shared. Having settled matters thus, the triumvirs then prepared for war against the assassins Brutus and Cassius, who were raising a Republican army in Greece. The Caesarians crossed the Adriatic and marched into Macedonia to confront the Republicans the following year (42 BC). Antony and Octavian fought two battles near Philippi, the first against

Cassius, the second, three weeks later, against Brutus: in both the Republicans were defeated, and the respective leaders committed suicide; captured officers were executed, while the rank and file were incorporated into the Caesarian army.

The Caesarians had drawn back from a private civil war in order to crush resurgent Republicanism, first in a military coup in Rome, then on the battlefield at Philippi. Lepidus had been marginalized by events. Antony had achieved temporary dominance by virtue of his successful military leadership. Octavian emerged with his power-base intact but his reputation tarnished. His alliance with the Senate in 44 BC followed by his abrupt volte-face and the military coup of 43 BC marked him as an ambitious opportunist without principle or honour. He was also an enthusiastic murderer. The bloody purge that followed the coup was in stark contrast to his adoptive father's policy of clemency, and his treatment of defeated enemies after Philippi was boorish and brutal; so much so, Suetonius tells us, that 'the prisoners, while being led off in chains, courteously saluted Antony as their conqueror, but abused Augustus [Octavian] to his face with the most obscene epithets.'(21) Weak, untalented, immoral, self-serving, arrogant, murderous: all these words applied to Octavian, and it is astonishing that this truly disgusting man has been admired by a succession of ancient historians mesmerized by the image-makers of the Augustan regime. He was in fact one of history's bloody tyrants.

The triumvirs now reapportioned their enlarged domain. Lepidus received Africa, Octavian took most of the West, including Rome and Italy, and Antony became responsible for the East. If some final showdown between the two leading triumvirs was inevitable, it was postponed for many years by the demands and distractions of their respective spheres. The division appeared to favour Antony. The East was richer and it offered an opportunity for military glory in the resurrection of Caesar's planned Parthian campaign. Octavian's share seemed, by contrast, both unglamorous and dangerous.

He first had to find land for the settlement of 100,000 Philippi veterans. The anger of Italian landowners was successfully exploited by Lucius Antonius, brother of Mark, who raised a revolt against the land confiscations and other repressive measures in 41 BC. This turned out to be a misjudgement: Lucius Antonius was besieged and defeated at

Perusia, and the war merely demonstrated the strength of support that Octavian enjoyed in the West. Lucius's brother, moreover, felt obliged to intervene, landing belatedly at Brundisium to challenge Octavian; but the soldiers of the two Caesarian armies fraternized and refused to fight, compelling their respective leaders to come to terms. The Pact of Brundisium in 40 BC renewed the Second Triumvirate, which was now sealed by Antony's marriage to Octavian's sister. The division of the Empire was renegotiated and modified in detail. There is evidence, however, of long-term damage to Antony's cause. His brother had raised rebellion on behalf of Italian landowners. Octavian had championed Caesarian veterans hungry for land. When the Caesarian general Calenus died shortly afterwards, all 11 of the Gallic legions he had commanded declared their allegiance to Octavian.

For the next ten years, though, Octavian was preoccupied fighting wars in defence of Italy. Between 42 and 36 BC he was at war with Sextus Pompeius, the surviving younger son of Pompey (the elder had been killed at Munda), who was operating from military bases in Sicily. Pompeius's naval operations threatened seaborne trade, especially the corn-supply to Rome, so his suppression was a military necessity. But Octavian's forces suffered reverses and the war dragged on. Marcus Agrippa now emerged as Octavian's leading lieutenant and party loyalist. At great expense and effort he established a new shipbuilding complex on the Bay of Naples, where an enlarged fleet could be constructed. This fleet, reinforced by ships sent by Antony (with whom a further renewal of the triumvirate had been negotiated at Tarentum in 38 BC), finally brought Sextus Pompeius to battle off Naulochus near the Straits of Messina in 36 BC and inflicted crushing defeat. A second major land settlement was now necessary as the forces assembled against Sextus Pompeius were demobilized. Octavian retained a large army, however, and a campaign of conquest was fought in Illyricum (the coastal region of the north-western Balkans) in 35–34 BC. But ambitious plans to push north towards the Danube were soon cut short. Relations with Antony had soured, and from 33 BC onwards Octavian was preparing for a new civil war.

Antony's attack on the Parthian Empire – like that of Crassus – had gone badly wrong. Though the lesson had been learnt that strong contingents of cavalry and light infantry were essential, Antony had opted for a direct assault on distant Persia, bypassing Mesopotamia. As winter closed in, his army found itself at the end of a dangerously long and exposed supply-line, having failed to bring the Parthians to battle. The relentless attacks of Parthian skirmishers on Antony's retreating column in the winter of 36–35 BC decimated his army. His power was diminished at the very moment that of Octavian, after the defeat of Sextus Pompeius, reached its peak. Sensing his vulnerability, Antony entered deeper into alliance with Cleopatra, the Greek queen of Egypt. While it is undoubtedly the case that Antony – like Caesar before him – was Cleopatra's lover, it does not follow that the alliance between Roman triumvir and Greek monarch was driven by lust. Rather, Antony required Cleopatra's military support for his Parthian campaign, and yet further support after his retreat, and this was paid for in a series of political concessions (the so-called 'Donations of Alexandria') by which Cleopatra's empire was to include Media, Parthia, Armenia, parts of Palestine and Nabataean Arabia, Cyprus, Cyrene, Syria and Cilicia. These territories – a mixture of Roman provinces, client-states and prospective conquests – were to be ruled either by Cleopatra herself, or by the couple's anticipated son, or by Ptolemy Caesarion, Caesar's son by Cleopatra. The ancient historian Max Cary sums up the implications laconically: 'Had all these transfers of territory been carried into effect, the result would have been to form an empire within the Roman Empire, and in all probability to disintegrate the Roman dominions into two rival states. Antony's complaisance to Cleopatra, if not actually treasonable, might easily be construed as such.'(22)

It was certainly so construed by Octavian's propagandists. Antony was stereotyped as a Roman corrupted by the decadence of the East and emasculated by a devious seductress. He was the heinous turncoat in a Manichaean struggle between us and them, civilization and barbarism, the West and the Orient. 'Opposing them [Octavian's forces at the naval battle of Actium] was Antony; with him, on board, he had Egyptians and the whole strength of the East, even to most distant Bactria; on his side was the wealth of the Orient and arms of varied design, and he came victoriously from the nations of the Dawn and the Red Sea's shore, followed – the shame of it! – by an Egyptian wife . . . The queen in the centre called up her columns by sounding the tambourine of her land . . . Her gods, monstrous shapes of every species, even to the barking Anubis, levelled weapons against Neptune, Venus, even Minerva herself.'(23) Thus the Augustan court-poet Virgil.

At first, Antony's portion of the triumviral carve-up may have looked tastier. While Octavian landed the unhappy task of dispossessing Italian landowners to make farms for soldiers, and an unglamorous but expensive and difficult war against Sextus Pompeius's sea-raiders, Antony seemed poised for glory in an eastern crusade. But things had worked out differently. The Republican opposition had been crushed, and peace restored to Italy and the West. Exhausted, Roman society had settled into relative stability. Octavian had been able to repackage himself: no longer a murderous civil war faction-leader, he now approximated to the image being conjured by court artists of a patriotic and paternal statesman. His popularity with both the propertied classes and the common people soared. But what truly mattered was his military power. Control of Italy and Cisalpine Gaul was a decisive advantage: these were still the principal recruiting-grounds of Rome's army, and from here came most of the men of the 45 legions and 500 warships at Octavian's command. These men were the military embodiment of the traditional *Romanitas* he claimed to represent in the struggle with Antony. The poet was not far wrong about Actium. Octavian's forces were united by language, religion and ideology in a way that Antony's polyglot army was not; Romans were a minority in the eastern army, and their discomfort among so many exotic allies was to be reflected in a wave of desertions in the days and hours before the battle.

The final breach had come in 32 BC. Antony had refused to see his wife Octavia after 35 BC. He had married Cleopatra and become the Egyptian queen's prince-consort under Greek dynastic law in 33 BC. He then divorced Octavia the following year. Not until 31 BC, however, was Octavian ready to move; only then was he confident that his Italian base was secure, his forces large enough, their cohesion and commitment certain. Antony and Cleopatra moved to block an assault on their eastern empire, so that the civil war, just as in 48 and 42 BC, came to be fought in Greece. But the eastern forces lacked centralized command and a common cause. Mismanaged and demoralized, their fleet found itself blockaded in the port of Actium on the north-west coast of Greece, where it ran short of supplies and was weakened by desertions. Antony attempted a mass breakout, but in the confused and desultory fighting that followed, only Cleopatra, Antony and some 60 ships broke through; the rest of the eastern fleet returned to port and soon surrendered.

Octavian marched overland to the East – through Greece, Asia Minor, Syria, the Levant, and finally to Egypt. He encountered little opposition. Antony's empire was a façade without substance. Once master and mistress had fled, the peoples of the East had no interest in resistance. Octavian's march was a triumphal procession in which the new ruler showed himself to his new subjects. When Octavian reached Egypt in 30 BC, Antony and Cleopatra committed suicide. Their conqueror was then master of the entire Roman world. And, though people could not at first be sure, the civil wars were finally over. The Roman Revolution was complete. The Senate had been overthrown and replaced by a military dictator, a regime of new men, and a policy of conservative reform.

CHAPTER 4

• • • • • • • • • • • • • •

The *Pax Romana,*
30 BC–AD 161

The new order: the reign of Augustus,
30 BC–AD 14

Octavian returned to Rome in 30 BC hugely popular. He would remain so for the rest of his reign. He was the Caesarian leader who would prevent oligarchic counter-revolution; the military strongman who guaranteed an end to war and a new period of peace and prosperity; and the conqueror able to crush foreign enemies and extend the borders of empire. But his authority was a constitutional anomaly, his real power-base the army, and many secret enemies lurked in the dark places of the Roman state. The fate of his adoptive father was a chilling warning. Octavian's aims, therefore, were essentially two. First, to demobilize surplus soldiers, concentrate a trimmed-down army on the frontiers, and thus demilitarize society and restore normal civil administration. Second, to reward his followers, conciliate defeated enemies, and forge a comprehensive political settlement that would reunite, enlarge and strengthen the Roman ruling class. Achieving all this would take time. Demilitarization was the first priority.

The Actium army was promptly demobilized in Octavian's third major land resettlement – only this time dispossessed Italian landowners were compensated. It has been estimated that in Octavian's three land resettlements of 41, 36 and 30 BC, 5 per cent of Italian land changed hands, 300,000 families received farms, and 150 million *denarii* was paid out. The victories the new veterans had won over foreign enemies – Balkan tribesmen and a Greek queen – were duly celebrated the following year (29 BC) in three triumphs for the Illyricum, Actium and Alexandria campaigns. Roman tradition did not permit triumphs for victories in civil war – but nor would it have suited a regime bent on conciliating old enemies to have crowed over the corpses of Brutus, Cassius, Sextus Pompeius and Mark Antony. Even so, in 28 BC, there was a purge of reactionary senators, 200 of whom were ejected from the house – though, in contrast to wartime purges, none were executed or lost their estates. The approach was clear: the victors would reap rewards, the regime would consolidate its grip, but erstwhile opponents would not be hounded to destruction, and those prepared to trim their politics might in time find ways to prosper.

Still, though, the regime lacked any appearance of stability. *Princeps* – leading man – was the term applied to Octavian, a title without constitutional significance whose adoption signalled the ruler's anomalous authority. There were two successive attempts – in 27 and 23 BC – to clothe the dictator's power with legal form and give credence to his spurious claim to have 'restored the Republic'. It was the first of these that conferred the new name 'Augustus' by which Octavian was henceforward usually known, a name which, having something of the sense of the English word 'venerable', symbolized the makeover that had transformed the ruler's image since the mid-30s BC. But the first settlement soon broke down over its expectation that Augustus's constitutional authority would depend on his holding successive annual consulships. This was unsustainable: it burdened the ruler with too much work, and, by blocking the ambition of so many potential candidates, risked alienating the senators. So after 23 BC Augustus rarely held a consulship (though from 19 BC he had a special seat in the Senate *between* the two consuls). Instead he enjoyed permanent *tribunicia potestas* (tribunician power), enabling him to posture as popular champion, and giving him the authority to convene the Senate, present legislation to the People, and function as a supreme court. He retained, moreover, the triumvirs' power of *commendatio* (recommendation), effectively the right to nominate candidates for magistracies. In the provinces, his power took the form of *maius imperium* (greater authority) over the proconsuls who governed senatorial provinces, and *proconsulare imperium* (proconsular authority) in the imperial provinces (and, unlike that of all others, his *imperium* did not lapse when he entered Rome). The distinction was between old provinces with only small garrisons (senatorial), and frontier provinces where the bulk of the army was now stationed (imperial). Augustus's direct control over the frontier provinces – administered by governors who were his *legati* (legates: representatives with delegated powers) – meant that he was, *de facto*, the commander-in-chief of the Roman army. More than that, he inherited the Late Republican warlords' role of army patron: he was responsible for pay, conditions, gratuities, and retirement packages; and, in recognition of this, the soldiers on enlistment swore an oath of allegiance to the emperor. Augustus was a military dictator masquerading as an elected politician. The substance and the forms of power diverged. But for the present most men preferred not to expose this truth: too much was at stake. When, occasionally, the façade was breached, the perpetrators were promptly struck down. And when this happened, the majority looked away, preferring peace, order, a career, an easy life. Politics were privatized: no longer a collective struggle over principle and policy, they became a matter of court intrigue for personal advancement – a squabble over spoils at the summit of the enlarged administrative hierarchy.

The hierarchy's basic structure was not new. Augustus's aim was to gull adherents of the old order with a semblance of continuity. But Republican institutions, as well as being open to wider recruitment, were now subject to careful regulation from above. After the purge of 28 BC, the Senate's numbers were further reduced in 18 and 13 BC, bringing an unwieldy assembly of a thousand or so down to around 600. There were strict qualifications for membership, the most important being a minimum property rating of 250,000 *denarii*. There was a steady infusion of new blood, of men promoted from among the most successful of the Italian municipal aristocracy, becoming first equestrians, then senators. The Senate became a mainly (but not exclusively) hereditary aristocracy of office dependent on imperial patronage. The second-division equestrian order was also regulated. The minimum property qualification was set at 100,000 *denarii*. Formal career paths were laid out, culminating in top imperial posts, such as the two prefectures of the Praetorian Guard, the imperial bodyguard troops in Rome, and the governorship of Egypt, a new imperial province which senators were not even permitted to visit.

Equestrians also now enjoyed the exclusive right to sit in the jury-courts. For both senators and equestrians – and many others of more modest status – the number and variety of posts to which they might aspire grew rapidly.

Though incorporating much of the former Republican infrastructure and its titles, government administration was so streamlined and expanded under the emperors as to constitute something substantially new. The imperial provinces each required a governor, responsible for justice, general administration, and military affairs, and a procurator, responsible for finance; each had their own staffs; each reported directly to the emperor. Rome, now an imperial capital of a million people, was administered by 'curators' (curatores) or 'prefects' (praefecti), permanently appointed and operating singly or in boards, each in charge of a department – water-supply, sewage, the corn dole, fire service, building control, police. The men under their charge included seven 500-strong cohorts of paramilitary firefighters and nightwatchmen (cohortes vigilum), and three 1,000-strong cohorts of front-line riot police (cohortes urbanae); these were in addition to the nine 500-strong cohorts of Praetorian Guard, the elite imperial bodyguard troops barracked in the city. At the highest level were men who attended upon the emperor in person, whether as counsellors of the consilium principis (perhaps best rendered as 'Privy Council'), or as members of the imperial household, including many freedmen (liberti: freed slaves), who, though present in aristocratic households generally, in this case soon acquired a sinister reputation as gatekeepers of the ultimate source of patronage.

Beyond Rome, in Italy, the Hellenized East, and the more Romanized western provinces, local government was in the safe hands of the gentry, who were enrolled on town councils by virtue of their property-ownership. These decuriones or curiales (as they came to be known in many western provinces) formed, in effect, the third tier of the Roman aristocracy. Concerned mainly with security of property, the defence of privilege, and their own personal advancement, the decurions were a class of imperial loyalists who could be relied upon to collect taxes, maintain order, and promote Romanitas. The conservative bloc they represented was reinforced by the numerous coloniae – new settlements of Roman citizens – founded by Caesar and especially Octavian-Augustus. As noted, there were perhaps 300,000 farms owned by Caesarian veterans in Italy, the security of their land titles dependent on the regime they had helped to found and to whose defence they were therefore committed.

Even among the free poor, the regime, as far as we can judge, was popular. Peace meant that farms prospered and the trades picked up. There was work, a market for produce, a measure of security, hope for the future. In Rome especially, but in other towns too, there was much work for builders and decorators. 'I found Rome built of bricks,' announced Augustus. 'I leave her clothed in marble.'(1) The exaggeration is excusable: we know of scores of monumental structures built, reconstructed or repaired in the city during Augustus's reign, including some of the greatest, the Temple of Jupiter on the Capitoline, the Temple of Apollo on the Palatine, and the Forum of Augustus with its dominating Temple of Mars the Avenger. We have Augustus himself to thank for much of the detail. An extraordinary contemporary document, 'The Achievements of Divine Augustus' (*Res Gestae Divi Augusti*), has survived almost complete in the form of a stone inscription from the walls of the Temple of Rome and Augustus at Ankara in Turkey. Originally, no doubt, it was publicly displayed in many parts of the empire. In it, the emperor lists the offices and honours he held, his personal expenditures for public purposes, and his deeds in war and peace. It amounts to a comprehensive political testament. It is mainly from the *Res Gestae*, for instance, that we learn that Augustan Rome was a city not only of great building projects, but also of handouts and spectacles. 'To the Roman plebs I paid 300 sesterces apiece in accordance with the will of my father . . . I paid out of my own patrimony a largesse of 400 sesterces to every individual . . . These largesses of mine reached never less than 250,000 persons . . . I gave a gladiatorial show three times in my own name, and five times in the names of my sons or grandsons . . . Twice I presented in my own name an exhibition of athletes invited from all parts of the world . . . Twenty-six times I provided for the people hunting spectacles of African wild beasts in the Circus, the Forum, or the amphitheatres, in which about 3,500 animals were killed . . .'(2) Work, bread and shows were the Augustan recipe for a compliant mob.

More than any of these groups, however – more than senators, equestrians, civil servants, decurions, veterans, farmers, the mob – the regime depended on its soldiers. The army was trimmed down to a permanent force of 28 (later 25) legions, each around 5,000 men, formed of long-service professionals, all of them Roman citizens. Each legion was divided into ten cohorts, and each cohort into six centuries, such that the basic tactical sub-unit was a century of 80 heavy infantry commanded by a centurion. Each legion also had a small cavalry unit for reconnaissance and communications, and strong field artillery, perhaps 60 light arrow-shooters, and 10 heavier stone-throwers. As well as approximately 125,000 legionaries, there were roughly equal numbers of auxiliaries, non-citizen troops of the kind traditionally raised from Rome's allies as cavalry, light infantry, and other specialists, but now organized as regulars and integrated into the standing army. Legionaries served for 20 years and enjoyed good pay and conditions of service; upon retirement they received grants of land or money generous enough to set them up as substantial members of the communities where they settled. Auxiliary service also offered good pay and conditions, plus, on completion of 25 years' service, the grant of Roman citizenship, a highly coveted privilege.

Half or more of the state's tax revenue was expended on the army. Much of the private wealth of the emperor – the profits of civil war now organized as a vast imperial estate – went to supplement this. The soldiers regarded the emperor as their commander-in-chief, swore allegiance to him, and remained deeply loyal as long as he remained an effective patron, a provider of pay, perks and pensions. At the core of the empire, then, was a state-army nexus of power. This was fuelled by a 'tax-pay cycle', in which the decurions of a thousand towns collected the local taxes across the empire, the state redistributed the revenues as payments to the army, and the soldiers spent their wages and thus pumped money back into the civil economy. The state-army nexus and the tax-pay cycle were essential characteristics of the Roman state between the 1st and 5th centuries AD.

Augustus stationed almost the whole of his army in the frontier provinces. For much of his reign the soldiers were engaged in the greatest campaigns of conquest in Roman history. In terms of territory won, Augustus was Rome's foremost empire-builder. The turmoil of the Late Republic had brought the expansionist dynamic that powered Roman society to a peak as successive warlords competed to accumulate plundered wealth through military victory. Augustus, in this respect, stood in the line of Marius, Sulla, Pompey and Caesar. The cost of populism had, in this time, become heavily inflated. In chapters 15–17 of the *Res Gestae* Augustus listed some of the staggering sums paid out in his reign: 280 million *denarii* in gratuities to citizens and soldiers; 215 million *denarii* in compensation to landowners for veteran settlements; 80 million *denarii* in subventions from the emperor's private resources to state coffers. These sums alone are equivalent to the wealth of 2,300 senators. Many other expenditures are listed in the *Res Gestae*, such as the 15 major construction projects recorded in chapter 19, and the 82 temples repaired in chapter 20. This unprecedented largesse could be paid for only by permanent war. Imperial expansion was, in any case, central to the regime's ideology. Its supporters had heady expectations of further glory and conquest. As Virgil explained, Rome's mission was to rule the world. The Augustan regime – a regime that trumpeted commitment to peace – was underwritten by sustained imperial violence.

Illyricum had been conquered in 35–34 BC, securing Italy's northeast frontier, and providing a firm launch-pad for subsequent Roman advances across the Balkans and towards the Danube. Egypt was annexed in 30 BC. The royal treasures were carted off immediately to pay Octavian's war-debts, and grain and tax began to flow from the land of the pharaohs to the Rome of the emperors. Thrace and Moesia (modern Bulgaria) were overrun in 29–28 BC, bringing the Roman frontier to the lower Danube. Augustus undertook a grand tour of Gaul and Spain in 27–26 BC, and a renewal of Caesar's stalled attack on Britain was openly canvassed. Instead, however, the focus shifted to Spain, where between 26 and 19 BC the conquest of the peninsula was completed, with the north finally subjugated and a new legionary base established at Leon, bringing to an end 200 years of Roman military operations against the Celtiberian tribes. Meantime, in 25 BC, the Salassi were crushed on Italy's north-western border, and Roman communications across the Alps to Gaul made safe. Armed diplomacy in the East secured peace with Parthia in 20 BC, symbolized by the much-acclaimed return of standards captured at Carrhae 30 years before. The northern frontier was extended to the upper Danube to create the provinces of Noricum and Raetia in 17–15 BC. The strategic offensive then reached its peak in the years 13 to 7 BC, with simultaneous invasions of Pannonia, to complete the subjugation of the Balkans, of Germany, conquered as far east as the Elbe, and of Moesia and Thrace, where a major rebellion had broken out. Facing massive armies commanded by the greatest soldiers of the age – Augustus's two stepsons, Tiberius in Pannonia, Drusus in Germany – the resistance of Rome's barbarian enemies wilted under the onslaught. Such huge territories were overrun in this final push that by 7 BC Augustus had doubled the size of the empire. Five hundred years of Roman imperialism had been brought to an extraordinary climax. The heady claims of Augustan propaganda seemed fully vindicated, both at home and abroad.

The culture of the Augustan Age has been admired for centuries. The Forum of Augustus, the *Ara Pacis* sculptures, and the poetry of Horace, Ovid and Virgil represent pinnacles of achievement. But richness of form cannot compensate for poverty of content. Augustan art served dictatorship and empire. Its themes are the vacuous propaganda messages of power. A cult of personality was constructed around the ruler, portrayed sometimes as a reincarnation of Aeneas or Romulus, legendary founders of nation and city, sometimes as *Pater Patriae*, the benevolent 'Father of His Country', sometimes as *imperator*, army commander and world conqueror. 'I received the title of Augustus by decree of the Senate,' the dictator proclaims, 'and the doorposts of my house were publicly decked with laurels, the civic crown was fixed over my doorway, and a golden shield was set up in the Julian Senate House, which, as the inscription on this shield testifies, the Roman Senate and People gave me in recognition of my valour, clemency, justice and devotion.'(3) National rebirth was a recurring motif – a new beginning after decades of discord and civil war. Traditional cults and values were revamped – the regime represented a return to the past, to the good old days of a Republic based on courage, duty and piety. The message was that the revolution was over: nobility could breathe easy, secure again in its privileges; the Augustan aristocracy of 'new men' now enthusiastically embraced the ancient aristocracy of blood; all could unite to advance the cause of Roman civilization against northern barbarians and oriental despots. On the *Ara Pacis* (Altar of Peace) sculptures, the imperial family and friends appear on the south frieze, the magistrates, senators and priests of Rome on the north, new regime and old nobility thus symbolically joined. Aeneas and Romulus, mythic and metaphoric forebears of Augustus, are depicted on the west panel, female personifications of Rome and Italy amid images of abundance on the east. In the niches of the colonnades in the Forum of Augustus were statues of Roman heroes, great figures from Republican history down one side, the ancestors of the Caesars down the other. Towering over them on the far side of the piazza was the Temple of Mars the Avenger, erected to celebrate the defeat of Caesar's assassins, men who are thus, by the victors' disingenuous implication, portrayed as wickedly bent on destroying the harmony of the state. If form alone is the criterion, much Augustan art is stunning. If content be the measure, it is a gallery of empty-headed propaganda.

But as Augustus approached his final decline, *Nemesis* struck. In AD 6 the Pannonians, crushed by the might of Tiberius's army in 12–9 BC, then crippled by military requisitions, rose in revolt. The Illyrians, conquered in 35–34 BC, immediately joined them. The occupation forces were wiped out, and Italy was threatened with invasion. Troops had to be redeployed from Germany, and only when Roman strength reached perhaps 100,000 men was it possible for the empire to go on to the offensive. Though the revolt in the Balkans had been defeated by AD 9, the weakening of the garrison in Germany necessary to achieve this proved fatal. To replace Tiberius and Drusus in Germany during the Balkan war, Augustus had appointed Publius Quintilius Varus, a man without experience of the country, who attempted to consolidate imperial control by imposing taxation and Roman jurisdiction on the recently conquered inhabitants. A young chieftain of the Cherusci tribe called Arminius, who had served as an auxiliary in the Roman army and been granted citizenship and equestrian status, was elected to lead a revolt. Varus and his three legions were lured into the Teutoburg Forest, where they were ambushed and destroyed by an army of German tribesmen. Some 25,000 soldiers perished with their commander, 10 per cent of the Roman imperial army, leaving a gaping hole in the empire's frontier defences. It was Rome's worst defeat since Carrhae in 53 BC, and the worst at the hands of northern barbarians since Arausio in 105 BC.

Suddenly the regime looked terribly fragile. When the news reached Rome, the Praetorian Guard was ordered on to the streets as precaution against any attempted coup. Provincial governors were retained in their posts so that the empire remained in the hands of proven loyalists. Special games were celebrated in honour of Jupiter to assuage divine anger and divert the mob. 'Indeed,' relates Suetonius in his biography of Augustus, 'it is said that he took the disaster so deeply to heart that he left his hair and beard untrimmed for months, and would often beat his head on a door, shouting, "Quintilius Varus, give me back my legions!"; and he always kept the anniversary as a day of deep mourning.'(4)

Augustus' reaction, if accurately reported, reflected the gravity of the defeat. The army had been pared down to the barest minimum needed to guard the thousands of miles of the empire's frontiers, and yet its strategy had remained relentlessly offensive, with tens of thousands of men engaged year-on-year in new wars of conquest. Demilitarization had been essential, both to reassure the ruling class that stability and normal government had been restored, and to cut costs and release funds for regime-building largesse. The consequent army reductions had left the empire without a strategic reserve, while the ideology of the regime and the expectations of its supporters – not least the all-important professional officer class – had propelled it into an unbroken succession of military adventures. The result was that the empire was militarily overextended, such that, because it lacked reserves, one major tactical defeat risked strategic disaster. It was fortunate, indeed, that Arminius's German host broke up after victory. The Germans were content to have destroyed their enemies, freed themselves of tax-collectors, and returned home rich in plunder. But Rome could not risk another Teutoburg Forest. Augustus halted offensive operations on all fronts. His successor – ironically the great soldier Tiberius – would maintain this policy. Not before AD 43 would the empire again mount a major military offensive. Even then, the invasion of Britain was an exceptional event, not the start of a new trend. In AD 9 the great epoch of Roman imperial expansion came to an end. The Empire, a product of 500 years of conquest, its size doubled in the 50 years of history dominated by Octavian-Augustus, would thereafter hardly grow at all. Here was a transformation of the greatest historical significance: AD 9 was nothing less than the central pivot on which the whole history of Rome turned. The empire had risen to its highest point. From this moment on, its historical trajectory flattened out. It ceased to expand. It had reached its limits. And in the course of time it would be revealed that the glory days were over for good, and that Rome was heading towards decline, fragmentation, and the eventual collapse of the Western Empire.

The limits of power: the Julio-Claudian emperors, AD 14–68

Power is never absolute. The Roman emperors were among the most powerful rulers in history, yet the survival of their regimes depended upon successful management of a complex of contradictory pressures. Often their position at the summit of the political order was precarious. Occasionally they were toppled. And the last of the Julio-Claudians so mismanaged the politics of empire that the dynasty was destroyed in civil war.

Not least among the problems was the succession. The army was the basis of power and could, if it chose, intervene to decide who should wield it; without a clear succession, therefore, the danger was that a dispute between rival candidates might lead to civil war. There was, of course, no constitutional precedent for succession to the Principate. Rome under the emperors was not an hereditary monarchy. The forms of power were still those of the Republic: ostensibly the 'leading man' received his authority from the Senate, and in theory any man could succeed him (or, indeed, none at all). In practice, however, the hereditary principle was strongly developed at the outset. It was helped by the common Roman belief that personal qualities could be inherited, such that ancestry and family were considered strong arguments for preferment. Of perhaps greater value was inheritance of the emperor's personal fortune and estate, making the prospective successor the richest man in the empire. If no natural son was available, the heir, in established Roman tradition, might be adopted, as Octavian had been by Julius Caesar. Either way, he would be advanced rapidly through a series of senior posts to gain appropriate experience and public recognition.

Augustus, whose health was poor, was preoccupied by the succession throughout his reign, advancing a series of candidates, all of whom save the last (reluctant) choice predeceased him. The emperor had no son of his own, but for many years personal antipathy prevented him supporting his stepson Tiberius, who, in many respects, was the obvious candidate. On both his father's and mother's side Tiberius was a member of the Claudii, an illustrious blue-blooded family that claimed its first consulship as early as 495 BC, and had a grand total of 28 consulships in all, plus five dictatorships, seven censorhips, and six triumphs. It was, in short, one of the oldest and most accomplished patrician families in Rome. Moreover, by AD 9, when his position as heir finally became unassailable, Tiberius was the most prominent figure in Roman public life after Augustus. The empire's greatest soldier, he had spent much of the previous quarter century on campaign, making peace with Parthia, conquering Pannonia, and winning many great victories in Germany. With no other suitable candidates remaining, and with a character and record above reproach, Tiberius was the man finally chosen by the ageing Augustus to succeed him. When the old emperor died, Tiberius had already been promoted to all the offices which in combination made him constitutionally *princeps*. The succession was therefore seamless.

Born a patrician, highly educated, culturally philhellene, philosophically in sympathy with the Stoics (who advocated willing acceptance of public duties), and ideologically a Roman traditionalist, Tiberius seemed a relic of the Republican Senate, a strange successor to Octavian-Augustus, the faction-leader and upstart dictator. Secure in his aristocratic status and personal accomplishments, Tiberius, with nothing to prove, aimed to rule as his superior intelligence and conservative instincts directed – avoiding military adventures, treating the Senate with respect, defending hierarchy, tradition and order. It proved to be a *modus operandi* that, however seemingly worthy, the *princeps*, perched on the pinnacle of power, could not sustain.

The essence of aristocratic politics was competition for high office and the power, wealth and honour which were its rewards. Under the Republic this competition had been mediated by the Senate, and, until the time of Marius at least, rivalry had been contained by the constitution's strongly collegiate character. The system broke down during the 1st century BC, to be replaced, under triumvirs and emperors, by a form of court government. Autocracy required the appointment of loyalists, so advancement came to depend on association with whichever was the dominant court faction. Since insiders had an interest in monopolizing the privileges of power, outsiders would find their careers stalled. They then had three options: to curry favour and somehow gain entry to the court faction; to restore the Republic and a collegiate system for allocating posts; or to overthrow the dominant faction and replace it, including perhaps the emperor himself. Thus, when aristocratic competition for office was displaced from Senate to court, parliamentary manoeuvres gave way to court factionalism. When intrigues developed into plots – real and imagined – the court struck back with purges and executions. The resultant bitterness fostered a new round of plotting.

Intrigue penetrated the court itself, where, as Tiberius visibly aged, three factions manoeuvred to secure the succession. When Tiberius

himself – worn out by failure, bored with court politics, fearful of
assassination – retired to the island of Capri in AD 26, the faction of
Sejanus became dominant. Sejanus, Prefect of the Praetorian Guard,
was left in effective control of the empire, trusted by Tiberius because
his equestrian status made him dependent on imperial patronage and
appeared to impose limits on ambition. His status, however, merely made
his dominance more hateful, and as Sejanus manoeuvred to strengthen
his position against rival factions, he came under suspicion. He must
have feared a future without Tiberius, when, as the former creature of the
tyrant, he would have been at the mercy of his enemies. He may have
been planning a coup to pre-empt inevitable downfall. We will never
know. Tiberius, certainly, was persuaded that Sejanus was plotting, and
in October AD 31 orders were dispatched from Capri for the arrest and
execution of the traitor. A letter of condemnation was read out in the
Senate in the presence of the unsuspecting prefect. The Guard had
already been stood down by its newly appointed commander, and the
Senate House surrounded by the paramilitary corps of *vigiles*. Sejanus
was dead by nightfall, and Macro the new Praetorian Prefect and effective
ruler of the Empire.

The state terror reached a new intensity. Tiberius, old, paranoid
and isolated, was easily persuaded of the guilt of suspects. Macro and his
protégé – Tiberius's nephew and prospective successor, the young Gaius
Caligula – were determined to maintain their dominance through the
short period of life remaining to the emperor. Their mechanism of power
was the treason trial. Informers (*delatores*) were encouraged to come forward and denounce suspects for 'diminishing the majesty of the Roman
People' (*maiestas minuta*). This vague, catch-all, essentially meaningless
charge was used to destroy a succession of prominent figures, the example
serving to intimidate other potential opponents. Great state trials continued through the remaining six years of the reign, a grinding machine
of terror to shore up Tiberius's principate, Macro's ascendancy, and
Caligula's succession. At the end, even the tyrant himself may have fallen
victim to his agent's bloody rule. He died at Misenum on the Bay of
Naples during an occasional visit to the mainland. Tacitus reports foul
play. The story goes that after the emperor's apparent death Caligula's
succession had been announced, but that Tiberius had promptly rallied
and ordered a meal. 'There was a general panic-stricken dispersal. Every

face was composed to show grief – or lack of awareness. Only Gaius stood in stupefied silence, his soaring hopes dashed, expecting the worst. Macro, unperturbed, ordered the old man to be smothered with a heap of bed-clothes and left alone.'(5)

Caligula was an inexperienced and mentally unstable young man. He owed his elevation – and early popularity – to his Julio-Claudian ancestry, being great-nephew of Tiberius, and great step-grandson of Augustus. His father Germanicus and grandfather Drusus had both been famous generals. Tiberius had been hated at the end, the terror casting a pall over official Rome, and the beginning of the new reign was celebrated with general enthusiasm. Yet Caligula's madness soon revealed itself. The contradiction between supreme power and personal insecurity quickly unhinged the ruler. Seriously ill in 37 BC, Caligula was disconcerted to discover that the business of government had continued perfectly well without him. Macro, his leading minister, fell under suspicion and was struck down. Other high-ranking courtiers were also purged. The court was filled with a coterie of aristocratic youth and celebrities of stage and stadium – nonentities whose presence would not expose the young emperor's inexperience and inadequacies. A series of flamboyant public events was organized – such as a military parade, led by Caligula dressed as Alexander the Great, which passed along a 5 km bridge of boats specially constructed for the purpose on the Bay of Naples. The ruling class – largely excluded from this travesty of government – was quickly alienated. Matters came to crisis-point in AD 39. Though details are obscure, it seems that Caligula faced a major plot, since we hear that both consuls were sacked and replaced by stooges, and that there were changes in military commands and several forced suicides. Among the victims of the purge were Caligula's brother-in-law and remaining sisters, and the Governors of Pannonia and Upper Germany, both big military provinces.

It must have dawned on Caligula that gestures were not enough to secure the allegiance of the governing class; the emperor had to prove himself fit to rule by real achievement. So Caligula planned a great campaign in the north, first to cow the German tribes and stabilize the Rhine frontier, then to conquer Britain. Though he came from a family of great soldiers, Caligula yet lacked military accomplishments of his own. Great victories in the North would restore his battered public image.

The campaign was a disaster. Though Caligula's generals won limited gains in Germany, the emperor was disgraced by personal cowardice, having to be passed to the rear over the heads of his soldiers at news of the enemy's imminent approach. Later, on the Channel coast, either the emperor lost his nerve entirely, or the soldiers, having no confidence in their leader, mutinied and refused to embark. Whatever the cause, instead of invading Britain, Caligula's soldiers were ordered to collect seashells on the shore, and these were sent back to Rome as spoils of a victory over Neptune.

In the winter of AD 40–41 a great plot formed to destroy the regime. Though most senators remained cravenly inert, a minority feared the damage to the empire and was prepared to act to restore good government. Many more probably knew of the plot but kept their silence. It was the army, though, that was decisive, especially men of the imperial bodyguard, whose adherence would maximize the chances of successful assassination. Caligula's arrogance, bullying and unpredictability had eroded the support of even his own police-chiefs – the prefects and tribunes of the Praetorian Guard – who were left fearful for their own safety. Other leading courtiers were also among the active conspirators. The rot had, in fact, eaten into the narrow coterie of family and friends around the ruler. Caligula sensed the danger. For three months after his return from the North he refused to enter the capital, instead issuing a string of alarming statements, threatening violent retribution on his enemies, offering himself as emperor of equestrians and people in opposition to the senators, and, perhaps most worrying of all, announcing that he had become a god. Late in AD 40 he launched a minor purge, but the regime's security apparatus was degrading, and only marginal figures were destroyed; the core of the conspiracy remained undetected. In late January AD 41, when Caligula retired from his seat at the Palatine Games to lunch and bathe, he was attacked in the tunnels beneath his palace by a group of army officers led by two tribunes of the Guard and hacked to death. Thus Caligula, as the historian Dio Cassius dryly observed, discovered by actual experience that he was not a god after all.

At first there was pandemonium. Someone dispatched a death-squad to kill the empress and her daughter. On the other hand, the emperor's German bodyguard went berserk, killed several senators in the games stadium, and seemed poised for a general massacre; only with difficulty were they restrained as city officials began to assert control. Fearful of general disorder, the consuls summoned the Senate to emergency session on the Capitoline, moved the city treasures there, and mobilized the Urban Cohorts to provide a defensive cordon. As debate began, some urged the restoration of *libertas* (liberty: the collective rule of the senatorial elite). The terror of Tiberius and the madness of Caligula had breached the central Augustan principle of polite deceit that was supposed to govern relations between *princeps* and Senate. The ten years preceding the coup of AD 41 had revealed tyranny behind the façade of Republicanism. The fear engendered made *libertas* an attractive option. Others, however, rallied around the rival candidatures of different senators, pursuing the self-interested factionalism now inherent in the Roman political system. The session became rancorous and inconclusive as it ground on into the night. It also became increasingly irrelevant, for the embryonic senatorial state on the Capitoline Hill was confronted by an alternative embryonic court on the other side of the city.

The Praetorian Guard had found Claudius – uncle of Caligula, nephew of Tiberius, step-grandson of Augustus – hiding in the palace, recognized him, and carried him off to their barracks. His presence was the occasion for another great debate on the future government of Rome, this time a debate not of politicians but of soldiers, indeed of guardsmen, the most pampered of the emperor's soldiers, enjoying easy conditions of service, high pay, generous donatives, and all the amenities and comforts of the capital city. These privileges were inextricably bound up with Julio-Claudian power: the Praetorians were creatures of Caesarian patronage. Claudius, the senior surviving male member of the imperial house, being the best candidate for emperor available, the Praetorian Guard ended their assembly by acclaiming a new *princeps*.

For a while, the farce continued. On one side of the city, an assembly of millionaires and career politicians, protected by a thin cordon of riot police, bickered over which of their self-interested cliques should form a government. On the other, several thousand hired thugs guarded an obscure middle-aged aristocrat as a growing trickle of supporters and sycophants arrived to pay homage. But it did not last long. Power flowed through the night from Senate to court. As news spread, the Caesarian mob rallied to the Julio-Claudian, the place-seekers headed for the barracks, and the cordon of outnumbered police around the Capitoline broke up, fearing a clash with the Guard. In the light of morning, their semblance of power dissolved, a gloomy little party of politicians and officers made its way across the city to concede defeat. Claudius was carried in triumph to the imperial palace on the Palatine. The coup of AD 41 had ended in Julio-Claudian victory. After Caesar's assassination in 44 BC, it had taken eight years to crush Republicanism. After Caligula's, it took just 24 hours.

The victor was a portly, twitching, stammering, somewhat debauched intellectual, who had been denied a conventional political and military career by his snobbish family because they were embarrassed by his 'physical and mental deficiency' (in fact, though we cannot be sure, Claudius probably suffered from cerebral palsy). Wrongly assumed to be stupid, relatively inexperienced and unknown, Claudius was easily caricatured by his enemies as a fool. Furthermore, he had now become the willing tool of insurgent soldiers, a figurehead ruler whose power rested on the naked coercion of an intimidated Senate. He was both Claudius the Fool and Claudius the Usurper. The new regime's spin-doctors had work to do. The danger became apparent the following year, when dissident senators and generals hatched a plot to bring one of the huge legionary armies stationed in the Balkans to Rome. The soldiers refused to march, and the coup collapsed after five days. Snatch-squads rounded up suspects. There were show-trials in the Senate. Bodies were dumped in the Tiber. All told, during Claudius's 13-year reign, 35 senators and 321 equestrians were executed for treason. His court was filled with equestrians, freedmen, provincials and others of secondary status whose loyalty could be trusted. Claudius rested uneasy on his throne, hated by many of his peers as a mediocrity and tyrant presiding over a regime of upstarts. It is for this reason that Claudius was both 'the last of the *populares*' and also conqueror of Britain.

Claudius bought popularity in the old-fashioned way. He paid the Praetorian Guard a donative of up to 5,000 *denarii* per man (Caligula had paid just 500). The rest of the army received a donative totalling almost 200 million *denarii* – virtually an entire year's tax revenue. The mob was bribed with cash handouts, grain doles, public-works programmes, and gladiatorial games. All this largesse drained the treasuries. The cost of Caesarian populism had traditionally been met by war booty, however, and war was precisely what Claudius's advisors proposed; and not only for the booty – also to legitimize the new principate, inspire party loyalists, and marginalize the malcontents and would-be plotters.

Britain was the obvious target. The expansion of the Catuvellaunian kingdom in the south east – at the expense of a Roman client-king – provided a handy *casus belli*. Caligula's officers had already done the staff-work – for the abortive invasion of AD 40. Britain was mysterious, dangerous, 'beyond Ocean', and in some sense unfinished business ever since the expeditions of Julius Caesar a century before. While an invasion of Britain was probably less risky than war in the East or in Germany, it could none the less be presented to the public otherwise: as one of the greatest of Roman military achievements. Also, the island was rich enough to subsidize Claudius's largesse.

The invasion was, as predicted, a spectacular success. Aulus Plautius and 40,000 men were landed in the early summer of AD 43. Shortly afterwards they won a two-day pitched battle against Caratacus and the main field army of the Catuvellaunian kingdom. Claudius then arrived in person to head the triumphal entry into the enemy capital at Camulodunum (Colchester) and receive the surrender of 11 British kings. It was, says Barbara Levick, Claudius's modern biographer, 'the greatest event of his reign' and 'one of his prime claims to rule, as his systematic exploitation of it shows'.(6) There were celebrations in Rome in AD 43 when news of the victory first reached the capital; more when Claudius arrived home in AD 44, having toured the western provinces on the way; and yet more when Aulus Plautius returned in AD 47, when the city boundary was extended in commemoration in AD 49, and finally when the captured British leader Caratacus was paraded through the streets of the city in AD 51.

Otherwise, on the frontiers, Claudian policy was conservative. It was the policy of the late Augustus and of Tiberius: to eschew further conquests, consolidate the frontiers, assimilate new subjects. Caligula and Claudius had broken with this policy in relation to Britain, but in both cases they were motivated not by strategy but by the political insecurity of their respective regimes. Once Claudius the Fool-Usurper had transformed himself into Claudius the Conqueror, he reverted to the policy of imperial retrenchment. The power of the empire was in part mirage. It appeared invulnerable and all-conquering. This appearance – what imperial statesmen sometimes call 'prestige' – was vital to its security. But in truth it had reached the limits of its capacity for expansion.

Campaigns were sometimes undertaken to straighten, shorten and otherwise strengthen existing frontiers, but even these were capable of provoking intractable resistance. Tacfarinas, a Numidian who had deserted from Roman auxiliary service, led a long guerrilla war in North Africa between AD 17 and 24. The reasons are obscure, but the disruption of traditional nomadic migration routes by Roman frontier operations may have been one of them. Heavy Roman taxation could also provoke revolt, as in Gaul under Florus and Sacrovir in AD 21, where again leadership was provided by elements in the Romanized elite who had been alienated by their erstwhile masters. Tiberius urged moderation upon imperial governors, aspiring to have his 'sheep shorn, not flayed'; but on the ground, where tax-collectors, recruiting officers, loan-sharks and slave-dealers battened on to the provinces under the protection of the Roman army, the reality was often very different. Rome ruled through fear. Fear was instilled by 'prestige': the conviction of the victims that the imperial state had the power to crush them if they fought back. And prestige depended upon victory. Military adventures beyond the frontier risked defeat, a haemorrhaging of men, a denting of prestige. Super-exploitation risked revolt, a diverting of men to internal security, an overextended army. The Claudian invasion of Britain was an anomaly, therefore, one driven by political necessity, not a wholesale return to the glory days of Pompey and Caesar.

Claudius ruled Britain, but not his own court. The dominant factions there were headed by two successive wives. The first, Messallina, was about 16 when she married the middle-aged Claudius shortly before his accession. She produced a son in AD 41, later named Britannicus, an obvious potential heir to the throne. But Messallina was a naïve, ambitious and reckless schemer, who eventually overreached herself. Though the events of her downfall are hard to decipher, she appears to have taken part in some sort of 'marriage' to her lover, and whether this was a prank or an attempted coup, it was certainly used by her enemies at court to destroy her. The couple were arrested and summarily executed by leading freedman Narcissus and a detachment of the Guard. Claudius's second wife, Agrippina, more mature and subtle but no less scheming than the first, manoeuvred to displace Britannicus in favour of her own son by a previous marriage, Lucius Domitius Ahenobarbus. Claudius was persuaded to adopt Ahenobarbus – who thus became Nero Claudius Caesar

– and to marry him to Messallina's daughter Octavia. Having consolidated her faction's power by forming an alliance with Burrus, Prefect of the Praetorian Guard, and fearing that Nero's hedonistic character might cause her husband second thoughts, Agrippina had no further use for Claudius. It is rumoured she murdered him by serving up a plate of poisoned mushrooms.

Nero was 16 when he became emperor, and for the first eight years of his reign the government was controlled by his former tutor Seneca, a Romano-Hispanic senator and intellectual, and Burrus, the Romano-Gallic equestrian who commanded the Guard. Both men were competent. Relations with the governing class were good. Appointments were not restricted to a narrow clique. There were no state trials of senators or equestrians between AD 54 and 62. But in the latter year Burrus died, Seneca retired, and Nero assumed personal responsibility for government. Few men elevated to such high office have been less suited. Nero was a vain, hedonistic, upper-class playboy with a distinctly psychotic personality. His relationship with his mother was probably incestuous and certainly highly charged. When she spitefully transferred her affections to Britannicus, Nero had his rival murdered at the dinner table. When she continued to scheme – or because he imagined she did – mother and son became increasingly estranged, until finally, in AD 59, Nero dispatched a death-squad to bludgeon her to death in the family villa on the Bay of Naples. When he assumed power in AD 62, he divorced his wife Octavia (who was later exiled and then executed) and married his mistress Poppaea Sabina (whom he would also later kill). At the same time he promoted Gaius Ofonius Tigellinus to command of the Praetorian Guard in place of Burrus. These three – Nero, Poppaea and Tigellinus – headed an all-powerful court faction devoted to private indulgence and public spectacles. The degradation of government was symbolized by Nero's personal addiction to the games and his ambition to win acclaim as an artist. His appearances culminated in AD 67, when, during a tour of Greece, all four major games festivals were celebrated in the same year, and the emperor was awarded all 800 prizes. The tactfulness of the Greeks was amply rewarded: imperial taxation was abolished in their province.

Roman traditionalists viewed it all with bitter contempt. The dominant faction had turned the state into a junket. Their purpose was simply to retain power, amass wealth, and pursue pleasure. Rome's pretensions to govern and civilize the world were made a mockery. But the regime might well have survived had it not threatened the property of the ruling class and the integrity of the empire. The crux of the problem was finance. The expenditures on luxury and largesse were vast. When, in AD 66, the Armenian client-king Tiridates made a state visit to Rome, for example, the expenses amounted to 200,000 *denarii* per day. Continual prodigious expense at the centre of the empire was met by rising exploitation in the provinces. The dangers inherent in this policy had been demonstrated often enough: the army was fully extended guarding the frontiers, and the reserves did not exist to suppress internal revolts without compromising border security. Super-exploitation – the flaying of sheep – risked revolts that might overwhelm the army: this, the lesson of the Teutoburg Forest, was as valid in AD 66 as in AD 9.

Already there had been a major revolt in Britain in AD 60 or 61. It was provoked by heavy-handed land seizures and debt-collection. Speci-fically, Nero's agents moved in to take over the territory of the Iceni when the client-king Prasutagus died. Their purpose was probably to add former royal land to the imperial estate, and to impose Roman taxation on everyone else. At the same time, multimillionaire creditors, like the leading minister Seneca, were calling in overdue debts, now grossly inflated by the crippling interest rates that prevailed in the Roman world, a form of legalized swindling with which the hapless British notables were probably unfamiliar until they received demand for repayment. The peasantry was oppressed by taxes, labour services, and, around the new Roman *colonia* at Colchester, the confiscation of their farms. When Boudica, the widowed queen of the Iceni, raised the banner of revolt, tens of thousands joined her. The rebel army defeated a legion and destroyed three towns before its annihiliation in battle by the Roman governor. Events might easily have turned out differently: the Romans had been heavily outnumbered in the final battle; had they been commanded by another Varus, the Roman occupation of Britain might have ended as abruptly as that of Germany.

No general lessons were drawn from the Boudican Revolt, however. Nor from a humiliating defeat suffered by the Roman army in AD 62 during its long-running war with Parthia over the status of Armenia (AD 53–63). It should have been clear that tax-rates were being ratcheted up to dangerous levels, and that the army was overextended. Taxation was almost certainly the issue which, in spring AD 66, ignited the greatest anti-imperialist revolt of the century. According to the Jewish historian Josephus, the Roman governor Gessius Florus had demanded 100,000 *denarii* from the treasures of the Temple in Jerusalem 'for Caesar's needs'. He may, under pressure from above, have been attempting to make good a shortfall in revenue due to an incipient tax strike. Anticipating resistance, he sent in the troops. Clashes with groups of demonstrators ended in massacre and provoked full-scale urban insurrection. Overwhelmed, the governor and his troops abandoned the city. When Cestius Gallus, Governor of Syria, tried to smash his way back with an army of 30,000 men in the autumn, he was defeated with heavy loss at the battle of Beth-Horon north-west of the capital and sent into headlong retreat. That winter, the revolt spread across Palestine, and tens of thousands were organized into revolutionary militias to resist the Roman army in the spring.

It took the Romans three years to recapture Jerusalem, and three more to suppress continuing residual resistance. The siege of Jerusalem in AD 70 turned into an apocalyptic confrontation between the haves and have-nots of the Roman Empire. The city was defended for almost five months by some 25,000 militiamen, mainly recruited from peasant villages and inspired by a millenarian message of imminent freedom from corrupt rulers, tax-collectors and landlords. They eventually succumbed to the overwhelming power of 60,000 professional soldiers, and were consumed by fire, sword, famine, pestilence and the cross. Handfuls escaped across the desert to continue the fight from remote fortresses, but these too, one by one, were suppressed – until, by AD 73, only Masada remained. Here, when the Romans broke in, they were confronted by an eerie silence, for the defenders, knowing their walls breached, had committed suicide in preference to defeat and slavery, and now lay dead, 960 of them, in rows, the men, women and children of each family side-by-side.

By this time, Nero, and with him the Julio-Claudian imperial dynasty, had perished. The Jewish Revolution, coming so soon after the Boudican Revolt, had alerted the Roman ruling class to the danger represented by the regime. Anxiety was compounded by the growing eccentricity, *luxuria* and corruption of the court clique. When fire swept through

Rome in AD 64, the government diverted suspicion from itself by initiating a ghastly anti-Christian pogrom. Meanwhile, debris was cleared from the gutted districts to lay out a vast new imperial palace and park complex, the grounds two, three, perhaps four times the size of the present Vatican, including a fabulous pavilion that became known as the *Domus Aurea* (Golden House), complete with revolving dining-room, and a colossal bronze statue of the emperor in the guise of the sun-god Apollo. But a plot to overthrow the megalomaniac dictator in AD 65 was betrayed, and some 30 eminent men – a mixture of career politicians, guards officers, Republican die-hards, intellectuals and literati – were driven to suicide or exile. Thereafter the regime remained suspicious, and the familiar machinery of state terror ground into action, fed by the work of informers, police and torturers. No high-ranking person, no aristocratic estate, was safe. Corbulo, greatest general of the age, victor over the Parthians in Armenia, was forced to commit suicide in the winter of AD 66–67.

When the emperor and his retinue were away touring Greece in AD 67, a new conspiracy was formed, this time extending outwards from Rome to encompass the governors and generals who commanded the main frontier armies. Upon his return to Italy early in AD 68, Nero was confronted by news that Vindex, Governor of Gallia Lugdunensis, had risen in revolt, supported by the Romano-Gallic leaders of three native tribes. A Romanized Gaul himself, he could not aspire to the imperial purple; instead, undoubtedly by prior arrangement, he called on Servius Sulpicius Galba, a 73-year-old senator from an old Republican family who was currently Governor of Hispania Tarraconensis, to accept the throne. But the revolt faltered. Vindex and his Gallic levies were defeated by loyalist troops from the Rhineland, and Galba, fearing the worst, retreated into the interior of his province. Had Nero and his agents acted quickly and efficiently, they might yet have saved themselves. But that was not their way. The politics of real power, when generals and armies were in play, were beyond them. When the commander of the Roman troops in Africa declared against the regime, Nymphidius Rufus, Tigellinus's fellow Prefect of the Praetorian Guard, turned traitor and bribed the guardsmen into declaring for Galba. The Senate followed suit. Nero was declared an outlaw, fled the city, and shortly afterwards committed suicide at a nearby villa even as rebel troops arrived to arrest him.

The Neronian regime had tested imperial power to its limits. These limits were essentially three: major wars of conquest risked overstretching the army and imposing crippling losses; excessive exploitation risked provincial revolt and an unsustainable burden of internal security; and court factionalism and state terror risked civil war by destroying the coherence of the Roman ruling class. Had the Jewish Revolt of AD 66–70 coincided with the Parthian war of AD 53–63, the empire could well have faced military disaster. As it was, the frontiers held, and internal order was restored. But the crisis in relations between court and Senate was not so easily resolved. In fact, the crisis spiralled rapidly out of control. As the Julio-Claudian dynasty plunged into the abyss, it dragged the Roman state with it. For the first time in a century, Italy was to be ravished by Roman armies from distant frontiers, come home to fight a brutal civil war for mastery of the empire.

The limits of Empire: the year of four emperors and the Flavian dynasty, AD 69–96

Galba, on hearing news of his elevation in Rome, recovered his nerve, emerged from the interior of his province, and set off for the capital. But he was destined for an unstable and short-lived reign. His supporters were an uneasy alliance of Praetorian Guardsmen, old-school senators, and career politicians from Spanish postings. The alliance was held together by the promise of immediate reward. But what was on offer to the officers of the Rhine, Danube and eastern legions? In fact, they were doubly disadvantaged under Galba: excluded from access to court patronage, their resentment and disloyalty could be anticipated, so that even posts they already held were under threat. First the Governor of Lower Germany was superseded, then the Governor of Upper Germany. Each of these men had commanded 20,000 legionaries, and in January AD 69, at the instigation of their senior officers, these soldiers refused to renew their allegiance to Galba and hailed Aulus Vitellius emperor in his place.

News of this revolt brought the tensions within Galba's government to a head. The new emperor's policy had been a disastrous mixture of sanctimony and corruption. The Praetorian Guard had been angered by Galba's refusal to pay their promised bribe. The officers from Spain were alienated by his nomination of another blue-bloodied senator like himself as prospective successor. So Marcus Salvius Otho, Governor of Hispania Lusitania, one of Galba's leading lieutenants and effective head of the 'Spanish' faction, went to the Praetorian barracks and offered to pay the soldiers. The guardsmen proclaimed Otho emperor and denounced his rival as an enemy. Galba, a bald and arthritic old man, was hunted down and lynched in the Forum. This resolution of the immediate crisis in Rome still, however, left two emperors in play within the empire, each representing a powerful bloc of politicians and officers, one rooted in Rome, Italy and Spain, the other in the Rhineland; and with each faction heavily armed, only war could decide which of them would prevail.

Otho, in control of Rome and given legitimacy by senatorial support, attracted the formal allegiance of most provincial governors and the practical assistance of the Danubian legions. His position – like that of Pompey in 49 BC – appeared, on the face of things, the stronger. But the Vitellians – like Caesar's Gallic War legions at the Rubicon – represented a coherent bloc of concentrated military power. Though Vitellius himself was grossly fat and debauched, he was merely a mask for the career ambitions of the Rhineland officers, skilled commanders of an experienced and loyal army. When the rival armies clashed near Cremona in northern Italy, legion against legion in a day-long battle amid the vineyards, the Othonians were defeated. Their 37-year-old leader, his fastidiously hair-plucked body crowned by a toupee to hide his baldness, committed suicide and so brought to an end his 95-day reign as Roman emperor. As the victorious army headed for the capital, the empire accepted the judgement of war, the Senate and most provincial governors switching allegiance for the third time in a year to acclaim Vitellius the new ruler.

The Vitellian revolution was in an important sense different from its immediate predecessors. The secret of empire, as Tacitus explained, was out: emperors could be made elsewhere than at Rome. The secret had been concealed behind a façade of Republican rectitude: Augustus had claimed to have 'restored the Republic', and his successors had maintained this fiction. The image had dissolved momentarily in AD 41, but even then military intervention had amounted to a brief, near-bloodless coup carried out by a few thousand guardsmen in Rome. Only now, in AD 69, was the full reality of the military dictatorship revealed. Vitellius was the 'Rhineland' emperor, a creature of the generals stationed there, a ruler brought to Rome by 40,000 frontier legionaries. His was the regime of a narrow faction, and, as with Galba and Otho, a purge was needed to consolidate its power, though this time, after civil war, a bloodier one. For the 'Germans' – despite their victory over Otho's alliance of 'Spaniards' and 'Danubians' – might yet be challenged in their turn. They knew that one other player remained in the game: Titus Flavius Vespasianus, the top Roman general in the East.

Vespasian cannot have considered himself in contention at the beginning of the crisis. He owed his current eminence – he was commander of the 40,000-strong army fighting the Jewish rebels in Palestine – to relative obscurity. Born into a small-town family of Italian landowners, army officers and businessmen, his grandfather had been a commoner, his father an equestrian, and Vespasian himself was a first-generation senator. The Flavian family was, in fact, a good example of the class of 'new men' from the Italian municipal aristocracy who had flourished under the new Augustan order. Such men tended to be more loyal agents of the Caesars than nobles from ancient families: they depended more heavily on the good favour of their patrons, and their ambition, in the nature of things, could hardly extend to the purple throne itself. By flattering tyrants and their flunkies, Vespasian had ascended the administrative hierarchy, survived the purges, and finally been promoted to the most senior of military commands – partly because he was not considered a political threat. Now, by one of history's ironies, he stood poised on the brink of supreme power.

For the 'Easterners', the news from Rome was gloomy: the victory of Vitellius meant direct Rhineland control over imperial patronage and a corresponding slump in the fortunes of men stationed in the East. Worse, it was rumoured that Vitellius would switch the western and eastern legions, forcing the latter to exchange the comfort and ease of city billets for wooden forts in a cold and wet German forest. But if the officers on the Rhine could create their own emperor, why not those in the East? The ancient sources aver that Vespasian was reluctant to accept a nomination, but this may have been a traditional deceit. Whatever, once widely canvassed as a candidate for the throne, no man could safely draw back: he was henceforward and forever tainted as politically suspect. The momentum towards an eastern military coup quickly became unstoppable, and Vespasian was propelled willy-nilly into a new civil war.

Perhaps by prior arrangement, perhaps through hurried last-minute negotiation, the Prefect of Egypt declared for Vespasian on 1 July AD 69, calling upon the soldiers and citizens of Alexandria assembled before him to swear allegiance. With Egypt secure, giving him two legions and the Nile grain-stores, Vespasian ten days later accepted the acclamation of his own army in Palestine. Shortly afterwards came further declarations in his favour, two of them, Syria and the Danube, representing decisive shifts in the balance of power. This support – the whole of the East and the Balkans, and two of the three main army groups in the empire – gave Vespasian a potentially winning hand, especially as the Flavian revolt seems to have taken the Vitellians by surprise, the discipline of the Rhineland legions having broken down after their arrival in Rome.

But Vespasian dithered. Before bringing on a decisive clash, he aimed to cut off Rome's grain-supply from Egypt, and to gather more support by sending an advance expedition through Asia Minor. His partisans, however, showed greater initiative. Antonius Primus, leader of the pro-Flavian revolt on the Danube, ignoring any orders he may have received from the East, crossed the Alps to invade Italy and fall upon the Vitellians while they were still in disarray. In the late autumn, the Rhineland and Danubian legions clashed again on the battlefield of Cremona, and this time the Danubians triumphed. As the Vitellians broke and ran, the Flavians massacred the fugitives and then looted Cremona. A second Vitellian force arriving from Gaul was beaten soon after, and a final attempt to block the snow-bound passes over the Apennines disintegrated as the Vitellian rank-and-file deserted. The 56-year-old emperor – whose 'ruling vices were gluttony and cruelty' according to Suetonius – made a final bid to save himself by cutting a deal with Vespasian's brother, who was acting as the family's representative in Rome. The deal collapsed when the Vitellian soldiery mutinied, stormed the Capitoline Hill, and lynched the Flavian leader. Antonius Primus's Danubians then pressed on to Rome, where they destroyed the remaining Vitellians in fierce street-fighting. Vitellius himself was dragged into the streets half-dressed and bloated with food and drink (Suetonius again), and there pelted with dung and filth, tortured by little sword cuts, and finally murdered on the banks of the Tiber. Afterwards, while their senior officers set up a provisional government headed by Vespasian's younger son Domitian, the Danubian soldiers celebrated by looting Rome. It was December. The empire now had its fourth emperor in a year – and Rome and the Italian towns had been twice plundered by the army that was supposed to defend them. Even now, though, the crisis was not over.

The splintering of the imperial elite and the distraction of the army in civil war had created openings for revolt from below. The discontent bubbling away under the oppressive Neronian regime now boiled over. The Jewish Revolution, a great rising of the rural poor, was entering its fifth year, and its greatest battle, the defence of Jerusalem, was yet to come. On the other side of the empire, in the Rhineland, there was mutiny in the regiments of Gaulish and German auxiliaries serving in the Roman army. The revolt was led by Julius Civilis, a Romanized Gaulish chieftain, and it tapped deep pools of bitterness in the frontier districts. Raising an army of mutineers and German tribesmen, and facing legionaries disoriented and demoralized by civil war, Civilis quickly established military dominance on the Lower Rhine, and soon had the major Roman base at Vetera under siege. His example, coupled with news from Rome – notably that the Capitoline Temple of Jupiter had been burnt down – inspired a wider revolt of Gaulish tribes led by other Romanized chieftains, namely Julius Classicus and Julius Tutor, supported by militant members of the druidic priesthood, who were predicting the conquest of Rome by the peoples of the North. The rebels now organized themselves into a proto-state – an 'Empire of the Gauls' – and such was the momentum of revolt in the frontier districts that many legionaries were won over (a high proportion of whom were no doubt of Gallic or German origin). If Rhineland soldiers could march on Rome and install an emperor, they could equally well stay at home and set up a rival empire there. Another secret was out: if emperors could be made elsewhere than at Rome, so too could empires.

The Empire of the Gauls was, however, a fortress of sand. When Classicus and Tutor attempted to win over the rest of Gaul at a great congress of the tribes at Rheims, they failed; the rebel empire remained confined to the Rhineland. Too many top-ranking Gauls had become stakeholders in the imperial system; or they feared the mutinous soldiery and Germanic tribesmen who formed Civilis's army; or, quite simply, they expected Vespasian to win. The rebel confederation itself began to break up. A rag-bag alliance of notables, mutineers and tribesmen, of

Romans, Gauls and Germans, it was never politically coherent and only briefly militarily effective. At the mere approach of loyalist legions under the Flavian general Quintus Petilius Cerealis in the summer of AD 70, the rebel legionaries deserted back to the Roman side. The Gauls under Classicus and Tutor were then defeated in battle outside Trier. Shortly afterwards the Germans under Civilis were also defeated near Vetera. Finally, far to the north, in the marshes of the Rhine and Meuse estuaries, the Batavians, the last of the rebels to hold out, were crushed in their turn. By this time also, Jerusalem had fallen to the army of Titus, Vespasian's elder son, who had assumed command in Palestine after his father's elevation; the Jewish resistance was down to a handful of remote desert fortresses. Broadly, by the beginning of AD 71, the empire was again at peace. But Flavian victory had been hard-fought, and there was no guarantee the peace would hold. Moreover, even if the worst of the crisis was over, there were immediate problems with an estranged governing class, a disloyal army, unsettled frontiers, and an empty treasury. In the longer term, two years of civil war, army mutinies and popular revolt had taught sharp lessons: the empire of the Julio-Claudians had been overexploited and overextended; a new, more cautious, more measured policy was essential. The mission of the new Flavian dynasty – if it was to survive – was to restore equilibrium to a system out of kilter.

AD 71, however, was a year for celebration. There had been victory over Vitellians, Jewish rebels and the Gallic Empire; and, as in 30 BC, with a real yearning for peace and order, there was the basis for an alliance between the new dynasty – that of an upstart military dictator, after all – and Rome's traditional elite. Triumphs were held for the capture of Jerusalem and the subjugation of the Batavians. The doors of the Temple of Janus were closed to symbolize the coming of peace. Major construction projects were launched – to rebuild the Capitolium, to inaugurate a new Temple of Peace, to sweep away Nero's palace, and to provide Rome with a great stone amphitheatre. The Colosseum was rich in symbolism. It was built on the site of Nero's ornamental lake: what had once been a monument to a tyrant's *luxuria* was now a place of free public entertainment. The construction work meant contracts for Rome's businessmen and workshops, while heavy labour was provided by slaves, many no doubt from Palestine and the Rhineland: the subjugated 'other' put to work in the service of the conquerors. The shows put on when the amphitheatre was complete – the first in AD 81 – were spectacles of power and empire: gladiator-slaves were decked out in the manner of Rome's historic enemies.

The new regime was popular at home. Though he developed a reputation for meanness – as expenditure was cut back to restore government finances – Vespasian himself was straight-dealing, unpretentious and tolerant of opposition ('I don't kill dogs for barking'). Few, anyway, were given cause to oppose. The old nobility had been reduced to a rump; the great majority of senators now were aristocrats-of-office raised up by the Caesars. The ideological republicans had shrunk into a small sect. The more thoughtful among the aristocracy sought refuge in philosophy. But the various brands on offer amounted to little more than a retreat from attempts to change the world into obsessive individualism. The Cynics denounced all government as corrupt and urged withdrawal from public life. The Stoics maintained that forms of government were dictated by divine reason, and favoured public service and political conformity. The Epicureans considered the pursuit of pleasure to be the greatest good. Though admired by some (the 'stiff upper lip' taught in British public schools probably owes something to the Stoics), these philosophies were essentially vacuous. They offered a choice of lifestyles, not an analysis of the world; they coated powerlessness in a patina of virtue. Vespasian could safely let the dogs bark. Treason trials were few in his ten-year reign. The regime's real anxiety was not the loyalty of aristocratic salons, but that of the military headquarters and army barracks.

Recalling its disloyalty under the Julio-Claudians, the Praetorian Guard was reduced in numbers and placed under the command of Vespasian's son Titus, who thus became in effect the Flavian chief-of-police. It was Titus, too, in his role as censor for that year, who carried out a purge of the Senate in AD 73–74, reducing its numbers overall, while promoting party loyalists, among them many generals. The new intake included numerous Italians and provincials. A typical member of the Flavian aristocracy was Gnaeus Julius Agricola. He was born in the Roman colony of Forum Julii in southern Gaul in AD 40, and was educated at the local Greek city of Massilia (Marseille). The Julius in his name implies an ancestor enfranchised by Julius Caesar and probable Gaulish descent. Both his grandfathers had been equestrians in the imperial service, and his father had been made a senator. Agricola himself ascended what had, by his time, become a conventional career ladder for sons of senators. He first served a military apprenticeship in Britain as a legionary tribune, participating in the suppression of the Boudican Revolt in AD 60/61. He was then successively quaestor in Asia in AD 64, tribune of the plebs in Rome in AD 66, and praetor, again in Rome, in AD 68. This qualified him for a senior army command, and Vespasian appointed him legate of the Twentieth Legion in Britain in AD 70–73/74. This was followed by a senior civil post, that of Governor of Aquitania in Gaul, where he served from AD 74 to 77. Experienced, reliable and, above all, loyal to the regime, he now reached the summit of a senatorial career, holding a consulship in Rome in AD 77 or 78. His proconsular status then qualified him for the most senior and highly coveted posts of all. Among the choicest plums at the time were the governorships of Britain and Syria, since both conferred command of three or four legions, a strong possibility of military action, and thus a chance of military glory. Agricola served a double term as Governor of Britain (AD 78–84), where he directed some of the most aggressive and successful military campaigns of the Flavian era.

We owe our knowledge of Agricola's career to the remarkable survival of a short account of his life written by his son-in-law, the historian Tacitus. The *Agricola* throws much light on the inner workings of the Flavian empire. As well as promoting a 'career open to talent' within the existing imperial hierarchy – somewhat in contrast to the factionalism prevalent under the Julio-Claudians – the Flavian emperors promoted loyalty and stability in the provinces through a deliberate policy of Romanization designed to raise up native elites. 'Certain domains,' Tacitus tells us, 'were presented to King Togidubnus, who maintained his unswerving loyalty right down to our own times – an example of the long-established Roman custom of employing even kings to make others slaves.'(7) An inscription found in Chichester in 1723 refers to this king. It tells us that a temple had been erected in honour of Neptune and Minerva, and for the well-being of the 'divine house' (the imperial family), under 'the authority of Tiberius Claudius Togidubnus, great king of Britain'.(8) The king's Roman-style name reveals that he received his citizenship under Claudius, but Tacitus implies that he ruled well into the Flavian period. The temple dedication referred to on the inscription makes clear his commitment to Romanization. Like pro-western 'modernizers' in today's Third World, Togidubnus rejected native culture in favour of an imported *Romanitas* associated with prosperity, civilization and power. The archaeology of the three towns within what may have been Togidubnus's kingdom – Chichester, Silchester and Winchester – has revealed early examples of classical town-planning and monumental architecture. At Fishbourne, moreover, a mile or so from Chichester, is the probable site of the king's palace. At first, in the 60s AD, a substantial masonry villa was constructed, including a bath-house and an enclosed courtyard, the so-called 'proto-palace'. Then, some time between AD 75 and 80, construction began of a new house on a vast scale, creating something without parallel anywhere west of Italy. Approached through parkland, a cavernous entrance-hall gave access across a formal courtyard garden to a grand audience chamber on the far side. Elsewhere in the four ranges of rooms around the courtyard were the private apartments of the king and his family, suites for relatives, guests and royal servants, and, of course, a bath-house. The whole complex was decorated with marble, mosaic and fresco. Classical sculpture, bronze pitchers, imported tableware and elegantly crafted dining couches no doubt completed the Mediterranean ambience. Covered colonnades, neat box-hedges and stone-lined drains did the same for the garden.

Romanization started at the top, but it trickled downwards, seeping through long-established networks of patronage to create a substantial pro-Roman bloc of privileged, powerful people in each locality. 'Agricola,' explained Tacitus, 'had to deal with men who, because they lived in the country and were culturally backward, were inveterate war-mongers. He wanted to accustom them to peace and leisure by providing delightful distractions . . . He gave personal encouragement and public assistance to the building of temples, piazzas and town-houses . . . he gave the sons of the aristocracy a liberal education . . . they became eager to speak Latin effectively . . . and the toga was everywhere to be seen . . . And so they were gradually led into the demoralising vices of porticoes, baths and grand dinner parties. The naive Britons described these things as "civilisation", when in fact they were simply part of their enslavement.'(9) As it happens, part of a dedicatory inscription from one of those piazzas, found during excavations at Roman Verulamium (St Albans) in 1955, bears the name of the great governor. Only five small fragments were recovered, so the reconstruction is uncertain, but it probably records the opening of the new stone-built civic centre, comprising a grand assembly-room and council offices on one side, three ranges of private offices and shops on the others, and a central open courtyard fringed by covered, colonnaded walkways. Such buildings – along with others of the standard Roman urban package: temples, bath-houses, theatres, amphitheatres, official motels – symbolize the Romanization of local elites below the level of kings.

Tacitus's real interest in the *Agricola*, however, was his father-in-law's military achievements; it was these that he and his audience considered the proper measure of greatness. Each year of his governorship, we learn, Agricola pushed forward the conquest of Britain: in AD 78 the conquest of Wales was completed with the defeat of the principal northern tribe and the occupation of Anglesey; in AD 79 Brigantia (northern England) was overrun; in AD 80 the Roman army advanced across Scotland beyond the Central Lowlands as far as the River Tay; in AD 81 a series of forts was built along the Forth-Clyde line; in AD 82 south-west Scotland was conquered; and in AD 83–84 an advance up the east coast brought the Roman army to the Moray Firth and a great set-piece battle against the Caledonian tribes at Mons Graupius. The tribes were routed and left a third of their 30,000 men on the hillside where they had made their stand. It seemed to Tacitus that 'Britain had been completely conquered'.

But it had not. No Caledonian delegation arrived to offer submission. The beaten warriors skulked in their Highland glens, but they did not submit. Agricola was forced to fall back on winter bases further south, the war unfinished. The following year he was replaced by a new governor with orders to remain on the defensive. A few years later the Romans withdrew from the far north. The unfinished earth-and-timber legionary fortress at Inchtuthil on the Tay, lynchpin of the defences on the south-eastern fringe of the Highlands, was dismantled and abandoned in the late 80s AD. Soon, all forts north of the Forth-Clyde isthmus had been evacuated, and the Romans held a new line across the Southern Uplands, anchored on Newstead, where excavation has shown an early Flavian fort overlain by a late Flavian one. Finally, even the Newstead line was given up, and the Romans fell back in *c.* AD 105 to a position along the 'Stanegate' on the Tyne-Solway line between modern Newcastle and Carlisle. Tacitus, knowing of the retreat when he came to write his father-in-law's biography, was outraged: Britain may have been completely conquered, but it was then, he lamented, 'immediately lost again'. What had gone wrong?

The historian's explanation is wholly unconvincing: it was, he claimed, down to the jealousy of the new Flavian emperor Domitian, younger son of Vespasian. 'He knew that there was nothing so dangerous for him as to have the name of a subject exalted above that of the emperor.'(10) This is nonsense. Agricola was an arch-loyalist. Imperial generals won victories on behalf of the emperor they served. Defeats and retreats were damaging to prestige. Tacitus's account, anyway, is vitiated by transparent special pleading: when the emperor is reported heaping public praise on the returning general, we are informed, without a shred of supporting evidence, that he merely 'pretended to be pleased when in fact he was deeply disturbed'.(11) In truth, the historical and archaeological evidence for Flavian frontier policy elsewhere shows that events in Britain conformed to a pattern.

The aim was not a return to the expansionism of the Late Republic. The Flavian emperors retrenched and consolidated. Vespasian, like Tiberius, was a veteran general when he came to the throne. Titus, his successor, was the conqueror of the Jews. Neither had anything to prove. Both understood that the empire was overextended, that further conquests could be justified only if they increased frontier security without imposing new demands on the army. Even so, the army was kept busy. Discipline was quickly restored by disbanding four or five disloyal legions and the mutinous Gallic and German auxiliary regiments, replacing them with new formations. The reformed army was kept close to the frontiers in an extended line; instead of large battle groups concentrated for offensive action, there were now numerous local packets deployed for defence. When offensives were launched, they were designed as localized initiatives either to suppress hostile border tribes or to create shorter, straighter, more defensible lines. Vespasian had only one less salutation as *imperator* than Augustus, but the objectives and scale of warfare were quite different. Roads and forts – the work of the spade – came to predominate over battle. Britain became a major theatre of offensive action only because the Boudican Revolt had effectively halted the Roman advance on an indefensible line: a long diagonal across lowland Britain from Exeter to Lincoln, with actively or potentially hostile hill-tribes to west and north. Vespasian therefore appointed a succession of fighting governors to continue the conquest of the island until the frontier rested on the sea, or at least ran on a short east-west line. On the German frontier, in the upper Rhine and Danube region, where the Flavians inherited a sharp re-entrant projecting into Roman territory, the line was pushed steadily forwards. Domitian initiated the main forward advance by attacking the Chatti on the middle Rhine in AD 83, an offensive designed to force this hostile tribe back from the frontier and establish a new Roman line east of the river. The re-entrant to the south was then gradually bitten off, shortening the Roman line and improving communications between the Rhine and Danube army groups.

Despite Flavian caution, however, the empire's defences remained under pressure. A new threat had arisen on the middle Danube: King Decebalus and the Dacians. For a generation, from AD 85 to 106, the Dacians were to be Rome's principal enemies. Their mountain kingdom – roughly corresponding to modern Rumania – was rich in gold, and the Dacian kings, under threat of Roman expansion in the Balkans, had welded the hill-tribes into a powerful centralized state. Their territory was difficult to penetrate and defended by numerous elaborate hill-forts. Their army was formed of barbarian warriors, fiercely independent, organized in tribal contingents, and wielding the horrendous *falx*, a two-handed cutting weapon comprising an inward-curving, razor-sharp blade fitted to a long wooden shaft (in later campaigns, Roman soldiers would wear metal arm-guards and helmets reinforced across the top with metal cross-bars as defence against the downward slicing blows of the *falx*). In AD 85 Decebalus led his army across the Danube into Moesia, killed the governor, overpowered various Roman garrisons, and plundered the province. Domitian ordered a punitive counter-offensive, but his invasion force was defeated in AD 86. It was two years before the Romans were ready for a more determined effort, but on this occasion they won a great victory at Tapae, a mountain pass deep inside Dacia which led into the heart of Decebalus's kingdom. Before this victory could be consolidated, however, revolt broke out in the Roman rear and the army had to be recalled.

The generals' plot of AD 89 was led by Lucius Antonius Saturninus, Governor of Upper Germany. It was probably a direct response to the regime's perceived incompetence in the war against Decebalus. If so, the recent victory may have tipped the balance against the plotters, for most of the empire remained loyal, including the Governor of Lower Germany, whose forces had suppressed the revolt even before Domitian himself reached the scene. None the less, it had been the most serious conspiracy of the Flavian period, and Domitian, less secure on the throne than either his father or brother had been, cracked down on potential opponents. Domitian, as the younger son, had never expected to become emperor. He had lived his life in the shadow of his more accomplished father and elder brother. Vespasian had saved an empire. Titus had won a war. Domitian was merely his father's son. The Flavian dynasty, moreover, was very new, just 12 years old, when the new emperor acceded. Domitian's war against the Chatti had perhaps been fought – like Claudius's war against Britain – in part to win the emperor his spurs. He celebrated victory by raising his soldiers' pay by one third (from 225 to 300 *denarii*). He donned the dress of a *triumphator* (the victorious general in a triumph), and adopted the title *Germanicus* (Conqueror of Germany). He spent heavily throughout his reign on handouts, games and monuments. Yet there was another side to Domitian's Caesarism: the triumphalism of Claudius was married to the megalomania of Caligula. September and October were renamed *Germanicus* and *Domitianus*. Poets called him *Dominus et Deus* (Master and God). At newly established games in honour of Jupiter, he presided in Greek dress wearing a crown. He constructed a massive imperial palace on the Palatine Hill, and another in the Alban Hills outside Rome. Politically insecure, the emperor strove to elevate himself above the body-politic. Fear turned Domitian into a demi-god.

It also made him dangerous and unpredictable; especially after the scare of Saturninus's coup. Informers were encouraged. Philosophers and astrologers were banned from Rome. Various politicians, generals and intellectuals were charged with treason and executed. Then, as so often, the terror began to devour its own children. Some close to the emperor came under suspicion and were cut down – two Praetorian Guard commanders, a top imperial freedman, and the emperor's own cousin, husband to his niece, who was charged with atheism. The terror was soon out of control. It began to consume the dominant court faction. A plot formed at the highest level in AD 96. It included senators, army officers, members of the imperial household staff, and the empress herself. The assassination was messy. One of the imperial staff, a man called

Stephanus, who was facing a charge of embezzlement, offered to kill the emperor. He was admitted to Domitian's bedroom on the pretext that he had uncovered a plot and possessed a list of names. He promptly stabbed the emperor in the groin as he was reading the document, but, having failed to kill him outright, was then grappled. Domitian might yet have survived, but others of the imperial household joined the fray, a junior officer, a freedman, the head-chamberlain, and one of the emperor's personal gladiators. Overpowered and stabbed seven times, Domitian, third and last of the Flavian emperors, finally succumbed. An aged and colourless senator, Cocceius Nerva, figurehead leader of the plot, was hailed emperor on the same day.

After a period of civil war, the Flavian emperors had at first pursued an essentially moderate policy at home and on the frontiers, one designed to restore the empire's equilibrium. The governing class, after a preliminary purge, was left unmolested. The talented were promoted and the ranks of the elite broadened. The Romanization of the provinces was pushed forwards. The mob was succoured and entertained. The soldiers were regularly paid and kept busy. There was peace, prosperity for some, security for the propertied. The mass social base of the imperial system was restored. Also, with mutineers and rebels rooted out, the army was returned to discipline. The frontiers were carefully guarded, and, where necessary, strengthened by limited campaigns to punish a hostile tribe or improve a badly placed line. But problems remained. Partly they were those of a ramshackle political structure in which successive dictators were raised up who lacked legitimacy. Domitian was such a man. 'Contrary to his natural inclinations,' explained Suetonius, 'shortage of funds made him predatory and fear made him cruel.'(12) Domitian's attempts to buy popularity with the soldiers and the mob drained his treasury of funds. The opposition he faced within the governing class made him stuff his court with favourites and impose a reign of terror on the city. These were the politics of a weak dictator; and the tensions they generated within the Roman imperial elite could be resolved only by Stephanus's dagger. But underlying these parochial concerns – beyond the goldfish bowl of court and Senate – were tensions of far greater moment; tensions that could not be so easily resolved; tensions that would ultimately bring the empire down. These arose from a slowly shifting balance of forces between the rulers of the empire on one side, and the empire's enemies, both within and beyond the frontiers, on the other.

Decebalus had revealed again the limits of imperial power. A 'rogue state' had challenged the masters of the world and survived. The prestige of the empire had been dented. Was the empire strong enough to batter the Dacians into submission? Did the *Pax Romana* still hold?

A brief golden age: Trajan, Hadrian and Antoninus Pius, AD 98–161

After the crisis of AD 66–70, it had been hoped that the Flavian victory might herald another century of peace and security like that after Actium. Rebels, mutineers and civil-war factions had been crushed, and, during the 70s AD, with order and discipline restored under strong rulers, the army pushed forwards again on the frontiers – in Britain, in Germany, in the East. Then things seemed to unravel in the mid-80s. The Dacians had invaded Roman territory and defeated Roman armies. Domitian had punished them, but left them unbroken, a great kingdom just over the Danube, a skulking menace in the vastness of the Carpathians. Instead of settling with Decebalus, he had been provoked by plotters into turning on his own people, and blood had flowed among the rulers of Rome in the 90s. From great victories to punitive raids and civil strife: the later years of Flavian rule seemed to follow a depressing, downward trajectory. Was Roman power waning?

Two of Rome's greatest emperors, ruling in succession, Trajan (AD 98–117) and Hadrian (AD 117–138), offered radically different solutions to the crisis of empire in the early 2nd century. The contrast reveals the uncertainty of an imperial ruling class past its peak: the uncertainty that occurs when unexpected weakness is exposed and the attempt to continue in the old way falters. The history, traditions and values of Old Rome denied this possibility: was it not the divinely ordained destiny of the race of Romulus to rule the world, 'to command the nations, to impose peace, to spare the submissive, to crush the proud'? Yet a different image of the future had intruded, one in which shadowy forms of barbarian hordes and insurgent masses appeared in the frame. Perhaps the priority was to stiffen the empire's defences, and to foster the loyalty, unity and commitment of those standing behind them; to draw a line across the world, 'separating Romans and barbarians', them and us, rallying all the human and material forces of the empire in the cause of civilization. To continue to conquer in the old way, or to build a new commonwealth of peoples: this was the choice represented, respectively, by Trajan and Hadrian.

Trajan's immediate predecessor, the emperor Nerva (AD 96–98), had been an old man of little account. Representing no one in particular, he had had no particular mission to perform. He had been an historical dud, a convenient fill-in while the Roman governing elite recovered its nerve and found a way forwards. Once they had, Nerva obligingly died. By then, his regime was tottering, propped up at the last minute by one of the few wise decisions he made: naming Marcus Ulpius Traianus his successor. Trajan was a true soldier-emperor. An experienced and successful career officer, he was, at the time of his accession, serving as Governor of Upper Germany, making him one of Rome's top generals and a man rooted in one of its three major army-groups. Though of Romano-Spanish origin, his family was already established in the Senate, so, if he was a soldiers' candidate, he was equally acceptable to the politicians. Having named this popular successor, Nerva could be left to die peacefully, which he did just a month or two later. Trajan, still in Germany, was immediately hailed emperor without opposition.

Like Tiberius or Vespasian – but unlike Caligula or Domitian – Trajan did not have to prove his fitness to rule, and happily dispensed with the flummery of power that lesser men found necessary. His court was simple, the etiquette minimal, his person approachable, straight-talking, on the level. In this respect he was a Roman of the old school. So, too, in other, more important respects: for Trajan was, above all, a general and a conqueror.

Strangely – for he is one of Rome's greatest emperors – our written sources for his reign are poor. Our principal source for his two great campaigns of conquest in Dacia is his own victory monument – Trajan's Column, which still stands in the centre of Rome, its outer surface adorned with a spiralling ribbon of carved stone, just under a metre wide, some 200 m in length, depicting more than 2,500 separate figures engaged in the successive stages of war. It is, of course, a tainted source. It depicts only Dacians dead and dying, never Romans, and we can guess that much else about the imagery is selective. Yet, close reading of the ribbon, of one image following another – supplemented by fragments of evidence from elsewhere – allows a tentative reconstruction of events in Dacia in AD 101–102 and 105–106.

A force of perhaps 100,000 men was involved. Their supply was a logistical challenge of the highest order. The key was to use the Danube to ship grain from the Black Sea, but the rapids at the Iron Gates were an insuperable barrier to up-river navigation until Trajan's engineers cut a canal to bypass the worst, and restored a towpath that was part-carved into the cliff-face and part-projecting on a cantilevered timber frame. Then troops, transports and equipment were concentrated, new store-bases, forts and signal-stations constructed. Finally, the army crossed on pontoon bridges, the legionaries wearing new reinforced helmets and arm-guards, amply supplied with high-tech artillery, and supported by numerous auxiliaries, including archers, slingers and armoured cavalry.

But Decebalus was a cunning old fighter. He withdrew deep into his mountains, burning the ground behind him, until he reached Tapae, where, posting his warriors on the slopes above the pass, soon turned into slides of mud by torrential rain, he held shut the gates of Dacia. The following year, Trajan attacked again, this time in two columns, one to hold the enemy at Tapae, the other to force a way through by a second route, outflanking the main Dacian defence. The Column shows the native hill-forts on the approach reduced one by one – testimony to the fort-busting power of Roman siege-assaults – as the protective shell around Decebalus's capital at Sarmizegethusa was cracked open. Then, at the eleventh hour, Decebalus sued for peace. He saved his kingdom from annexation, but it was reduced to client status, and he was compelled to demolish his remaining hill-forts and accept a Roman garrison at his capital. Presumably the Dacian resistance had been strong enough to prevent outright victory, the capital perhaps just beyond Trajan's grasp at the end of a second summer.

Three years later, Decebalus felt strong enough to break free. He first took the commander of the Roman garrison at Sarmizegethusa hostage. But the general, an old friend of Trajan, killed himself to leave the emperor free to act. Again, two columns invaded, moving fast, reducing hill-forts in rapid succession, fighting with greater brutality than ever against men now deemed rebels. This time the Dacian capital was besieged and captured, though the king fled into the mountains, hotly pursued by Roman cavalry. The images on the Column are graphic: we see the king on the ground, isolated, surrounded, knife poised to take his own life, as so many of his followers had already done; meantime, towns and villages are torched, fugitives cut down, captives rounded up and dragged into slavery; and then an image of the dead king's head, held aloft before Trajan's assembled army.

In 1965, in a field in northern Greece, the tombstone of a Roman soldier was found: it was that of the man who had captured Decebalus and carried his severed head to Trajan. It read: 'He was made a *duplicarius* [junior NCO] by the divine Trajan in the Second Pannonian Cavalry, and then an *explorator* [scout]. He was decorated twice in Trajan's Dacian and Parthian wars. He was promoted to *decurio* [senior NCO] in the same cavalry regiment because he captured Decebalus and brought his head to Trajan at Rannistorum. He was honourably discharged by Terentius Scaurianus.'(13) This, of course, was the ultimate victory: the enemy dispersed; his capital taken; his leader slain; his territory plundered, laid waste, stripped of men. Dacia was ethnically cleansed, its people enslaved, at least 50,000 of them, though possibly, if there is no error in transmission of the written source, as many as 500,000; others, no doubt, were driven into the wilderness, where they perished. New settlers were introduced, and a new Roman province built, with roads, towns, pastures, salt-works and gold-mines.

The conquest of Dacia was celebrated in the old-fashioned way. A corrupted written source records the haul as 2.25 million kg of gold, 4.5 million kg of silver, and 500,000 slaves. Assume a simple transmission error and we might reduce these astronomical figures to a tenth of the size; even then, they represent, at the equivalent of around 675 million *denarii*, more than the whole sum of disbursements recorded by Augustus in the *Res Gestae*. We see something of this booty still preserved in surviving monuments of stone. A new commercial harbour, nearly one kilometre across, with berthing for 100 ships, ringed by great warehouses, was built at Portus near the Tiber mouth: a guarantee of the city's grain-supply. A massive public bath-house was erected, no doubt with deliberate symbolic intent, on the ruins of Nero's Golden House on the Esquiline Hill. Ancient slums were cleared in the zone immediately north of the Forum, and a great chunk of the Quirinal Hill, to a maximum depth of 38 m, was cut away, creating a wide open space, 200 m by

120 m, for the greatest of Trajan's buildings. The space was filled by a new imperial forum and basilica, the latter 80 m long by 25 m wide and lavishly decorated with imported marble columns. Beyond the basilica, on the western side of the complex, was a pair of libraries, and these framed the famous Column, allowing visitors to the library a close view of the sculpted scenes of the emperor's Dacian wars. Behind the imperial forum, resting against the cut-away hill to the north, a multi-storey complex of vaulted passageways, arcaded shops and luxury flats was built. Trajan's Markets still survive as the best place in the modern city to get a sense of what it was like to walk the streets of ancient Rome. There was a message in all of this. Trajan's answer to the crisis of empire was the familiar one: war is glorious, and it is conquest that yields security and riches. The empire was not weakening: Rome was still an earth-shaking colossus striding the globe.

But the richest rewards, as always, glittered beyond the haze of the eastern deserts. Here, the Flavian policy of border annexations had brought the legions up to the Parthian frontier. Then Trajan had ordered the annexation of Nabataean Arabia (centred on the great caravan city of Petra) in AD 105–108. Soon a new road was being built, linking Syria with Petra, Aqaba and the Red Sea. Tension mounted. In AD 110, Osroes succeeded to the throne of Parthia, a king committed to aggressive defence. The pro-Roman puppet ruler of Armenia was ejected and replaced by a kinsman of the Parthian king. Trajan, no less aggressive than Osroes, champion of traditional imperialism, victor over Decebalus, set himself the ultimate challenge: a great war of conquest in the East to eliminate the Parthian threat forever. Concentrating massive force – eight legions plus supporting auxiliaries (80,000 men) – he unleashed a military blitzkrieg in AD 114, overrunning Armenia, descending into northern Mesopotamia, sweeping up hasty declarations of allegiance from the Parthian client-kings in his path. The following year, his army raised to 13 legions (130,000 men), he pushed on south, down the lower Tigris and Euphrates, finally to reach the Gulf, the whole of Mesopotamia under his control. It was a dizzying achievement. The Land of Two Rivers was among the oldest, richest and most heavily populated centres of civilization in the world. It had been the supply-base of numerous great empires over millennia of time, but no Roman – not Sulla, Crassus, Pompey, Caesar, Antony or Octavian-Augustus – had ever come nearly so far.

That winter of AD 115/116, Trajan appeared greater than them all: a new Alexander.

But Alexander had fought two great battles of annihilation against the armies of the Persian Empire before he marched on Babylon. His enemies' military power had been broken before he took their capital cities. Trajan's achievement was puny by comparison. He had not yet faced the Parthian army at all – that enemy was still very much at large. His communications stretched back over hundreds of miles of river, desert and mountain. Vast populations were held in thrall by relative handfuls of soldiers. The Roman defence-line was wafer-thin. In the vast expanses of the East, the social and military weight of eastern humanity threatened to swamp the scattered pockets of Roman officials and soldiers among them. And so it came to pass. In AD 116, the Parthian Empire struck back. The main royal army, mustered on the Iranian plateau, swept down the passes of the Zagros Mountains, assailed the Roman supply-line, and crushed the battle groups sent against them. The ancient cities of Mesopotamia exploded into revolt: Roman garrisons were massacred, and Trajan was soon embroiled in a war of sieges to hold and retake key strategic centres. Meantime, deep in the Roman rear, a revolt among the Jews of Cyrene quickly spread to Jewish communities in Egypt, Cyprus and eventually Palestine itself. Finally, gut-wrenching news filtered through to the embattled army commanders in Mesopotamia that there was trouble in Britain and on the Danube: frontiers stripped of men for Trajan's eastern war were now exposed to attack as enemies learned that the army was bogged down. Trajan headed for home, leaving Hadrian, his principal lieutenant, in charge in the East. But on the way, in August AD 117, he fell ill and died. And, with the whole East in flames, his attempt to resolve the crisis of imperial overstretch by a return to untrammelled expansionism had died with him. Roman imperialism had lurched forwards, kangarooed and crashed.

The roots of Trajan's failure were deep. Ancient military imperialism was dynamically expansionist because it paid for itself and yielded a profit: it generated in plunder and tribute more than it cost. If this had not been so, it would have ruined the states that engaged in aggressive war, and impoverished their ruling classes – in which case there would have been neither the incentive nor capacity to wage it. Quite simply, war and empire were profitable. But only up to a point.

Everything depended on whether the land fought over could yield a return. Empire and civilization were based, broadly, on plough agriculture. Regions of intensive cultivation, supporting large populations and numerous settlements, produced surpluses that could be expropriated as booty, taxes, rents, tithes, interest and labour services. But the lower the level of agricultural development, the more marginal the potential gains. Beyond the plough-lands, in the marshes, forests, mountains and deserts of true *barbaricum*, regions populated sparsely by nomads, pastoralists and scattered crofters, there was little portable wealth. Here, moreover, armies could be swallowed up in great tracts of uncharted wilderness, starving at the end of long, fragile supply-lines, harassed by elusive guerrilla bands, bogged down in unwinnable and pointless wars. Heavy investment in men and hardware might count for little in such environments, even be liabilities. War and empire in the wilderness were not profitable, for there was little profit to be had; they were merely a drain on the plough-lands of the hinterland required to support the effort of conquest. Everywhere, the Roman Empire reached its natural limits where the ploughed met the unploughed, ancient agriculture bordered primitive wasteland, civilization confronted barbarism – in the mountain ranges of north-west Africa, at the desert fringes of Libya, Egypt, Palestine and Syria, along the Danube and in the Rhineland of continental Europe, and in the hill-country of northern Britain.

Almost everywhere: the exception was the narrow border with Parthia. Here, in contrast, the enemy was a rival empire, another super-power based on plough-agriculture. Rome and Parthia confronted one another in a corridor of cultivated land which ran north-west to south-east along the river lines of the upper Tigris and Euphrates. Invasions on this route were hedged with hazard. Elsewhere, on every other frontier, Rome now held the outer line of the plough-lands, and her army was stretched thin along it, often dangerously so. Yet to mount an invasion of Parthia, she had to mass great forces, for the strength of any army was sapped with each march forwards, by attrition in the field, and by the guards and garrisons that had to be left in the rear. Parthia's vast spaces, the great distance to her heartlands, the invincibility of her armoured cavalry and horse-archers on the open steppe, these things made a Roman conquest of the Orient a supreme military challenge. Repeatedly, since Crassus at Carrhae in 53 BC, the limits of Roman imperial power had been tested against the Parthian Empire, and each time they had been reached far short of any final victory. Rome was at an impasse on the eastern front: though able to contain it, she lacked the means to overthrow the Parthian Empire. Trajan had tried harder than any of his predecessors: his failure in consequence was more complete.

Publius Aelius Hadrianus, like Trajan, was Romano-Spanish. The two men were, in fact, related, and after Hadrian's father had died when the boy was ten, he had been entrusted to Trajan's care. Much later, he was married to Trajan's great-niece, Sabina, a loveless marriage without affection or issue, but one convenient in fixing Hadrian's position at the centre of his patron's network. Close family ties made Hadrian trustworthy, but he was also intelligent, well educated and energetic, a man suited to high responsibility. By the time of his elevation in AD 117, he was already a veteran general, having served in all three of Trajan's wars – as a staff officer in the Second Dacian War, a legionary commander in the Third, and, successively, as Governor of Syria and then commander-in-chief during the Parthian War. Even so, the accession was murky and contested. Nor is it difficult to guess what issue lay at the heart of the bloody clash at the top that inaugurated Hadrian's principate.

The written sources for Hadrian's reign are little better than those for Trajan's, and we have few details of the generals' plot of AD 117. Before reaching his capital, Hadrian's Praetorian Prefect had arrested, condemned and executed four of Trajan's leading marshals, charged with plotting against the new emperor. Probably, with some reason, they had argued that Hadrian was neither the appointed successor, nor an appropriate candidate. Trajan's death had been sudden. No heir had been publicly announced – perhaps for fear of igniting animosities among the army commanders. But Hadrian was the late emperor's ward, favourite, nephew by marriage, and commander-in-chief in the East, so perhaps his inheritance was implicit. The formal announcement, however, and the passing on of the imperial signet-ring had been a death-bed scene witnessed only by Trajan's wife, Hadrian's mother-in-law, the Praetorian Prefect, and a personal servant of the emperor – who, suspiciously, died suddenly soon after the event. The succession document bore his wife's, not Trajan's, signature. Was Hadrian, perhaps, a usurper? The new emperor was certainly at pains to win approval. He spent almost a month among the soldiers before arriving in the capital, determined first to show his face to the frontier legions and collect their acclamations. Then, a shower of largesse: large donatives were paid to the soldiers and the city mob; 'coronation gold', a tax traditionally paid at the accession of a new emperor, was remitted for Italy and reduced in the provinces; and all debts to the state were cancelled, at the spectacular cost of 225 million *denarii*.

The root of both the plotters' malevolence and the emperor's anxiety lay, almost certainly, in a deep split within the army command about the military débâcle in the East and the future direction of the empire. For Hadrian had resolved to pull out and consolidate. More than that: to stamp this policy on the empire forever. The contrast between the politics of Trajan and those of his protégé could not have been more radically different. Two men, both reared in the same stable, the one the pampered favourite and intimate of the other, reached diametrically opposed conclusions about how the empire should be governed. And while both were ideologically driven, Trajan's vision was a reactionary one, an attempt to return to the glory days of war and conquest, whereas Hadrian was a radical trying to make sense of new realities and fashion a new model empire. It was perhaps crucial that he was a provincial emperor. Reared in Spain, he had travelled during his career in Gaul, Germany, the Balkans, Asia Minor, the Levant and Mesopotamia. Italy, for him, was just one among the many provinces of the empire. He was the first emperor for whom the traditional imperial title *pater patriae* (father of his country) – which, like his model, Augustus, he adopted only at the end of his reign – meant not merely protector and patron of Rome and Italy, but of all the provinces of the empire. He wished to raise all to the same level of peace, prosperity, good governance, urban life and classical culture; to create a commonwealth of peoples enjoying the benefits of the *Pax Romana* and united by their allegiance to emperor, empire and Roman values. Thus would the empire grow stronger within. Thus would its people more willingly shoulder the burden of defence. Thus would the frontiers – now better defined, fortified and garrisoned – more easily be held. Hadrian set out to create a dichotomous world, in which the difference between civilization and barbarism was to be made sharper, the boundaries between them more rigid and immutable. It was a vision and a policy for an empire that had reached its limits.

Hadrian spent much of his reign travelling. But while his predecessors had sometimes done this in order to make war, Hadrian travelled in order to govern. The restless energy of the top commander that he had been became that of the visionary statesman, the nation-builder, the modernizing reformer, determined to see everything for himself, to make assessments on the spot, and to set in train the great projects needed to remake the world. He first toured the western provinces – the Rhineland, Britain, Gaul, Spain and Mauretania (Morocco) – in AD 120–123. Then he visited the Greek cities of Asia Minor, Old Greece and Sicily in AD 124–126. After two years in Rome, his third trip took him to Africa in AD 128. His fourth, in AD 129–131, was again to the East, to revisit Athens, and then on to Antioch, to Palmyra and Damascus, to Jerash and Petra, to Jerusalem, to Alexandria in Egypt and Cyrene in Libya.

Everywhere he went the emperor seems to have left an indelible mark: the archaeology of the Roman Empire still bears, on the frontiers and in the great classical cities, the imprint of Hadrian the Builder. He had made himself known already to the legions in the East and on the Danube, so in the early years of his reign he visited the men stationed on the Rhine, in Britain and in North Africa. Over some ten years Hadrian completed a great tour of inspection of the entire army and frontier system. 'He personally viewed and investigated absolutely everything,' explained Dio Cassius, 'not merely the usual installations of the camps, such as weapons, engines, trenches, ramparts and palisades, but also the private affairs of everyone, both of the men serving in the ranks and of the officers themselves – their lives, their quarters, their habits – and he reformed and corrected in many cases practices and arrangements for living that had become too luxurious. He drilled the men for every kind of battle, honouring some and reproving others, and he taught them all what should be done.'(14) The praises of the commander-in-chief, witness to a military tattoo at Lambaesis legionary fortress in North Africa, were proudly recorded on the base of a stone column: 'You did everything in orderly fashion. You filled the field with manoeuvres. Your javelin hurling was not without grace, although you use javelins which are short and stiff. Several of you hurled your lances equally well. And your mounting was smart just now and lively yesterday. If there was anything lacking, I should notice it; if there were anything conspicuously bad, I should point it out. But you pleased me uniformly throughout the whole exercise. My legate Catullinus, *vir clarissimus*, devotes equal care to all the branches he commands . . . Your prefect evidently looks after you carefully. I bestow upon you a largesse . . .'(15)

But it is the frontier defences that most visibly record the emperor's passing. Open lines controlled by forts, signal-stations and patrols were replaced by continuous linear barriers formed of ditches, palisades and walls. Hadrian's Wall in Britain is the supreme and best-studied example. Extending 73 miles (117 km) from Newcastle to Carlisle, it comprised a stone wall up to 3 m thick and perhaps 4.5 m high, with small forts for around 30 men every mile, and observation turrets every third of a mile. It was fronted by a wide, deep, V-shaped ditch, and between wall and ditch was an entanglement of forked and sharpened branches – the Roman equivalent of barbed wire. Gateways at the milecastles provided the only approved crossing-places, such that traffic over the border could be controlled and tolls perhaps levied on traders. Outpost forts were built north of the wall to facilitate long-range patrolling. The system of milecastles and turrets – though without the wall between – was extended far down the Cumberland coast. As work progressed, plans were modified: the thickness of the wall was reduced; sections built originally of turf were replaced in stone; a continuous linear earthwork (the Vallum) was dug to the south, defining a broad belt of land behind the wall as a 'military zone'; and, most importantly, a series of regimental forts were built along the line of the wall, at first 12, eventually 16, putting 6 or 7,000 auxiliary troops on the frontier line itself.

Debate about the purpose of the wall continues. The recent discovery of the thicket of spikes along its front implies a military purpose. But contemporary Roman military doctrine had it that pre-emptive and punitive aggression was the best form of defence, so the wall was more likely intended as a police and customs barrier. Even this, perhaps, is to over-rationalize a profoundly political project. If Trajan offered battles and military glory, Hadrian offered instead great buildings, monuments to imperial grandeur, a symbolic marking out of boundaries, a way of 'separating the Romans from the barbarians'. Hadrian's frontier works, moreover, were part of a larger package. It had been necessary to settle the soldiers – with bribes, flattery and hard work. But then, having ritually charged the boundaries of the empire by marking them with lines of earth and stone, Hadrian turned his attention to the people within, the subjects of Rome, all of whom were now to become stakeholders and loyalists in an imperial commonwealth. The showcases of the new world order would be, of course, the cities of the empire.

Here, not only was Hadrian's the vision, but very often so too were the plans, the blueprints, the engineering needed to monumentalize it in stone. Hadrian, it seems, was something of an architect. His masterpiece was the Pantheon in Rome. In it, the structurally redundant pillars of Greek temple architecture were abandoned, and the central shrine, released from its cage, became the whole building. But instead of a traditional box, the full potential of the Roman vault was realized, and the shrine was built as a huge dome, one describing a complete and perfect circle from apex to floor and from side to side. The huge span, an awesome 43.20 m, has been surpassed only in modern times, an achievement made possible by having an immense ring of concrete as foundation, by the use of top-quality Roman mortar, and by a careful grading of the thickness and types of material used in constructing the dome from top to bottom.

Rome, as ever, was intended as a model for the provinces. Hadrian, as he travelled, initiated great building projects in city after city. Today, when we visit ruined Roman cities around the Mediterranean, a good proportion of what we see belongs to the 'golden age' of Hadrian and Antoninus Pius, his immediate successor. Over several decades, the down-town areas of scores of imperial cities were transformed into building sites and recast with new complexes of monumental classical architecture and baroque decoration. Take Athens, for example, an old Greek university town that was a special favourite of the philhellene emperor. Close to the ancient agora, he built a library complex, more than 120 m by 80 m in extent, complete with walled garden, lily-pond, surrounding colonnades, and sitting-out places. On the edge of the city, he completed – 600 years after the foundations were laid – the Temple of Olympian Zeus, one of the largest classical temples in the world, of which 17 towering Corinthian columns still stand. More than that, in the area around the temple, he laid out an entire new city suburb, memorializing this achievement in a stone arch positioned between the old and new cities: 'This is Athens, the ancient city of Theseus' reads the inner face, 'This is the city of Hadrian, not of Theseus' reads the outer. The past – the glory that was Greece, the fount of classical civilization, the foundation on which Hadrian planned to build – this was honoured. But it was added to, made yet grander, renewed by Hadrianic monuments which appropriated that past to the exigencies of the present. Here, however, in his great projects of acculturation, no less than Trajan in his of subjugation, Hadrian discovered that empire had limits.

Not for the first time in the history of the Empire, the Jews of Palestine proved themselves the hardest rock of resistance. For 200 years, the peasants of Galilee and Judaea had rejected the temptations of *Romanitas*, and withstood the insults and bullying of its local agents. At root, they knew, Rome meant the rule of landlords, tax-collectors and government soldiers. The trinkets and trappings were mainly for the rich. The new gods were pagan idols offensive to the righteous. Here, for Hadrian, on the other hand, was a worm of corruption within his commonwealth, a class of men whose boorishness could feed an irrational opposition and a weakening of the body-politic. In AD 70, the Jewish Temple in Jerusalem had been destroyed, the Temple tithe diverted to Jupiter, and a Roman legion stationed on the Temple Mount. Yet, Judaism and a Jewish national identity had survived, even in Roman-occupied Jerusalem, where at least seven synagogues remained. The race, the monotheism and the nationalism of the Jews made them an enemy within, and Hadrian came to Jerusalem in AD 130 determined to destroy them, to ethnically cleanse his empire, to obliterate an ideological alternative, to impose by force the Graeco-Roman norms that had become compulsory.

Jerusalem was re-founded as a Roman colony – Aelia Capitolina – and a temple for the worship of Hadrian-Jupiter was built on the Temple Mount. The practice of circumcision – the single most distinctive marker of Semitic identity – was banned on pain of death. Hadrian declared himself successor to Antiochus Epiphanes, the Greek ruler who had tried to destroy Judaism three centuries before, and he erected a monument to Pompey, the first Roman enemy of the Jews. Alexandria and Cyrene, Greek cities devastated in the Jewish Revolt of AD 115–118, were conspicuously reconstructed. By AD 132 the Jews had been goaded into revolt. In scale, duration and ferocity, the resistance fully matched that of AD 66–73. Led by Bar-Kokhba, 'Son of the Star', a new Jewish messiah who was to prove himself a brilliant guerrilla commander, and by the radical-nationalist rabbi Akiba, the revolutionaries took immediate control of Jerusalem, restored the worship of Yahweh, and issued coins announcing the 'Redemption of Israel'. Quickly reinforced by returning emigrés and a general rising in the countryside, the rebels overwhelmed local Roman forces. Two legions were not enough. The empire was trawled for troops. With fresh legions poured into the war zone, Jerusalem was retaken; but the rebels re-established themselves at Herodium and various remote desert cave-complexes. It took four years to crush the revolt entirely. By the time it ended, in AD 136, 50 fort-resses and 1,000 villages had been destroyed, and 500,000 people killed or enslaved; Palestine, Dio Cassius tells us, was left a wilderness of wolves and hyenas feeding on corpses.

By now, Hadrian, back in Italy, was embittered and dying. His vision of a commonwealth of peoples had been consumed in the Palestinian apocalypse: all that remained there was the arrogance of foreign overlords and pagan gods. His relations with his commanders and officials had soured. The emperor's philhellenism, his open homosexuality, his public affair with the beautiful Greek youth Antinoös, the creation of a cult in his honour after he was drowned in the Nile: all this offended the sensibilities of conservative members of the Roman governing class. It seemed to many to symbolize the decadence of the regime. The withdrawal from Mesopotamia, the failure to advance elsewhere, the freezing of the frontier lines, the favouritism towards Greeks, the diluting of Roman citizenship, the spilling out of imperial wealth on the embellishment of provincial cities: all highly questionable. It was not just Jewish freedom-fighters who contested the Hadrianic vision; so, too, did the Old Guard at home.

Hadrian retreated to the grand country residence he had built for himself at Tivoli, in the hills a short distance from Rome, a palace and garden-city modelled on Athens and Alexandria, sprawling across some 300 hectares (making it not much smaller than Rome itself). He seemed no longer to care. He named as successor a handsome young fop with a reputation for idleness, self-indulgence, and reading love poetry and cookery books while reclining on scented cushions strewn with flowers. Presumably he was the old man's fancy. The fop predeceased his master. Hadrian then adopted an old friend: Titus Antoninus – soon to be Antoninus Pius – and thereafter relapsed into bitter apathy and derangement, awaiting death – sometimes, it is said, trying unsuccessfully to hasten it – a man psychologically and politically broken by the contradictions of an empire at bay.

Antoninus Pius (AD 138–161) was mercifully free of ambition, whether of Trajanic or Hadrianic type. The spirit of the age was mediocrity, and Antoninus was a fitting figurehead. Neither great generals, nor revolutionary leaders, nor reforming ministers were needed; merely an administrator who would do nothing to upset the geopolitical equilibrium. Expansion had ended, but retreat had not yet begun. This was the essence of Gibbon's golden age: 'In the second century of the Christian era, the empire of Rome comprehended the fairest part of the earth, and most civilised portion of mankind. The frontiers of that extensive monarchy were guarded by ancient renown and disciplined valour. The gentle, but powerful, influence of laws and manners, had gradually cemented the union of the provinces. Their peaceful inhabitants enjoyed and abused the advantages of wealth and luxury. The image of a free constitution was preserved with decent reverence: the Roman Senate appeared to possess the sovereign authority, and devolved on the emperors all the executive powers of government. During a happy period of more than fourscore years, the public administration was conducted by the virtue and abilities of Nerva, Trajan, Hadrian, and the two Antonines.'(16) Peace, order, wealth, civilization: the 2nd century empire certainly offered these. But all the while the mole of history was at work. Several phases passed in quick succession: the exhaustion of expansion under Trajan; the consolidation of frontiers under Hadrian; an equilibrium of forces under Antoninus; and then, under Marcus, a collapse along the upper Danube and a great flood of German tribesmen into northern Italy.

On the surface, all seemed calm. Almost everywhere there was peace. The only major campaign of Antoninus's reign was in northern Britain, a push forwards to take in the Southern Uplands and form a new line between the Forth and the Clyde. The reasons are obscure, but they were surely to do with improving frontier security; not that it worked, whatever the plan may have been, for the Romans were back on Hadrian's Wall a generation later. Elsewhere, it was a matter of small local campaigns and police operations – the straightening out of a stretch of frontier in Germany, a war against mountain 'brigands' in Mauretania, a tax revolt in Egypt: routine stuff. Meantime, across the empire, materialized in the archaeology of ten thousand Roman sites, the imperial economy was booming. Basilicas, temples, bath-houses, theatres, amphitheatres and shopping malls went up in town centres. Grand town-houses filled the suburbs, while villas were built on nearby country estates. Local aristocrats thus equipped themselves to shuttle comfortably between the amenities, social round and public duties of the town, and the relative tranquillity of their rural seats. A Mediterranean ambience was universal. A single Graeco-Roman cultural *koine* defined the elites of the empire. Everywhere it was colonnaded courtyards, frescoed and mosaic-floored living rooms, gardens filled with classical statuary, box-hedges and marble fountains. People drank wine, conversed in Greek or Latin, made offerings to Jupiter, and read – or claimed to read – the classics. Trade and the crafts flourished, and so did the larger farms with a surplus to sell and good roads or waterways to take it to market: for the empire and its civilization, the soldiers and the elite, the forts and the towns, all needed an unceasing supply of grain, meat, salt, cloth, leather, timber, stone, pottery, ironwork, bronze, silver, gold, and much else.

Yet the true stakeholders were a minority. The majority were slaves, serfs, poor peasants, or at best middling peasants with enough for themselves and their families but little to spare. These were perhaps three-quarters or more of the empire's people. They were the producers from whom surplus was creamed in tax, rent, interest and forced labour – the surplus that was invested in forts, towns and villas, the surplus that made empire and civilization possible. As things stood, though the empire brought no benefit, though it offered only a life of toil and trouble to the mass of rural people, nonetheless it generally left them enough to carry on, enough for some sort of life. But the balance was a fine one. The margin of safety for millions – the margin between how much went in tax and what was needed to feed a family and stock a farm – was perilously narrow. Tip the balance just a little, and millions might plunge to ruin.

For the state, too, the balance was fine, the margin of safety narrow: it currently took just enough in tax to support the minimum of soldiers needed to man the empire's defences. But the line – thousands of miles of stone, earth, iron and flesh – was stretched thin. Dangerously thin, as the skies darkened in the far north.

CHAPTER 5

• • • • • • • • • • • • • • •

The decline and fall of the Western Roman Empire

The military monarchy: Marcus Aurelius, Commodus and Septimius Severus, AD 161–211

Marcus Aurelius (AD 161–180) was a child of the *Pax Romana*. Like Trajan and Hadrian, he was Romano-Spanish, his elevation a further testament to the 'provincialization' of the imperial elite. Brought up and educated in the circle around Hadrian, he studied under top philosophers, became a convinced Stoic, and produced his own tract, *Meditations*, which has survived. Then he spent 23 years serving Antoninus Pius, 15 of them as a close advisor. He embraced the Hadrianic vision of the empire as a commonwealth of peoples, and, under Antoninus, tried to live up to the Stoic ideal of public service and *noblesse oblige*. True to the spirit of the age, his succession was seamless. Made Antoninus's adoptive son, married to his daughter, advanced through a series of top political posts, he already enjoyed full imperial power at the time of his patron's death. The accession was therefore automatic and uncontested. Though ostensibly sharing power with Lucius Verus – also Antoninus's adoptive son and nominated successor – the latter was a weak and dissolute young man, and it was always Marcus Aurelius who truly ruled. Yet Marcus stands as a figure of Tolstoyian tragedy, for his probity and good intentions were of no account in a reign dominated by storm and strife. Overextended, no longer subsidized by war and plunder, sinking slowly in the global geopolitical balance, the empire was invaded and devastated on a scale not seen since the time of Hannibal.

The first year of the new reign was a disaster. The Tiber burst its banks and flood-damage was widespread. Famine gripped parts of Italy. Border wars erupted in Britain and Upper Germany. Worst of all, King Vologases III overran Armenia, installed a Parthian puppet, defeated the Governor of Cappadocia, and then swept on down into Roman Syria, scattering the legions before him. It took time to organize a Roman counter-attack – not least because Lucius Verus was put in nominal command – but when it came, a steady succession of victories pushed the Parthians back, out of Armenia in AD 163, out of northern Mesopotamia in AD 164, and finally out of southern Mesopotamia also in AD 165; the Romans even penetrated into Media in the Zagros Mountains in AD 166.

Parthia was a declining power. Its occasional acts of aggression were the spasms of a weak, and weakening, political order. Momentary successes were due to surprise, and once Rome's legions were marshalled, the Parthian forces were invariably unable to meet them in pitched battle. But, just as Trajan had been in AD 115, Lucius Verus was overextended with his army on the Gulf. Of this, the young emperor was oblivious: he toured the Greek cities of the East calling himself *Armeniacus, Hercules Pacifer, Parthicus Maximus, Medicus* (Conqueror of Armenia, Hercules the Peacemaker, Great Conqueror of Parthia, Conqueror of Media). Marcus also celebrated, holding a triumph in Rome, taking the title *pater patriae* (father of his country), and giving his two sons the title *Caesar*. But Marcus, if not his co-emperor, understood the limits of power, and the eastern settlement he imposed reflected this: Armenia was restored as a Roman buffer state, but there was no repeat of Trajan's mistake in trying to hold Mesopotamia; the Romans pulled back to a safer line that could be held in strength. Even so, fate charged a terrible price for the Parthian War.

In AD 165, in the sweltering heat of the Mesopotamian summer, a deadly contagion was imported into the camps of the Roman army. It may have started at Seleucia, a city sacked by the Roman army in violation of an agreement. The story went around that a soldier had broken open a casket in the Temple of Apollo and unwittingly released 'a pestilential vapour'. The contagion kept its grip through the winter, and then flared up again the following summer. The Roman army retreated in a chaos of physical and moral collapse. The survivors reaching Syria brought the plague with them, and during AD 167 it swept across the Roman world. We do not know what it was. The Greek doctor Galen records fever, pustules, skin rash, and the spitting of blood. Perhaps it was smallpox. What is clear is that it was both virulent and persistent, a spectre of death haunting the army barracks and urban backstreets through all the long years of Marcus's reign and into the next. 'From the frontiers of the Persians to the Rhine and Gaul,' reported the historian Ammianus Marcellinus, 'the foul touch of the plague polluted everything with contagion and death.'(1) 'Such great pestilence devastated all Italy,' explained Orosius, 'that everywhere estates, fields and towns were left deserted, without cultivators or inhabitants, and relapsed into ruins and woodland.'(2) An outbreak in AD 189 – perhaps of the same contagion – killed 2,000 people a day in Rome. Some communities may have lost 25 per cent or more of their population. The plague emptied the tribute-bearing farms and frontier-holding forts of the Roman Empire with a power Vologases could never have imagined.

The same year the plague reached Italy – already weakened by bad harvests and famine several years running – a huge force of Germans crossed the Danube, defeated a Roman army of 20,000, passed over the Julian Alps, and descended into northern Italy. Led by Ballomar, King of the Marcomanni, they were a great tribal confederation that included Marcomanni, Quadi, Vandals and Lombards. Nothing like it had been seen since Marius had defeated the Cimbri and Teutones 250 years before. Roman countermeasures were desperate. Slaves, gladiators and brigands were enrolled in the army. Germanic barbarians were recruited. Reinforcements were rushed in from the East. The palace treasures were sold off at auction to raise funds. Marcus Aurelius took the field in person (as, again, did Lucius Verus, though he died soon after, in AD 169). For several years fighting raged across the empire's Danubian provinces, and then, in AD 172–175, the emperor carried the war forwards into Germany. His aim was perhaps to destroy German military power so completely that no further invasion of imperial territory would be pos-sible; perhaps also to create a buffer zone north of the Danube that would protect Roman territory. But forward aggression brought new enemies into the fray – notably the Sarmatians – and the war dragged on. A pause in AD 175–177 was followed by renewed fighting against Marcomanni, Quadi and Sarmatians in the final years of Marcus's reign.

The world was changing fast. The barbarian peoples of the North had evolved from loose tribal associations into proto-states ruled by kings. Contact with Rome had been a decisive influence. The emperors offered a model of autocratic power to tribal leaders. Subsidies and diplomatic missions enhanced the power of Roman clients. A steady flow of luxury goods, whether traded or given in gift-exchange, increased the patronage of those who controlled them. Above all, the threat posed by the Roman imperial army encouraged confederation, a forging of larger polities, obedience to kings who, by commanding thousands instead of hundreds, could offer both protection and plunder. In the past, great German leaders like Arminius, the victor over Varus at the Teutoburg Forest in AD 9, had been the elected commanders of temporary alliances; now, increasingly, they were reigning monarchs whose power lasted as long as they could keep their thrones. The Germans had become more redoubtable foes. Ten years fighting in the forests and mountains of the North had taught hard lessons. Rome, too, had to change. After the stopgap measures of AD 167, longer lasting reforms were set in train. It was in Marcus Aurelius's German wars that what has been called 'the military monarchy' first took shape.

The authority of the state over the bodies and property of its citizens was increased: birth registers were introduced; control over the estates of minors was taken from families and given to civil servants; fathers lost control of the rewards paid to sons on military service. In this and other ways, intermediary institutions – families, guilds, local towns – were displaced as the central state entered into a direct relationship with the civilians on whom it depended for tribute and recruits. Central government interfered increasingly in local affairs: the cost of games and shows was tightly regulated; expenditure on public buildings was reined in; new burdens were imposed on towns and villages, including the provision of food, lodging and transport to the army. Resources were not to be wasted on largesse and grandeur; they were to be husbanded for the war effort. Devastated border areas were repopulated by defeated barbarians, organized in tightly regulated communities under obligation, in return for their land, to perform military service. Other defeated barbarians were enrolled directly into the standing army.

Much has been written about the 'barbarization' of the Roman army. In fact, the army had always recruited barbarians, and if the proportion was now increased, this was a prerequisite of imperial survival. When, as sometimes happened, revolts broke out among barbarian soldiers, these invariably were rooted in specific abuses, not in some general 'nationalist' aspiration to bring down the empire. The army was reformed in other ways, too. New regional commands were created, with control over army groups extending across several provinces, and some units were withdrawn from the front-line to form mobile reserves stationed in back-areas. Promotion on merit became more common. The army, always the principal avenue of social advancement, became yet more open to promotion from the ranks, with numerous equestrian officers reaching the highest positions in Marcus's service. Inherited rank mattered less; the embattled empire put a premium on professionalism.

Centralized power, cuts in municipal spending, an increase in the burdens imposed on citizens, new barbarian frontier settlements, the reorganization of the army, new military strategies, a career more open to talent: all these are features of the emerging military monarchy. The essence of it was a shift of wealth and power away from citizens, families, towns, even the provinces as a whole – away, that is, from what might be called 'civil society' – to the state, the army, the frontiers, and the imperial aristocracy. Here was the first stage in a long process in which the burden of imperial defence – previously subsidized by plunder from wars of conquest – was shifted from expropriated foreign enemies to the civilian population of the empire itself. By one of history's many ironies, Marcus Aurelius, the would-be philosopher-king, was experienced by most of his subjects as a ruthless warlord.

In another respect, too, events in Marcus's reign heralded the epoch of imperial decline. The empire still retained battlefield dominance. It would continue to do so until at least the campaigns of Belisarius in the second quarter of the 6th century AD. The combination in Late Roman and Early Byzantine armies of accumulated military expertise, superb drill and discipline, high-tech armour and weaponry, and first-rate organization, logistics and engineering usually ensured tactical success, even against numerically much superior opponents. The problem was strategic: concentrated force could be applied only in one or two places at any time, leaving the rest of the empire – whose frontier lines were thousands of miles long – relatively exposed. With the empire's military centre of gravity temporarily in the East during Marcus's Parthian War, the defences of continental Europe had been weakened, and it was then that the Germans had broken through. Once the weight of the army had been shifted back, not only were the Germans driven out, but the war was successfully carried into their homeland. This see-sawing of military strength would characterize the whole history of the Late Empire; ever shifting from one threatened front to another, the emperor's mobile army groups would no sooner have plugged one gap than another would gape open elsewhere. This, moreover, was not simply a military problem: the chronic threat of localized frontier collapse that henceforward afflicted the empire imposed a huge strain on its political structure.

The first responsibility of the state, after all – of any state – was to protect the national territory. A state which could not do this lost legitimacy. From the time of Marcus onwards, emperors were rarely able to ensure comprehensive, all-round security. The military monarchy was forced to prioritize, concentrating men, military hardware, supplies and financial reserves where they were most needed. This draining of resources to the main battlefronts left officers defending other frontiers dangerously weak. Forts, towns and villas were open to attack. A century of stable frontiers, fixed garrisons and local recruitment, moreover, had forged strong bonds between soldiers and the districts where they served. Many men were defending families, homes and farms nearby. The growing centralism of the Roman state was therefore contradicted by the growing regionalism of its army groups. The military monarchy aimed for a more centripetal empire as the state apparatus at its command was pulled apart by centrifugal forces. The rebel officers of Late Antiquity – like those of AD 69 – may often have been motivated by careerism. Their prospects of advancement dimmed during years passed in garrison forts that were distant from the emperor, the mobile army, and fields of victory. Promotion was faster on active service under the eye of the commander-in-chief. But whatever personal motives drove the successive military revolts of the period, sections of the civil elite often gave strong support: a usurper emperor, one who used local revenues for local protection, often seemed a better prospect than a 'legitimate' ruler a thousand miles away.

In AD 175, Avidius Cassius, the leading commander under Lucius Verus during the Parthian War, and afterwards effective plenipotentiary for the whole of the East, rose in revolt. Marcus Aurelius had never visited the East. Lucius Verus had earned only opprobrium. The region had been devastated by plague. It had also been drained of tribute and man-power to defend the West against the Germans. Avidius Cassius found a mass base in both the army and the eastern elite for his challenge. In fact, the revolt collapsed after three months when its leader was assassinated by a centurion. Even so, the legitimate regime had received a shock, and Marcus spent a year touring the East, purging the army and administration of rebels, rallying loyalist support, and presenting himself as 'Saviour of the West' and 'Beneficent Conciliator of the East'. To strengthen the dynasty, his teenage son Commodus was first made consul, then styled *Augustus* and granted tribunician power, and finally, in AD 177–178, advanced to formal equality with his father as co-emperor. The political situation stabilized – for the moment. But an old fissure had reopened. If a fracturing of the Roman imperial aristocracy on regional lines was a recurring feature of Late Antique politics, the greatest fracture line of all, and the one along which the empire would eventually divide for good, was that between East and West. It had been there in the struggles between Caesar and Pompey, Octavian and Antony, Vespasian and Vitellius. The revolt of Avidius Cassius was not on this scale – but it was the dress rehearsal for a major struggle 20 years later.

The Antonine regime survived the coup of AD 175 because the imperial elite remained broadly united behind Marcus Aurelius. By the time of his death in AD 180, not only was the East resettled, but the German War effectively won. His son and successor, eager to escape the inconveniences of frontier life and return to the pleasures of the capital, quickly imposed a settlement. The Germans, drained by the violence, were ready to make peace on Roman terms. Deserters and prisoners were to be returned, contingents of mercenaries supplied, and an annual corn tithe paid. War on Rome's allies was banned, partial disarmament imposed, and the time and place of tribal assemblies regulated. In return for accepting this client status, all Roman garrisons were to be withdrawn from German territory, and Roman subsidies would be paid to native rulers. Again, as in the East, the policy was not to conquer but to pacify; not, that is, to risk overextending Roman lines, but to liquidate military threats and restore the old frontiers. Marcus Aurelius had done his work well: the Rhine-Danube line was destined to hold, more or less, for two generations.

The son was a striking contrast to the father. Returning in haste to Rome, he sacked old ministers, promoted favourites, showered the mob with handouts, and indulged his personal fascination with the games. Commodus had himself portrayed as the Greek hero Hercules. The emperor appeared in person in the Roman arena. Gladiators were included among his courtiers. Not for a century had Rome seen such rampant faction and corruption at court, and nowadays, in a more army-dominated empire, less tolerance was granted to playboy emperors. The reign of Commodus was punctuated by plots and purges, the first, involving the emperor's sister, as early as AD 182. The tension inside the palace reflected the fears of courtiers subject to a mentally unstable master whose favour was whimsical and unpredictable – not least because Commodus's instinctive response to waning popularity was to sack and execute a leading minister. Within five years of his succession, Commodus faced a major military revolt. The commanders of the British and Danubian legions sent troops to Rome to overthrow the government of the Praetorian Prefect Tigidius Perennis. Commodus, true to form, abandoned Perennis to his fate, allowing him to be outlawed by the Senate and then lynched by a detachment of soldiers.

Because on this occasion the emperor himself survived and the soldiers returned to their frontier bases, factional politics quickly revived. Isolated from the governing class by a wall of contempt and hostility, Commodus turned to those outside it. Finally, in AD 187, a freedman called Cleander from Phrygia in Asia Minor, formerly the emperor's Chamberlain, was made Praetorian Prefect. The appointment broke the monopoly over this office of the equestrian order. Cleander, moreover, used his position to enrich himself and his entourage by selling magistracies, governorships, honours, legal decisions, and anything else in the gift of government. There were no less than 25 consulships awarded in a single year. Freedmen became senators. The whole finely graded Roman imperial system of rank and privilege was threatened. For a time, terror kept the lid on opposition in the capital, but growing disorders in the provinces gave urgency to the crisis of leadership. Border wars erupted in Dacia, Germany, Mauretania and, above all, Britain, where military mutinies increased the threat to frontier security. Meantime, deep within the empire the rising burdens of the military monarchy provoked popular revolt.

Around AD 187 an army deserter-turned-bandit called Maternus spread 'insecurity throughout Gaul and Spain'. Details are minimal. The revolt is described as a 'war of deserters' which involved 'countless numbers plaguing Gaul'. This looks like a serious outbreak of peasant revolt, in which army deserters reinforced endemic social banditry, and the two fused with wider rural discontent to mobilize large numbers and create a mass resistance movement. Were this not the case, it is unlikely that the classical writers would have recorded the event at all. They report, moreover, that large-scale military operations were required to suppress the rebels, and that before this could be done, Maternus had marched towards Rome with the explicit intention of assassinating Commodus and replacing him as emperor. In the event, Maternus was betrayed, captured and beheaded, and his movement dissolved back into the countryside from which it had emerged. But the rising was a measure of growing stress within imperial society. There would be many more like it in Late Antiquity.

Meantime, increasingly insecure, Commodus became megalomaniac and murderous. Contemporary inscriptions show him claiming a ludicrous list of names and titles: *Lucius* (his personal name), *Aelius* (Hadrian's family name), *Aurelius* (Marcus's family name), *Commodus* (another personal name and the one by which we know him), *Augustus* (emperor), *Herculeus* (reincarnation of Hercules), *Romanus* (embodiment of Rome), *Exsuperantissimus* (supreme being), *Amazonius* (conqueror of the Amazons), *Invictus* (unconquered), *Felix* (blessed by the gods with good fortune), and *Pius* (faithful and dutiful). The months of the year were to be renamed in the emperor's honour. Rome was henceforward to be called *Colonia Commodiana*. The emperor's features now graced the old Colossus of Nero. Coins announced a new golden age of peace and prosperity (*felicitas saeculi*). Or they referred to the loyalty (*fides*) and unity (*concordia*) of the army under the leadership of His Highness the Supreme Being (*summus exsuperantissimus*). In December AD 192 the emperor appeared in the arena in the guise of Hercules and slew a large number of wild beasts. He then announced that he would appear before the Roman people on New Year's Day as both consul and gladiator. He missed the appointment. Terrified by his lunacy – that it would destroy them all – Commodus was assassinated by his closest courtiers. A bizarre alliance of equestrian prefect, freedman-chamberlain, pro-Christian concubine and professional wrestler organized to strangle the emperor in his bath-tub.

The Praetorian Prefect Laetus then offered the throne to an elderly senator with a distinguished record of imperial service. Pertinax was duly acclaimed by the Guard and formally empowered by the Senate. But he afterwards paid the soldiers only half their promised donative, and, when faced with mutiny in consequence, executed some rebels on the evidence of a slave. Laetus then led a second attempt against the emperor: a detachment of soldiers entered the palace, and Pertinax, who had reigned for just three months, was cut down by a member of his own German bodyguard. The Praetorian Guard were then in control of the capital, and their only interest lay in maximizing the amount they could extort for their services. The empire was put up for auction at the Praetorian Barracks. The price reached 6,250 *denarii* per man, and the matching offer of Marcus Didius Julianus, a wealthy senator, was preferred over that of his rival, since the latter was Pertinax's father-in-law, who, it was feared, might seek vengeance for his relative's murder. The Guard carried Julianus to the Senate and secured ratification of their decision.

The Guard was less successful, however, in its attempts to disperse the large numbers of demonstrators who then besieged the palace. The new regime's opponents passed a resolution calling on Pescennius Niger, the Governor of Syria, to intervene in defence of constitutional government. Around the same time, Septimius Severus, Governor of Upper Pannonia, called on his troops to avenge the murder of Pertinax and punish the arrogance of the Guard; he was immediately acclaimed emperor. Clodius Albinus, the Governor of Britain, meanwhile, was acclaimed by the legions in Britain. The Roman Empire faced a second 'Year of Four Emperors'. It had shattered in an instant into regional fragments, the rule of Julianus and the Guard in Rome contested by rival usurpers representing, respectively, the Eastern, the Danubian and the British legions. The high command and officer corps of each army group viewed its rivals with suspicion and jealousy; each faction was determined to win the empire for itself, lest it be uncoupled from the gravy train of promotion and largesse; each, too, found wider support among local landowners and city authorities, eager to ensure that revenues and soldiers were not siphoned away to fight distant wars. As in AD 69, a corrupt regime and a military coup had destroyed the legitimacy of central government, opening a contest for power which revealed the hidden fracture-lines cutting across the empire.

Severus had the advantage of a central position. He was also cunning, ruthless and decisive. He secured his right flank by bribing Albinus with the title of *Caesar* and the prospect of eventual succession. He then force-marched his army across the Alps into northern Italy, capturing Ravenna and its fleet. Julianus attempted to improvise a defence of Rome, but late payment of their donative and the prospect of a clash with the Danubian legions drained the Praetorians' enthusiasm for war. Severus offered the guardsmen their lives if they handed over the murderers of Pertinax and stood themselves down. The Guard took their chance: Severus was proclaimed emperor, and Julianus was outlawed and murdered in his palace. Severus was then formally invested with imperial power by a delegation of 100 senators at a meeting outside Rome – the visitors having first been searched for hidden weapons, the emperor receiving them surrounded by 600 bodyguards. Severus then approached the city. The Praetorians were paraded without arms, demobilized, and exiled beyond 160 km from Rome. A new Guard was recruited from frontier legionaries. The Senate was conciliated: Severus justified his actions as the avenger of Pertinax; he promised to rule according to the principles of Marcus Aurelius and not to execute any senators; two of his daughters were married to the two senators nominated for the consulship the following year. He appealed, too, for the good favour of the People, with handouts, games, and a care for the bread-supply. There was a civil war going on: Severus needed all the friends he could get; above all, he needed a secure capital before turning to confront his main enemy: Pescennius Niger.

The eastern legions were no match for the Danubians in a straight fight, but Niger enjoyed widespread support in the East, and his strategy was a sensible one of proactive defence. His appeal to the officers, officials and client-rulers of the eastern provinces was compelling: local resources for local defence; Italy, the Danube, the Rhineland, distant Britain, these were foreign countries. The East he turned into a fortress, establishing two strong lines of defence, one at the Straits, the second at the passes into Syria over the Taurus Mountains. Severus forced the first line by seizing the city of Perinthus, crossing the Hellespont, and capturing Cyzicus on the far side. He then pushed inland and defeated Niger again at Nicaea, at which point the eastern forces fell back on their second line. Three battles in AD 193 thus gave Severus control of Asia Minor. The following year he turned Niger's defence of the mountain passes, crossed into Syria, and won the fourth, and decisive, battle of the campaign at Issus. Niger himself was run down and killed by Severan cavalry. His head was displayed at Byzantium – gateway to the East and still holding out under siege – for the edification of its defenders. The victor remained a further year in the East. Cities that had supported Niger – especially Antioch – were devastated, plundered, and permanently reduced in status. Those that had supported Severus were promoted to colonies and given construction subsidies. The property of Niger's supporters was confiscated and added to the imperial estate. Recalcitrant local tribes were suppressed. Formal peace was made with Parthia. Only in the winter of AD 194–195 did Severus finally head west, returning to Europe after completing his eastern campaign by capturing – and devastating – Byzantium.

Victory gave confidence to the new regime. Caracalla, Severus's eight-year-old son, was made Caesar, displacing Albinus, whose support was dispensable after the destruction of Niger. Seeking legitimacy, the dynasty now claimed descent from Marcus Aurelius; and who, in the circumstances, would see fit to deny it? Emperor-worship replaced the cult of the standards in the legions. Severus's Syrian wife was honoured as *Mater Augusti* (Mother of Emperors) and *Mater Castrorum* (Mother of the Military Camps); soon it would emerge that she was actually a goddess, Juno Caelestis, Juno of the Heavens, no less, a Romanized version of the ancient Punic Tanit who was worshipped in Severus's native North Africa. The emperor and his family were being elevated into gods on earth; the imperial cult was assuming central ideological significance; older concepts like the Senate and People of Rome were being supplanted. The military monarchy was acquiring a religious form.

Albinus, the former ally now redundant, was recast as usurper and outlaw. But he, like Niger in the East, had a strong base of support among the officers and landowners of the north-west provinces, and his supporters promptly reiterated their acclamation of him as emperor. But Albinus was fighting against the odds. Though he crossed the Channel with the bulk of the British army, he won only modest support from the legions on the Continent; notably, the great army-bases on the Rhine stood aloof. Even so, nothing was certain in the shifting sands of civil war. Severus had problems in his rear: rumours of disloyalty demanded a flying visit to Rome, a studied display of magnanimity, and a fresh dole-out to the mob.

And when the campaign was resumed and battle finally joined out-side Lyons on 19 February AD 197, matters were long in the balance. Severus led his men into a trap – a minefield of concealed pits harbouring sharpened stakes – and was himself at one point in grave danger when thrown from his horse. The battle lasted through the day, and the casualty list was horrendous. But the British legions finally broke and ran, and as they did so, battle turned to massacre. Albinus himself was trapped in a building and committed suicide. The body was brought to Severus – who 'feasted his eyes on it' according to the historian Dio Cassius. The head was cut off and sent for display in Rome. The rest of the corpse was trampled and degraded before being tipped into the Rhône, along with the bodies of Albinus's murdered wife and sons. Lyons, meantime, suffering the fate of Antioch and Byzantium, was put to the sack. Severus's police agents then fanned out across Gaul, Spain and Britain to track down and destroy the broken remnants of Albinus's party. Thus did the Roman imperial elite – which prided itself on bring-ing civilization to the world – conduct its private feuds.

Severus, master of the world, commander of its most powerful army, could now dispense with the niceties of diplomacy and law. The military dictatorship, which had been ashamed to speak its name for two cen-turies, now openly declared itself. The spirit of the age would be encap-sulated by Severus many years later in oft-quoted deathbed advice to his sons: 'Live at peace with one another, enrich the soldiers, and despise everyone else.'(3) A united dynasty and a loyal army: these were now the very essence of Rome – and certainly all that was necessary to power. The rest existed only as the servants and suppliers of the all-powerful state. The Senate, once courted and honoured, was cowed into obedience with a purge of former supporters of Niger and Albinus: 64 members were brought to trial, and 29 condemned to death and loss of estates. The purged Senate was then neutered, losing its power to propose legislation and appoint magistrates. The legal fiction of a 'restored Republic' was finally dissolved. As the Senatorial Order sank – its members even lost their immunity from torture in treason cases – the inexorable rise of the Equestrian continued. New provinces and legions were now commanded by equestrians instead of senators. The Praetorian Prefect became a high court judge, the head of the civil service, and the emperor's overall deputy. The old state treasury (*aerarium*) was downgraded into the city finance department for Rome, and an enlarged imperial treasury (*fiscus*) henceforward received the revenues from both imperial and senatorial provinces, and from the emperor's private estates. The streamlining of the dictatorship involved a stripping away of its Republican crust.

The army, meantime, was purged, enlarged and reformed. Just 25 legions strong at the end of Augustus's reign, Marcus had raised it to 30, and now Severus increased it again to 33. One legion was stationed at Albanum a mere 32 km from Rome: reinforcements if needed for the reconstituted Praetorian Guard, the Urban Cohorts, and the Nightwatchmen stationed in the city. Within the army, aristocratic privilege, a barrier to talent and efficiency, was further broken down. The Praetorian Guard was now recruited from across the army, becoming a kind of officer training corps, from which men promoted from the ranks might eventually graduate as centurions. The status of junior officers was elevated, as centurions, previously always commoners, were sometimes promoted to equestrian rank, making them eligible in due course for further promotion to tribune or prefect. Terms improved also for the rank and file. Pay was increased – from 375 *denarii* for legionaries and 1,250 for guardsmen to 500 and 1,700 respectively. Legionaries were granted the right to marry during service, so that the offspring of relationships with native women would have Roman citizen status. Veterans' privileges were extended to include, for instance, a lifetime's immunity from personal service in their native towns after retirement. Amenities were improved at army bases – in North Britain, under Severus and his immediate successors, inscriptions record new or reconstructed barrack-blocks, bath-houses and aqueducts, as well as drill-halls, armouries, headquarters-buildings and granaries. It was not quite a new model army, but it was an army thoroughly reformed and rededicated to the service of the emperor.

All of this cost. So, too, did a generous programme of largesse and public works. Six bounties paid to the mob and the soldiers are estimated to have totalled some 220 million *denarii*. There were lavish games in Rome. The *fiscus* funded the imperial post – an empire-wide system of roads, state motels and changing stations. It also paid out to revive the old *alimenta* system, whereby loans of capital were made to support Italian farmers, and the interest on these provided a primitive form of social security for the support of poor citizen families. Not least, Severus mounted a huge building programme, both in Rome and in favoured cities of the empire. North Africa especially benefited – above all, Leptis Magna, the emperor's home town.

Severus has been acclaimed as 'the black emperor'. The fact that Severus was African has been cited as evidence that Rome was colour-blind, free of racism, a genuinely multicultural commonwealth. Septimius Severus was no more 'black' than Julius Caesar. Politically, culturally and racially, he was part of the broad Mediterranean elite that ruled the Roman Empire. Just as the blood of Etruscans and Samnites flowed in the veins of Italian nobles (like Augustus or Vespasian), and that of Celts and Iberians in those of Spanish ones (like Trajan, Hadrian and Marcus), so did the blood of Berbers and Carthaginians flow in the veins of an African noble like Severus. Yet, no less than any of his prede-cessors, Severus was classically educated, thoroughly Romanized, and, one has to assume, every bit as contemptuous of barbarians, peasants and slaves as other members of his class. We are told that 'he retained a trace of an African accent into old age'.(4) No doubt: he probably knew Libyan, Punic and Greek as well as Latin, and it would have been most surprising if the Latin of Leptis Magna had sounded like that of Rome; an 'African accent', in other words, was a Roman provincial accent, not a foreign one.

Leptis was one of the three great cities that formed Tripolitania (today the north-west coastal region of Libya). Like nearby Oea and Sabratha, it was a great entrepôt, receiving grain and olive oil from the rich estates along the coast, and, from trans-Saharan desert caravans, salt, gold, semi-precious stones, ivory, slaves, wild animals for the arena, and natron for use in embalming and glassmaking. Already fabulously rich, Leptis scaled new heights of grandeur when its most illustrious son became emperor. A great marble-faced complex – forum, basilica, colonnaded street, four-way arch – was constructed by the Wadi Lebda which led down to the harbour. The harbour itself was lined with new warehouses and provided with a new lighthouse at its entrance. A circus for chariot racing was built beside the amphitheatre on the edge of town.

Despite the lavish spending, the regime remained solvent; indeed, Severus's successor inherited a bulging *fiscus*. The Severan military monarchy had achieved a spectacular resolution of the financial crisis that had almost crippled imperial defence under Marcus Aurelius. Like the great civil wars of the Late Republic, those of AD 193–197 had effected a massive transfer of wealth from the defeated to the victors. The wreckage of army-camps and sacked cities had yielded rich booty. The estates of the dead and the fled had been annexed to the imperial estate. The post-war police terror had produced further crops from the condemned and expropriated. Severus had emerged from his wars against Niger and Albinus richer than all his predecessors, and a special treasury, the *res privata principis*, was established to handle the new acquisitions. His regime had triumphed by plundering the estates and cities of the empire – by waging war not only on civil war factions, but on civil society itself. Added to this were new hauls from foreign war. With his domestic enemies dead, the governing class cowed, the army thoroughly reformed, and revenues pouring into the treasury, Severus had been able to take the offensive in the East, where the Parthians, seeking to benefit from the Roman civil war in the West, had launched an attempt to recover lost territory. In the late summer of AD 197, Severus had marched his Danubian veterans and three new legions raised in his Balkan power-base to confront the traditional enemy. As so often when faced by all-out effort, the Parthians melted away before the Roman advance, and Mesopotamia was overrun. Now, as before at Antioch, Byzantium and Lyons, the streets of Ctesiphon succumbed to an orgy of massacre, destruction and looting by Severan soldiery. The war then followed a familiar pattern: the opening blitzkrieg was followed by a tedious war of sieges, while Roman strength was sapped by disease and long supply-lines. Even so, Parthian power was crumbling – it was destined to succumb to the Sassanians, a new breed of invading warlords from Iran, within a generation – and Severus held on to far more of Mesopotamia than any of his predecessors. It was easily enough of a victory to merit a grand tour of the eastern provinces – Syria, Palestine and Egypt (AD 199–202) – before returning in triumph to Rome, where the booty of the war was consumed in handouts, games and monuments.

At the beginning of the 3rd century AD, the Roman Empire looked stronger than ever. The civil wars were over. The Parthians had been crushed. Northern Mesopotamia had been annexed. The army had been enlarged and professionalized. The treasury was full. There was a construction boom in the imperial cities. Streams of merchant ships crisscrossed the Mediterranean. Farms were peaceful and prosperous.

And yet so little was truly secure. The military monarchy had imposed heavy burdens on the people of the empire. Discontent festered in remote villages. The pressure valves of constitutional opposition had been shut down – the rotting heads and mangled corpses of the dictator's enemies discouraged criticism. The ruler, the court, the upper echelons of the state machine, the army high command, these commanding heights of power were no longer rooted in the institutions of civil society. Little vestige of accountability remained. The state had been elevated above society – dominating, exploiting, siphoning resources. It had become an end in itself, a self-perpetuating mechanism of power. The empire had thus acquired a distorted form, its parts unbalanced and out of kilter, the head swelling as the limbs shrivelled.

Even before the old dictator died, in the bogs and glens of the British North the imperial leviathan, lashing out into the mist and drizzle, was reduced to despair by bands of blue-painted skirmishers. Slowly dying, gout-ridden, carried about on a litter, Septimius Severus remained to the end a man of blood and iron. 'Let no one escape utter destruction at our hands,' was the chilling injunction to his men; 'let not the infant still carried in its mother's womb, if it be male, escape from its fate.'(5) But they did escape, and it was Severus who was taken by fate, early in AD 211, at the city of York, shortly before the new campaigning season opened. Maybe, after all, blood and iron would not suffice to save the Empire.

The Anarchy: from Caracalla to Diocletian, AD 211–284

For the conqueror of Mesopotamia, the British war of AD 208–211 was a dismal business. The empire's north-west frontier had been troubled since the 180s AD. Mutiny and civil war had so weakened the army there that Roman commanders had been reduced to bribing barbarian chieftains to keep the peace. Severus would have none of it, and saw as well a chance to get his sons, Caracalla and Geta, away from Rome and toughen them up with some soldiering. His preparations were thorough. Tens of thousands of men were massed on Hadrian's Wall. South Shields was remodelled to hold a three-month grain supply. A fleet was assembled to transport men and stores up the east coast of Scotland. As the army marched, new roads were cut through forests, causeways laid across marshes, bridges thrown over rivers. Perhaps it was just too thorough, for the tribesmen avoided pitched battle and waged guerrilla war. The struggle was already in its third year when Severus died, and the chances of decisive victory seemed remote. The Romans had failed in these northern wastes before, retreating under Domitian in the 80s AD, and again under Marcus in the 160s AD. Elsewhere, too, campaigning outside the limits of plough-cultivation, in the mountains, forests and deserts beyond the frontiers, they had often found themselves in a military morass. We do not know what advice the two young emperors were given by the generals after Severus's death, but some surely doubted the wisdom of the war. It probably looked unwinnable. The Highlands were hard to control. The tribes were desperately poor. There was little booty. Meantime, the army, its prestige compromised by failure, was thousands of miles from Rome, the Balkans and the eastern frontier. That was dangerous. Whatever was said, Caracalla and Geta would have needed little encouragement to pack for home. They made peace with the Caledonian tribes, dispersed the field army, and returned forthwith to Rome.

Severus had named his sons joint heirs, and on his deathbed had enjoined them not to quarrel. But deep hatred divided them. They travelled separately on the journey home, kept separate courts within the palace, and even discussed splitting the empire in two. The matter was resolved when Caracalla had his brother murdered – stabbed to death by army officers, it is said, having fled through the palace into his mother's arms. Caracalla went immediately to the Praetorian Barracks to secure the allegiance of the Guard. 'With you I pray to live or, if need be, die,' announced the emperor, though he wisely added, 'Yours are all the treasures of the state'(6) – specifically, higher pay and better rations. Then he went to the Albanum Barracks, where the legion his father had stationed near Rome was based. At first the gates were closed against him, but, again, an offer of higher pay promptly secured the soldiers' allegiance. Soon, around the empire, frontier legionaries were being assembled on their parade-grounds to be told of the army pay-rise, to damn the traitor Geta, and to swear devotion to Caracalla. Many stone-cut records of these events, so-called 'loyalty inscriptions', have been found at army bases. Meantime, Geta's friends and allies were destroyed in a savage purge (one source inflates the total slain to 20,000).

Insecurity and inflated spending were hallmarks of Caracalla's reign. The power of the internal security apparatus – essentially an empire-wide network of military police and paid informers – was increased. The army pay-rises were underwritten by hefty tax increases. The inheritance and manumission taxes paid by Roman citizens were increased from 5 to 10 per cent, and Caracalla's famous citizenship edict of AD 212, by which all free persons in the empire became citizens, was intended to increase the numbers obliged to pay. *Aurum coronarium* – the 'coronation gold' traditionally paid only on the emperor's accession and often in practice remitted – became a recurring extraordinary levy. The coinage was debased: a new double-*denarius* was issued at a lower weight (and therefore silver content) than the two *denarii* it supposedly represented. All these schemes transferred surplus from civil society to the state and its army. By these means the cost was met of the military-bureaucratic complex over which Caracalla presided: not only army pay-rises and rewards to favourites, courtiers and loyalist officers; also the 'bread and circuses' and monumental building that appeased and awed the mob; and the bribes and subsidies to border chieftains that were a growing feature of imperial defence.

Once things were settled in Rome, Caracalla spent his time with the army, fighting first in Germany (AD 213), then in the East (AD 215–217). His methods were a mix of vanity, intrigue and brute force. Modelling himself on Alexander, he adopted Macedonian dress, created a 16,000-strong phalanx, and tried to fix up a marriage alliance with an eastern princess. He employed secret diplomacy to buy off potential enemies and isolate the more intractable. His armies were then free to crush, successively, German tribesmen, Egyptian tax-rebels and Parthian garrisons. Even so, the emperor did not inspire confidence, and his position was gravely weakened in the winter of AD 216–217 when he ordered a retreat in the face of an impending Parthian counter-offensive. Caracalla was assassinated by a common soldier in April AD 217.

For a moment the grip of the Severan dynasty was broken. The eastern army hailed one of its own generals emperor. But Macrinus ruled for only a year. He succumbed in June AD 218 to a military revolt orchestrated by the leading women of the ousted House of Severus. Though Septimius's widow, Julia Domna, was dead, her sister, Julia Maesa, was very much alive, and her two daughters, Julia Soaemias and Julia Mammaea, each had a son – and therefore a 'legitimate' Severan heir. Determined to maintain the pre-eminence of the family, Julia Maesa roused her Syrian supporters to revolt (she was from the eastern city of Emesa), bribed the soldiers to overturn Macrinus, and placed one of Septimius Severus's two great-nephews on the throne.

The 'Syrian' faction were unfortunate in their chosen instrument. Elagabalus, who had taken the name of the eastern sun-god of which he was chief priest, was a religious fanatic. Established in Rome from early AD 219, he continued to don the fantastic garb of an eastern priest, filled the court with a retinue of religious charlatans and cranks, and ordered the Senate to elevate the cult of the Unconquered Sun into the principal state religion. In the bizarre theocratic dictatorship of Elagabalus, devotion was the principal qualification for high office, and an actor became Praetorian Prefect, a charioteer headed the Night-watch, and a hairdresser supervised the corn-supply. Accounts of the fertility 'rites' enacted at court lost nothing in the retelling in Rome's salons and bars. By the summer of AD 221, Julia Maesa was manoeuvring to destroy her grandson and replace him with his less colourful cousin. The blow fell in March AD 222. The Praetorians were bribed, Elagabalus and his mother murdered, and the rest of the court hunted down and killed. The theocratic dictatorship collapsed in a day, and Severus Alexander was hailed emperor.

The principal qualities of the new emperor were that he was a relatively 'normal' Roman youth, he was easily controlled by his female minders, and he was not Elagabalus. Even so, the Syrians were discredited and had ground to make up; behind the cardboard ruler they schemed to rebuild their power. The tension that had recently developed between the traditional aristocracy of office represented by the Senate and the military-bureaucratic complex of court and army recruited from the Equestrian Order was eased. Senators were readmitted to the highest councils of the state, and previously reserved equestrian offices – crucially that of Praetorian Prefect – were opened to them. The mob, too, was courted in the usual way, with handouts and public works. Court expenditure, on the other hand, was reined back, and new taxes were levied on the rich. The Syrians were eager to make themselves popular.

The real danger, however, was not at home but abroad. Decisive shifts in the balance of geopolitical power were taking place in both the East and the North. The military monarchy had effected a significant redistribution of resources from civil society to the state, and an enlarged and reorganized army had enabled it to crush domestic and foreign enemies.

But, locked into an eternal military struggle with her neighbours, Rome could only ever gain temporary respite through her victories; indeed, these very victories provided the spur to her enemies to regroup, rearm, and return to fight again. Severus's conquest of Mesopotamia in AD 197–199, and Caracalla's successful defence of it in AD 215–217, had shattered the cohesion of the fast-decaying Parthian Empire. In the 220s AD it had splintered into rebellious provincial fragments. Among the local potentates who then contended for power was one Artaxerxes, Prince of Persepolis, ancient homeland of the Achaemenids, who, 500 years before, had ruled the greatest empire on earth. After smashing the Parthian king in pitched battle in AD 227, Artaxerxes overran Mesopotamia and reached the borders of Syria and Asia Minor in the succeeding three years. As the new 'Great King' or 'King of Kings', Artaxerxes laid claim to the empire of his ancestors – a domain that had embraced the whole Eastern Mediterranean as far as the Aegean. The wreckage of empire wrought by Severus's legions a generation before had produced its Nemesis. The spirit of Cyrus, Darius and Xerxes walked again: an aggress-ive, boasting, thrusting imperialism that mirrored that of Rome: the Sassanid Empire.

Severus Alexander's attempts to negotiate were ignored, and Roman forces had to be rushed to the East. The campaign was mismanaged and losses were heavy on both sides. Both empires, too, were soon distracted by more pressing problems elsewhere, and the war, which had begun with such grandiose aims in AD 230, had petered out by AD 233. But the relocation of the court to Antioch, and the shift of crack Danubian units to the East, had gravely weakened the empire's European defences. German tribes penetrated the frontier screen and plundered territory along the Rhine and Danube. Such news cannot have played well in the ranks of soldiers recently transferred from the Balkans to the East: their families and farms at home had been exposed by their absence fighting a 'foreign' war. When court and army relocated again to the North, the centrifugal tensions within the Roman state came to a head. Severus Alexander was eager to cut a deal with the tribes. His mother, Julia Mammaea, wanted to escape the miserable northern forests. The court – or so it seemed to some – was run by women and stuffed with foppish eastern favourites. The 'Germans' had had enough of the 'Syrians'. In March AD 235 the Danubian soldiers acclaimed one of their own emperor: Maximinus Thrax, Maximinus the Thracian, a huge peasant-soldier who had risen from the ranks to top command. The eastern troops panicked and fled. Severus Alexander and his mother were murdered in the base-camp at Mainz.

Maximinus (AD 235–238) represented the military monarchy in its most extreme form. A farmer's son from a Balkan village, he was a rough career-soldier who had lived his whole adult life in the army. Immediately threatened by plots, one organized by a group of senatorial officers, another by eastern generals, the opposition was ruthlessly crushed. The candidate of the Rhineland and Danubian legions, he then went onto the offensive in the North, smashing the German tribes in pitched battle. Agents, meantime, were dispatched across the empire to rake in revenue to support the war effort. Within just three years, these policies had provoked a fresh revolt.

The military monarchy was falling apart, the state sinking into anarchy. The enemies of the empire were growing stronger. Current tax revenues were inadequate to support the size of army required to keep them out. Legions, in consequence, had to be constantly shifted to deal with one emergency after another. Such redeployments frequently created new openings that led to localized collapses and the devastation of Roman territory. This in turn undermined the cohesion of the imperial ruling class, which fragmented into regionally based factions, each eager to concentrate revenues and soldiers in defence of local territory. Centrifugalism become an inherent feature of the empire in decline, and the attempt of successive regimes to suppress it further undermined imperial defence by diverting troops to internal security.

For the rich landowners of Roman Africa, the German tribes might as well have been on the moon. When the financial procurator threatened aristocratic estates in his efforts to fill the emperor's war-chest, he provoked a property-owners' revolt. A group of young bloods assassinated the procurator and declared emperor an octogenarian nobleman of impeccable pedigree and distinguished service currently serving as provincial governor. Gordian I (AD 238), acting with a vigour that belied his age, immediately dispatched a band of armed partisans to Rome to overthrow the government, while appealing to the rest of the empire for support. All save Spain, Dacia and Pannonia declared for Gordian – a measure of the fear for person and property engendered by the brutal

Maximinus regime. But the property-owners' revolt was a castle of sand. The civilians could not defeat the army. Just 22 days after it began, the revolt in Africa was over, and both Gordian I and his son – named co-emperor and therefore recorded by history as Gordian II – were dead.

In Italy, at first, matters took a different turn. Here the Gordianic faction was headed by an energetic provisional government dominated by senators: the so-called Board of Twenty. Exploiting widespread hostility within the military to the dominance of the German faction, the Board had been busy turning paper support into armies. Undeterred by the setback in Africa, they now elevated two of their own number, Balbinus and Maximus, to the throne. Then, in response to protests from soldiers and the mob against the restoration of senatorial rule, they added a third: Gordian I's 13-year-old grandson, who thus became Gordian III. Meantime, the regime prepared to meet the onslaught of Maximinus's legions. The Board of Twenty's show of force was promptly rewarded. Maximinus was held at the fortified city of Aquileia on the north-east coast of Italy. Unprepared for a long siege, he quickly ran out of food, at which his soldiers mutinied, murdered him in his bed, and transferred their allegiance to Gordian III (AD 238–244).

For a moment it appeared that, against the odds, the civilians had won. A property-owners' revolt against the demands of the military monarchy had produced a government of senators in Rome. It was an illusion. The military were the dominant partners in the victorious faction and they had no intention of sharing power: the Praetorian Guard murdered Balbinus and Maximus, dumped their bodies in the street, and declared Gordian III sole emperor – an event signalling the true collapse of the property-owners' revolt. A military monarch – and his minders – again reigned supreme.

The German and civil wars had weakened the frontier defences. In the East especially, from which the army had marched off to Germany in the winter of AD 233–234, the situation was dire. The Sassanids had invaded Syria and were within reach of Antioch. Though a Roman counter-attack mounted in AD 243 was spectacularly successful, the army's logistics broke down, the troops went hungry, and an ambitious general, Philip the Arab, seized his opportunity to incite the troops against the boy-emperor and have him murdered. The fates of Maximinus Thrax and Gordian III revealed a new feature of the anarchy. The soldiers had grown accustomed to making and unmaking emperors. They expected their leaders to keep them well supplied, to lead them to victory, to safeguard the interests of the army. When they failed to do so – as they often did in the troubled times of the mid 3rd century AD – they found themselves at the mercy of serial mutineers.

The reign of Philip the Arab (AD 244–249) exemplified the whole nexus of contradictions that had produced the anarchy. Peace was made with the Sassanids only to be followed by three years of war on the Lower Danube, where new enemies, peoples migrating from the depths of Eurasia, were pushing against the frontiers of the Empire. Then, while celebrating the apparent return of peace on Rome's one-thousandth birthday in AD 248, the regime was hit simultaneously by three army revolts – on the Danube, in Cappodocia, and in Syria – and a new invasion by Carpi, Goths and Vandals on the Lower Danube. Lack of money was at the root of all these conflicts. The Danube revolt had been triggered by arrears of pay, the eastern revolts by ruthless tax-collecting, the barbarian incursions by failure to pay a promised subsidy. It was a classic 'scissors' crisis: in one place mutiny and invasion over payments not made, in another revolt against revenue collection. Here, in a sense, is written the whole history of the decline and fall of Rome.

The man sent to restore order on the Danube drove out the barbarians and paid the soldiers their arrears. They responded by acclaiming him emperor, and though the general tried to decline and protested his innocence to Philip, he was hopelessly compromised and found himself propelled willy-nilly into a struggle for power. It was Philip, however, who was defeated and killed when the two armies clashed, and Decius Trajan (AD 249–251) became emperor. Decius was unusual among 3rd century emperors in being a distinguished senator linked by marriage with an old Italian aristocratic family. His relations with the Senate were therefore cordial. He could not, however, eschew military affairs; to base oneself in Rome and rule as a civilian politician was no longer an option. It was again the Goths on the Lower Danube who posed the principal threat. The barbarians had crossed the ice-bound river in force during the winter of AD 250–251. The city of Philippopolis had been captured and put to the sack. But when Decius engaged the Gothic host in a great battle in the marshes of the Danube Estuary, he was betrayed by one of his own subordinates. The details are obscure. It appears that two of the enemy's battle-groups had been repulsed, and Decius was advancing to attack a third, expecting support from the force commanded by Gallus, Governor of Moesia. But Gallus made no move as Decius's men marched into a bog and were destroyed by Gothic archery. The emperor's body was never found. Gallus (AD 251–253) was proclaimed in his place. Had the traitor done a deal with the Goths? Or had he merely sensed an opportunity in the chaos of battle? Whatever, the incident seems evidence of deep rottenness within the Roman state. In the succeeding two decades, it would bring the Empire close to collapse.

Gallus did not last long. He seems to have been paralyzed by indecision in the face of Gothic raiders, a new Sassanid offensive in the East, and a severe epidemic of plague. By the winter of AD 253–254 the frontier legions were in revolt. Gallus was defeated by Aemilianus and the Danube army, and then murdered by his own troops. But Aemilianus (AD 253) reigned for just three months before he was deserted and murdered in his turn, as the soldiers switched allegiance again, this time to the usurper Valerian, marching on Italy at the head of the Rhineland army. The anarchy was fast accelerating into a chaos of warring factions. The Roman imperial elite was imploding even as its enemies poured across crumbling frontier defences. The end of the empire seemed possible. In response to escalating crisis, a critical decision was taken by the new regime. The political order would be adapted to reflect the centrifugalism now endemic in the overextended empire. Valerian (AD 253–260) appointed his son Gallienus (AD 253–268) co-emperor, first with the junior rank of Caesar, later the more senior one of Augustus. Shortly afterwards the empire was effectively divided in two, with the East allocated to Valerian, the West to Gallienus. Henceforward there were two courts, two armies, two centres of power, one facing the Sassanids in the East, the other the barbarians in the North.

Valerian went out to the East in AD 256 or 257. Establishing his headquarters at Antioch, he first repelled a Sassanid incursion under Shapur I, then turned to deal with a new threat on the coasts of Asia Minor, where Borani and Goths were mounting seaborne raids. But the expedition had to be aborted when plague broke out in the army and, at the same time, news arrived that Shapur had returned to the offensive. Shifting front yet again, Valerian marched into Mesopotamia, hoping, by devastating his enemy's territory, to force upon him a negotiated peace. Little else was possible, for the Roman forces were at their limit. Barbarian raiders threatened in the rear. The communication lines were long and exposed. The army was withered by plague, climate, battle casualties and garrison duty. Shapur agreed to negotiate, but then, treacherously, seized Valerian, who died soon afterwards in Sassanid captivity (AD 260). Though a victim of deceit, Valerian had been driven to destruction – driven to take the risk that led to his destruction – by military weakness.

Gallienus could offer no assistance from the West. The Rhine defences had collapsed completely in AD 258. The Franks broke through in the north and overran much of Gaul and Spain. The Alamanni attacked in the south and invaded Italy over the Alpine passes. The following year, Carpi, Goths, Marcomanni, Quadi and Sarmatians assailed the Danube line, while rebel legions declared against Gallienus in the Balkans. Battling to restore control here – partly by ceding territory to King Attalus of the Marcomanni in return for his allegiance – Gallienus lost the western portion of his territory. The military collapse on the Rhine, at a time when the emperor, fully committed on the Danube, could offer no help, triggered a civil war. Officers and landowners in Germany, Gaul, Spain and Britain rallied around the usurper-emperor Postumus. Gallienus's belated efforts to suppress the revolt were beaten off, and the rebels quickly consolidated their territory into a secessionist 'Gallic Empire', destined to endure for 15 years. A complex military crisis had thus exploded across the Western Empire in AD 258–259, destroying its political and military coherence. Simultaneous pressure at several points on his overextended lines had exhausted Gallienus's diplomatic and military resources, leading to multiple breakthroughs on the frontier. This in turn had shattered the unity of the western ruling class as regional fragments abandoned allegiance to the central Empire and reorganized in their own defence.

Meantime, with no support from the West, the eastern Roman generals were unable to save Antioch, the ancient capital of Syria and one of the greatest cities of the Empire. A makeshift emergency government was then constructed by the eastern generals around two young usurper-emperors. Gallienus opposed this move: he had lost the revenues and legions of half the West; now he was threatened with the loss of the whole East; he risked being reduced to a Balkan-based rump as he faced the barbarian hordes massed along the Danube. Macrianus, the leading

Roman general in the East, and the two eastern emperors, who were his sons, marched west to confront Gallienus, but they were defeated and killed somewhere in the Balkans. Macrianus's eastern colleagues, on the other hand, succeeded in defeating Shapur and driving the Sassanids back. This left the Eastern Roman Empire intact and, for the moment, relatively safe for the rebels, since Gallienus could hardly contemplate an invasion of Asia. Instead he sought an ally: a client-ruler rich and powerful enough to act as an effective counterweight to both the Sassanid Empire and the rebel regime: Odenath of Palmyra.

A great trading city on the northern edge of the Arabian Desert, Palmyra had grown rich on the caravan trade passing from Mesopotamia to Syria; it was a vital link between the Mediterranean and the Orient bringing highly prized luxuries like perfume, spices and fine textiles to Roman markets. Palmyra, however, was a society under stress. The Sassanids coveted the wealth of the trade routes. Incessant warfare had disrupted the caravans. The Romans were no longer able to protect their allies. So the traditional caution of traders preoccupied with making money had given way to a brooding hawkishness in the city. The potentate of Palmyra had declared himself a king and built an army. Palmyrene gold, after all, could buy many soldiers. Odenath had already seen off a Sassanid army. The city had therefore become a player in the power-politics of the age – one important enough to be noticed and courted by a Roman emperor based in the distant Balkans. Gallienus, in return for an alliance, recognized Odenath as King of Palmyra and declared him Duke of the Roman East. Thus legitimized, Odenath went on to the offensive, winning over many Syrian cities, for whom he now appeared the most promising protector, and capturing Emesa, capital of the embryonic Eastern Roman Empire, whose leaders were promptly put to death. Soon the King of Palmyra was effective master of the Roman East.

The Palmyrene Empire was no mere bubble. It had expanded to fill the vacuum left by the collapse of Roman political and military power in the East, and it was now sustained by the tribute from a hundred fabulous cities. But it was rather less than the super-state that Odenath, dizzy with success, now took it to be. Like others before him who had possessed Syria, he could not resist the temptation of Oriental conquest, and now hurled his army into Mesopotamia. Though knocked back at first, the Sassanids later rallied and repelled the Palmyrene invaders, while far in

Odenath's rear Gothic raiders, seizing the moment, attacked Asia Minor and penetrated as far as Cappadocia. In the winter of AD 266–267, his royal prestige tarnished, Odenath was assassinated in a court plot by a Palmyrene nationalist faction eager to assert independence from Rome. Zenobia, Odenath's former second wife, henceforward ruled as regent on behalf of her infant son Waballath. Gallienus refused to recognize the new regime, but his attempt to suppress it militarily was defeated. The embattled Balkan emperor had tried to prop up imperial authority by cultivating an eastern client-state. But Roman power was so hollowed out that nothing had remained in the East to contain the client-state's expansion and hold its rulers in check. Now the Kingdom of Palmyra, like the Gallic Empire in the West, stood independent of Rome.

The Gallic emperor, indeed, had played much the same role in the history of the West in the 260s AD as the Palmyrene king in that of the East. Gallienus's forces had been kept at bay, and domestic usurpers suppressed. The Franks and Alamanni had been expelled, and the Rhine defences restored. The coasts had been secured against seaborne raiders. The currency had been improved and commerce revived. The property-owning classes and the cities of the West had been given good reason to remain loyal. Gallienus meantime remained hopelessly embroiled in the Balkan inferno. AD 262 was an especially black year, as a new wave of plague swept across the empire, and the Goths devastated Thrace, Macedonia and Greece. By forced marches the emperor crossed and recrossed his shrunken domain, plugging one gap only to find another had swung open in his rear. The Goths were no sooner expelled from the Balkans than they were attacking Asia Minor, where they captured and plundered the great city of Ephesus, already racked by earthquake and plague. In AD 268 the barbarians came again in massive force, both Heruli and Goths, attacking by land and sea, sweeping aside local Roman forces, plundering at will the cities of the Aegean. This time Gallienus caught and smashed them in pitched battle – but it was to be his last fight.

The general Gallienus had left to guard Italy had risen in his rear. The emperor raced back to confront the rebels, putting Milan under siege, but some of his own officers too were traitors, and when the emperor rode out alone to reconnoitre a reported enemy sortie, he was assassinated. The empire he left behind seemed on the edge of the abyss. The West was controlled by Gallic emperor Victorinus, the East by the Palmyrene regent Zenobia, Italy by a third rebel regime. The North was threatened again by Alamanni and Goths. Earthquake, plague and war had devastated the empire. Taxation, requisitioning and compulsory services were crushing. The treasury was empty, the currency worthless. When the Balkan army chose Marcus Aurelius Claudius – Claudius Gothicus, as he would become known – to be the new emperor, many must have wondered whether he might not be the last. Yet, despite everything, this Balkan army, all that now survived of the once-mighty Roman imperial state, represented a kernel of military power that was uniquely strong – a nucleus about which the empire could still be reconstructed.

The forces ranged against Rome were still highly disparate and localized. They lacked organizational coherence, transcontinental reach, any real vision of an alternative world. The Roman ruling class – or rather the high command of the military monarchy that formed its inner core – retained such resources of centralized political and military power that the greatest of disasters could still be set right. The barbarians could invade and raid while the emperor's war-machine was distracted, but they could not hold ground when it returned. Equally, rebels could carve out a regional domain when the legitimate emperor was fully committed against foreign invaders, but he, needing the resources of a united empire, was bound to come for them sooner or later. That is why usurpers usually attacked the central empire: the political game they played was, in the long run at least, an all-or-nothing gamble. Unless destroyed by foreign enemies – and they were yet too diffuse – the empire, however much divided, tended to re-cohere. Regionalism was still counterbalanced by a yet more powerful centralism.

The military monarchy, moreover, under the stress of war during Gallienus's long reign, had become tougher. Senatorial generals had finally disappeared completely; all senior officers were now professional men of equestrian status promoted from the army's ranks. The senators had also lost control of many provincial governorships, again to equestrians. The central state's military-bureaucratic complex was expanding at the expense of an established civilian aristocracy that had once monopolized high office. An in-service staff college had emerged for promising centurions who were in training for higher (equestrian) commands. Many new mounted regiments were raised (called simply *equites*), and the old mounted detachments of the legions were reconstituted as independent units (called *promoti*). The idea was to create a field-army with an elite core of fast-moving, hard-hitting shock cavalry. The military dominance of the heavy-infantry legions, the basis of Roman military power since the 6th century BC, was over. To fund the reformed army, the state operated an emergency finance regime. As well as heavy – sometimes crippling – levels of taxation, requisitioning and labour services, deliberate debasement of the currency effected a direct transfer of wealth from civil society to the military-bureaucratic complex. In AD 235 the silver content of the *denarius*, the basic Roman monetary unit, had been 1.3 gm; by AD 253, it had fallen to 0.8 gm; by AD 268, it was reduced to 0.1 gm – the state, in other words, was melting down coins collected in taxation, increasing the base-metal content, and reissuing an increased number with the same nominal value.

Gallienus had pared the military monarchy down to its essence. After him, a succession of three great soldier-emperors from the Balkan army – Claudius Gothicus (AD 268–270), Aurelian (AD 270–275) and Probus (AD 276–282) – used this streamlined instrument to restore, stone by stone, the edifice of imperial power. First, Claudius Gothicus re-established control over the empire's central zone by overthrowing the usurper regime in Rome, ejecting Alemannic invaders from northern Italy, and breaking up a massive Gothic onslaught by land and sea against the cities of the Aegean. The emperor then succumbed to plague. He was succeeded by his second-in-command. Aurelian maintained the momentum of the counter-offensive in the West. Having finished with the Goths on the lower Danube, the emperor turned his attention to the upper Danube, under attack from several Germanic confederations. Taken by surprise, the emperor suffered defeat at Placentia in northern Italy, a setback which immediately prompted revolt in Rome by senators opposed to the rule of the soldier-emperors. The rebels had moved too soon. The Germans were crushed in two big battles, and few of the raiders escaped home. Aurelian then marched on Rome and smashed the revolt. While there in AD 271, convinced of the imperial capital's chronic vulnerability, he ordered the construction of one of Late Antiquity's greatest monuments. The Aurelian Wall around ancient Rome was 19 km long, 3.6 m thick, and 6 m high. It had 18 gateways, the four main ones double-arched, and both here and at regular intervals around the circumference there were square projecting towers. The work, which continued for years, was carried out by slaves and conscripts. The monument symbolized the empire's insecurity, its great reserves of strength, and the subordination of its once pampered citizens to the dictates of a war-economy.

Zenobia meantime had openly thrown off Palmyra's formal subordination to Rome. Aurelian anyway wanted to restore the flow of eastern tax revenues to the central treasury. Shifting the bulk of his Balkan army to the East, he planned a two-stage offensive to collapse the Palmyrene Empire: first the outlying territories of Egypt and Asia Minor, only loosely held in thrall by Palmyra, were to be wrested back; then the Syrian heartland would be stormed. The plan was sound. The presence of the emperor with a strong army restored the confidence of the eastern cities in Roman power. A lenient policy towards reformed rebels encouraged rapid realignment. The professional skill of Roman generals in combined-arms operations soon gave them mastery of the battlefield. The Palmyrenes depended for success on the charge of elite units of superheavy cavalry – so-called 'cataphracts', where the rider was encased in armour, and sometimes his horse as well. Lighter, faster and highly trained, Aurelian's Danubian and Moorish cavalry would fall back before the cataphracts, drawing them forwards, wearing them out under the heat of a Syrian sun, breaking up their close-order formation. The Roman infantry provided a solid defensive line. The Roman cavalry would then launch decisive counter-attacks when their opponents' exhaustion and disorganization were at a peak. Antioch fell. Then Emesa. Zenobia withdrew to Palmyra itself. The Romans closed in, bribing local tribes to desert, beating back a Sassanid relief force. Famine broke out in the city. As her empire disintegrated, Zenobia fled. Palmyra then surrendered on terms. Zenobia's leading counsellors were tried and executed. She was caught, spared, and kept for display in a later Roman triumph. The Palmyrene Empire had collapsed in a year (AD 271–272). Though a fresh nationalist revolt brought Aurelian racing back the following year, it was easily crushed; and this time the city was put to the sack.

Then Aurelian turned to deal with the western secession. The Gallic Empire had, in fact, entered its terminal crisis some years before. The succession to Postumus had been contested, and Victorinus had soon been killed. Tetricus reigned as the third Gallic emperor in just three years. Spain had returned to its former allegiance. Provence had also been lost. Now the Germans were on the offensive, and Tetricus was unable to keep them out. The Gallic Empire thus lost its *raison d'être* – its superior ability to defend property – and local support fell away. Aurelian, momentarily free of commitments elsewhere, chose this moment to attack, and he emerged victorious from a long and bloody battle at Châlons when Tetricus himself deserted to the enemy and his army broke up in confusion (AD 273).

When Aurelian returned to Rome in early AD 275 to celebrate a double triumph over the Palmyrene and Gallic Empires, he took the title 'Restorer of the World' (*Restitutor Orbis*). It seemed no exaggeration. Aurelian's were the greatest victories since the time of Septimius Severus. They had achieved one of the most complete turnarounds in Roman history: from the brink of complete disintegration in AD 268 to an empire reunited behind secure frontiers in AD 274. More than that. The financial crisis was eased as the army returned to barracks and tax revenues flowed in again from East and West. The currency was reformed. Debts were cancelled. Corn doles resumed. The Tiber was dredged and its banks restored. The cult of Sol, the Roman Sun-god, was promoted as a supreme state religion, the divine embodiment of the resurrected empire. Aurelian, the soldier-emperor risen from the ranks of Gallienus's Balkan army, was now father of his country, an old-style Caesar, a true *popularis*.

Ambition lured Aurelian back to the East in AD 275, this time to launch an aggressive war to recover Mesopotamia. He never had his chance. A petty palace squabble exploded like a bomb and blew Aurelian's court to pieces. An official accused of lying tried to protect himself by fabricating a capital prosecution list that included several leading officers. They in turn murdered Aurelian in self-defence. The conspiracy had no wider basis, and the army high command, having no desire to upset the Aurelianic system, deferred the decision about a successor to the Senate. The latter, equally wary, prevaricated. Renewed pressure on the frontiers soon forced an appointment, but the reigns of Tacitus (AD 275–276), an elderly senator, and Florianus (AD 276), a close relative, were messy and short. The army quickly reasserted its authority when the Aurelianic frontier settlement came under threat, and Probus, formerly Aurelian's right-hand man, succeeded.

Probus (AD 276–282), third and last of the great Balkan soldier-emperors, successfully defended the restored Aurelianic Empire. He, like his predecessors, spent almost the whole of his reign on campaign, fighting Germans in the Rhineland, Vandals on the Danube, Nubians at the southern limits of Egypt, bandits in rural Turkey, and new usurper-emperors in the former Gallic Empire.

Despite his energy – perhaps, in a sense, because of it – Probus was brought down by a mutiny in the Balkan army in AD 282. The soldiers assassinated their emperor in protest against being put to work on land reclamation and other public works. The leader of the coup, Praetorian Prefect Marcus Aurelius Carus, was destined to reign only briefly, however. Having made his two sons Caesars, he left Carinus in charge of the West, and himself headed east in company with Numerianus. Yet again, the allure of eastern glory drew a Roman emperor to Mesopotamia; for the Balkan soldier-emperors of the 270s and 280s AD that allure was a curse. Probus, like Aurelian, had been planning a great eastern war when he was killed, and now Carus, though his army captured the Sassanid capital at Ctesiphon, was suddenly struck down, perhaps by a freak accident, perhaps by foul play. His son was murdered soon after. So the Balkan generals, as they had done so often before, convened an army council to decide the future of the empire. Again they chose one of their own to lead them: an Illyrian soldier of modest birth who had risen through the ranks to the command of the household troops: Gaius Aurelius Valerius Diocletianus. We know him as Diocletian. He was one of Rome's greatest emperors. Elevated on 17 November AD 284, he reigned for over 20 years, after which he voluntarily stepped down, later to die peacefully in his bed. Though no one could have known this at the outset, his accession marked the end of Rome's long crisis, its decades of anarchy, and inaugurated a period of concentrated reform and political consolidation which amounted, in effect, to a Late Roman counter-revolution.

The Late Roman counter-revolution: Diocletian, the Tetrarchy and Constantine the Great, AD 284–337

Republican and Early Imperial Rome had been subsidized by the profits of war. New conquests sustained the expansion of the system. But the cost of empire and civilization was high, and only plough-agriculture could generate sufficient surplus. Therefore, the Roman Empire reached natural limits once it had conquered the plough-lands and its frontiers came to rest on untamed wilderness. The profits of war then ceased to flow, and the shortfall was made up in higher taxes, labour *corvées*, and military requisitioning. The empire became a finely balanced military-supply economy in which a base of peasant labour-services and tribute-payments supported an imperial infrastructure of army, forts, towns, villas, propaganda monuments, and 'bread and circuses'. The balance was repeatedly upset by military pressure on the frontiers. Simultaneous threats on different fronts frequently overstretched the empire's military resources to breaking point. This destroyed the unity of the imperial ruling class, leading to usurpation, secession and civil war as regionally based factions attempted to organize their own defence. The resource crisis also increased the pressure on civil society, as the embattled state struggled to supply itself through taxation, conscription, requisitioning, and currency debasement. The 3rd century anarchy was, in essence, the crisis of a system of ancient military imperialism that was unable to expand and therefore unable to sustain itself without eroding its own socio-economic base. The Late Roman counter-revolution – which began under the Balkan soldier-emperors and was completed under Diocletian and Constantine – was the response of the military monarchy, representing the core section of the imperial ruling class, to this crisis. And in the absence of forces capable of destroying the military monarchy in the late 3rd century AD, whether foreign invaders or internal rebels, the counter-revolution allowed the Western Roman Empire to survive for another century and a half – though in a distorted and crisis-racked form, and at enormous cost to its people.

The counter-revolution was not a planned programme of reform, but a series of radical *ad hoc* changes imposed from above in response to successive crises. The effect was cumulative as the changes were consolidated into a new system, and the pace of change gathered momentum, especially after AD 284. The pattern under Diocletian and Constantine was similar to that under Octavian-Augustus: in both cases, improvisation under the stress of war and revolution was subsequently consolidated into a new political order. The term 'Principate' is commonly used to describe the Augustan system; some historians favour the term 'Dominate' for that of Diocletian. Peter Brown has highlighted the importance of the latter transition by dubbing it the 'Late Roman Revolution', and this term, despite recent revisionist emphasis on 'continuity', is embedded in the literature. But the implication is wrong: the Roman imperial ruling class was not overthrown; on the contrary, the essence of the change was for its power to increase substantially at the expense of subordinate social groups. Such was the gravity of the 3rd century crisis that revolution may indeed have occurred had there been a revolutionary class capable of carrying one out. But there was none. The gentry were scattered across a thousand cities, the peasants across a hundred thousand villages. Whatever discontent there was – and all the evidence suggests there was much – it was not organized into a political force capable of overthrowing the imperial ruling class and remodelling society. Instead of revolution, the state – centralized, bureaucratic, militaristic – grabbed a higher proportion of the available surplus to support its core activity (defence) and to cement together its power-base (the imperial aristocracy, the state bureaucracy, the army high command, the Church hierarchy, and key client-groups like the soldiers and the populations of major cities).

The result was the relative impoverishment of towns and villas, provinces and countryside, gentry and peasants. The military aristocracy was the winner, civil society the loser: a non-revolutionary outcome to the crisis of the 3rd century best described as 'counter-revolution'. But as such, it left the contradictions that had produced the crisis unresolved. The intensified accumulation of surplus by the state – a process driven by military competition – was irrational in so far as it undermined the ability of the Late Roman economy to reproduce itself. Civil society was overtaxed, eroding its ability to sustain the military-bureaucratic complex in the long run. Indeed, not only could the Late Roman counter-revolution not resolve the contradictions of imperial decline, the victory of the state over civil society intensified them by increasing the amount of surplus that was siphoned upwards. The military-bureaucratic complex expanded by consuming its socio-economic capital. Increased state power may have suppressed the political symptoms of decay that had been so evident in the 3rd century, but beneath superficial calm the rate of decay accelerated and eventual collapse became more certain.

For most of the first 14 years of his reign, Diocletian was busy on campaign, facing the usual combination of frontier incursions and usurper emperors. But by AD 298, he and his colleagues (for by then he had been joined by three co-emperors) had succeeded in suppressing resistance in

Britain, Gaul, the Rhineland, the Balkans, Egypt, and the East. The hardest struggle had been in the West, where a combination of peasant revolt, seaborne raiding, and fighting along the Rhine had produced a powerful usurper regime based in Britain and northern Gaul, headed first by Carausius, then Allectus. This regime was established in AD 286, and though it soon lost northern Gaul, it successfully repelled an invasion of Britain in AD 293; the rebels did not finally succumb until AD 296. By this time Diocletian had reorganized his government into a 'Tetrarchy' (Rule of Four). In AD 285 he had made Maximian – also, like his patron, an Illyrian soldier – his adoptive son and co-emperor with the rank of Caesar. The following year Maximian was promoted to the higher rank of Augustus, thereby becoming Diocletian's equal, and the empire was divided into two zones of responsibility: Maximian took the West (with his capital at Milan), Diocletian the East (Nicomedia). In AD 293 a Caesar was appointed to assist each of the Augusti, Constantius in the West under Maximian, Galerius in the East under Diocletian. The arrangements were sealed by dynastic marriages and appropriate titles, the empire was sub-divided into four zones of responsibility, and it was proclaimed that in due course the senior emperors would resign and their juniors succeed and appoint new subordinates. In place of regional usurpers, there were to be regional emperors. Instead of wars of succession, there was to be a seamless sequence of Caesars becoming Augusti and raising up new Caesars.

But the Tetrarchy's stability depended on the consent of a small group of top men who knew each other, worked well together, and had combined to defeat a series of common enemies. The centrifugalism inherent in the empire could not be dissolved by a constitutional gimmick. Nor could the realities of power be altered by a change of titles. The tetrarchs claimed divine origins and took the title *Dominus* (master). Everything associated with an emperor became *sacrus* (sacred) or *divinus* (divine). Prostration before the ruler became a feature of court etiquette – a practice traditionally disparaged by Greeks as *proskynesis*, by Romans as *adoratio*. The ruler became distinguished by special dress, by a decorum associated with his person, and by maintaining a symbolic separation and distance between him and others. The men of his inner household – the freedmen, slaves and eunuchs of the Bedchamber (*cubiculum*) – became powerful figures at court. This was the style of true monarchy, of absolute rule, of 'divine right'; a style wholly at odds with the Graeco-Roman tradition of personal familiarity and Republican dignity. Yet it reflected not strength, but weakness; it was an exaggerated assertion of power against the odds. It reflected also the relative independence of the state, which had been raised up above society and lacked any real accountability to those it dominated. Yet emperors could not become gods simply by claiming themselves to be them. Names and titles are simply that: only power can give them substance. In fact, the Tetrarchy was doomed to fail at its first test, when Diocletian and Maximian retired in AD 306, and their Caesars' right to succeed was immediately contested by rival candidates and liquidated in civil war.

Other reforms were more durable. To one of Julius Caesar's centurions, the Late Roman army would have been unrecognizable. Old units were divided and many new ones formed, and a plethora of regimental titles reflected the diversity of origins. *Scholae palatinae* were elite household troops. *Protectores domestici* were the officer cadets of in-service training units. *Cunei equitum* or plain *equites* were newly raised elite cavalry, and *auxilia* their infantry counterparts. *Legiones*, *alae* and *cohortes*, on the other hand, indicated regiments that had evolved out of old-army units of that name, while *vexillationes* had been formed from detachments of these. There were also units entitled simply *milites* (soldiers), *numeri* (numbers of men), or even just *gens* (perhaps best translated 'friendlies'). To these type-designations were added regimental names: the *Cornuti* were the horn-blowers, the *Bracchiati* armlet-wearers, the *Lanciarii* lancers, the *Herculiani* followers of Hercules (and therefore Maximian's Own), and the *Ioviani* followers of Jupiter (Diocletian's Own).

Typically, regiments were of cohort or battalion size, varying between 300 and 1,000 men, with perhaps 500 as an approximate average on active service. Regiments were commanded by *praepositi*, *tribuni* and *praefecti*. They were formed into brigades of many different sizes, the composition liable to vary over time, especially in the case of the field army. And here was another difference from the old army. A broad distinction arose between *comitatenses*, field-army troops (so called because originally they had been the 'companions' of the emperor on campaign), and *limitanei*, the more static garrison troops who manned the frontiers; the former were commanded by *comites* (counts), the latter by *duces* (dukes). The highest command positions – the field-marshals of the Late

Roman army – were the *magistri equitum* (masters of horse) and *magistri peditum* (masters of infantry). All officers, moreover, were now career professionals; the days when senior commands were routinely held by aristocratic politicians were long gone.

Having evolved during the anarchy, this new army was far better adapted than the old to contemporary conditions. Nor is there any evidence to support the oft-repeated claim that the Late Roman army was less professional than the old legions. Grand strategy had changed. That of the 2nd century had been based on fixed frontiers held by strong forward garrisons combined with pre-emptive aggression against neighbouring 'rogue states', with heavy-infantry legions providing the key strike-force. That of the 4th century was based on defence-in-depth and counter-attack by mobile field-armies organized around a core of elite shock cavalry. The network of roads behind the frontiers had been greatly elaborated to facilitate redeployment to confront intruders. The belt of forts in frontier regions had grown thicker and denser, providing strongholds, store-bases and assembly-points for defending forces. The forts were stronger. Military architecture was now heavily defensive, with thick, high walls, narrow, heavily defended gateways, numerous projecting towers, and sometimes wall circuits that followed the high ground. New equipment was introduced. Some cavalry now fought as *cataphracti* or *clibanarii* – heavily armoured in the manner of medieval knights. Infantry weapons included a torsion-powered, hand-held crossbow known as a *manuballista* (hand-ballista), lead-weighted javelins called *martiobarbuli* (barbs of Mars), and a long slashing sword, the *spatha*, previously reserved to cavalry. The archaeological record implies a high-tech, fully professional army. It reveals a network of defence-works – walls, forts and roads – more extensive and better constructed than anything otherwise known in the ancient world. Nor does the written record imply less than the highest standards of military efficiency. When the Roman army went into battle on anything approaching equal terms, it almost always won. The only real problems were recruitment and logistics: there were not enough soldiers.

Conscription was more widely used. Sons of veterans in particular were legally obliged to follow their fathers into the army. Law codes imposed fearsome penalties for draft-dodgers. Barbarians were frequently recruited, not least to fill the ranks of elite units. Military service was often imposed as a condition of peace or of resettlement in Roman territory; but there were also many willing volunteers. On the other hand, the so-called 'barbarization' of the army was neither new nor an aspect of 'decline'. The Romans had always recruited from native populations on the fringes of their empire. (Indeed, it is hard to think of an empire which has not done this.) Instances of disloyalty or inefficiency were very rare; much less common, in fact, than mutiny by Roman citizen-soldiers. The real distinction was between recruitment into regular Roman units – whether of empire citizens or foreign barbarians – and the employment of barbarian mercenary contingents commanded by independent chieftains. The latter – known as *foederati* – became important only after the Battle of Adrianople in AD 378. Eventually they would indeed play a decisive role in the destruction of the Western Roman Empire. But that was not a matter of the Roman army being 'barbarized'; it was a matter of the Roman army ceasing to exist at all.

For the present, the recruitment of more regular soldiers depended upon improved supply. To this end, Diocletian and his colleagues effected a lasting reform of the entire imperial bureaucracy. Our knowledge depends in large part on the survival of an extraordinary ancient text: the *Notitia Dignitatum* (*List of High Offices*). This lengthy document, illuminated with depictions of badges of office, appears to provide a complete list of the military commanders and senior administrators of the Late Roman Empire. It dates to *c.* AD 395–420, though the accuracy of the record even for this period is variable. The list seems to have been updated in some places but not in others, so the information presented may not always be contemporary. Also, the list may sometimes reflect claims and intentions rather than realities. Even so, much in the list can be corroborated from other sources, and the quantity of information provided is very high. We get a complete breakdown of each man's command, his regiments and forts if a general, his civil service departments if a minister. Careful *Notitia* scholarship, moreover, can yield rich information about earlier periods – sometimes taking us back to the time of Constantine, Diocletian, even Gallienus; the nomenclature of regiments, for example, very often gives away their date of origin. What the *Notitia* most certainly reveals is the thoroughgoing centralization of empire which took place under Diocletian and Constantine.

State bureaucracy in the Early Empire had been minimal. Provinces were large yet had small staffs. Efficient local government was the key, and this was in the hands of the decurions, part-time officials and councillors recruited from the gentry. Diocletian hugely increased the central bureaucracy. Each of the four tetrarchs had his own *comitatus* (mobile court). The empire was divided into large territorial prefectures under senior *praefecti*. Provinces were grouped together as 'dioceses' under *vicarii*. Many provinces were subdivided. Britain had been one province until the time of Septimius Severus, who made it two, and then Diocletian split each of these, making four. Each required its own governor and staff. The men appointed were usually professional civil servants of equestrian status rather than senatorial politicians. There were two parallel hierarchies, one military, one civil, both of them technocratic rather than political in spirit, and in each case men got on largely through experience, seniority, hard work, and winning favour with superiors. One estimate is that a diocesan vicar was served by around 300 officials, a provincial governor by 100; on that basis, Diocletian's reforms may have added 10 to 15,000 officials to the government payroll.

The lower bureaucracy remained a local affair, but the decurions had been displaced. Public office had become arduous, expensive and unpopular, and in late antiquity there were no compensating rewards. Efficient imposition of rising state demands earned opprobrium, not praise. Often decurions were frustrated by popular resistance – but any shortfall earned a forced levy on their own estates. Local councillors risked ruin in the public service while making themselves hated by their fellow citizens. Many qualified men, in consequence, tried to evade service, and successive legal edicts from on high denounced their negligence, threatening dire penalties. Filling the gap in local administration were the *principales* or *decemprimi*, the top group of richest men, perhaps one in ten of a town's decurions. These were given special powers to administer in default of a full council. Naturally they used these powers to shift burdens on to others; specifically to protect their own property at the expense of lesser gentry and the peasantry. The rise of the *principales* is clearly represented in the archaeology of Late Roman towns: the evidence is still there for basic urban infrastructure, but most of the grand houses of the gentry lie abandoned, town life having lost its attractions.

The main job of the *principales* was to impose a new tax system. During the anarchy, debasement and inflation had destroyed the tax-pay cycle on which military supply depended, and officers on campaign had used forced requisitioning (without payment) to support their troops. Such erratic and uneven burdens were unsustainable. Monetary and tax reform was essential. Diocletian introduced two new taxes, one levied on *capita* (heads), thus a *capitatio*, the other on *iuga* (taxable units of land), thus a *iugatio*. The former was a poll tax, a levy on existence itself, and a particular burden on large peasant families, who would pay for each of their grown-up children. The latter was a property tax, which, bureau-cratically administered from above, took inadequate account of differ-ences in land quality and of variations in yield from year to year, and, moreover, no account at all of the overall size of holdings, such that rich and poor paid the same percentage. The *capitatio* was paid in coin, the *iugatio* at first in kind, later also in coin. Reform of the coinage was therefore an essential corollary. The standardization of AD 294 was based on 60 gold coins per half kilogramme and 96 silver coins per half kilogramme of the respective metals. Local issues ceased, though many official mints were established. But would the new coinage be any more resistant to debasement and inflation than its predecessors? Diocletian's central plan included an attempt at price control. His Price Edict of AD 301 has survived, and, being immensely detailed about goods and prices at the time, is an invaluable source. But the severity of the penal-ties proposed for violators is no doubt inversely related to the Edict's effectiveness. Without regulation of supply and means of enforcement, official prices were widely ignored, and the Edict stands as a supreme example of an historical document that records intention not reality. The new coinage fared little better, and further reforms were soon necessary. A greater success was the establishment of government factories to supply the troops directly with arms, armour, uniforms and equipment: many are recorded in the cities of the empire by the *Notitia*.

To facilitate censuses, tax collection, and state control over labour, peasants were ordered to return to their places of origin and remain there: henceforward many were classed as *coloni*, effectively serfs tied to the land by law, a condition which greatly strengthened the power of landlords, since peasants were no longer free to move in search of an improved tenancy. Other occupations also became hereditary. Among those whose labour the state now attempted to direct were decurions, soldiers and their sons, shippers, boatmen and carters, workers in the new state factories, and various categories of artisan and trader. The sources are scanty and do not allow us to distinguish between intention and reality, and in particular to estimate the overall degree of the state's success. But the aim is clear.

Within the limits imposed by a pre-industrial economy, the Late Roman state had some of the characteristics of modern totalitarian systems. A greatly enlarged apparatus was created to regulate and exploit civil society more effectively, and to harness and channel resources to support the military-bureaucratic complex that controlled the empire. Centralized control was established over local government, the tax system was overhauled and improved, state factories were set up, and military conscription and tighter control of labour imposed, such that military supply greatly improved. But clear limits to state power are apparent in the raucous tone of many repressive laws, the inflationary collapse of the new coinage, and the total failure of price controls. More seriously, however, to the extent that Diocletian was successful, there was a heavy price to be paid, at least in the long term, in growing economic decline, social discontent, and popular hostility towards the state, its officers and its mission.

One reform that did not outlast Diocletian was the Tetrarchy. Diocletian (willingly) and Maximian (under duress) resigned in May AD 305. Constantius became Augustus in the West, Galerius in the East. Constantius, who was ailing, requested the release of his son Constantine from service in the East, but Galerius, suspecting that the young man was being groomed for the succession in violation of tetrarchic arrangements, refused to release him. Constantine escaped nonetheless, attending his father's deathbed in York in July AD 306, where he was promptly hailed Augustus by the Roman army in Britain. The usurpation destroyed at a stroke the delicate balance of the tetrarchic system and unleashed a complex and protracted struggle for power. Britain and Gaul adhered to Constantine; Spain and Africa to Maxentius, son of Maximian; Italy to the legitimate tetrarch, the Caesar Severus, who was also backed by Galerius in the East.

Maximian returned to office from retirement – playing the Augustus to his son Maxentius's Caesar – and Severus was quickly defeated, giving the rebels control of Italy. Galerius then attacked the Maximian/ Maxentius faction from the East. Both parties wooed Constantine, but he accepted the suit of the latter, an alliance sealed by the marriage of Maxentius's sister to Constantine. Galerius's invasion in AD 307 proved abortive. Despite this, the central bloc promptly imploded: Maximian was estranged from his son and fled to join Constantine. Galerius, seizing the moment, called a conference of the former Augusti at Carnuntum on the Danube late in AD 308. Diocletian persuaded Maximian to retire again. Licinius was appointed western Augustus. Constantine was recognized as Caesar. Maxentius was declared a usurper. Before any action on these redrawn battle-lines, however, Maximian, politically unstable to the end, self-destructed by initiating a plot to overthrow Constantine which backfired badly and resulted in his own enforced suicide (AD 310). The Tetrarchy, despite Carnuntum, had obviously broken down irrevocably. Whatever had been agreed, no one trusted anyone else, and one of the key players, Maxentius, had not been included at all. Constantine, for example, was threatened by Maxentius, who was laying claim to the whole of the West, but at the same time feared that a victory by the Galerius-Licinius bloc over Maxentius would lead directly to an attack on himself. It was around this time that Constantine made a momentous decision: he was going all-out to win sole autocratic power.

Three strands of evidence suggest this shift: a pre-emptive strike against Maxentius; a clear change in Constantinian propaganda; and the inauguration of a politico-religious revolution. Formally in alliance with Licinius, in AD 312 Constantine invaded Italy with the declared intention of destroying the usurpation of Maxentius. The defenders, taken by surprise, fell back to the outskirts of Rome, and here, at the Milvian Bridge, one of history's most decisive battles was fought. Maxentius seems originally to have planned a defence of the city, but collapsing prestige and the threat of revolt from within forced him to lead his army into open battle. The armies clashed at a place called Red Rocks, a defensible defile between hills and the River Tiber where Constantine had judged he could hold Maxentius's assault with part of his army. Once battle was joined, Maxentius learnt that the rest of Constantine's army was attacking his rear, and there was heavy fighting at the Milvian Bridge leading back into the city. Trapped, Maxentius's army still fought well, but it finally broke up, and, as it did so, thousands, including the defeated emperor, were cut down or drowned trying to escape across the river. Constantine's victory was total. He was master of the Western Roman Empire. But there was more to his victory than speed and tactical finesse.

Constantine had already begun to claim descent from Claudius Gothicus – a genealogical fiction that represented a *pre*-tetrarchic claim to legitimacy. He also announced that Sol Invictus, the All-conquering Sun, a favourite deity of Aurelian, was his special protector – rather than Hercules, who had been the patron of the now disgraced western tetrarch Maximian. Constantine was creating a new dynastic propaganda that elevated him above all his contemporaries, implying that they, whether usurpers or legitimists, had more recent, and therefore inferior, claims. And there was something more. Cheerfully oblivious of any inconsistency as he mixed the ingredients of a rich ideological brew, the emperor had his men fight at the Milvian Bridge with the *Chi-Rho* (the first two letters of his name in Greek) monogram of Christ painted on their shields. Lactantius tells us this was due to a dream before the battle in which God instructed Constantine to have this done. Eusebius reports that Constantine had been inspired by a cross of light seen emblazoned across the sky. Probably he did indeed have some sort of conversion experience. Certainly he was under strong Christian influence, not least that of his mother Helena, who had already converted. Later, for sure, his Christianity was clear, consistent and committed, encouraged, no doubt, by a spectacular sequence of victories that brought him to supreme world power in AD 324.

Whatever personal engagement there may have been, however, it was the power of the Church at the beginning of the 4th century AD that made Constantine's decision possible. Its significance can hardly be exaggerated. The Battle of the Milvian Bridge was one of history's great turning-points. It was the first victory by a major political leader fighting as a Christian, and, because it set Constantine on course for empire-wide supremacy, it led directly to the eventual triumph of the Church across Europe. In February AD 313 Constantine issued the famous Edict of Milan granting religious toleration across the empire, thus legalizing Christianity and facilitating its rapid development henceforward as the religion of court, army and civil service. By the end of the 4th century, the emperors had unleashed a full-scale offensive against the old religion, handing over the estates, treasures and sanctuaries of the pagan temples to the Christian Church, which in return preached that obedience to and service under state authority were holy duties. This alliance of Church and State was, of course, an essential, defining feature of the medieval West. It is important, therefore, to ask: what lay behind Constantine's religious revolution?

Christianity had been founded in the 50s AD by an itinerant mystic who preached in the synagogues and public auditoria of the cities of the Roman East. A Hellenized Jew, he had grafted ideas about saviour deities and the afterlife that were widespread in the Greek-speaking world at the time on to a set of stories, at first orally transmitted but gradually taking on a written form, about a Jewish village prophet of the 30s AD called Jesus Christ (Jesus the Messiah). St Paul – as we know him – made the startling discovery that Jesus was a god in human form; that he was literally *the* 'Son of God', not simply, as any Jew might be metaphorically described, *a* 'son of god'. Jesus's mission, it turned out, had not been to lead the Jews in a national struggle against Roman imperialism and Jewish collaborators; rather, his kingdom not being of this world, it had been to make converts and save souls, guiding humanity on to a path of righteousness that would guarantee resurrection and eternal life after death. The defeat and destruction of the Jewish national revolutionary movement in AD 70 – including, we must assume, the Jewish Christian sect – cleared the decks for the advance of Pauline 'Catholic' Christianity. Rooted in the cities of the East, where Gentiles as well as Jews had been converted, it survived the holocaust in Palestine. More than that, by denationalizing and spiritualizing Jesus, Paul had effectively severed Christianity's roots in Judaism, transforming it from a national religion concerned with the struggle against oppression in Palestine into a universal one concerned with personal salvation. As such, it was ideologically equipped to deal with the shattering disillusionment that followed the Jewish defeat. Still, though, and for long afterwards, it remained mainly a religion of the poor, especially the urban poor. A central tenet of Early Christianity – in contrast to most pagan religions – was that all were equal before God, that earthly possessions were of no account, and that differences of rank and property would not be recognized in the afterlife. The Early Church retained an egalitarian spirit. It offered solace to slaves and commoners in a world corrupted by class oppression. It was therefore viewed with suspicion by authority, and was periodically the target of persecution.

The Great Persecution of AD 298–313 was only the last of many. It was triggered when pagan priests blamed failed omens on the presence of profane persons at a ritual attended by Diocletian and Galerius in AD 298. Diocletian ordered all public servants to perform sacrifice to the pagan gods (considered sacrilege for a Christian) on pain of flogging and dismissal. Not until AD 303, however, was a full-scale pogrom unleashed. Imperial edicts were posted ordering the surrender for burning of all copies of scripture, the dismantling of churches, the banning of Christian meetings, and loss of rank and denial of legal rights to all Christians. The edicts gave the green light to reactionary local officials and urban mobs. In Nicomedia, the eastern capital, the local church was destroyed, the bishop executed, and the imperial household purged. Eusebius kept an accurate record of martyrdoms for his diocese in Palestine: one execution under the first edict; two under the third; one under the fourth; and eight more when six young men presented themselves shouting out that they too were Christian. Overall, when the authorities attempted to implement the edicts forcefully, while some Christians recanted, handed over scriptures, and made sacrifice, many refused and were imprisoned, sometimes tortured, occasionally executed. The Church was left with a catalogue of martyrs to parade. Though many fair-weather friends departed during the storm – leaving a legacy of deep division among Christians – the Church emerged defiant. The Great Persecution was another of Diocletian's failures.

Large-scale, top-down, empire-wide persecutions were rare. That of Diocletian may indicate the state's insecurity as it attempted to drive through reforms which attacked whole sections of civil society. The persecution created an enemy within and an intimidating, witch-hunting atmosphere. The potential effects were various: to assuage public anxiety in a period of turmoil by placating angry pagan gods; to provide scapegoats, castigate deviance, and encourage uniformity and obedience; above all, to expose the actually disloyal and terrorize the potentially disloyal. It seems improbable that Christians were a real threat. Christian pacifism has only rarely been a discouragement to military service, and the Church hierarchy certainly did not have subversive political aims, merely an interest in protecting itself and enlarging the social space it occupied. Certainly, the Church was a large, well-organized, empire-wide institution, with bishops meeting regularly in provincial capitals, and metropolitan bishops in major centres emerging as powerful figures, the effective leaders of tens of thousands of Christians in places like Rome, Carthage, Antioch and Alexandria. But if, in some sense, the Church was 'a state within a state', that need not weaken the cohesion, loyalty and political will of the Roman body-politic. Indeed, it was a potential ally, and, ironically, more so after the Great Persecution than before. The Church had demonstrated its strength. It had shown that it could not be broken by direct state assault. What the moderation of local authorities, the resistance of the Christian communities, and the relative lack of anti-Christian pogroms in the cities had revealed was that central government was weak and the Church strong. The persecutors found themselves opposed by a powerful public opinion, including sections of the military-bureaucratic complex itself.

Its bargaining position strengthened, the Church was now poised to cut a deal with the state. It was clearly the largest single ideological apparatus in the Roman Empire, and the state could hardly expect to function effectively without its co-operation. On the other hand, if the state became the patron of the Church, a great network of preachers and adherents might be converted into enthusiasts for secular authority. Though a minority overall, Christians were strategically concentrated in the towns, always the locus of power in the ancient world. Their theology's distinctive combination of universal appeal and monotheistic intolerance meshed well with the centralizing aims of the Late Roman state, allowing Christian emperors to demonize pagan usurpers as enemies of God. Moreover, the Christian vision of a heavenly hierarchy seemed to mirror, and thereby legitimize, the imperial order on earth. At the very least, being 'the heart in a heartless world', Christianity offered personal solace in a world full of fear, giving many men the will to carry on, and some the courage to fight heroically in the empire's defence. Constantine's religious revolution, in short, was an event of substance and great moment. Within a few decades of the Milvian Bridge, the Church had been transformed into what it would remain for more than a millennium: the principal ideological apparatus of the medieval states of Europe.

The Church embraced by Constantine in AD 312 was, however, a flawed instrument. Always split into theological factions, the Great Persecution had hammered wedges deep into the cracks. The 'Catholic' moderates of the North African Church were willing to readmit those who had caved in – those who had handed over copies of scripture to be burnt (thus *traditores*). The 'Donatist' radicals were not. The Catholic party was that of the government, the urban elite, and the great land-owners. The Donatists were a party of village priests and the rural poor. The left-wing of the party included bands of militants who attacked landlords and debt-collectors. The conflict between the rival churches erupted over a bitterly contested election to the vacant metropolitan see of Carthage. The emperor was invited to arbitrate. Constantine had little choice. If his vision of a powerful, united, conservative Church working for the defence of the empire was to be realized, orthodoxy and obedience had to be imposed; otherwise, so far from being an ally, the Church might become a vehicle for the empire's subversion from within. Henceforward, church councils were regularly convened, often with the emperor chairing in person, in an effort to heal schism. The first, the Council of Rome in AD 313, ruled against the Donatists. The second, the larger Council of Arles in AD 314, attended by 33 bishops, confirmed this ruling. It made little difference: Donatist agitation continued, there was rioting in Carthage, and in AD 321 the authority of the church councils was enforced by state repression. Church and State became, for the first time, allies in the persecution of 'heretics'. Donatism yielded a second gallery of martyrs. The rift in the North African Church deepened.

In the struggle against paganism, by contrast, the emperor enjoyed further spectacular success. The campaign of AD 312 had delivered the West to Constantine and the Church. That of AD 324 delivered the East. Relations with Licinius had steadily deteriorated. There had been a flurry of fighting in the Balkans in AD 316. Constantine had appointed consuls without the approval of his ostensible colleague. Licinius had resumed the persecution of Christians within his territory. When Constantine felt ready to launch a full-scale invasion, the western bishops were sum-moned to give their blessing, the emperor was provided with a special campaign tent to serve as a portable chapel, and the army marched bear-ing the Labarum, a sacred imperial standard emblazoned with the *Chi-Rho*, with its own guard of 50 picked men. Licinius, by contrast, chose to fight under the totems of the old pagan gods.

They did him little good. Like the campaign of AD 312, that of AD 324 was a Constantinian blitzkrieg. A series of victories gave Constantine's army control of the Balkans, and when he immediately ferried his men across to Asia Minor, Licinius sued for peace. His surrender was accepted, but he was promptly executed on the victor's orders. Constantine – the first Christian emperor – was master of the entire Roman world. Political authority was restored to a single, supreme, military dictator. The empire was again a unified war economy. The reformed military-bureaucratic complex of Diocletian dominated civil society. Paganism withered in the shadow of Constantine's Church. The Late Roman counter-revolution was complete.

All that glisters is not gold, however. The reforms of the soldier-emperors – Gallienus, Aurelian, Probus, Diocletian, Constantine – had bought the empire time. But the price, largely hidden from history, certainly for long unpaid, was high. The siphoning of surplus upwards – from towns, estates and farms – sustained the military-bureaucratic complex only by consuming the economic foundations of the empire. The contradictions of imperial decline were not resolved. On the contrary, the stronger the state, the more efficient the exploitation; and the more efficient the exploitation, the faster the decay. The Roman Empire was being hollowed out.

Town and country in decline: the House of Constantine and the House of Valentinian, AD 337–378

Let us recall a story told earlier. In the winter of AD 187–188, a man called Maternus, whom the ancient sources describe as a 'deserter' and 'bandit', set out for Rome at the head of an improvised army with the intention of assassinating Commodus and replacing him as emperor. Such was the 'insecurity throughout Gaul and Spain' and the 'countless numbers' mobilized that a major military operation was necessary to suppress the revolt. Maternus himself was betrayed, captured and beheaded.

About 20 years later, in AD 206–207, we hear that a man called Bulla or Felix was at large in Italy at the head of a band of some 600 men. For two years he 'continued to plunder Italy under the very noses of the emperor and a multitude of soldiers'. He is reputed to have sent a message to the Roman authorities saying, 'Feed your slaves to stop them becoming bandits.' And later, after capture, when asked by his Roman interrogator, the Praetorian Prefect Papinian, 'Why did you become a bandit?', to have answered, 'Why are you a prefect?'(7)

Scattered references to banditry pepper ancient accounts of the anarchy. Philip the Arab (AD 244–249) stationed units in Italy as a defence against 'robbers and pirates'. Probus (AD 276–282) campaigned against a bandit-chief called Lydius, whose army of peasant outlaws had evicted the Roman authorities from much of the countryside of Lycia and Pamphylia in southern Turkey. The Isaurians, whose mountain territory lay immediately to the east, were also, it seems, out of control. The ancient sources demonize the Isaurians as bandits, pirates and serial rebels, reporting numerous campaigns against them down the centuries. Diocletian, in AD 284–285, ordered the suppression of rebels known as *bagaudae*. This is the first of many references to *bagaudae* in the ancient sources. They mounted a series of rebellions in Gaul, Spain and possibly Britain between the late 3rd and mid 5th centuries AD. Even when not specifically referred to, we can sometimes assume their identity. Ammianus Marcellinus, for example, our best historical source for the 4th century AD, refers mysteriously to 'many battles fought in various parts of Gaul' early in the reign of Valentinian (AD 364–375), but these he considers 'less worthy of narration' than fights with Germanic tribesmen, it being 'superfluous to describe them, both because their outcome led to nothing worthwhile, and because it is unbecoming to prolong a history with ignoble details.'(8) Here, surely, are *bagaudae* waging guerrilla war: something likely to bore and irritate an aristocratic army officer and military historian like Ammianus.

Later, in the 5th century, references to *bagaudae* become frequent and explicit. Risings are recorded in Gaul in AD 407–417, 435–437, 442 and perhaps 448; in Spain in 441, 443, 449, 454 and 456; and possibly in Britain in 408. These references imply revolts serious enough to warrant intervention by imperial troops – and therefore notice from historians. The further implication is that banditry was extensive and endemic in much of the countryside of the Western Roman Empire during the 5th century. Eric Hobsbawm has argued that rural 'social banditry' is, in fact, a normal state of affairs in pre-capitalist class societies where those who work the land are exploited by landlords and governments. Mostly it exists only as a nagging irritant, for the bandits rarely amount to more than one in a thousand of the rural population, and a typical band

numbers no more than 10 or 20 hiding out in some remote spot and supporting itself by preying on big estates, tax collectors and rich travellers.
Recruited largely from the rural underclass of escaped slaves and serfs,
army deserters and fugitives from the law, and impoverished crofters
unable to make a living on the land, the bandits still remained part of
peasant society, enjoying a measure of protection and support – even
sometimes being lionized as champions of the poor. As such, if conditions in the countryside worsened considerably, and if the state's repressive power weakened, social banditry could flare into peasant revolt.

Bulla's two recorded statements reveal radical consciousness.
Occasional references to the practices of *bagaudae* reveal the same.
The senator and poet Rutilius Namatianus records that his relative
Exuperantius, in suppressing bagaudic revolt in Gaul in AD 417, had
'restored the laws and brought back liberty, and did not allow the Bretons
to be slaves of their own domestics'.(9) The world, it seemed, had
momentarily been turned upside down. It was not law and liberty as such
that needed restoring, of course, only the law and liberty of the ruling
class. That much is clear from another reference. A comedy written by an
unknown author around the same date makes jokes about life beside the
Loire, where men live by popular laws, peasants make speeches, capital
sentences are pronounced under an oak tree and recorded on bones,
and 'anything goes': a satire, apparently, not on a world without law or
liberty, but on one without landlords, tax-collectors and police.

A similar spirit was at large in the countryside of Roman North Africa.
Here wandering bands of poor peasants were inspired by the simple
rural piety of the Donatist Church. Known as *circumcelliones* in reference to the shrines of martyrs where they gathered, they had their own
communal organization, collective rituals, and distinctive style of dress.
Many courted martyrdom – even a bitter enemy like St Augustine
conceded that 'they lived as robbers but died as *circumcelliones* and were
honoured as martyrs'.(10) Sometimes, crazed by religious enthusiasm,
whole groups would commit suicide by jumping off a cliff or setting fire
to themselves. Others plundered villas and churches. Some organized
collective resistance to debt-collectors. One source records bands of
circumcelliones forcing rich men out of their carriages and making
them run behind while their slaves took their seats. The combination of
social and religious radicalism attested by the ancient writers appears

to make the *circumcelliones* precursors of the millenarian sects of the Middle Ages.

If rural banditry and revolt were as endemic as they seem in the Late Roman Empire, it is not difficult to suggest reasons. In AD 238 the villagers of Scaptopara in Thrace petitioned the emperor to complain that soldiers and officials attending an annual festival nearby regularly demanded accommodation and supplies without payment. So heavy was the burden that many villagers had abandoned their ancestral farms and let their fields return to waste. Earlier complaints had prompted the provincial governor to issue an edict ordering that the villagers be left alone. But it had provided only temporary respite, and soon the problem was as bad as ever. Little wonder: soldiers and officials took their lead from their masters. Two contemporary historians, Dio Cassius and Herodian, describe the financial ruthlessness of the military monarchy and its consequences. 'Nobody in the world should have money but I,' Dio has Caracalla (AD 211–217) exclaim, 'so that I may bestow it on the soldiers.' Later, facing the censure of his mother for excessive expenditure, he is said to have exhibited his sword and declared, 'Be of good cheer, mother, for as long as we have this, we shall not run short of money.'(11) Herodian compares the ravages of Maximinus Thrax (AD 235–238) to a barbarian invasion: 'Maximinus, after reducing most of the notable houses to poverty . . . began to lay hands on the public treasuries. He expropriated whatever public moneys there were – funds which had been collected for the grain-supply, or for distribution to the people, or earmarked for shows or festivals. Dedications in temples, statues of gods, honours to heroes, and whatever embellishment there was of a public nature, or adornment of a city, or material out of which money could be made – he melted all of it.'(12) Dio and Herodian lament especially the spoliation of aristocratic estates, but, in speaking up for the property rights of their class, they illuminate the exploitation of all. Yet more informative are surviving Roman law codes.

The Theodosian Code (published in the East in AD 438) was a fairly comprehensive record of laws issued in the previous 40 years, and a more patchy record of laws from the time of Constantine onwards. The Justinianic Code (AD 529) and the Justinianic Digest (AD 533) superseded the earlier code, eliminating obsolete laws and amending, abbreviating and reordering those that remained in force; thus, like the Theodosian

Code, these documents also preserve many laws dating back to the early 4th century AD. The law codes are key sources for official policies, the detail of administration, the social structure, and aspects of everyday life in town and country. It is from the law codes that we learn that many of the peasants had become *coloni*: though terms and conditions varied from place to place, generally, it seems, this meant they were serfs, that is, men who were tied to the service of a particular estate. For the state, this had the advantage that taxes and labour services could be more easily levied. For the landlords, it denied tenants their principal means of redress – seeking a better tenancy elsewhere – and thus allowed the rate of exploitation to be ratcheted up. But if the law, in recording the rise of serfdom, implies growing oppression in the Late Roman countryside, it also, in its frequent references to *agri deserti*, alerts us to one of the fatal consequences of this. *Agri deserti* meant 'abandoned fields': land that it had once been profitable to cultivate now too burdened with tax, rent, debt and labour service to be viable. A.H.M. Jones, the great historian of the Late Roman Empire, estimated that perhaps the poorest 20 per cent or so of land went out of use. He argues that, while some land may have been abandoned due to shortage of agricultural labour or in some areas to insecurity, in the main it was caused by the high and increasing rate of taxation, which reduced the net return on marginal land to vanishing point. Archaeology supports the notion of a slow-working agricultural depression in the Late Empire, beginning as early as the 2nd century in places, becoming more widespread in the 3rd, gathering strength through the 4th, and bringing whole regions to ruin in the 5th.

The evidence for most parts of the empire remains anecdotal and impressionistic, but that for Roman Britain is based on systematic surveys of excavation data. A sample of 78 Romano-British villas revealed a steady climb to a peak in occupation around AD 325 – the true 'golden age' of villa civilization in Britain, when many sites had been expanded into great country houses with suites of dining-rooms, bedrooms and baths opening on to colonnaded gardens. Thereafter, however, there was decline: some villas had been abandoned as early as AD 350, more than a third by 375, and well over two-thirds by the end of the century. Around AD 400, in fact, all building-work had ceased on villa sites, and within a decade or so elite occupation had been completely terminated. Occasional claims for 'continuity of occupation' turn out to be unfounded: at a handful of sites there is evidence that former country houses were converted into working farms; there is not a single site in the entire British archaeological record where elite occupation at a villa can be demonstrated as late as AD 425.

Decline is also apparent among the villages, hamlets and farmsteads where the Romano-British peasantry dwelt. A survey of 177 sites spread randomly across the country revealed that, between a 2nd century AD peak and the late 4th century, some 37 per cent of settlements were abandoned. A more detailed survey of 317 sites in the Severn Valley and Welsh Marches region showed a drop of 27 per cent over a similar period. Shortly after AD 400, moreover, virtually all Romano-British rural sites appear to have been abandoned; only gradually over the succeeding decades does a new rural settlement pattern emerge in the archaeological record. All of the evidence – increasing peasant resistance, complaints about exploitation, references to *agri deserti*, the end of the villas, the abandonment of native rural settlements – confirms the impression of a generalized and steadily worsening agricultural depression in the Late Roman Empire.

Little wonder, then, that the decurionate was in crisis. The law codes list a series of edicts making service on local town councils compulsory and imposing stiff sanctions on absentees. Traditionally the gentry – legally defined by regular censuses as men endowed with estates and other property of a certain minimum value – had served willingly on local councils, often competing energetically for elected office and distinguishing themselves in acts of public benefaction. The provincial towns of the 2nd century AD, with their basilicas, temples, baths and fine houses, were monuments to the civic-mindedness of this class. But as the military monarchy battened on to civil society, as taxes, requisitions and *corvées* fell more heavily, as resentment and resistance mounted, public service became more burden than honour, and many men withdrew, eschewing politics, administration and the law, retreating into the country, where they managed their estates and embellished their villas. The state pursued them there, demanding a return to duty. When some avoided service by joining the army, the civil service or the clergy, the law thundered against them: such persons were to be tracked down, dragged back, forced to perform their municipal duties. Centrally appointed town governors – *curatores* – were dispatched to administer the municipalities. Boards of ten – *decemprimi* – were formed of the leading local notables – *principales* – and given authority to impose on their more junior colleagues and enforce attendance and service. But edicts and orders from on high constitute intentions, not reality, and the archaeology of the towns of the Roman Empire argues for failure and a steady decline in urban life.

Across the empire, the great age of urban public building came to an end with a final flourish in the early 3ʳᵈ century AD. At Leptis Magna in Libya are to be found the ruins of some two dozen major public buildings erected between the reigns of Augustus and Severus. Every imaginable type of Roman public architecture is represented: forums, basilicas, temples, baths, theatres, amphitheatres, circuses, monumental arches, public fountains and shopping malls. The ruins are dominated by the Augustan-period theatre, the Hadrianic public-baths, and the imperial forum, colonnaded street and harbour-works of Septimius Severus. Then it all stopped. Almost nothing was built thereafter, with the notable exceptions of a circuit of defensive walls enclosing most (but not all) of the existing city in *c.* AD 250–350, and the conversion of some pagan temples into Christian churches in the later 4ᵗʰ century AD. Leptis, more-over, is typical. Except for refurbishments, conversions and defence-works, urban building virtually ceased in most provincial towns after the early 3ʳᵈ century AD. The evidence from 17 Romano-British towns has been collated and analysed. It reveals that the towns were growing from the late 1ˢᵗ to the early 3ʳᵈ century AD, with heavy expenditure on public buildings in AD 75–150, followed by the construction of elite town-houses in AD 150–225. The middle years of the 3ʳᵈ century, however, were a time of crisis, with a collapse in civil construction and diversion of resources into building town walls. There was some recovery in the early 4ᵗʰ century, but this was limited and faltering, with no return to the boom conditions of the 2ⁿᵈ century, and virtually all construction work had ceased by AD 400. Population levels mirrored this decline in build-ing: they reached a peak in the early 3ʳᵈ century, retained this level for about a century, but then declined dramatically – down more than a quarter by AD 350, more than a half by AD 375, and collapsing to a mere eighth of peak levels by the end of the century.

We cannot know how successful were the Late Roman state's efforts to dragoon reluctant gentry into taking their seats in local council chambers.

What we do know is that the infrastructure of the towns in which those chambers lay was degrading from the early 3rd century onwards. Indeed, in the course of the 4th century, most towns in the Western Roman Empire lost their distinctive urban characteristics. Typically, by *c.* AD 400, a Late Roman 'town' comprised a circuit of strong walls, often enclosing only a small inner enclave, within which most public buildings were in a state of ruin, and most private houses abandoned or taken over by lower-class 'squatters'. Often there is evidence for some sort of administrative centre, one or two churches, a few grand residences, perhaps a large warehouse or two, a small garrison of soldiers, and a much-reduced plebeian population of artisans, traders and labourers. Heaps of stinking refuse and sewage frequently clogged the empty houses, yards and back-streets of abandoned districts. Populations of a few hundred were probably common.

Town and country were in crisis. Municipal aristocrats rarely came to town, were no longer interested in public building, and more often than not failed to maintain their residences. But at their country seats, too, there were problems: not at first perhaps, but certainly from the mid 4th century onwards, landowners discovered that the burdens on estates meant dwindling returns. Soon the great country houses were too expensive to maintain: frescoes flaked and were not replaced; mosaics were holed and badly patched; the water-channel got blocked and the bath-house ran dry. Beyond, in the villages, there was grinding poverty and sullen resentment. Some of the outlying farms were in ruins, the fields overgrown; others were short of labour, animals, equipment, and the resources and will to make good. Many peasants had simply fled, disappearing perhaps to another estate, perhaps to eke out a living in the wilderness, perhaps to join the outlaws and hold up travellers on the remoter roads. There were, in short, three worlds of Late Antiquity: the world of the imperial grandees, of emperors, generals, courtiers and bishops; the world of the provincial gentry, of ruined towns, crumbling villas and bankrupt estates; and the world of the peasantry, of tax, rent, debt, *corvées*, and a desperate struggle to survive on the margins of existence. Because these three worlds were linked, because grandees needed gentry to manage their empire, and peasants to create its wealth, the great edifice of Roman imperial power was, by the 4th century, resting on a foundation of crumbling sand.

The Western Roman Empire endured for as long as it did only because its myriad discontents could never be organized into a revolutionary force capable of challenging the military-bureaucratic complex. Decurions might abscond to their country seats and there grow bitter as ancestral estates decayed. But, divided between a thousand local-government districts, their outlook was ever a parochial one, and the decurionate never coalesced into a national class. Peasants might flee to join a band of outlaws, or even, on occasion, rise in revolt *en masse* and, for a while, drive the bailiffs, tax-collectors and recruiting-officers away. But peasants, too, lacked national organization; without some catalyst of unity – the leadership of an urban class or the inspiration of a revolutionary ideology – they remained preoccupied with farm, fields, the village, the eternal cycle of the seasons. The socio-economic base of the Late Empire rotted away, therefore, largely unseen, beneath the gaze of history, and only indirectly were the effects felt amid the froth of events – in a renewal of dynastic strife, in religious conflict, and in the growing threat posed by the barbarians hammering at the gates.

Behind the internecine conflict that tore apart the House of Constantine was the old problem of regionalism in an overextended empire. Constantine attempted to satisfy the need for local emperors without the attendant danger of usurpation by restricting power to members of his own immediate family. Conflict erupted nonetheless. The emperor's eldest and most accomplished son, Crispus, was suddenly and inexplicably executed by his father in AD 326. Fausta, the emperor's wife, followed shortly after (probably charged with adultery). Though he had advanced his three remaining sons and a nephew to supreme power by the time of his death in AD 337, his carefully crafted partition of the empire between the four was immediately rejected by the army, which refused to recognize any but the three sons of Constantine as emperors. Territory was reapportioned: Constantine, the eldest, took Britain, Gaul, Spain and the Rhine frontier; Constans, the youngest, Italy, Africa, the Balkans and the Danube frontier; and Constantius, the East. But civil war soon broke out between Constantine and Constans, and when the former was defeated and killed, the latter amalgamated his brother's territories with his own (AD 340). Ten years later, in AD 350, Constans was overthrown by Magnentius, one of his own senior commanders, but the Balkans revolted against the usurper and declared allegiance to Constantius, who promptly invaded from the East, defeated Magnentius, and reunited the empire under his sole authority (AD 353). Finally, Constantius II had two of his own leading subordinates arrested and executed, one in AD 354, the second in AD 355. Unsurprisingly perhaps, the last of the sons of Constantine emerged from almost two decades of intermittent civil war with a well-deserved reputation for paranoia and ruthlessness.

The only prominent surviving male member of the House of Constantine apart from the emperor himself was now Julian, the son of a half-brother of Constantine the Great killed by the army in AD 337. Julian himself had been saved by his youth (he was only six at the time). Constantius, preoccupied with the defence of the East against the Sassanids, needed a colleague to guard the Rhine frontier, and, though ever suspicious, came to depend heavily on his cousin. Julian was made Caesar (junior emperor) in Gaul and Germany in AD 355. His mission was to restore the damage after deep and devastating barbarian raids, and then to take the offensive in order to break the power of the Germanic 'rogue state' of the Alemanni. He won a spectacular victory at the Battle of Strasbourg in AD 356, and proved himself also an efficient administrator, restoring city defences, establishing military supply-bases, and cracking down on corruption in the Roman administration. We have a detailed account because the historian Ammianus Marcellinus, formerly one of Julian's officers, was an admirer for whom Julian's career was especially heroic, edifying and pivotal. In Ammianus's detailed narrative we gain insight into the mechanics of making emperors. Julian's success consolidated his base – and heightened the suspicions of his master. When Constantius II demanded the dispatch from Julian's army of four crack units – as a test of loyalty? to weaken a potential usurper? or simply because he needed them? – Julian (or so Ammianus leads us to believe) wished to comply. But Julian's supporters refused – it would weaken them politically against Constantius, and militarily against the Germans. Yet to refuse was to revolt. Thus, in a classic confrontation over the deployment of scarce military resources, fuelled by mutual suspicion, Constantius and Julian were propelled towards civil war. In AD 360 Julian was hailed emperor by his supporters. Constantius refused recognition as a co-equal, and both sides prepared for war. Only the death of Constantius the following year prevented a clash of arms. The elevation of Julian, in the event, passed peacefully.

His short reign amounted to a doomed reaction against the Constantinian order. The sons of Constantine had pursued a Christianizing policy, banning pagan sacrifices, closing temples, granting tax immunity to the clergy, funding the building of churches. Also, like their father, they intervened frequently in Church affairs in the interests of unity. Their ideal was a single Church preaching a uniform message. Their fear was that a divided Church might become a vehicle for political opposition. But schism was a perennial feature of the Early Church. Sometimes, notably among the Donatists in North Africa, sectarian faction gave expression to popular discontent and threatened to erupt into class warfare. More often, splits in the Church reflected rivalries within the ruling class. This was surely the case in the bizarrely obscure, yet intractable, theological dispute between Arians and Catholics in the East. The argument revolved around the relationship between God the Father and God the Son, and whether the latter was of the same priority and substance as the former. The priest Arius had argued that God the Father came first. His bishop, Alexander of Alexandria, had denied this. Constantine had attempted to heal the rift at the great Council of Nicaea in AD 325. Attended by around 250–300 bishops, a moderate majority had united around a compromise formula destined to become one of the cornerstones of Catholic theology: the Nicene Creed. But the compromise spawned a party of extreme rejectionists on either side, and bitter disputes raged in the Eastern Church until the end of the 4th century AD.

The controversy was fuelled by the fast-growing wealth of the Church. Control over valuable assets was at stake. The patronage of the House of Constantine quickly transformed the Church into a major legal authority, a political power, and a privileged corporation with a huge property portfolio. The great monuments of the age were usually churches. Major foundations included: in Rome, the Mausoleum of Helena, the Lateran Basilica, and St Peter's on the Vatican Hill; in Constantinople, the Church of Santa Sophia; and in Jerusalem, the Church of the Holy Sepulchre. Constantinople, built in AD 324–330, was of special significance. It was a 'New Rome' with its own Senate, but it was conceived and built as a thoroughly Christian city. It was not just a monument to its founder, a celebration of victory over a pagan enemy (Licinius), a fortified palace complex, and a city with an excellent harbour that was highly defensible, strategically located, and destined to become one of the greatest in world history; it was also a symbol of the new Christian Empire that it had been Constantine's work to create.

The rise of the Church elevated the bishops to the imperial aristocracy. Increasingly they were recruited from among the grandees, and certainly all were able to take their place among them. Bishops, positioned at the head of a rigid ecclesiastical hierarchy, managed large estates, were numerous at Court, and dominated their home towns, where they conferred benefactions, largesse and favours. Clashes between Donatists and Catholics, Arians and Alexandrians, were, in part at least, struggles between aristocratic factions for wealth and power.

So, too, were clashes between Christianity and paganism. The new religion was associated with the court, the army, and the new men who formed an aristocracy of merit around the emperor – with, that is, the military-bureaucratic complex that controlled the empire. Throughout Roman history new nobles had been resented by old, aristocrats of office by aristocrats of birth. It was true in the conflict between patricians and plebeians in the 5th and 4th centuries BC, and again in the civil wars between Caesarian 'new men' and the Senate in the 1st century BC. It had fuelled the opposition to the military monarchs and soldier-emperors of the 3rd century AD. Now, in the 4th, the conflict took the particular form of religious strife, in which the old order – traditional landowners and hereditary peers – rallied to the defence of the pagan cults. They found their champion in the emperor Julian (AD 361–363).

His short reign, though, must be judged a miserable failure. His attempt to restore the old religion by withdrawing the privileges of the Church and lavishing largesse on the temples amounted to little more than a temporary blip. The programme was curtailed by the emperor's early death and the strong Christian reaction evoked in his successors. Julian came to grief – as so many of his predecessors had done – in the East. Resuming Constantius's interrupted war, he marched his army deep into Mesopotamia, but was defeated by the Sassanid strategy of scorched earth and guerrilla warfare (AD 363). During a night attack on the Roman camp, Julian led out a sortie without waiting to put on his armour and was shot and mortally wounded, dying a few hours later. The House of Constantine was finally extinguished.

Embroiled in a losing war, the generals at first chose the stopgap emperor Jovian to lead them, fearing that the split between mainly

Christian appointees of Constantius and mainly pagan appointees of Julian might blow the high command apart; now was not the time for theological dispute. Jovian dutifully cobbled together a peace agreement with the Sassanids and pulled the army out of Mesopotamia. The following year he died (whether naturally or not is unclear), and the generals assembled again to choose an emperor. Valentinian, the son of a peasant who had risen to become a general, was selected, a man who, according to Ammianus, 'hated the well-dressed and educated and wealthy and well-born'.(13) He took as co-emperor his younger brother Valens, giving him responsibility for the defence of the East while he took charge in the West. Both men were firm Christians. Their elevation meant that the pagan revival was dead. Religious compromise was thrown to the winds. Militant Christianity – and the military-bureaucratic complex – resumed its forward march. The old order was sidelined again by the dominant power-nexus of court, army, Church, and the aristocracy of merit.

For more than ten years, moreover, Valentinian (AD 364–375) and Valens (AD 364–378) suppressed internal opposition and defended the frontiers of the empire. When Valentinian died – in an uncontrollable fit of rage, it is said, while negotiating with some barbarian leaders – he was succeeded by his sons Gratian (AD 375–383) and Valentinian II (AD 375–392). But Gratian was a teenager, Valentinian a child, and they were in fact ciphers for their uncle, Valens: figurehead rulers to secure the House of Valentinian against usurpers in the West. Then, suddenly and cataclysmically, the regime was destroyed in a huge and terrible battle against the Goths at Adrianople on the lower Danube in AD 378.

Adrianople was the greatest Roman defeat since Cannae. But whereas, in its ascent to global power, Rome had rebounded from Cannae to win final victory against Hannibal, now, in its decline, it would never recover from Adrianople. The haemorrhaging of men that it suffered on that bloody field would be fatal. The Late Roman counter-revolution had put massive strain on the empire's economic and social foundations. As civil society decayed, tax revenues and reserves of men dwindled, and the military balance swung, slowly but inexorably, away from Rome and in favour of the increasingly well-organized and well-equipped barbarian confederations of Central Europe. The empire, in short, was bleeding to death. Adrianople was the moment when the crisis matured and history turned.

As the Huns advanced westwards across South Russia, the resistance of the (eastern) Ostrogothic and (western) Visigothic kingdoms collapsed. Large masses of displaced people, led west by the Visigothic chieftains Fritigern and Alavivus, appealed to the Eastern Roman Emperor Valens for admission to the Balkans. Their request was granted: they could settle on abandoned land in frontier Thrace in return for military service. In the late autumn of AD 376 the Goths were ferried across the Danube. Some immediately went east to serve in the Roman army. Others were settled around the city of Adrianople in central Thrace. Most, however, were left in refugee-camps in northern Thrace, without adequate food supplies, and prey to exploitation by corrupt Roman officials. The starving Goths were traded dog-meat in return for selling their families into slavery. The rate was one dog per slave.

Anger sometimes boiled over. There were armed clashes. As order broke down, the shattered remnants of the Ostrogothic people, led by the chieftains Alatheus and Safrax, crossed the Danube into Roman territory, swelling the numbers of refugees – and Gothic warriors. When the corrupt Roman military commander in Thrace murdered the escort of the two Visigothic leaders as they dined with him during negotiations, revolt exploded across the refugee-camps and beyond. The Gothic settlers at Adrianople and the Goths sold into slavery joined the revolt. So, too, did some of the provincials, including Thracian miners who had recently been rounded up and returned to work by the Roman authorities. The whole of Thrace was soon under the control of the insurgents. Landlords, tax-collectors and corrupt contractors fled. Local villas were plundered for food.

Valens arrived on the scene with the bulk of the Eastern Roman army in May AD 378. Though reinforcements had been promised from the West, he was confident he could win alone. Leaving their heavy baggage at Adrianople, the Romans advanced the 13 km to the Gothic camp, a great defensive wagon laager. The day was hot. When the Romans arrived, they were tired, thirsty and hungry. The land around the Gothic camp had been scorched, so there was no food to be had. There was then more delay, as abortive negotiations were dragged out by the Goths – deliberately, it seems, for the men defending the laager were awaiting the return of their cavalry, away foraging when news had come of the Roman advance.

Finally it began. The account in Ammianus is confused, but it seems that Valens ordered a massed assault on the Gothic laager, and as this became bogged down, more and more of his men were fed in, until no reserves were left. Then, with the entire Roman army committed, the Gothic cavalry reached the battlefield and charged into the exposed enemy flanks and rear. Surrounded and slowly compressed into an ever-smaller space, with neither room to manoeuvre nor opening to escape, the emperor Valens and some two-thirds of the Eastern Roman army perished on the battlefield.

The Goths declined to attack either Adrianople or Constantinople – 'I am at peace with walls,' Fritigern is reported saying – and the revolt was contained in Thrace. But the loss of manpower had inflicted irreparable damage. Never again would a Roman citizen army fight a major battle in Europe. Henceforward the defence of the West would depend on the services of barbarian mercenaries. Adrianople had revealed the rotted condition of Roman imperial society: the alienation of its own people; the corruption of its officials; and the sinking numbers, efficiency and morale of its fighting forces. In the chaos and carnage of that baking early summer's day, the world changed. Soon, the East, with its vastly superior estate, would cut the West adrift, leaving it starved of resources to die a lingering century-long death. But it would be the barbarian war-bands recruited to fill the gaps in the battle-line left by Adrianople that would be the instrument of termination.

End of Empire: from Theodosius to Romulus Augustulus, AD 379–476

As the Goths destroyed the Eastern Roman army at Adrianople, the Germans stood poised on the Rhine and upper Danube to invade the West. They, too, were in flight from the Huns; they, too, had nowhere else to go. Gratian, desperate for a reliable colleague to take charge in the East, summoned Theodosius from his Spanish estates (to which he had retired after the execution of his father) and appointed him Augustus at Sirmium in the Balkans in January AD 379. Theodosius ruled in partnership with the House of Valentinian until the deaths of Gratian in AD 383 and Valentinian II in AD 392. He remained stoutly loyal, twice intervening against usurpers in the West, first Maximus in AD 388, then Eugenius in

AD 394. Thereafter he ruled as sole emperor over both East and West;
the last to do so, for at his death in AD 395 the empire was divided, never
to be reunited.

Theodosius's greatest challenge was to create a new army. He did so
with ruthless efficiency. Draft-dodgers were combed out of offices and
farms. Penalties were imposed on officials who tried to fob off recruiting
officers with cooks, bakers and shop assistants. The mutilated – men
would cut off their own thumbs to disqualify themselves – were forced
to serve. Barbarians were enrolled on easy terms: a man might return
to his tribe when he chose provided he supplied a substitute. But the
units raised were inexperienced and unenthusiastic, and there were
not enough of them: the simple fact was that the losses suffered at
Adrianople could not be made good by traditional recruitment. The solution was to hire barbarians to fight barbarians – *en masse*.

The Roman army had always recruited barbarians on the empire's
frontiers. Some had acquired Roman citizenship and joined the legions.
Many more had fought as 'allies' (*socii*), such as the Gallic and German
cavalry employed by Caesar. Later, under Augustus and his successors,
these 'friendlies' had been enrolled in regular auxiliary units, led by
Roman officers and organized, trained and equipped to fight in Roman
style. In the crisis of the 3rd century, however, when campaigning was
relentless and attrition high, emperors had begun settling barbarians
wholesale in frontier areas in return for military service (when they were
known as *laeti*), or hiring the services of barbarian war-bands for the
duration of a war (*foederati*). These emergency measures were manage-
able: the standing army was still formed of regular Roman soldiers, who
formed a large majority of the empire's fighting men, whereas the barbarians took service only intermittently, when called upon, and as a
supplement to the main force. It was this that changed after Adrianople.
Such was the empire's desperate need of men that barbarian federates
soon predominated over regular forces; such was the need, moreover,
that the terms of service the emperor was compelled to offer amounted to
a surrender of political authority.

Gratian and Theodosius made peace with the Goths. Many of the
Visigoths still wished to settle, and they were welcomed along the lower
Danube, where they filled much of the long gap left in the Roman frontier-
line after Adrianople. Theodosius's court poet praised his patron for

populating a deserted country with former enemies. But the peace of AD 382 left these Goths governed by their own chiefs, subject to their own laws, and performing military service as allied contingents under their own leaders. The Gothic federate settlement of northern Thrace in AD 382 was something new: a state within a state, an armed body of men that lived on Roman territory but remained independent of Roman authority. The mechanism by which the Western Roman Empire would eventually break in pieces had begun to operate.

There was no alternative. Traditional recruitment could not make good the losses of Adrianople, and the federate system was a successful alternative. Without it, the empire would have succumbed sooner. In AD 386 an Ostrogothic assault on the lower Danube was thrown back by the Roman commander in Thrace – presumably at the head of an army of Visigothic federates. Eight years later, at the Battle of the River Frigidus, it was Theodosius's Gothic federates who crushed the army of the western usurper Eugenius, reunited the broken empire, and ensured the final victory of the Christian Church over pagan reaction.

That crisis had been brewing for years. Neither of the western emperors had a strong base. Gratian was young, educated and a sports-lover; he preferred the company of senators and intellectuals to that of military men. His brother, Valentinian II, was still a child. When the Roman army in Britain proclaimed Magnus Maximus emperor, Gratian's soldiers mutinied and killed him (AD 383). Theodosius rushed to restore stability, granting recognition to the new emperor, while shoring up the power of Valentinian's regime in the Balkans. At first Maximus kept the peace, and the empire was ruled by a triumvirate of three emperors. But the defence of Britain, the Rhine and the upper Danube were heavy burdens on the western provinces. Maximus is charged in the ancient sources with raising income by arraigning wealthy men on trumped-up capital charges to secure the confiscation of their estates. Elevated by the officers and landowners of the West to provide greater security, Maximus was driven to plunder their property to maintain the army at the necessary level. This contradiction could be resolved only by war. But when Maximus invaded Italy, determined to gain control of rich heartland provinces, Theodosius marched against him. Maximus was defeated, forced to surrender, and then immediately executed.

Theodosius remained in Italy for three years, leaving the East under the nominal rule of his son, Arcadius, who had been proclaimed Augustus in AD 383. When he departed in AD 391, he left the young Valentinian II in the care of the Frankish field-marshal (*magister militum*) Arbogast. The arrangement broke down the following year: Arbogast quarrelled with his charge and killed him; he then proclaimed an upper-class intellectual and government official called Eugenius emperor in his place. Theodosius was compelled to march west again, determined to uphold the legitimate political order, restore the dominance of the military-bureaucratic complex, and defend the Church against pagan revival. The struggle for the heart and soul of the empire which had dominated elite politics for a century now reached its bloody climax. There was much at stake at the Battle of the River Frigidus in AD 394.

The pagan prejudices of the old western aristocracy had taken a battering from the House of Valentinian. Gratian had dropped the imperial title *Pontifex Maximus*, removed the Altar of Victory from the Senate House, and confiscated the revenues of the Vestals and other pagan priesthoods in Rome. The petitions of pagan senators were ignored, whereas the outspoken Bishop of Milan, one Ambrose, was a close advisor of the emperor. In the East, Theodosius proved himself an equally resolute defender of both Church and Catholic orthodoxy (as represented by the Nicene Creed). He issued an edict in AD 380 which recommended the Catholic faith to all his subjects and proclaimed those who resisted 'heretics'. In AD 381 he ordered all churches be handed over to Catholics and banned any other religious meetings. The Council of Constantinople in May AD 381 reaffirmed the Nicene Creed and encouraged purges of nonconformists. In all, Theodosius enacted no less than 18 edicts against heretics during his reign, usually only amounting to bans on meetings and the confiscation of premises, but sometimes, in the case of obscure (and radical) sects, ordering them to be hunted down and exterminated. Then, with the Church united, the target shifted from heretics to pagans. In AD 391 the emperor issued an edict from Milan banning all sacrifices and closing all temples. The following year, from Constantinople, a supplementary edict extended the ban to private ritual in the home, the penalty for violation being the confiscation of the property where the offence occurred. The Theodosian religious reform therefore threatened a major shift of wealth and power from one section of the Late Roman elite to another. It represented a further squeeze by the military-bureaucratic complex of generals, administrators and bishops linked with the court on landowners, hereditary estates and the old political establishment associated with the pagan priesthoods. This was the context for the revolt of Arbogast and Eugenius.

Eugenius restored the Altar of Victory to the Senate House. Arbogast threatened to stable his horses in churches and conscript the clergy into the army. The usurpers drew on three decades of accumulated bitterness against the House of Valentinian. Under them, the pagan aristocracy was roused for a final battle in defence of the ancient gods of Rome. The enemy was the semi-barbarian Christian 'new men' of Theodosius's Eastern Empire. It was a measure of the age, however – of the withered power of Rome – that the leading champion of classical paganism was a Frankish general, and that the battle-line of Roman Christianity would be filled by federate Goths.

Arbogast knew his business. He chose a strong defensive position at the narrow entrance to an Alpine pass beside the River Frigidus, blocking the route of Theodosius's army into Italy. He built a wooden fort with palisade and towers on high ground, and deployed his army in front of this, its flanks secure, its front protected by secondary earthworks. Theodosius was compelled to launch a frontal assault. Some 20,000 Gothic warriors mounted a series of attacks through the day, but all were beaten back, and by the end some 10,000 of them had fallen. The westerners celebrated. The eastern generals urged retreat. But Theodosius persisted – spending the night, it is said, in fitful sleep and prayer – and the following day the attack was renewed. The westerners were caught off-guard and weakened by defections (of Christians from the pagan ranks?), but the battle again raged for hours all along the line. Victory came when the Alpine Bora – a gusting cyclonic wind – whipped dust into the faces of the western troops, who, physically and mentally exhausted, broke and ran. The rout turned into massacre, the wooden fort on the hilltop was burnt, and the western leaders perished, Eugenius by decapitation, Arbogast by suicide. The Christian God appeared to have answered his faithful son's prayers: Theodosius and his Church controlled the entire Roman world.

A few months later, Theodosius was dead. The empire was immediately divided – in the event, for the last time – between his two sons, the

18-year-old Arcadius (AD 395–408), who already ruled in the East, and the 11-year-old Honorius (AD 395–423) in the West. Neither emperor, even later when grown to manhood, was fit to govern; instead, the East was ruled by a succession of civilian ministers, the West by a succession of generals, sometimes of barbarian or part-barbarian origin. The dying Theodosius had made Stilicho, the son of a Vandal father and Roman mother who had commanded the eastern army at the Frigidus, guardian of both his sons. But the succession settlement was doomed from the outset: by the end of the 4th century AD, the Eastern and Western Empires had become separate entities, a split symbolized by the East's immediate rejection of Stilicho's regency.

East and West had always been different. The former was highly urbanized and prosperous, with a mainly Greek-speaking elite, and a history of civilization stretching back thousands of years. The latter was composed mainly of former barbarian lands where towns, classical civilization and the Latin language had arrived only with the Romans themselves. The foundation of Constantinople as a new imperial capital – complete with a government infrastructure to rival that of Rome – had merely widened an already existing political, socio-economic and cultural gulf. Crucially, on a crude estimate, while the East yielded about two-thirds of the empire's total tax revenue, it required only about one-third of the imperial army for its defence. Except for the Syrian front facing the Sassanids, and the lower Danube front facing the Goths, both heavily defended, the Eastern Roman Empire was relatively secure against attack. The West's Rhine and upper Danube frontier, on the other hand, ran right across continental Europe. The East, therefore, subsidized the defence of the West. Between the two regions lay the Balkans: a mountainous area with poor communications, restless imperial subjects, only superficial Romanization, and endless fighting due to barbarian incursions across the Danube and successive civil wars. The Balkans, then, was a barrier: and on the other side of the barrier were two very different worlds. When the eastern aristocracy rejected the authority of Stilicho and vested power in the hands of local politicians, it was protecting itself against the demands liable to be placed upon it by a western-based regent intent on the defence of the Rhine, the upper Danube and Italy. Not only was Stilicho denied the revenues of the eastern cities; his access to traditional army recruiting-grounds in the Balkans was contested by Constantinople.

As the East retreated into a form of Splendid Isolation, the Battle of the West began. It centred first on the Balkans and the threat posed by King Alaric of the Visigoths, who was at large in the region seeking a homeland for his people. While offering minimal assistance to Stilicho, the eastern regime sought to protect itself by bribing Alaric to go elsewhere, thus deflecting Gothic aggression away from Constantinople (and towards the West). Stilicho struggled to protect Italy and eject the Goths from the Balkans. When he failed – despite having defeated them on the battlefield more than once – he cut a deal: it was agreed in AD 405 that Alaric and his people would settle in Illyricum and that the king would be paid to keep the peace and guard Italy as *magister militum* of Illyricum. Stilicho's weakness thus compelled him to concede a huge new federate settlement – a new state within a state – as the only way to protect the western heartland.

Even before the agreement could be finalized, the Rhineland defences collapsed under a great surge of invading Alans, Burgundians, Sueves and Vandals, who poured across the frozen river in the winter of AD 406– 407. As the hordes entered imperial territory, they took different routes, some penetrating deep into southern Gaul and eventually Spain. Britain, cut off, raised a usurper, Constantine III, to organize the island's defence. Alaric compounded the crisis by demanding immediate payment of nearly 2,000 kg of gold in return for peace. The disaster shattered confidence in Stilicho's government. He had many enemies in the western aristocracy, men who resented his barbarian origins, his dependence on Germanic troops, his intimacy with Alaric and the Goths. Now, as Stilicho struggled desperately to raise money and soldiers, the young emperor Honorius was persuaded that his military commander was plotting against him. In AD 408 Stilicho was overthrown in a palace coup orchestrated by a civilian minister, Olympius, who probably represented a faction of Roman courtiers and aristocrats hostile to 'barbarian' influence. Stilicho was executed, the families of federate soldiers were massacred, and the soldiers themselves fled to join Alaric.

The coup was a disaster. Its effect was to destroy the only solid pillar that had remained of the Western Empire's state edifice: the power-nexus represented by Stilicho and his barbarian soldiers and allies. Olympius lacked the social, political and, above all, military support to establish a stable regime: he represented nothing more than the blind reaction of an embittered court elite whose world was falling apart. The succeeding ten years was a chaotic period of palace coups, usurper revolts and military defeats. When Alaric's offer of peace in return for land and gold was rejected, the regime's hollowness was at once exposed. The Goths marched on Rome and threatened to sack the city, forcing the Senate to pay out 5,000 lbs kg in gold, 30,000 lbs kg in silver, and much else in kind (AD 409). The power of the King of the Goths symbolized the rotten condition of the empire. With its resource-base crumbling and its military power shrivelled, the West had become entirely dependent on alliances with barbarian federates. The hordes breaking across the frontiers could be resisted only by hiring other hordes to fight them. To defend itself the empire had to authorize the construction of mini-states within its territory. The distinction between friends and enemies blurred. Alaric was sometimes an open enemy threatening pillage, sometimes a robber-baron extorting protection money, sometimes a highly paid mercenary captain. Weak and reactionary, the Western regime continued to wobble between conciliating and insulting Alaric. Finally, in AD 410, having placed the city under siege for the third time since Stilicho's death, Alaric stormed into Rome and put it to the sack.

The psychological shock was immense. It was the first time in 800 years that a barbarian enemy had captured Rome. Alaric quickly withdrew with his booty, shortly afterwards died, and was succeeded by a brother, Athaulf, who decided in AD 412 to quit Italy and try his luck in Gaul. Even so, there could hardly have been a more potent symbol of imperial decline and of the degree to which the Western Empire had become prey to roving war-bands. Traumatized, sections of the fragmented western elite now coalesced around a new strongman: from AD 411–421, though the emperor Honorius continued to reign, the effective ruler of the West was a Roman general from Illyricum called Constantius. His pre-eminence was consolidated by the award of patrician status in AD 415, his marriage to the emperor's half-sister Galla Placidia in AD 417, and, shortly before his death, his coronation as Augustus by his brother-in-law.

The Western Empire's centre of gravity had shifted from the Balkans to its western provinces. The British usurper Constantine III had invaded the Continent in an attempt to restore Roman rule in Gaul and Spain, but his would-be empire quickly fell apart, with the secession of Britain and Brittany, a revolt by his own commander in Spain, and a large Burgundian settlement on the west bank of the Rhine. Into this maelstrom plunged Constantius in AD 411, determined to wrest back control of the western provinces for the legitimate regime of Honorius, now based mainly at Ravenna in northern Italy. Constantine III was besieged and eventually captured at Arles; he was dispatched to Italy and later executed. Gerontius, the rebel commander in Spain, found his army melting away, was forced to retreat, and later perished in a mutiny. The barbarian settlers, on the other hand, proved more intractable. They asserted their independence by creating their own usurper emperor – Jovinus – and only by hiring the services of Athaulf's Goths, recently arrived in Gaul, was Constantius able to extinguish this new revolt. The Burgundian settlement was already too well rooted to be removed, however: the first of the Germanic states that would form the post-imperial world had come into existence. Soon there was a second. Having broken with his erstwhile ally Athaulf, Constantius had driven the Goths into Spain. This threatened the recent carve-up of territory in the peninsula by the barbarian hordes. When Athaulf was assassinated in AD 415, the Goths, under their new leader Wallia, were re-hired and charged with restoring imperial authority in Spain. This done, they were granted a permanent home in Aquitania (AD 418).

Relative stability returned for a time to the Western Roman Empire. But the face of it had been transformed. The *Notitia Dignitatum*, in the copy that survives, was regularly updated for the Western Empire until *c.* AD 425. Of the 180 field-army units listed, only 85 had been in existence before AD 395. The army seems, in other words, to have lost over half its strength – and in Gaul, in fact, almost two-thirds. The Rhineland frontier-army, moreover, is almost non-existent: in contrast to the scores of regiments listed for the Danube, a mere handful is recorded on the Rhine. The change was permanent. The tax-base of the Western Empire was fast degrading. In addition to the chronic problems of overtaxation, *agri deserti*, popular resistance and collapsing state authority, there was now the additional problem that great swathes of imperial territory had been surrendered, either because, as with Britain and parts of Spain, no resources were available for recovery, or because, as with Burgundy and Aquitaine, barbarian settlements had been granted. Even areas still under Roman control were often so devastated by war that they could pay nothing and their taxes had to be remitted. And despite the depth of the Western Empire's crisis, many of the richest potential taxpayers avoided paying. Even the preamble of a contemporary law records how 'the power-ful refuse and the rich reject' payment of taxes. Sometimes immunity was granted in return for service and support. But other times the authorities simply lacked any means of enforcement. Often local administration was little more than a racket run by the rich themselves. Under a weak state, the rich evaded tax one way or another, and the burden fell ever more heavily on the poor. But they, too, could resist.

A key ancient source for social conditions in the mid 5th century AD is the Gallic monk Salvian's tract *Concerning the Government of God*. Salvian condemned the entire Late Roman establishment as oppressors of the rural poor: the rich were guilty of gross injustice and acted like a pack of brigands; Roman officials were corrupt, the taxes they imposed crippling; businessmen practised fraud and perjury; soldiers were plun-derers. The result, wrote Salvian, was that the oppressed poor would flee for refuge to the *bagaudae* or the barbarians. Though given to rhetorical exaggeration, Salvian's picture is borne out by other sources. References to the *bagaudae* reach a peak in the 5th century AD. We hear elsewhere of peasant communities willingly placing themselves under the authority of barbarian rulers. Nor was Salvian the only radical churchman denouncing the wickedness of the age. The Donatist Church still thrived in North Africa, and Pelagianism was widespread across the West. Pelagius was a British-born monk who argued that people had free will, could choose to act righteously, and in this way accumulate enough heavenly credit to ensure salvation. In contrast to conservatives like Augustine, who believed that sin was inevitable and God's grace could be earned by faith and obedience alone, Pelagius maintained that people were responsible for their own actions and it was deeds not words that counted: a much harder road for the rich to tread, since it required them not merely to pro-fess to *be* Christian, but also to *act* Christian.

We see much circumstantial evidence for the economic and social decay implicit in Salvian's account. After AD 395 the government aban-doned the issue of base coinage except for tiny *nummi*, and issues of silver became sparse and occasional. Only gold was minted regularly in large quantity – *solidi* (staters), *semisses* (half-staters) and *tremisses* (third-staters). The old tax-pay cycle that had driven the military-supply economy and pump-primed a host of subsidiary commercial exchanges was grinding to a halt. Of monumental building there was almost none; even in the great imperial capitals like Rome, Milan, Ravenna, Trier and Arles, buildings of the mid 5th century AD are virtually non-existent. Most towns, if they survived at all, had shrunk into small defended enclosures, usually centred on an episcopal church.

Constantius died in AD 421, Honorius two years later. The rule of the House of Theodosius was briefly disrupted by the usurpation of the emperor Johannes (AD 423–425), but was then restored with the elevation of Valentinian III (AD 425–455), son of Galla Placidia, nephew of Honorius. Valentinian was another boy-emperor, and his mother acted as effective regent. The new regime was threatened, however, by a new strongman: Aëtius. Having spent some years in his youth as a hostage of the Huns, when he formed a close relationship with their royal family, Aëtius had in recent times been acting as Roman ambassador to the Hunnic court. When news reached him of the coup at home, he enlisted the support of his Hunnic allies in negotiating a role for himself in the new government. For many years thereafter the politics of the western court was dominated by a factional struggle between the supporters of Galla Placidia and those of Aëtius. But his powerful allies gave Aëtius the edge. A leading figure in the politics of the Western Empire from AD 425 onwards, Aëtius enjoyed supreme power from AD 434 until his murder in AD 454. His long supremacy was dominated by the loss of North Africa, the attempt to maintain Roman influence in Gaul, and by the impact of the Huns on the disintegrating empire.

Large areas of Spain had remained under the control of Vandals and Sueves after the withdrawal of Wallia's Goths in AD 418. The Vandals were settled mainly in the south, and in AD 429 a huge horde, recorded as 80,000 in total, so including perhaps 20,000 warriors, crossed the Straits of Gibraltar into North Africa. A new, massive, highly disruptive folk-movement was under way. Though, unusually, we have a precise figure for the size of the horde at the beginning of the expedition, numbers are likely to have fluctuated greatly thereafter. Some will have settled quickly. Others will have broken away in subsidiary movements. More may have arrived later in secondary waves. Some, perhaps many, who were not Vandals at all, but soldiers of fortune picked up along the way, may have joined. Numbers and movements will have been influenced, too, by the rivalries of chieftains within the horde, each seeking to build and maintain his retinue by accumulating land, gold and men in a dynamic and highly fluid struggle for power. Perhaps, indeed, when Gaiseric, the Vandal king, decided to invade, his initial intention was only to raid and sate his warriors' appetite for plunder before returning home to Spain. But the Vandals were lured on by the rich pickings of Roman North Africa, one of the great centres of classical civilization, and one little affected by the centuries of war that had ravaged Europe and the East. By AD 435 the Vandals were in control of Morocco and Algeria, and stood poised on the edge of the Tunisian heartland of Rome's African empire. In AD 439 the great city of Carthage, ancient capital of the Province of Africa, and in recent times one of the well-springs of Late Roman Christianity, fell to the Vandals. There was no possibility of dislodging them. Attempts by expeditionary forces from both East and West to do so were beaten off. Soon the Vandals were attacking Sicily, Sardinia, Corsica, and eventually even Rome itself.

The Western Empire was, by mid-century, too embroiled in Gaul to challenge the Vandal advance. The Huns had been transformed from allies of the Western Empire into terrifying enemies. When a Christian hermit dubbed Attila 'the Scourge of God', the Hunnic king adopted the title with relish. He and his people, in the literature of the day, became synonymous with ugliness, filth, cruelty and ruthlessness. The Huns – illiterate, nomadic, pagan – were portrayed as the apocalyptic antithesis of civilization, religion and culture. Contemporaries viewed the decisive battle at Châlons in AD 451 between the Romans and the Huns as an awesome collision between civilization and barbarism. Yet Attila was a monster created by Rome.

The Kingdom of the Huns had evolved quite suddenly in the second quarter of the 5th century into a fast expanding and predatory empire. Militarily formidable, the Huns lacked political coherence. With their origins in the nomadism of the Central Asian steppes, they were essentially loosely organized and highly mobile masses of light horse-archers. They moved into Eastern and Central Europe as the resistance of the Goths collapsed, and then, intent on feeding off the riches of classical civilization, they began levying protection money. Repeatedly, when threatened elsewhere, Constantinople faced demands for payments to keep the peace in the Balkans, payments that became a regular and rising subsidy to the King of the Huns: 350 lbs of gold a year in the AD 420s; 700 lbs kg of gold a year in the AD 430s; 2,100 lbs of gold a year in the AD 440s, plus an immediate one-off payment of 6,000 lbs to seal the new agreement. Roman prisoners also became a source of income: they were ransomed for first 8, then 12, gold staters per man. For the Roman Empire this was, if unavoidable, disastrous. The subsidies fed the rising power of the Hunnic King, whose capacity to reward his followers, cement their allegiance, and recruit and arm fresh forces was enormously enhanced. By the middle of the 5th century AD, Attila controlled a huge Central European empire. Roman gold had created a barbarian super-state.

In AD 447 Attila attacked across the Danube again. The Romans were defeated, and, after further Balkan devastation, Constantinople yet again accepted the Huns' terms, which this time included the cession of a huge belt of territory on the south bank of the Danube 'five days' journey in depth'. Then, suddenly, Attila's attitude to the Eastern Empire changed from predatory menace to conciliation. Eager to turn West, he secured his rear by offering Constantinople a moderate final settlement. Why he turned West, we do not know. Certainly, the Huns knew much about Gaul: many had fought there as federate allies of Aëtius in the AD 430s and 440s, participating in his campaigns against Visigoths, Franks, Burgundians and *bagaudae*. Probably, quite simply, the riches of Gaul, even the impoverished Gaul of Late Antiquity, seemed to offer more lucrative returns than the bribes and plunder to be had in the Balkans.

The pretext for invasion was a dispute between two Frankish chieftains on the lower Rhine, one of whom appealed for support to Aëtius, the other to Attila. The Huns moved first. A great invasion force first crushed the King of the Burgundians and conquered Eastern Gaul. It then split into three armies, one to protect the Huns' Frankish allies and guard Attila's right flank in the north, another to hold down the Burgundians and guard the left flank in the south, the third to push forwards in the centre towards Orleans, the territory of the Visigoths, and the prospective conquest of Western Gaul. But as Aëtius and King Theodoric of the Visigoths advanced against him, Attila fell back eastwards, ordering a concentration at Châlons-sur-Marne – a central position to which his northern and southern armies could march, and an area of wide open country ideal for massed cavalry action.

Châlons was a medieval battle. Both armies formed up in three separate battle-groups, and each fought its own engagement. The great majority on both sides were barbarian warriors organized in clans and tribes under kings and chieftains. Aëtius and the regular Roman troops were deployed on the right of the Romano-Gothic line, Theodoric and the Visigoths on the left, with the Alans (whose loyalty was suspect) sandwiched in the centre. Attila commanded the Huns in the centre of his own line, while Ostrogoths, Gepids and other subject peoples of his empire formed the wings. The battle, fought with aggression and determination on both sides, lasted two days. On the first, Attila launched furious but unsuccessful attacks on the Romans and the Alans, but the Ostrogoths on his right flank collapsed before the onslaught of Theodoric's Visigoths. Exposed to the danger of a devastating flank attack by Gothic cavalry on his embattled centre, Attila engineered a fighting retreat to his fortified camp, keeping the Goths at bay with massed archery. The following day he stood on the defensive in a great wagon laager. In the centre was a huge pyramid of wooden saddles. Around it were ranged the king's spoils and wealth. Perched on the sides were his wives. And on the summit was Attila himself, directing the battle, but ready to be consumed in a vast conflagration should the laager fall. The pyramid was his funeral pyre.

It was not needed – not yet. The Romano-Gothic army was traumatized by its grim struggle. Its assaults on the second day of the battle were repulsed, and Attila was allowed to extricate his army and escape eastwards. Perhaps, indeed, Aëtius wished it so. Roman power, reduced largely to a matter of bargains and bribes, had come to depend on a balance of power among the barbarian polities that now dominated Europe. With Attila so diminished, perhaps it was better that he survived as a counterweight to the Romans' victorious Visigothic allies. In the event, however, Attila died two years later, and his empire, which had formed so fast and covered such a swathe of Europe, fell to pieces as its subject peoples rose in revolt against their masters.

Aëtius too died soon after the battle. The butt of much jealousy at court, where many spoke against him, the mighty general was suddenly accused of treason and murdered by the emperor (AD 454). The emperor himself was shortly afterwards assassinated in a revenge killing by Aëtius's retainers (AD 455). There followed a rapid succession of undistinguished emperors, nine (more or less) legitimate rulers in 21 years, of whom no less than six died violently. The dominant figure, Ricimer, the last of the great generalissimos of the Late Western Empire, was, like Stilicho half a century before, a barbarian. Making and unmaking emperors, embroiled in endless court intrigue, constantly shoring up the rickety edifice of power that supported him, Ricimer presided helplessly over the final collapse of the Western Empire. He represented a wafer-thin carapace of military strength hollow beneath: a court, several capital cities, some thousands of armed men, an historic claim to world empire – but, lacking any real economic, social or political base, liable to crumble to nothing at the slightest blows.

These fell swiftly. Diplomacy and carefully controlled projections of such military force as remained allowed the Western Empire to preserve fragments of authority across its former domains for a time. But gains were momentary. When Vandal raiding was extended into the Eastern Mediterranean, it provoked a joint operation by both Eastern and Western Empires in AD 468, but it ended disastrously, and Vandal power in the Mediterranean was further entrenched. There were energetic Roman campaigns in Gaul in the late 450s AD, but within a few years the expanding Visigothic kingdom had taken Arles, an imperial capital, the principal seat of what had remained of Roman authority in Gaul, one of the greatest centres of classical culture in the West. More often than not, territory was absorbed rather than conquered. Gallo-Roman landowners agreed, through force of circumstance, to divide their estates with barbarian 'guests'. Germanic kings converted, became patrons of the Church, and entered into alliance with local bishops. The infrastructure of estates, churches and urban-based administration and tax-collection were appropriated by the new rulers. A classic reversal took place: once the empire had sought to 'Romanize' the barbarian chieftains it conquered; now the barbarian conquerors of the empire helped themselves to the *Romanitas* of their new subjects. Before long, Germanic kings were busy at the game of making and unmaking Roman emperors.

The death of Ricimer, the last of the great strongmen of the West, in AD 472 heralded the end. The Western throne was disputed between the remnants of the Roman aristocracy, the Germanic kings and Constantinople. There were five emperors in as many years. The last was Romulus Augustulus (AD 475–476). His authority over Italy rested on the support of King Odoacer and his Germanic federate army. When the king demanded for his followers the same treatment as had been granted to their compatriots in Gaul – a one-third share in estates – he was rebuffed. He responded by removing the emperor and seeking to place himself on the throne. When his appeal to the Eastern Emperor for recognition and legitimacy was turned down, he restyled himself 'King of Italy'. The Western Roman Empire had ceased to exist. Its territories had become a patchwork of barbarian kingdoms.

The Vandals ruled Africa, Sicily, Sardinia and Corsica. Odoacer ruled Italy, Illyricum, and what was left of Raetia and Noricum. The Visigoths ruled a huge area centred on south-west Gaul. The Burgundians held most of the rest of Gaul, except for Brittany, which had been settled by British exiles, and the lower Rhine, which was Frankish. A small Romanized enclave controlled by Syagrius in northern Gaul was absorbed by the Franks in AD 486. The Visigoths ruled most of Spain, except for the north-west, where there were Suevian and native Vascon territories. Britain was divided into numerous, obscure petty-states, some British, some Anglo-Saxon. In many places, a Romanized elite culture survived under the authority of new rulers. But even this was gradually transformed – given new shapes and meanings in a changed and changing world. And elite culture is not the same thing as Roman imperial power and a social order based on cities, villas, and a municipal oligarchy of landowning gentry. The Roman Empire defined in these terms had been in decline since expansion ended in the 2nd century AD. If it survived beyond the 5th century in some form in the East – a much-mutated form – it did so only because the West had been cast adrift. Once, Rome had been powerful enough to conquer the East and take possession of its riches. Now, without those riches, Rome could not stand, and the Western Roman Empire was consumed by its barbarian enemies amidst the indifference of its people. The story that had begun at Rome in 753 BC ended there in AD 476.

Timeline

Dates, authorities and events which are uncertain or mythical are given in square brackets. Dates which are approximations only are marked 'c.' for *circa*. Names of legitimate rulers are given in italics. Names of usurpers and *de facto* rulers are given in round brackets. Major period subdivisions are given in bold. Approximate modern geographical equivalents for ancient regions are given in brackets.

Date	Ruling authority	Event
[1184 BC]	[*Aeneas*]	[Fall of Troy and flight of Trojans: new settlement in Latium]
[753 BC]		[Foundation of City of Rome]
[753–716 BC]	[*Romulus*]	
c. 750–625 BC	Latin chieftains	Rome develops from hilltop farming village into chieftain's hillfort dominating several miles of countryside
[716–673 BC]	[*Numa Pompilius*]	
[673–642 BC]	[*Tullus Hostilius*]	
[642–616 BC]	[*Ancus Marcius*]	
c. 625–509 BC	Etruscan kings	**The Regal Period** Rome refounded and developed as Etruscan city-state with monumental public architecture
[616–578 BC]	*Tarquinius Priscus*	
[578–534 BC]	*Servius Tullius*	
[534–509 BC]	*Tarquinius Superbus*	
c. 509 BC		Monarchy overthrown in aristocratic revolution
c. 509–367 BC	Patrician oligarchy	**The Early Republic** Rome evolves from narrow patrician oligarchy to more open patrician-plebeian oligarchy limited by popular institutions as result of the Struggle of the Orders
c. 506 BC		Battle of Aricia: Greek victory over Lars Porsenna frees Latium of Etruscan domination

Date	Ruling authority	Event
c. 499–493 BC		First Latin War
c. 499 BC		Battle of Lake Regillus: Roman victory over Latins
c. 494 BC		First revolutionary secession of Roman plebs
c. 493 BC		Treaty of Cassius ends Latin War and settles Latium
c. 483–474 BC		First Veientine War
c. 477 BC		Battle of Cremera: Etruscan victory over Roman Fabii clan
451 BC	Decemvirate	Rome ruled by emergency Committee of Ten Twelve Tables laws enacted
c. 449 BC	Consuls, Senate and People of Rome	Second revolutionary secession of Roman plebs Crisis ended by Valerio-Horatian laws
c. 437–435 BC		Second Veientine War: Romans gain Fidenae
c. 406–396 BC		Third Veientine War: Romans capture and destroy Veii
390 BC		Battle of the Allia: Gauls defeat Romans Brennus captures and plunders Rome
c. 384 BC		Trial and execution of popular leader Marcus Manlius Capitolinus
367 BC		Licinio-Sextian laws open consulship to plebs and effectively end the Struggle of the Orders
367–133 BC		**The Middle Republic**
343–341 BC		First Samnite War
c. 340–338 BC		Second Latin War: Latins defeated and Latin League suppressed
327–304 BC		Second Samnite War
321 BC		Battle of Caudine Forks: Samnite victory over Romans
298–290 BC		Third Samnite War
295 BC		Battle of Sentinum: Romans defeat Italian confederation
287 BC		*Plebiscita* (enactments of Assembly of the Plebs) gain equal status with *leges* (laws passed by Assembly of the Centuries on advice of Senate)
282–272 BC		War against Tarentum
280–275 BC		War against Pyrrhus
275 BC		Battle of Beneventum: narrow Roman victory over Pyrrhus after two narrow defeats
272 BC		Fall of Tarentum: Roman garrison installed

Date	Ruling authority	Event
264–241 BC		First Punic War
263 BC		Tyrant of Syracuse accepts Roman client status
262 BC		Battle of Heraclea Minoa: Roman dominance on land in Sicily established
256–255 BC		Abortive Roman invasion of Africa (Tunisia)
241 BC		Battle of Aegates Islands: Roman naval victory ends Carthaginian settlement in Sicily
240–237 BC		Mercenary War at Carthage: Romans seize Sardinia and Corsica
229–228 BC		First Illyrian War
225 BC		Battle of Telamon: Romans defeat Gauls and proceed with colonization of Cisalpine Gaul (Northern Italy)
221 BC		Hannibal acclaimed Carthaginian commander in Spain
221–219 BC		Second Illyrian War
219 BC		Hannibal captures Saguntum
218–202 BC		Second Punic War
218 BC		Battle of Trebia: Hannibal wins control of Cisalpine Gaul (Northern Italy)
217 BC		Battle of Lake Trasimene: Hannibal wins allegiance of some North Italian states
216 BC		Battle of Cannae: Hannibal wins allegiance of some South Italian states
215–205 BC		First Macedonian War
209–206 BC		Scipio destroys Carthaginian Empire in Spain
204–202 BC		Scipio leads invasion of Africa (Tunisia)
202 BC		Battle of Zama: Scipio defeats Hannibal
200–196 BC		Second Macedonian War
197 BC		Battle of Cynoscephalae: Roman legions defeat Macedonian phalanx
197–179 BC		Second Spanish War
196 BC		Flamininus' proclamation of freedom for Greek cities
192–188 BC		War against Antiochus of the Seleucid Empire (Syria)
189 BC		Battle of Magnesia: Romans defeat Antiochus Devastation of Galatia (Central Anatolia)
171–168 BC		Third Macedonian War
168 BC		Battle of Pydna: Romans defeat King Perseus of Macedonia

Date	Ruling authority	Event
167 BC		Enslavement of Epirus (Albania)
154–133 BC		Third Spanish War
150–146 BC		Fourth Macedonian War
149–146 BC		Third Punic War
146 BC		Destruction of Corinth and Carthage
142–133 BC		Siege of Numantia
139 BC		Final Roman conquest of Lusitania (Portugal)
136–132 BC		First Sicilian slave war
133–30 BC		**The Late Republic**
133 BC		Pergamum bequeathed to Rome
133–132 BC		Tribunate and assassination of Tiberius Gracchus
125–121 BC		Roman conquest of Gallia Narbonensis (Provence)
123–122 BC		Tribunate and assassination of Gaius Gracchus
112–105 BC		War against Jugurtha in Numidia (Algeria)
103–101 BC		Second Sicilian slave war
102–101 BC		Marius defeats Cimbri and Teutones at Battles of Aquae Sextiae and Vercellae
100–88 BC	(Supremacy of Marius)	
100 BC		Army veterans demonstrate in Rome: Marius's political supremacy established
99 BC		Army veterans reimpose order in Rome
91–88 BC		Social War: Italian allies defeated but Roman citizenship conceded
89–84 BC		First Mithridatic War
88 BC		Sulla carries out first conservative coup in Rome
87–84 BC		Sulla's eastern command
87 BC		Marius and Cinna lead popular counter-coup in Rome
87–84 BC	(Supremacy of Cinna)	
83–80 BC		Civil War
82–81 BC		Battle of the Colline Gate: Sulla defeats *populares*, enters Rome, carries out second conservative coup, and purges opponents in 'proscriptions'
82–79 BC	(Supremacy of Sulla)	
80–72 BC		War against Sertorius in Spain
77–72 BC		Pompey's Spanish command
74–63 BC		Third Mithridatic War
73–71 BC		Italian slave revolt under Spartacus
73–71 BC		Verres's governorship in Sicily

Date	Ruling authority	Event
71–70 BC		Crassus and Pompey carry out anti-oligarchic coup in Rome
71–63 BC	(Supremacy of Crassus and Pompey)	
67 BC		Pompey defeats pirates
66–63 BC		Pompey's eastern conquests
63 BC		Catiline conspiracy
59 BC		Formation of First Triumvirate of Caesar, Crassus and Pompey
59–53 BC	(First Triumvirate)	
58–51 BC		Caesar's conquest of Gaul
56 BC		Pact of Luca confirms First Triumvirate
53 BC		Battle of Carrhae: Crassus defeated and killed by Parthians
52 BC		Revolt of Vercingetorix in Gaul Assassination of Clodius and riots in Rome
49–45 BC		Civil War after Caesar crosses Rubicon and invades Italy
48 BC		Battle of Pharsalus: Caesar defeats Pompey and secures East
48–44 BC	(Supremacy of Caesar)	
46 BC		Battle of Thapsus: Caesar defeats Pompey's supporters in Africa (Tunisia)
46 BC		Caesar becomes dictator for ten years
45 BC		Battle of Munda: Caesar defeats Pompey's supporters in Spain
44 BC		Caesar becomes dictator for life Assassination of Caesar
43 BC		Antony, Octavian and Lepidus form Second Triumvirate and carry out Caesarian coup in Rome
43–31 BC	(Second Triumvirate)	
42 BC		Battles of Philippi: Caesarians defeat Republicans
41 BC		Revolt of Lucius Antonius against Octavian
40 BC		Pact of Brundisium restores Second Triumvirate
38 BC		Pact of Tarentum renews Second Triumvirate
36 BC		Battle of Naulochus: Octavian's fleet defeats Sextus Pompeius
36–35 BC		Antony's abortive invasion of Parthia
35–34 BC		Octavian's conquest of Illyricum (Yugoslavia)
31 BC		Battle of Actium: Octavian's fleet defeats Antony and Cleopatra

Date	Ruling authority	Event
30 BC		Octavian conquers Egypt: Antony and Cleopatra commit suicide
30 BC–AD 235		**The Early Empire**
30 BC–AD 68		Julio-Claudian Dynasty
30 BC–AD 14	*Augustus*	
29–28 BC		Conquest of Thrace and Moesia (Lower Danube)
27 BC		Octavian's first constitutional settlement: takes title 'Augustus'
26–19 BC		Conquest of Spain completed
23 BC		Augustus's second constitutional settlement
20 BC		Recovery of Roman standards from Parthians
17–15 BC		Conquest of Noricum and Raetia (Upper Danube)
12–9 BC		Conquest of Pannonia (Middle Danube)
12–5 BC		Conquest of Western Germany
AD 6–9		Pannonian Revolt
AD 9		Battle of Teutoburg Forest: three legions destroyed under Varus and Roman rule ended in Germany
AD 14–37	*Tiberius*	
AD 17–24		Revolt of Tacfarinas in Numidia
AD 21		Revolt of Florus and Sacrovir in Gaul
AD 26–31	(Supremacy of Sejanus)	
AD 31–37	(Supremacy of Macro)	
AD 37–41	*Caligula*	
AD 40		Abortive German and British campaigns
AD 41		Assassination of Caligula and usurpation of Claudius
AD 41–54	*Claudius*	
AD 43–51		Conquest of Southern Britain
AD 53–63		Parthian War
AD 54–68	*Nero*	
AD 54–62	(Supemacy of Burrus and Seneca)	
AD 60/61		Revolt of Boudica in Britain
AD 64		Great Fire of Rome
AD 65		Conspiracy of Piso
AD 66–73		First Jewish Revolt in Palestine
AD 67		Nero's tour of Greece
AD 68		Nero overthrown in military coup
AD 68–69	*Galba*	

Date	Ruling authority	Event
AD 69	*Otho* *Vitellius*	Year of Four Emperors: civil war and two Battles of Cremona
AD 69–96		Flavian Dynasty
AD 69–79	*Vespasian*	
AD 70		Siege and destruction of Jerusalem
AD 70		Revolt of Civilis: Empire of the Gauls
AD 71–84		Conquest of Wales, Northern England and Southern Scotland
AD 78–84		Governorship of Agricola in Britain
AD 79–81	*Titus*	
AD 81–96	*Domitian*	
AD 83		War against Chatti in Rhineland
AD 85–89		First Dacian War
AD 89		Conspiracy of Saturninus
AD 96		Assassination of Domitian
AD 96–98	*Nerva*	
AD 98–117	*Trajan*	
AD 101–102		Second Dacian War
AD 105–106		Third Dacian War
AD 105–108		Annexation of Nabataean Arabia
AD 114–117		Parthian War
AD 115–118		Revolt in the Jewish Diaspora
AD 117–138	*Hadrian*	
AD 117		General's plot against Hadrian
AD 120–123		Hadrian's tour of the western provinces
AD 124–126		Hadrian's first tour of the eastern provinces
AD 128		Hadrian's tour of Africa
AD 129–131		Hadrian's second tour of the eastern provinces
AD 132–136		Second Jewish (Bar Kokhba) Revolt in Palestine
AD 138–192		Antonine Dynasty
AD 138–161	*Antoninus Pius*	
AD 161–180	*Marcus Aurelius*	
AD 161–169	*Lucius Verus*	
AD 161–166		Parthian War
AD 165–167		Great Plague
AD 167–175		German War
AD 175		Revolt of Avidius Cassius
AD 177–180		Resumption of German War
AD 180–192	*Commodus*	
AD 182		Fall of Perennis

Date	Ruling authority	Event
AD 187–188		Revolt of Maternus in Gaul
AD 192	*Pertinax* *Didius Julianus*	Assassination of Commodus: soldiers 'auction' Empire
AD 193–197		Civil war
AD 193–235		Severan Dynasty: 'the military monarchy'
AD 193–211	*Septimius Severus*	
AD 193–195	(Pescennius Niger)	Severus's defeat of eastern rival
AD 193–197	(Clodius Albinus)	
AD 197		Severus's defeat of western rival
AD 197–199		Parthian War
AD 206–207		Bandit-chief Bulla at large in Italy
AD 208–211		War in Northern Britain
AD 211–217	*Caracalla*	
AD 211–213	*Geta*	
AD 212		Caracalla's citizenship edict: all free persons in empire become legally Roman
AD 213		German War
AD 215–217		Parthian War
AD 217–218	*Macrinus*	
AD 218–222	*Elagabalus*	
AD 222–235	*Severus Alexander*	
AD 227		Artaxerxes destroys Parthian and founds Sassanid Empire
AD 230–233		Sassanid War
AD 234–235		German War
AD 235–284		**The Anarchy**
AD 235–238	*Maximinus Thrax*	
AD 238	(Gordian I) (Gordian II) (Balbinus) (Maximus)	Revolts in Africa and Italy against Maximinus
AD 238–244	*Gordian III*	
AD 242–244		Sassanid War
AD 244–249	*Philip Arabicus*	
AD 249–251	*Decius Trajan*	
AD 251–253	*Gallus*	
AD 253	*Aemilianus*	
AD 253–268	*Gallienus*	
AD 253–260	*Valerian*	Division of empire into western and eastern commands
AD 258–259		Collapse of western frontier defences
AD 260		Formation of secessionist 'Gallic Empire' Valerian's defeat, capture and death in East

Date	Ruling authority	Event
AD 260–269	(Postumus)	
AD 260–261	(Macrianus) (Quietus)	Rebel 'Eastern Roman Empire'
AD 261–267		King Odenath of Palmyra recognized as client ruler of East by Gallienus
AD 267		Odenath assassinated and power usurped by Queen Zenobia
AD 267–272	(Zenobia)	Rebel 'Palmyrene Empire' in East
AD 268		Revolt in Italy combined with Gallic Empire in West and Palmyrene Empire in East reduces Gallienus's legitimist regime to Balkan rump: Gallienus assassinated
AD 268–270	*Claudius Gothicus*	
AD 268–271		Re-establishment of Rhine frontier
AD 269–271	(Victorinus)	
AD 270–275	*Aurelian*	
AD 271–272		Liquidation of Palmyrene Empire
AD 271–273	(Tetricus)	
AD 273		Liquidation of Gallic Empire
AD 275–276	*Tacitus*	
AD 276	*Florianus*	
AD 276–282	*Probus*	
AD 282–283	*Carus*	
AD 283–285	*Carinus*	
AD 283–284	*Numerianus*	
AD 284–476		**The Late Empire**
AD 284–305	*Diocletian*	
AD 286–305	*Maximian*	Division of empire into western and eastern commands
AD 287–296		Secessionist rebel regime based in Britain
AD 287–293	(Carausius)	
AD 293–305	*Constantius* ('Caesar') *Galerius* ('Caesar')	Two senior and two junior emperors form Tetrarchy (Rule of Four)
AD 293–296	(Allectus)	
AD 294		Diocletian's monetary reform
AD 296		Liquidation of rebel regime in Britain
AD 298–313		Great persecution (of Christians)
AD 301		Diocletian's Price Edict
AD 305–311	*Galerius*	
AD 305–306	*Constantius I*	
AD 306		Elevation of Constantine: collapse of Tetrarchy
AD 306–363		House of Constantine

Date	Ruling authority	Event
AD 306–337	*Constantine the Great*	
AD 307–312	*Maxentius*	
AD 308–324	*Licinius*	
AD 308		Pact of Carnuntum achieves temporary peace among imperial rivals
AD 312		Battle of Milvian Bridge: victory of Constantine over Maxentius also victory of Christianity over paganism
AD 313		Edict of Milan ends persecution of Christians Council of Rome
AD 314		Council of Arles
AD 324		Defeat of Licinius in East: Constantine supreme across Roman Empire
AD 324–330		Foundation of Constantinople
AD 325		Council of Nicaea
AD 337		Death of Constantine and division of empire among sons
AD 337–340	*Constantine II*	
AD 337–350	*Constans*	
AD 337–361	*Constantius II*	
AD 340		Civil war: defeat and death of Constantine II
AD 350		Civil war: defeat and death of Constans
AD 350–353	(Magnentius)	Usurper regime in West
AD 355–360	*Julian* ('Caesar')	Division of empire between Julian in West and Constantius in East
AD 356		Battle of Strasbourg: Julian defeats Germans
AD 360		Usurpation of Julian: death of Constantius prevents civil war
AD 361–363	*Julian*	
AD 363–364	*Jovian*	
AD 364–392		House of Valentinian
AD 364–375	*Valentinian I*	
AD 364–378	*Valens*	
AD 375–383	*Gratian*	
AD 375–392	*Valentinian II*	
AD 378		Battle of Adrianople: Goths destroy Eastern Roman army
AD 379–450		House of Theodosius
AD 379–395	*Theodosius the Great*	
AD 380		Catholic orthodoxy proclaimed in Eastern Roman Empire
AD 382		Gothic federate settlement in Thrace
AD 383–388	(Magnus Maximus)	Revolt in West against House of Theodosius

Date	Ruling authority	Event
AD 391		Pagan sacrifices banned and temples closed across reunited empire
AD 392–394	(Eugenius)	Revolt of Arbogast and Eugenius in West against House of Theodosius and Christian Church
AD 394		Battle of River Frigidus: Theodosius defeats western pagan revolt
AD 395		Death of Theodosius: final division of Roman Empire into western and eastern halves
AD 395–423	*Honorius* (in West)	
AD 395–408	*Arcadius* (in East) (Supremacy of Stilicho in West)	
AD 405		Gothic federate settlement in Western Balkans
AD 406–407		Collapse of Rhine frontier: barbarian invasion of western provinces Revolt of Constantine III in Britain Burgundian federate settlement in eastern Gaul
AD 408		Fall of Stilicho in court coup: purge of 'barbarians' in Roman service
AD 408–450	*Theodosius II* (in East)	
AD 410		Sack of Rome by Alaric the Goth
AD 411–421	(Supremacy of Constantius in West)	
AD 418		Pacification of West: Gothic federate settlement in Aquitaine; Vandal and Suevic settlements in Spain
AD 423–425	(Johannes in West)	
AD 425–455	*Valentinian III* (in West)	
AD 429		Vandal invasion of North Africa
AD 434–454	(Supremacy of Aëtius in West)	
AD 438		Publication of Theodosian law code
AD 439		Fall of Carthage to Vandals
AD 451		Battle of Châlons: Attila the Hun's invasion of West defeated
AD 457–472	(Supremacy of Ricimer in West)	Rapid succession of short reigns by ineffective emperors
AD 476		Overthrow of Romulus Augustulus, last Western Roman emperor, and establishment of Kingdom of Italy by Odoacer

References

The list of references is divided into two parts. I first list the translations actually used, then give page references for the direct quotations that appear in the text. Where secondary sources are cited, the full reference will be found in *Bibliographical notes*.

Classical sources

Ammianus Marcellinus, *The Later Roman Empire, AD 354–378*, trans. W. Hamilton, 1986, London, Penguin.

Anonymous, *Lives of the Later Caesars*, trans. A. Birley, 1976, London, Penguin.

Appian, *The Civil Wars*, trans. J. Carter, 1996, London, Penguin.

Apuleius, *The Golden Ass*, trans. R. Graves, 1950, Harmondsworth, Penguin.

Caesar, *The Civil War*, trans. J.F. Gardner, 1967, Harmondsworth, Penguin.

Caesar, *The Conquest of Gaul*, trans. S.A. Handford and J.F. Gardner, 1982, Harmondsworth, Penguin.

Horace, *The Odes of Horace*, trans. J. Michie, 1967, Harmondsworth, Penguin.

Livy, *The Early History of Rome* (Books 1–5), trans. A. de Sélincourt, 1960, Harmondsworth, Penguin.

Livy, *Rome and Italy* (Books 6–10), trans. B. Radice, 1982, London, Penguin.

Livy, *The War with Hannibal* (Books 21–30), trans. A. de Sélincourt, 1965, Harmondsworth, Penguin.

Livy, *Rome and the Mediterranean* (Books 31–45), trans. H. Bettenson, 1976, London, Penguin.

Pliny the Younger, *The Letters of the Younger Pliny*, trans. B. Radice, 1969, London, Harmondsworth.

Plutarch, *Plutarch's Lives*, trans. J. Dryden, revised by A.H. Clough, undated, London, Dent.

Polybius, *The Rise of the Roman Empire*, trans. I. Scott-Kilvert, 1979, Harmondsworth, Penguin.

Sallust, *The Jugurthine War and the Conspiracy of Catiline*, trans. S.A. Handford, 1963, Harmondsworth, Penguin.

Suetonius, *The Twelve Caesars*, trans. R. Graves, 1957, Harmondsworth, Penguin.

Tacitus, *The Agricola and the Germania*, trans. H. Mattingly and S.A. Handford, 1970, Harmondsworth, Penguin.

Tacitus, *The Annals of Imperial Rome*, trans. M. Grant, 1977, Harmondsworth, Penguin.

Tacitus, *The Histories*, trans. K. Wellesley, 1986, Harmondsworth, Penguin.

Thucydides, *History of the Peloponnesian War*, trans. R. Warner, 1972, London, Penguin.

Virgil, *The Aeneid*, trans. W.F. Jackson Knight, 1958, Harmondsworth, Penguin.

Primary source collections

N. Lewis and M. Reinhold, *Roman Civilization, Volume I: Selected Readings: the Republic and the Augustan Age*, 1990, New York, Columbia University.

N. Lewis and M. Reinhold, *Roman Civilization, Sourcebook II: The Empire*, 1966, New York, Harper & Row.

London Association of Classical Teachers (LACTOR 4), *Inscriptions of Roman Britain*, ed. V.A. Maxfield and B. Dobson, 1995 (3rd edn), London.

London Association of Classical Teachers (LACTOR 11), *Literary Sources for Roman Britain*, ed. J.C. Mann and R.G. Penman, 1985 (2nd edn), London.

Quotations

Prologue

1. Virgil, *The Aeneid*, 172–173.
2. Virgil, *The Aeneid*, 149.
3. Virgil, *The Aeneid*, 223.
4. Virgil, *The Aeneid*, 338.
5. Livy, *History of Rome*, Book 1, 17–18.
6. Quoted in Crawford 1992, 9.
7. Livy, *History of Rome*, Book 1, 18.

Chapter 1

1. Virgil, *The Aeneid*, 175–176.
2. Horace, Book 1, Ode 7, 31.
3. Plutarch, *Romulus*, 36.
4. Livy, *History of Rome*, Book 1, 79.
5. Cary 1935, 77.
6. Polybius, *History of Rome*, Book VI, 312–317.
7. Quoted in Cornell and Matthews 1982, *Atlas of the Roman World*, 41.

Chapter 2

1. Livy, *History of Rome*, Book 8, 177.
2. Cornell 1995, 367.
3. Thucydides, *The Peloponnesian War*, Book 2, 147.
4. Plutarch, *Pyrrhus*, 55.
5. Plutarch, *Pyrrhus*, 58.
6. Finley 1968, 74.
7. Finley 1968, 87.
8. Polybius, *History of Rome*, Book 1, 61.
9. Polybius, *History of Rome*, Book 1, 65–66.
10. Polybius, *History of Rome*, Book 2, 140.
11. Livy, *History of Rome*, Book 21, 23–24.
12. Harris 1985, 205.

13. Livy, *History of Rome*, Book 21, 41–42.
14. Livy, *History of Rome*, Book 31, 27–28.
15. Polybius, *History of Rome*, Book 18, 511–513.
16. Polybius, *History of Rome*, Book 18, 516.
17. Quoted in Crawford 1992, 59.
18. Harris 1985, 225.

Chapter 3

1. Brunt 1986, 2.
2. Pliny the Younger, *Letters*, 105–106.
3. Plutarch, *Tiberius Gracchus*, 132.
4. Appian, *Roman History*, Book 1, 5.
5. Apuleius, *The Golden Ass*, 169–170.
6. Brunt 1986, 92.
7. Quoted in Lewis and Reinhold 1966, 353–354.
8. Cary 1935, 312–313.
9. Plutarch, *Gaius Marius*, 100.
10. Quoted in Lewis and Reinhold 1990, 396.
11. Plutarch, *Pompey*, 385–386.
12. Quoted in Cooley and Cooley 2004, 21.
13. Quoted in Cooley and Cooley 2004, 53.
14. Plutarch, *Pompey*, 425.
15. Plutarch, *Pompey*, 432–433.
16. Sallust, *The Conspiracy of Catiline*, 178.
17. Parenti 2003, 87.
18. Sallust, *The Conspiracy of Catiline*, 219–220.
19. Appian, *The Civil Wars*, 87–88.
20. Cornell and Matthews 1982, 70.
21. Suetonius, *Augustus*, 57.
22. Cary 1935, 442.
23. Virgil, *The Aeneid*, 222.

Chapter 4

1. Suetonius, *Augustus*, 66.
2. Quoted in Lewis and Reinhold 1966, 9–19 *passim*.
3. Quoted in Lewis and Reinhold 1966, 19.
4. Suetonius, *Augustus*, 62.

5. Tacitus, *Annals*, 226.
6. Levick 1993, 148.
7. Tacitus, *Agricola*, 64.
8. LACTOR 4, 88.
9. Tacitus, *Agricola*, 72–73.
10. Tacitus, *Agricola*, 91.
11. Tacitus, *Agricola*, 91.
12. Suetonius, *Domitian*, 297.
13. Quoted in Connolly 1988b, 25.
14. Quoted in Lewis and Reinhold 1966, 507.
15. Quoted in Lewis and Reinhold 1966, 509.
16. Gibbon, *The History of the Decline and Fall of the Roman Empire*, Chapter 1.

Chapter 5

1. Quoted in Jackson 1995, 174.
2. Quoted in Jackson 1995, 174.
3. LACTOR 11, 38.
4. Quoted in Birley 1999, 35.
5. LACTOR 11, 38.
6. Quoted in Parker 1935, 90.
7. Quoted in de Ste Croix 1981, 477.
8. Quoted in de Ste Croix 1981, 478.
9. Quoted in de Ste Croix 1981, 478.
10. Quoted in Raven 1969, 140.
11. Quoted in Lewis and Reinhold 1966, 429.
12. Quoted in Lewis and Reinhold 1966, 430.
13. Ammianus Marcellinus, *History of Rome*, Book 30, 406.

Bibliographical notes

The scholarship on the history of Rome is vast; it would take many lifetimes to read it all. The rate of output, moreover, despite a long-term decline of the classics in schools and universities, has continued to rise: more new books on ancient history and classical archaeology now appear each year than ever before. This is not necessarily unalloyed progress. While knowledge of the ancient world certainly increases, understanding may not. Old texts are read more critically; new ones are unearthed in the desert; more settlements, cemeteries and hoards are revealed by archaeology. But while mastery of a growing body of evidence is one thing, the ability to fit it into a wider historical context is quite another. The first is mainly a matter of specialist scholarship; the latter requires social theory, and this, in the last generation, has been under sustained intellectual attack. Much recent secondary literature reflects the current postmodernist fashion for deconstructing unitary grand narratives and proclaiming instead a multiplicity of voices and discourses. While understanding of some aspects of the past has been advanced, our ability to fit all the pieces together into meaningful patterns has actually regressed.

The following notes, therefore, both because the literature is so vast and because so much is of limited value, are far from a comprehensive bibliography. I have restricted myself to the texts which I know and have found useful. The result is that readers are given a good indication of the sources of information and ideas mined for this book. They are also provided with some strong recommendations for further reading.

Books relevant to the content of more than one chapter are discussed in the general sections. Those used only in relation to one chapter – even if they in fact cover a longer period – are discussed in the relevant chapter sections. The editions cited are those actually used – the copies on my bookshelves.

General history and analysis

I still rate M. Cary's *A History of Rome, down to the reign of Constantine* (1935, London, Macmillan) the best narrative history (and, as it happens, the original better than Scullard's revised version). H.H. Scullard's *A History of the Roman World, 753 to 146 BC* (1980, London, Methuen) and *From the Gracchi to Nero: a history of Rome from 133 BC to AD 68* (1959, London, Methuen) are detailed traditional narratives, though, unlike Cary, interpretation is weak. E.T. Salmon's *A History of the Roman World, 30 BC to AD 138* (1968, London, Routledge) is also sound. M. Le Glay, J.-L. Voisin and Y. Le Bohec's *A History of Rome* (2001, Oxford, Blackwell) is a well-established, though somewhat eccentric, textbook. T. Cornell and J. Matthews's *Atlas of the Roman World* (1982, Amsterdam, Time Life) is more than its title implies, being a sound narrative history with good use of archaeological evidence. M. Grant's *The Routledge Atlas of Classical History* (1994, 5th edn, London, Routledge) and C. Scarre's *The Penguin Historical Atlas of Ancient Rome* (1995, London, Penguin) are also useful. M. Crawford's *The Roman Republic* (1992, London, Fontana) and C. Wells's *The Roman Empire* (1992, London, Fontana) are valuable companion volumes, offering concise, up-to-date scholarly overviews. Encyclopaedic coverage is provided by *The Cambridge Ancient History*, volumes 7 to 12. Essentially a series of extended essays by leading specialists, some providing narrative, others discussing themes, the *CAH* is an exceptionally comprehensive reference. Interesting for their materialist analysis, though very dated, are M. Rostovtzeff's *Rome* (1960, Oxford, OUP) and *Social and Economic History of the Roman Empire* (1926, Oxford, Clarendon). C.G. Starr's *The Roman Empire, 27 BC – AD 476* (1982, Oxford, OUP) is another stimulating overview. G.E.M. de Ste Croix's *The Class Struggle in the Ancient Greek World* (1981, London, Duckworth) is a superb and seminal Marxist analysis of classical antiquity. P.A. Brunt's *Social Conflicts in the Roman Republic* (1986, London, Hogarth) is a concise yet penetrating analysis of both the Struggle of the Orders and the Roman Revolution. L. Keppie's *The Making of the Roman Army: from Republic to Empire* (1984, London, Batsford) is a sound account of the evolution of the army up to the 1st century AD. P. Connolly's *Greece and Rome at War* (1981, London, Macdonald) uses archaeological evidence to trace the history of the Roman army from its origins to the fifth century AD. D. Williams's *The Reach of Rome: a history of the Roman imperial frontier, 1st–5th centuries AD* (1996, London, Constable) is excellent on the history and archaeology of the frontiers. P. Matyszak's *The Enemies of Rome: from Hannibal to Attila the Hun* (2004, London, Thames & Hudson) provides a handy set of narratives, but without any real understanding of the forces at work. E.N. Luttwak's *The Grand Strategy of the Roman Empire, from the 1st century AD to the 3rd* (1979, Baltimore, Johns Hopkins) is an analysis of Roman imperial defence policy.

General archaeology and culture

P. Jones and K. Sidwell's *The World of Rome: an introduction to Roman culture* (1997, Cambridge, CUP) is excellent, while P. Connolly and H. Dodge's *The Ancient City: life in Classical Athens and Rome* (1998, Oxford, OUP) is very good on the archaeology of ancient Rome. Though old, J. Carcopino's *Daily Life in Ancient Rome: the people and the city at the height of the empire* (1956, Harmondsworth, Penguin) is a superb window on everyday life. M.I. Finley's *The Ancient Economy* (1992, London, Penguin) is invaluable in the light it throws on how the ancient world actually worked. J. Ferguson's *The Religions of the Roman Empire* (1970, London, Thames & Hudson) is sound, as is K. Dowden's *Religion and the Romans* (1992, Bristol, Bristol Classical). R. MacMullen's *Paganism in the Roman Empire* (1981, New Haven, Yale) tries to get beneath the skin of Roman religion. R.E.M. Wheeler's *Roman Art and Architecture* (1964, London, Thames & Hudson) remains a superb short introduction. M.I. Finley's (ed.) *Atlas of the Classical World* (1977, London, Chatto & Windus) is a good general archaeological reference. On the archaeology of Italy generally, T.W. Potter's *Roman Italy* (1987, London, British Museum) offers a good overview. On Pompeii, A.E. Cooley and M.G.L. Cooley's *Pompeii: a sourcebook* (2004, London, Routledge) is a useful collection of inscriptions, and M. Grant's *Cities of Vesuvius: Pompeii and Herculaneum* (1976, Harmondsworth, Penguin) is still a fine general introduction to the archaeology. Also good are J.J. Deiss's *Herculaneum: Italy's buried treasure* (1989, California, John Paul Getty Museum) and A. Wallace-Hadrill's *Houses and Society in Pompeii and Herculaneum* (1994, Princeton, Princeton University). Among the countless studies of other regions, provinces and cities of the Roman Empire, I have found the following useful: S. Keay's *Roman Spain* (1988, London, British Museum); A. King's *Roman Gaul and Germany* (1990, London, British Museum); N. Lewis's *Life in Egypt under Roman Rule* (1983, Oxford, Clarendon); S. Raven's *Rome in Africa* (1969, London, Evans Brothers); P. Salway's *A History of Roman Britain* (1997, Oxford, OUP); and Iain Browning's three studies, *Palmyra* (1979, London, Chatto & Windus), *Jerash and the Decapolis* (1982, London, Chatto & Windus), and *Petra* (1989, 3rd edn, London, Chatto & Windus). On the other hand, Richard Reece's *My Roman Britain* (1988, Cirencester, Cotswold Studies) can be recommended to all those who wish to avoid misuse of archaeological evidence.

Prologue

The two key texts for the mythological account of the origins of Rome and the Romans are Virgil's *The Aeneid* (trans. W.F. Jackson Knight, 1958, Harmondsworth, Penguin) and Book 1 of Livy's *The Early History of Rome* (trans. A. de Sélincourt, 1960, Harmondsworth, Penguin). Useful critical discussion of these texts can be found in J. Griffin's *Virgil* (1986, Oxford, OUP), R. Jenkyns' *Classical Epic: Homer and Virgil* (1992, London, Bristol Classical Press), and P.G. Walsh's *Livy: his historical aims and methods* (1989, Bristol, Bristol Classical Press). M.C. Howatson's (ed.) *The Oxford Companion to Classical Literature* (1989, Oxford, OUP) is also useful. There are handy short summaries on the sources for early Roman history in M. Cary's *A History of Rome down to the reign of Constantine* (1935, London, Macmillan), R.M. Ogilvie's *Early Rome and the Etruscans* (1976, London, Fontana), and M. Crawford's *The Roman Republic* (1992, London, Fontana).

Chapter 1

R.M. Ogilvie's *Early Rome and the Etruscans* (1976, London, Fontana) is a generally sensible short introduction to the period *c.* 650 to 390 BC, but it is overly preoccupied with some rather arcane scholarly debates, and the interpretation of events is often weak. A far more reliable and up-to-date study is T.J. Cornell's *The Beginnings of Rome: Italy and Rome from the Bronze Age to the Punic Wars (c. 1000–264 BC)* (1995, London,

Routledge); a recent work of high scholarship, this is now the main academic reference for the history of early Rome. M. Pallottino's *The Etruscans* (1955, Harmondsworth, Penguin) is still a good introductory book, while A. Boëthius's *Etruscan and Early Roman Architecture* (1978, Harmondsworth, Penguin) is a standard work, and N. Spivey's *Etruscan Art* (1997, London, Thames & Hudson) is a concise introduction. R.R. Holloway's *The Archaeology of Early Rome and Latium* (1996, London, Routledge) is a comprehensive and well-illustrated summary of archaeological evidence, while T.W. Potter's *The Changing Landscape of South Etruria* (1979, London, Paul Elek) summarizes the results of a major landscape project immediately north of Rome. Victor Davis Hanson's *The Western Way of War: infantry battle in Classical Greece* (1989, London, Hodder & Stoughton) is an excellent analysis of hoplite warfare. The Celtic or Gaulish background is well covered in T.G.E. Powell's *The Celts* (1983, London, Thames & Hudson), B. Cunliffe's *The Ancient Celts* (1999, London, OUP), and S. James's *Exploring the World of the Celts* (1993, London, Thames & Hudson).

Chapter 2

W.V. Harris's *War and Imperialism in Republican Rome, 327–70 BC* (1985, Oxford, OUP) is a masterful study in which the evidence is assembled to demonstrate Republican Rome's essentially aggressive and predatory character. E.T. Salmon's *Roman Colonisation under the Republic* (1969, London, Thames & Hudson) is the standard work on colonies. J.G. Pedley's *Paestum: Greeks and Romans in Southern Italy* (1990, London, Thames & Hudson) provides an insight into the archaeology and multicultural civilization of southern Italy. R. Meiggs's *Roman Ostia* (1973, Oxford, OUP) is the standard work on this very important site. J.K. Davies' *Democracy and Classical Greece* (1993, London, Fontana) and F.W. Walbank's *The Hellenistic World* (1992, London, Fontana) provide good introductions to the Greek world, while M.I. Finley's *A History of Sicily: Ancient Sicily to the Arab Conquest* (1968, London, Chatto & Windus) contains rich insights into the decay of Greek civilization. Possibly the two best books on the Punic Wars are B. Craven's *The Punic Wars* (1980, London, Weidenfeld & Nicolson) and A. Goldsworthy's *The Punic Wars* (2000. London, Cassell). The ancient accounts in Polybius (*The Rise of the Roman Empire*, trans. I. Scott-Kilvert, 1979, Harmondsworth, Penguin) and Livy (*The War with Hannibal*, trans. A. de Sélincourt, 1965, Harmondsworth, Penguin) are highly accessible. A. Goldsworthy's *Cannae* (2001, London, Cassell) offers a vivid reconstruction of ancient combat.

Chapter 3

The literature on the Late Republic is huge. R. Syme's *The Roman Revolution* (1960, Oxford, OUP) is seminal. T. Holland's *Rubicon: the triumph and tragedy of the Roman Republic* (2003, London, Little, Brown) has been deservedly praised: when has Roman history ever been such a compelling and convincing read? M. Parenti's *The Assassination of Julius Caesar: a people's history of ancient Rome* (2003, New York, New Press) is an excellent read and a refreshingly acerbic indictment of the Late Republican ruling class, but the analysis of Caesar and what he represented is naïve. K. Hopkins's *Conquerors and Slaves* (1978, Cambridge, CUP) is an excellent analysis of slavery under the Republic by someone who is both classicist and sociologist. Also valuable on slavery are K. Bradley's *Slavery and Rebellion in the Roman World, 140 BC – 70 BC* (1989, London, Batsford) and *Slavery and Society at Rome* (1994, Cambridge, CUP). The standard work on the vexed question of citizenship is A.N. Sherwin-White's *The Roman Citizenship* (1973, Oxford, OUP), while J.P.V.D. Balsdon's *Romans and Aliens* (1979, London, Duckworth) is a superb exposé of the snobbery and prejudice that permeated Roman society. Several of the leading figures of the Late Republic have attracted modern biographies. Among the more important are Peter Greenhalgh's *Pompey: the Roman Alexander* (1980, London, Weidenfeld & Nicolson) and Christian Meier's *Caesar* (1996, London, Fontana), though J.P.V.D. Balsdon's *Julius Caesar and Rome* (1967, London, English Universities) and Michael Grant's *Julius Caesar* (1972, London, Granada) are good, concise, serviceable accounts.

Chapter 4

There are good biographies of all the Julio-Claudian emperors, notably P. Southern's *Augustus* (1998, Routledge, London), B. Levick's *Tiberius the Politician* (1986, Beckenham, Croom Helm), A.A. Barrett's *Caligula: the corruption of power* (1993, London, Batsford), B. Levick's *Claudius* (1993, London, Batsford), and M.T. Griffin's *Nero: the end of a dynasty* (1987, London, Batsford). Also of great value are D. Earl's *The Age of Augustus* (1968, London, Elek) and the excellent Open University sourcebook by K. Chisholm and J. Ferguson, *Rome: the Augustan Age* (1981, Oxford, OUP). P. Garnsey and R. Saller's *The Roman Empire: economy, society and culture* (1987, London, Duckworth) is good on the mechanics of the Early Empire. G. Woolf's *Becoming Roman: the origins of provincial civilisation in Gaul* (1998, Cambridge, CUP) is a scholarly study of the Romanization process, while M. Millett's *The Romanization of Britain: an essay in archaeological interpretation* (1992, Cambridge, CUP) is equally good but using archaeological evidence. The First Jewish War and the Palestinian background are covered in my *Apocalypse: the great Jewish revolt against Rome, AD 66–73* (2002, Stroud, Tempus). Trajan's Dacian Wars are well covered by a combination of Frank Lepper and Sheppard Frere's *Trajan's Column* (1988, Gloucester, Alan Sutton), a scholarly study of the sculptures, and Peter Connolly's *Tiberius Claudius Maximus: the Legionary* (1988a, Oxford, OUP) and *Tiberius Claudius Maximus: the Cavalryman* (1988b, Oxford, OUP), which are popular illustrated books aimed at older children.

Chapter 5

The best narrative account of the first part of this period is H.M.D. Parker's *A History of the Roman World from AD 138 to 337* (1935, London, Methuen), whereas a more thematic approach to the same period is offered by P. Southern's *The Roman Empire from Severus and Constantine* (2001, London, Routledge). Overlapping with these studies but taking the story up to the beginning of the 7th century are the magisterial volumes of A.H.M. Jones, *The Later Roman Empire, 284–60: a social, economic and administrative survey* (2 vols, 1986, Oxford, Blackwell), and *The Decline of the Ancient World* (1966, London, Longmans), which is effectively a précis of the former. Another narrative history, J.B. Bury's *History of the Later Roman Empire from the death of Theodosius I to the death of Justinian* (2 vols, 1958, New York, Dover), covers the period AD 395 to 565, again in exceptional detail. Other important studies of the period include P. Brown's *The World of Late Antiquity* (1971, London, Thames & Hudson) and *The Making of Late Antiquity* (1993, London, Harvard), A. Cameron's *The Later Roman Empire, AD 284–430* (1993, London, Fontana) and *The Mediterranean World in Late Antiquity, AD 395–600* (1993, London, Routledge), and B. Ward-Perkins's *The Fall of Rome and the End of Civilisation* (2005, Oxford, OUP). M. Maas's *Readings in Late Antiquity: a sourcebook* (2000, London, Routledge) is a handy collection. Good imperial biographies for this period include A.R. Birley's *Septimius Severus: the African emperor* (1999, London, Routledge), S. Williams's *Diocletian and the Roman Recovery* (2000, London, Routledge), A.H.M. Jones's *Constantine and the Conversion of Europe* (1948, London, Hodder & Stoughton), J. Holland Smith's *Constantine the Great* (1971, New York, Charles Scribner's), and S. Williams and G. Friell's *Theodosius: the empire at bay* (1994, London, Batsford). R. MacMullen makes many interesting observations in *Corruption and the Decline of Rome* (1988, New Haven, Yale University). My *The Decline and Fall of Roman Britain* (2000, Stroud, Tempus) offers an archaeological case-study, and the archaeology of Late Roman towns generally is covered in John Rich's (ed.) *The City in Late Antiquity* (1992, London, Routledge) and J.H.W.G. Liebeschuetz's *The Decline and Fall of the Roman City* (2003, Oxford, OUP). E. Hobsbawm's *Bandits* (1972, Harmondsworth, Penguin) is an important work of historical sociology with real value in understanding the hidden history of the Late Roman Empire. N. Cohn's *The Pursuit of the Millennium: revolutionary millenarians and mystical anarchists of the Middle Ages* (1970, London, Paladin) may be useful in getting a grip on the true character of groups like the North African *circumcelliones*. Disease and Roman responses to it are covered in R. Jackson's *Doctors and Diseases in the Roman Empire* (1995, London, British Museum).

Index and glossary

An index should be useful. Therefore, only substantive references have been included; minor passing references have generally been ignored. Where subjects are discussed at length, full page runs are given. The index also functions as a mini-glossary, providing summary descriptions and definitions. Historical figures are listed under the name by which they are best known; unless otherwise stated, they can be assumed to be Roman. Most towns, provinces and regions are shown on the maps and have not been included in the index unless the text offers more substantive information. Entries are usually in English, occasionally in Latin, according to what seemed most logical. Some references are subsumed under general categories, such as Temple of Jupiter under Rome. References under general categories are listed in text rather than alphabetic order. Where possible, I have tried to index discussion of key themes, so the index includes some abstract-noun concepts, of which the most important is Roman imperialism.